Epics of Empire and Frontier

A book in the Latin American and Caribbean
Arts and Culture publication initiative.
Latin American and Caribbean Arts and Culture is
supported by the Andrew W. Mellon Foundation.

Epics of Empire and Frontier

Alonso de Ercilla and Gaspar de Villagrá as Spanish Colonial Chroniclers

Celia López-Chávez

UNIVERSITY OF OKLAHOMA PRESS : NORMAN

Excerpts of *La Araucana* in English translation are from *A Translation of Alonso de Ercilla's "La Araucana"* by Louis Carrera. Published 2006 by RoseDog Books. Copyright © Joan Carrera Memorial Scholarship Trust. Reprinted with permission. Revised by Celia López-Chávez.

Excerpts of *Historia de la Nueva México* are from *Historia de la Nueva México, 1610: A Critical and Annotated Spanish/English Edition* by Gaspar de Villagrá. Ed. by Miguel Encinias, Alfred Rodríguez, and Joseph P. Sánchez. Copyright © 1992 University of New Mexico Press, 1992. Reprinted with permission.

Library of Congress Cataloging-in-Publication Data
Names: López-Chávez, Celia, author.
Title: Epics of empire and frontier : Alonso de Ercilla and Gaspar Pérez de Villagrá as Spanish colonial chroniclers / Celia López-Chávez.
Description: Norman : University of Oklahoma Press, 2016. | Includes bibliographical references and index.
Identifiers: LCCN 2015040527 | ISBN 978-0-8061-5229-5 (hardback)
Subjects: LCSH: Spanish poetry—Classical period, 1500–1700—History and criticism. | Ercilla y Zúñiga, Alonso de, 1533–1594. Araucana. | Villagrá, Gaspar Pérez de, 1555–1620. Historia de la Nueva México. | Literature and history—Latin America. | Colonies in literature. | Indigenous peoples in literature. | Spaniards in literature. | Imperialism in literature. | BISAC: LITERARY CRITICISM / European / Spanish & Portuguese. | HISTORY / Latin America / Mexico. | HISTORY / Latin America / South America. | POETRY / Epic.
Classification: LCC PQ6066 .L68 2016 | DDC 860.9/003—dc23
LC record available at http://lccn.loc.gov/2015040527

The paper in this book meets the guidelines for permanence and durability of the Committee on Production Guidelines for Book Longevity of the Council on Library Resources, Inc. ∞

1 2 3 4 5 6 7 8 9 10

To Tom,
who made the "epic" meeting between
south and north possible.

It is my (perhaps illusory) hope that a history of the imperial adventure rendered in cultural terms might therefore serve some illustrative and even deterrent purpose.

Edward W. Said

Contents

Illustrations

Figures

Color Plates

Map

Acknowledgments

As with any multiyear research project, there are many people to thank and there is always the fear of leaving out names. I want to thank Dr. Rick Hendricks for his invaluable help with the translation of most of the text that I originally wrote in Spanish. His advice relative to events and sources of New Mexican history is also much appreciated. My Spanish colleagues Genoveva Enríquez and Pilar Lázaro de la Escosura have been of great help at the Archivo General de Indias in Seville, as well as Alberto González Bay at the Biblioteca Nacional in Madrid. I appreciate the assistance of the archivists at the Archives of the Universidad de Salamanca and the Biblioteca Nacional in Santiago de Chile. I thank my Chilean colleagues Leonardo León Solís, Luz María Méndez Beltrán, Sergio Grez, Pablo Lacoste, Alicia Salomone, Sarissa Carneiro, Rolando Carrasco, and Carlos Ruiz Rodríguez, who shared their research and interpretations of *La Araucana* and Ercilla with me. Dr. Nasario García and the late Dr. Anthony Mares read parts of the manuscript and made suggestions. I also thank University of Oklahoma Press acquisitions editor Alessandra Jacobi Tamulevich. My gratitude to manuscript editors Emily Jerman Schuster and Katrin Flechsig for the care and time they put into this project. English being my second language, I much appreciate their copyediting. My thanks to Luther Wilson for his support, as well as to Dr. Ursula Shepherd of the University of New Mexico, who has supported this and my other research and teaching projects with great enthusiasm. I thank my friends Patricia Gay, Margo Chávez-Charles, Laia Obregón Dans, Diana Córdova, Marcia Glenn, and Javier Lorenzo for their interest and encouragement through the writing process. I also appreciate the support of my family in New Mexico: Nicolasa Chávez, Noé García Chávez, Alexina García Chávez, and Allen Sprowl. My sisters, Silvia López Camporro and Mirian López Camporro, shared their love and humor with me during the writing process and lifted my spirits in New Mexico and from their homes in Argentina. Finally, my gratitude to Dr. Thomas Chávez, my partner and best friend; his knowledge of New Mexican history and support in so many different ways allowed me to finish this project. His tenacity, positive attitude, and excellence as a historian have been an inspiration to me.

~

Regarding translations from Spanish to English in this book: Quotations from secondary works published in Spanish were translated by Dr. Rick Hendricks and me. The English translation of the poem *La Araucana* by Louis Carrera was, until 2014, the only published English translation of the complete poem in book form. I have revised Carrera's edition in many lines cited throughout this book. Although the result is not perfect, I hope it will not hinder readers in their enjoyment of this book.

Epics of Empire and Frontier

Introduction

At the beginning of the twenty-first century, the indigenous Mapuche people in the Arauco region of Chile were once again experiencing militarization against them, just as their ancestors had centuries before during the Spanish conquest. In the 1960s, the famous Chilean singer and activist Violeta Parra gave voice to the pain of the historical occupation in Arauco, which began in the mid-1500s, through her lyrics: *"Arauco tiene una pena/ que no la puedo callar/ son injusticias de siglos/ que todos ven aplicar/ nadie le ha puesto remedio/ pudiéndolo remediar/ Levántate Huenchullán!"* "Arauco feels a pain/ that I cannot keep silent/ it is the injustices of centuries/ that everyone comes to apply/ no one has given it relief/ if relief can be given/ Rise up, Huenchullán!" To the cry of "land, justice, and liberty," the Mapuche people are demanding the restoration of indigenous rights, especially the right to possess ancestral Indian land (the Mapuche people claim 2,500 hectares).[1] Today, there is still no relief for these Chileans from the conflict resulting from the occupation of Indian lands. The Chilean government has responded with armed force to their attempts to regain possession of ancestral lands.

The Mapuche communities most active in this clamor—Wincul Mapu, Chekenko, Temucuicui, and Wañaco Millao—are in the *comuna* (a district similar to a county) of Ercilla. The comuna bears the name of Spanish poet Alonso de Ercilla, who wrote about the area and its conquest—in which he participated—in his epic poem *La Araucana*. The comuna that experienced trauma during the conquest continues to witness protests and violence. On January 3, 2008, the Mapuche Indian Matías Catrileo Quezada was shot in the back by members of the Chilean national police force.[2] In the eyes of indigenous Chileans, the death of Catrileo was like that of Caupolicán, a Mapuche military leader whom the Spaniards executed in 1558, or like that of Galvarino, a Mapuche warrior whose hands were first amputated as an example to the rest of the Indians before he was hanged in 1557.[3]

The amputation of Galvarino's hands recalls another set of amputations from this period of Spanish conquest—the amputation in New Mexico of one foot of each male Indian over the age of twenty-five who survived the battle of Acoma

Pueblo in 1599. Governor Juan de Oñate gave the order as punishment for the rebellion and to set an example for the rest of the Indian pueblos of New Mexico.[4] Poet Gaspar de Villagrá wrote about the battle of Acoma in his epic poem *Historia de la Nueva México.* One morning in January 1998, four hundred years after the battle, the large bronze statue of Oñate in the village of Alcalde, north of Santa Fe, was discovered to have had its right foot cut off.[5]

Clearly, the consequences of a conquest that began four and a half centuries ago, and that was followed by other conquests, continue to play out in Chile and New Mexico. After independence from Spain, the Indians of the former Spanish empire continued the struggle to claim their ancestral territory and their identity, facing national armies and then economic interests that went (and go) beyond the borders of nations—and that today are part of another type of imperialism.

Current events demonstrate that *La Araucana*'s themes of loss and tragedy are prevalent today: "estamos esperando que se pacifique la Araucanía" (we are waiting for the pacification of the Araucanian region), the Chilean government has said.[6] The situation is doubly tragic when we consider that in an attempt to subdue Mapuche protests, the national Chilean government has applied the Law of Internal Security in 1997, and the Antiterrorist Law in 2002 and 2004. Both laws originated during the dictatorship of Augusto Pinochet (1973–90).[7]

Literary critic Gilberto Triviños confirms that if there is a place in which that tragic loss is reflected, it is in "literary space,"[8] and if the founding of the Chilean nation is characterized by a "nacimiento trágico" (tragic birth), *La Araucana* "no es el poema del nacimiento épico de una nación sino la escritura estremecida de una violencia fundadora" (is not the poem of an epic birth of a nation but the trembling writing of a founding violence).[9]

The *Historia de la Nueva México* ends with a long description of the violent battle between the Spanish and the natives of Acoma Pueblo. Like *La Araucana,* the *Historia* is a poem that reflects tragedy and loss, and, as such, it could be considered the tragic beginning of the historical memory of contemporary Chicanos/as and Nuevomexicanos/as.[10] The *Historia* has been characterized as an epic "rooted in misunderstanding" and that ends "without closure."[11] There is more agreement among scholars that *La Araucana* serves as a foundational text of Chile than that the *Historia* is a foundational text of New Mexico, as will be seen.

This volume presents an analysis of Spanish imperialism and Indian resistance that took place in two frontier spaces of colonial Spanish America. Epic poetry is used as a source, specifically the poems *La Araucana* by Alonso de Ercilla (1569, 1578, 1589), about the conquest of Chile on the southern frontier of the empire, and the *Historia de la Nueva México* by Gaspar de Villagrá (1610), about the conquest of New Mexico on the northern frontier of the empire, in what is today the Southwest of the United States. In this historical study, concepts from literary criticism are fundamental. Literature and history unite in an attempt to explain processes that range from the agenda of a particular writer as a representative subject of his or her time to the consequences of imperial policy in regions far from the large colonial centers. This is not an attempt to defend a literary text as a source of absolute historical truth. Instead, it is an attempt to demonstrate the importance of the analysis of epic poetry as narrative material for the historian.

Epic poetry, as a blend of fiction and nonfiction, can provide insights into the values, attitudes, perceptions, and observations of a historic period or moment in time. This volume's view of historical events and processes through the lens of epic poetry and other primary documents aligns it with other scholarly works published on epic poetry, especially in the past twenty years. When examined as a cultural production and a complex genre of colonial literature, epic poetry offers a richer perspective to colonial studies. As scholar Elizabeth Davis states, we "can no longer ignore the epic" if we want to study and understand Spanish culture through literature. Similarly, it is impossible to ignore the fact that epic poetry is inevitably connected to imperial power.[12] It is in this direction that this book proposes to contribute to recent scholarly studies on epic poetry, with a strong emphasis on the intersection of history and epic poetry at the frontiers of the Spanish American empire.

Davis dedicates part of the introduction of her book *Myth and Identity in the Epic of Imperial Spain* to reviewing the circumstances that have dampened interest in reading and analyzing epic poetry of the Spanish Golden Age—though *La Araucana* has received ample attention from its first editions onward. The "lack of context" necessary to understand epic poetry is in part the reason for that "inattention," according to Davis.[13] This volume aims to offer a context, and also to add to the effort of rescuing epic poetry from what scholar Raúl Marrero-Fente calls "a marginal place within colonial discourse."[14] He adds that "the exclusion of the epic genre from colonial studies has left a gap that must be filled in order to create a broader framework in which to view and analyze colonial writing in Latin America."[15]

The scholarly attention paid to Spanish colonial epic poetry in the past twenty years—especially to *La Araucana*—is still paltry compared with what has been published on chronicles and *relaciones*. There is still more to look at in the epic. The comparison here of a well-known and studied epic poem such as *La Araucana* with a less-known and studied one such as the *Historia* by Villagrá, and the idea of focusing the comparison on the themes of empire and frontier is, hopefully, one of the main contributions of this volume to the use of epic poetry in this revision of colonial studies.

The seminal studies on epic and empire by James Nicolopulos,[16] David Quint,[17] and Elizabeth Davis have served this volume as important bases for understanding the theory and practice of Renaissance epic poetry and as essential works of literary criticism that add to the historical analysis. These and other works are indispensable in setting up a theoretical framework from literary criticism, which no solid analysis of history, epic poetry, and empire should overlook. All three scholars have included the two poems analyzed in this book in their own studies in the context of other classical and Renaissance epic poetry (*La Araucana* more extensively than *La Historia de la Nueva México*). Ercilla and Villagrá employ allegories, supernatural elements, and stories and themes in their poems that imitate classical works in the same genre, specifically those by Virgil, Ariosto, and Lucan. The imitation of the classics was an important aspect of Renaissance poetics. In addition, in the case of Villagrá, a clear imitation of Ercilla is also present. The analysis of those elements by literary critics helps the historian to understand and identify what is imitation and what responds to the conventional formula of the epic genre.

Furthermore, themes that apparently are a product of imitation can also be considered part of a historical reality inherent in any imperial endeavor—that is, a product of a clash between invader and invaded. One example is the theme of greed, a universal in time and space in matters of conquest and empire. Another example is the description, ubiquitous in any epic, of a huge battle, preferably a naval battle. The theme of imperial conquest and the conquerors' interactions with the "other" (the invaded) may be a product of imitation of previous epic poetry, but it is also inherent in the case of sixteenth-century Spanish conquest. The space and time may shift, but epic poetry always contains some universal themes connected to the human condition. In addition, in the case of Spanish epic poetry of the sixteenth century, the conventional Greek and Roman epic formula of including prophecies and genealogies was also present, reminiscent of the link of the Habsburg monarchy of Spain to the Holy Roman Empire.[18]

The purpose of the present volume is to offer a postcolonial critique of the historical events contained in the poems by Ercilla and Villagrá. It analyzes colonial history from an interdisciplinary perspective with a specific look at the frontier spaces where events narrated in the poems took place. The use of epic poetry as a source seeks to demonstrate the importance that literary texts originating in a specific historic context can have for an understanding of the Spanish imperial presence in the Americas, and in this specific case, in the northern and southern frontiers of Spain's American empire in the sixteenth century. In the process, it is hoped that the analysis and comparison of both poems will help elucidate the connection between political conquest and Spanish cultural practices.

Studies by literary critics such as those mentioned above and others cited throughout the book will be used to compare and contrast their conclusions in a broader historical context, one expanded in time and space. Although the epic poetry born in the Americas shares the conventional formula of the genre, the American soil gives its specific imprint to the poets' lines. In the past two decades, studies of *La Araucana* and *Historia de la Nueva México* have been centered on concepts such as the poems as foundational texts, the myth of the hero, the imitation of the classics through the presence of conventional epic themes and elements, and the ambiguity—and inconsistency—of the poets in choosing the side of the empire or that of the natives. This book will enlarge upon previous works by combining their information with a comparison of the poems sprung from two different regions: the southern and northern peripheries of the Spanish colonial empire. The two poets were soldiers who participated in their respective conquests, and although the events took place in the same century, the legal framework of the two conquests differed. This political reality is reflected in each poem, one written about a conquest at the beginning of the reign of Habsburg king Felipe II, and the other written about a conquest that took place at the end of his reign.

The regions where those conquests took place were not just any place. From the time of the arrival of the first Europeans in the sixteenth century, the two regions were characterized by their far distance from the centers of Spanish imperial power. These spaces were seen by the metropolis and its authorities—specifically the viceroys of New Spain in the north and of Peru in the south—as "frontier" zones, which is a Western or European concept; that is, zones beyond "civilization." For natives, the concept of "frontier," as such, did not exist. From the imperial point of view, if one managed to dominate the frontier zone and its resources, including its Indians, one could continue even "farther beyond." This volume pays special attention to the concept of that geographical space which the Spanish knew as "frontier." The concept of place became an important subject in the poems to the point that, perhaps, we might consider the frontier space as the main protagonist in each text. Furthermore, it can be argued that both regions today continue to be frontier zones, considering what the descendants of the natives of the respective regions are claiming in terms of identity and rights, or if we look carefully at the role of the two regions (New Mexico in the United States and the Araucanía of Chile) in the national historical memory of each nation.

Other scholarship that contributes to the analytical framework of this book is found in the works of Edward Said, José Rabasa, Rolena Adorno, Serge Gruzinski, and Michel de Certeau. Each of these scholars has inspired this author to offer a new perspective, to be applied in this case to the comparison of Ercilla and Villagrá's poems within the global/imperial, regional/frontier, and personal approaches. Regarding the imperial theme, Edward Said defines "empire" in his book *Culture and Imperialism*. He reflects on the idea that domination of a space and its people is implicit in the concept of empire. Although he refers to empires of the nineteenth century, his definition is applicable to sixteenth-century European imperialism, a fact that demonstrates that the imperial model has not changed in three centuries. According to Said, imperialism is "the practice, the theory, and the attitudes of a dominating metropolitan center ruling a distant territory; 'colonialism' . . . is the implanting of settlements on distant territory."[19]

From the standpoint of geography, Said adds the idea of "geographical inquiry into historical experience" and affirms that "the earth is in effect one world, in which empty, uninhabited spaces virtually do not exist." According to Said, we are not out of or beyond geography, therefore "none of us is completely free from the struggle over geography."[20] Struggle over geography is, according to Said, "complex and interesting because it is not only about soldiers and cannons but also about ideas, about forms, about images and imaginings."[21] It is precisely from this perspective that a rereading of the poems of Ercilla and Villagrá is proposed, using a spatial approach and making geographical space an essential factor in the intersection of history and epic poetry.

José Rabasa's conclusions about colonial space and the redrawing of the world map add to Said's point when he explains the differences between the discourse of Christopher Columbus and that of Hernán Cortés, the latter representing a second period in the "invention of America." Rabasa states that in the years that passed between Columbus's enterprise and that of Cortés, "the map of the world was redrawn, but the intent to find a western route to Asia remained in both discourses."[22] Similarly, the colonial discourses presented in the two poems analyzed here show a further redrawing of the map, adding the frontier spaces of the far north of New Spain and the areas of central and southern Chile to the imperial map. Rabasa mentions that Cortés's plans for the colonization of Asia placed "Tenochtitlán and New Spain, and no longer Hispaniola, as an intermediate region between the two ends of the Old World."[23]

As I continue with this line of analysis, the "new frontiers" of north and south, and the histories related in the two poems, appear to indicate a third period in the "invention of America." I posit the rereading of the two poems in the context of the addition of "new spaces" to the imperial map, a reading that acknowledges the importance of the route to Asia prevalent in the discourse of the two poems. By the beginning of the seventeenth century (given that Villagrá's poem was published in 1610) there still existed a colonial discourse with objectives similar to those of Columbus, except that the frontiers—from the European perspective—had moved.

The concept of "Europe and its others," in vogue in the colonial discourse of the sixteenth century, is also essential to an analysis of the poets' observations on the native cultures of Chile and New Mexico. Rabasa states the importance of identifying the Eurocentric world view in Spanish texts: "the force and effectiveness of images that fabricated new realms of reality that are still influential today."[24] In addition, all classical or Renaissance epics relied heavily on the opposition between an empire and "the other."

Ideas and images that appear in the poems represent political and social values and practices of the time and space in which the poets lived. Each text bears the clear hallmarks of its historical period—political-legal, military, and religious traits—but also those determined by the specific characteristics of each frontier space. Thus, to borrow from Victor Burgin, epic poetry, considered as a form of cultural representation, "cannot avoid involvement with social and political relations and apparatuses."[25] This book attempts to see the two poems as cultural pieces representative of a historical period but also as the colonial literary texts that they are. In and of themselves they are "a social practice," to use a concept of scholar Rolena Adorno. In other words, literary discourses "do not describe events; they *are* events, and they transcend self-reference to refer to the world outside themselves."[26] Colonial literary texts, including the two poems of this book, are written "with the objective of influencing readers' perceptions, royal policies, and social practices."[27] Therefore, one of the objectives of this book is to analyze the poems in the context of Adorno's theory.

It is in this framework of literature as "social practice" that the two poems gain meaning for the historian. Both poems had relevance as historical sources, not only in their own time but centuries later and up to the present day. The epilogue shows how the poems have been interpreted and assimilated by different generations of scholars and readers. The poets' identities have been transformed by the historical and contemporary memory of the people whose cultures and regions have inherited those poems. Their political message goes far beyond a single time period.[28] The rereading of the two poems, therefore, is presented from the perspective of a twenty-first century reader seeking meaning and relevance in accordance with the signs of our own times.

Returning to the concept of space previously mentioned, the present analysis considers the spatial theme at three levels: empire, frontier, and individual. In the case of this last level, my approach is to look at the lives of the poets in relation to their words. They wrote from a specific story and background but also as world citizens who traveled beyond their place of birth. As subjects of the Spanish empire, they lived, worked, and wrote in and about two different regions, different hemispheres, and different areas of the then-known world. The analytical approach used here implies the idea of flows of people, information, and knowledge across long distances and cultures. The book follows this perspective using the thesis of historian Serge Gruzinski. The concept of a global world after the expansion of the Spanish empire became common currency in the works of the first chroniclers. In their texts, the word "world" appeared frequently and the writers included themselves in a larger, planetary context, the "universal context of the monarchy."[29] Gruzinski writes about chroniclers, but in this volume it will be shown that his thesis can also be applied to Ercilla and Villagrá.

Thus, our two poets pertain to a group of writers who encompassed more than a single place and culture. Their biographies and the stories told in their poems are interconnected. It is impossible to separate the literary analysis from the historical analysis. Therefore, it is key to combine the fields of literature and history and their respective critical camps. It is then hoped that the result of this interdisciplinary approach is a new historical interpretation of the two literary pieces. In the words of Michel de Certeau, "the exercise of appropriate methods," in addition to creating an analysis that follows a "set of practices," is what gives value to a historical analysis.[30]

A historical study is not the product of "a personal philosophy" or "the resurgence of a past reality"; rather, it "is linked to the complex of a specific and collective creation"; it is precisely "the *product* of a *place*."[31] It is hoped that this volume accomplishes the purpose of being a historical analysis that falls within Certeau's definition. With respect to being the "product of a place," it must be noted that with contemporary methodological advances it is almost impossible to separate history from literature. Both have been characterized as "branches of the same tree." Author Russel B. Nye has aptly said that both history and literature constitute an "attempt to gain from experience some kind of insight into the quality, mood, tempo, and personality of life—not just the *fact* of the past but the *feel* of it."[32] After all, as Nye affirms, history and literature ask the same questions about the nature of man (with his term "man" understood as both men and women): "Their ultimate aim is to provide man with knowledge of himself by knowing what men have been and done—and, hopefully, perhaps why."[33]

More than ever, the modern historian must provide answers to the human uncertainties of the present. The legacy of the past in the present is not necessarily obvious, nor is the link evident: "scholars need to dig in the past in order to see the connection between it and our present.[34] In this context, I reflect on three general matters. First, the literary texts analyzed here reflect a colonial discourse characterized by Eurocentrism. Second, that mentality still has remnants today in the manner in which some studies simplify the complex colonial reality,[35] and with that in mind, this book seeks to overcome that ethnocentrism to the extent possible. Third, both poems follow an imperial model whose development implied a broader process with widespread consequences. Thus, as scholar Walter Mignolo affirms, the imperial model is "a process of Westernization of the planet," which is to say that the conquest and colonization of America must be understood as part of a "history of planetary consciousness that is irrefutably linked to the processes of colonization."[36]

At this point, it is important to present a general view of the historical circumstances in which each epic was published, as well as to clarify some concepts, such as frontier and space, used frequently in this book. *La Araucana* by Alonso de Ercilla was originally published in three parts: part 1 in 1569, part 2 in 1578, and part 3 in 1589. The poem depicts the Spanish conquest of Chile's central and southern regions between 1536 and 1559 and the resistance of the Araucanian people. In 1597, three years after Ercilla's death, the three parts were published together, along with some additions by the poet. The conquest described in *La Araucana* occurred under the leadership of two governors: Pedro de Valdivia and García Hurtado de Mendoza, although Ercilla only participated in the events during the governorship of García Hurtado.

Meanwhile, the year that the complete text of *La Araucana* was published, Governor Juan de Oñate in the northern part of the Viceroyalty of New Spain was preparing his expedition into what is today the state of New Mexico and the Southwest of the United States. Gaspar de Villagrá, who participated in that expedition as captain and *procurador general* (judge), wrote his epic poem *Historia de la Nueva México* to recount the early history of Spanish settlement directed by Oñate between 1598 and 1599. The events included in the poem also present some details of the Spanish occupancy of the region starting in 1540. The poem was published in Alcalá de Henares, Spain, in 1610.

The two extremes of the Spanish empire in the Americas began to be explored at almost the same time, with the exploration of Chile being a little earlier than New Mexico. Around the mid-sixteenth century, the Spanish conquest in South America had expanded as far as present-day Chile, with a timid attempt at occupation in the south. In what is today the U.S. Southwest, Spanish exploration had arrived at the present-day states of Arizona, New Mexico, Texas, Oklahoma, and Kansas.

In 1541 Pedro de Valdivia founded the city of Santiago de la Nueva Extremadura in today's Chile in the southern hemisphere, while in the north in the same year Francisco Vázquez de Coronado arrived at what was then called Quivira (present-day Kansas). The silver mines of Zacatecas in New Spain began to be exploited in 1546, and a rich ore strike led to the permanent establishment of Spaniards there and eventually to further expansion north. But the Spanish presence north of Zacatecas also provoked decades of resistance by the Chichimeca Indians. Between 1581 and 1593, other expeditions were sent north to what is today New Mexico, but it was the expedition of 1598 commanded by Juan de Oñate that finally established a permanent settlement. Meanwhile, on the Chilean frontier, the Spanish conquest encountered continued resistance by the Araucanians. The Spaniards advanced toward southern Chile, founding the colonies of Concepción, Imperial, Angol, Villarrica, and Valdivia. Ironically, although 1598 marked the beginning of Spanish colonization and expansion in New Mexico, on the Chilean frontier this year represented the beginning of Araucanian military victories. Between 1598 and 1622 they would not give the Spaniards a moment's respite.[37]

As noted previously in this introduction, the theme of physical space has a special place in this analysis. For this reason, this book is divided into two parts: "The Empire" and "The Frontier." The article "Space and the Rhetorics of Power in Colonial Spanish America" by scholars Santa Arias and Mariselle Meléndez offers a definition and characteristics of "space" in Spanish colonial America that are applicable to this volume's analysis. The authors draw from Michel Foucault's critical theory on space, Henri Lefebvre's characterization of space, and Doreen

Massey's observations in her book *Space, Place, and Gender*, to characterize space in the colonial discourse as an area of ground or expanse where humans interact. Such space is full of symbolism and power relations.[38] Because "space influences the way in which we think about the world and others," the obvious result is that "our view of the world and the people who inhabit it is marked by cultural and ideological baggage, which seriously influences how we describe or define others."[39] In the colonial texts of Spanish America "space (geographical, physical, and cultural) is at the center of all textual constructions, from the literature of exploration, to the autobiographies of nuns."[40]

This characterization can also be applied to our two Spanish colonial epic poems. In the analysis of the space of empire—imperial space—as depicted in the two poems, two subthemes appear: the characteristics of the sixteenth-century Spanish monarchy and legal framework of the conquest. These subthemes are to some extent determined by the content of both poems, but at the same time they constitute two key elements when it comes to understanding the nature of Spanish colonial imperial space. The space of empire, as portrayed in the poets' lines, is full of political meaning and marked by power relations.

The second part of the book, "The Frontier," is framed by frontier space, which, like the space of empire, has physical, cultural, and political dimensions. In this volume, "frontier" denotes a space in flux, in which the stability of colonization has not yet been fully achieved. Álvaro Félix Bolaños offers three useful definitions relevant to the concept of frontier space as applied in this book. He defines *frontier* as "an open space penetrated by European colonization"; the *Western city* (that is, founded by the Spanish in the Americas) as "an enclosed space inside that frontier whose existence guarantees the success of the 'conquest,'" and *colonial status quo* as "a state of social pacification considered desirable by the colonizer."[41]

Both poems refer to the establishment of Spanish cities: San Gabriel on the northern frontier and Concepción on the southern frontier. However, despite how much the poets may emphasize that those Spanish settlements meant a guarantee of "successful conquest," the historical facts show that they did not represent stability, much less a "colonial status quo." The characteristics of those two settlements were not identical. San Gabriel was more a Spanish campsite than a city, and Concepción was more of a fortress. The point is that in both frontiers these settlements were a promise rather than a reality. As scholar Julie Greer Johnson states, Spanish American cities were symbols of Spanish imperialism, and their designs "were imposed upon even the most unpretentious settlements," some of them in spaces of "isolation and peril, such as Concepción."[42]

Geography and landscape; that is, a physical space and its natural characteristics, frame the analysis in part II of this book. If the law and the global monarchy are the referents in the first part, then in the second part, the central element is the land upon which the colonizer set foot. The colonized is also part of the analysis, for the land on which the foreigner walked cannot be understood without the presence of the native cultures that inhabited it from ancestral times. The analysis in part II is based on the description of geography as an essential theme of colonial discourse and in particular in the two poems, with special attention to the physical space and its natural resources as the stage for a violent encounter.[43]

In addition, the theme of the Indians in their natural landscape, as well as the Spanish *entrada* and the ritual taking of possession by the invader, are important components of the analysis in part II. Specific geographic landmarks made frontier space either accessible or impenetrable, containable or beyond control for the colonizer. This is the theme of the final chapter. In other words, the analysis of the two poems envisions the frontier as an active protagonist, as the geographical and cultural space in which the encounter between peoples took place, especially the possession by force of the one and the inevitable resistance of the other.

If the analysis in part I makes it possible to visualize the imperial message of the two poems and the legal framework of the conquest, part II attempts to show the actor—the colonized and the colonizer (including both poets in this last group)—setting foot on the space, meeting, and deciphering each other. If both poems seem to emphasize and even honor the colonized, the analysis "from" and "in" the space shows that the central character continues to be the colonizer. It is hoped that the reader will find in part II a response to the questions and concepts presented in part I. After all, it was on the soil of the Americas, specifically in frontier space, that laws and decrees from the distant monarchy came to have meaning for the soldier-colonizer, or, to the contrary, became completely impossible to obey. In other words, the second part of the book is an attempt to answer the question: how do the two poems, in a frontier space, reflect the idea of empire conceived by Spain? The role of the poets as participants in their respective conquests is explored in response to this question. While biographies of the poets are beyond the scope of this book, the appendix summarizes the most important events in their lives, framed by the larger historical context of the conquest of each frontier.

Nevertheless, it is important to reflect on two concepts: The frontier is a Western idea perceived from the point of view of modern western New Mexico and central and southern Chile. From the native perspective, there was no "north" and "south" of an empire. The concept of frontier, or frontier space, is presented here because Spanish imperial literary sources are being analyzed. The poems originated in and for the empire, and with particular intentions that have to do with the agenda of the two writers who wrote from the Spanish perspective. Therefore, if there is one limitation in the analysis offered in this book, it is that of studying the poems from the perspective of the conqueror and not the conquered. One can anticipate that in the lines where each poet attempts to give space to the voice of the Indian, that voice is conditioned by his own ethnocentric vision. Nevertheless, to the extent possible, the analysis attempts to provide some response to questions related to perception from the perspective of "the other," or of the conquered.

Essential to defining frontier space is its counterpart: temporal space. Temporal space is understood for the purpose of this analysis as a historical period or moment in time in which the events take place. It must be emphasized that the spaces examined here existed as a function of events that took place during the first century of Spanish conquest. The frontier in the Spanish-American colonial space of the sixteenth century was not the same as that of later centuries. The concept of frontier has frequently been defined and analyzed for periods subsequent to the first stage of the conquest. But this book uses a definition determined by a different historical reality, marked especially by the moment when Spaniards attempted to establish their first permanent settlements in the most distant spaces, north and south, of the viceroyalties of New Spain and Peru. Hence, the analysis that historians have provided for the seventeenth and eighteenth centuries, while valuable, does not apply to the situation of the north in 1598 and 1599 and the south in the 1530s and 1540s. The theme of frontier space in the north and south, at a precise historical moment, remains complicated to analyze and therefore deserves to be examined in more depth.

The frontier space of the north, for purposes of this book, is considered as "starting from the south (from Mexico City) to the north," as the anthropologist Alfredo Jiménez has put it.[44] This definition has to do with a viceroyal space and history that "began in the sixteenth century and demonstrates an ongoing process," meaning that the frontier is conceived and understood from the perspective of Mexico City. Jiménez elaborates on this point of view:

> From the great city there extended a limitless panorama toward the *interior* of the continent, and this perspective also makes it possible to trace the beginning of the process to Prehispanic times when Mesoamerica, as an area of indigenous civilization, had in Mexico City–Tenochtitlán its most powerful capital. Then, in colonial times, there opened to the north an infinite frontier inhabited by nomads, with no more enclaves of agriculturalists than those represented by the Pueblo Indians of New Mexico and Arizona.[45]

This concept of a frontier space in which the Spanish conquest of New Mexico developed, specifically the first Spanish settlement of New Mexico, provides one of the physical or geographic contexts of this book. This definition incorporates the Spanish conquest within a framework that goes beyond the history of the frontier as understood from the viewpoint of the United States (the Spanish

Borderlands). It connotes a "larger system"; that is, "the far north of a continental empire,"[46] not the Southwest of North America. In this context the first Spanish settlements also concord with the idea expressed by Bernd Schröter, that "every process of expansion linked to colonization implies the formation of a frontier."[47]

Likewise, the Chilean frontier is conceived of and understood following the same conceptual framework, meaning that Chilean historians identify Araucanía as "frontier space."[48] In Chile, as in the far north of New Spain, that space is a "zone of contact" between two culturally different worlds that in the end became related. As the Chilean historian Jorge Pinto Rodríguez affirms:

> Although far from the centers where political decisions were made and almost on the periphery of the world that defined itself as civilized, frontier spaces appear to have given rise to many varied relationships, which offer evidence of the connection that existed between Indian and non-Indian societies.[49]

The first years of Spanish settlement in the frontier spaces of the far north of New Spain and the center and south of Chile developed within a framework of relationships characterized by two circumstances. On the one hand, there were periods of peace (depending on the number of Indians who accepted domination without resistance) and of war (when the Indian response was not submission). On the other hand, there was a desperate Spanish search for gold. In both north and south, the Spaniards hoped to find another rich New Spain or Peru.

In both cases, the two frontier spaces have been referred to as "peripheries," from the point of view of the world called "civilized." Nonetheless, these zones were neither marginal nor passive but areas that, although far from colonial centers, responded to forces both external and internal. The decisions made in the political centers exerted influence on the frontier zones, which at the same time created their own dynamic. Nothing in the frontier spaces was static or passive; the contrary was true in every way. Peripheries, yes, in the sense of the space most distant from the colonial centers, but also to be understood as zones with their own dynamic linked to larger processes.

This does not imply, however, that the reality of all frontier spaces of the Spanish colonial empire was the same. Therefore, this book does not aim to compare two frontier spaces by attempting to look for similarities that did not necessarily exist. Instead, this book simply observes and contemplates frontier spaces to the extent that the sources, in this case epic poetry, permit it to do. Thus, the "far north of New Spain" and the regions of central and southern Chile served as inspiration for Spanish-American epic poetry. These spaces were the most distant zones that the Spanish imperial presence had reached, with more or less permanent settlements in the north and south of the two continents between 1540 and 1599. Those peripheries adopted the shape of an appendage in the north along both sides of the Rio Grande, and in the south along the Chilean

coast and between the coast and the Andean foothills. A look at the map of
the territories covered by the Spanish in the Americas—through exploration,
missionary work, and settlement—in the second half of the sixteenth century,
clearly shows that the northern and southern frontier spaces were similar in
shape. The north was delimited by the presence of the sedentary Indian Pueb-
los. The south was constrained by the geographical features of the region, espe-
cially the mountains to the east and the Biobío River, which became the natural
divider of Spanish and Araucanian dominance. Depending on the Araucanian
advances, Spanish settlements would survive or not south of the river.

To conclude the discussion of frontier space as applied to the analysis in this
book, it is important to mention its use in comparison with that of *borderland*,
a concept used in U.S. Western history and also by literary critics, especially
in the field of Chicano literature. Borderland and frontier space have similar
definitions: the farthest lands with a Spanish presence to the north and south of
the Americas. This interpretation works as a compromise between what literary
critics who deal with the American Southwest behold and what historians who
deal with Latin America behold.

In this context, the analysis of a frontier space is a little more complex in the
case of the *Historia* than in the case of *La Araucana*. The *Historia de la Nueva
México* is a literary and historical text shared by two nations and two differ-
ent cultural heritages: the Hispanic American–Chicano/a of the United States
and the Spanish American of Mexico and Latin America. As scholar Francisco
Lomelí has mentioned, from a historical and literary perspective, Villagrá's
poem "falls somewhere in between the historical cracks of two future nations
by being perceived as neither one nor the other,"[50] until after the 1970s when the
poem acquired greater interest with the development of Chicano literary history.
Without denying the importance of the *Historia* in Chicano literature, the cur-
rent volume attempts to remind readers, through the analysis of the themes of
empire and frontier, that the *Historia* is indeed an important text for the analysis
of Latin American colonial history. Giving *La Araucana* and the *Historia* the
same degree of importance—as texts born in a frontier space of the Spanish
empire—makes it possible to give the *Historia* a more global dimension. As will
be seen in the epilogue, the *Historia* holds a special place in the literary history
of Chicano and Hispanic literature. However, it can also be seen and analyzed as
a poem, with the continental and global dimensions that it merits.

It is precisely this argument that determined that this book should include
an epilogue. It seemed appropriate and necessary to complete the postcolonial
analysis by looking at the legacy of the poems in the context of their respective
regional and national identities in the current countries where the conquests
took place (Mexico/United States and Chile). The word "legacy" is used here in
the sense of the influence the poems have had on posterity, as cultural material

with a political message. *La Araucana*, for example, is considered a "jewel" of Spanish literature, a "great example" of the most elegant use of the Castilian language, and it has been called the "national poem" of Chile for its content that praises the native Chilean. Today, however, many specialists see the poem as an imperialist poem of the sixteenth century that represents, in the final analysis, more of a paean to empire than a paean of admiration for the Araucanian Indians.

Historia de la Nueva México is considered today to belong to the classics of Hispanic American literature, written by a Mexican criollo from a Western, Christian perspective. At the same time, the poem is, for authors and literary critics in the United States, the first example of "Mexican American or Chicano literature." Therefore, although for Hispanic American or Latin American literature the poem clearly follows the canons, model, and values of a text of Spanish origin born in the Americas and with a clear imperial tinge, from the point of view of "the north," the poem represents the proud literary and cultural origin of a minority, and, as such, it is hard to square with imperial values.

The topic of frontier is in fact what inspired this book project in the first place. This analysis proposes a new way of looking at the two poems from the frontier perspective, and it is hoped that the reader will find answers in this book to questions such as:

> Is it possible that the very genesis of these poems in a frontier reality has led them to move, over the centuries, from one culture to another, from one model to another, from one identity to another?

> If each poem is the result of a frontier reality, is this what influences the role the poems have had in the construction of memory of their respective peoples?

> If the theme of frontier is such an important part of the colonial discourse that it emanates from the poems, might frontier be the real protagonist of these examples of epic?

Last, it is important to clarify that this volume does not offer a detailed study of the use of the epic as a literary genre; to the extent that the analysis demands it, the reader is referred to specific sources in the bibliography. The poems of Ercilla and Villagrá constitute examples of the traditional Renaissance epic that uses the Americas as inspiration.[51] The fact that they are poems with American themes does not mean that they fully reflect the essence of the Americas. Nevertheless, both *La Araucana* and the *Historia* relate themes that give the poems an identity distinct from European Renaissance epic poetry. The frontiers in which events took place were and are part of a different landscape: an American landscape. Both poems exhibit certain characteristics of the Spanish colonial epic that "leave a record of the Spaniard's awe (conquistador and poet) before the 'new lands.'"[52]

Ercilla and Villagrá chose the epic genre as the most appropriate format to write about their respective conquests. Publications of other epic poetry in the second half of the sixteenth century and beginning of the seventeenth century demonstrate that the genre was still in vogue. According to Spanish literary scholar Isaías Lerner, there were two reasons for the renewed interest in the epic genre: one was "the new dissemination during the Renaissance of works and genres practiced by the classical literatures," and the second, which may be considered a result of the first, was the publication in Italy of works such as *Orlando Furioso* (1516) by Ludovico Ariosto, which "offered new possibilities of artistic and thematic renovation for a genre that was paralyzed by the prestige of the Greek and Latin masterworks."[53] *La Araucana* and the *Historia* belong to the period of a resurgence of interest in the epic as a result of the Renaissance, and it is in this context that we should view them.[54]

Most epic poetry with American themes was published between the 1560s and 1630s, and as late as 1673. Scholar Alfred Arteaga argues that the *Historia* and its telling of Oñate's conquest of New Mexico did not play an important role in the "national character of Spain or Mexico" and that "its sole impact has been in New Mexico."[55] Arteaga adds: "Nor does it figure in the cultural history of the United States,"[56] although there are signs that this trend is changing. The lateness of publication of the *Historia* is what, according to Arteaga, caused it to be unknown in its time, not achieving the popularity of *La Araucana*. There could be many reasons why the *Historia* was not popular at the time, but what cannot be ignored is that in the twentieth and twenty-first centuries scholars have been paying attention to its role in the literary and historical memories of New Mexico, Mexico, Spain, and the United States. Moreover, the formation of a Spanish nationality from the sixteenth century on cannot be understood without the Americas. Spanish nationality was reinvented after the conquest of the Americas. Therefore, American-themed epic poetry—including *La Araucana* and the *Historia*—must be considered part of that phenomenon.

Scholar Paul Firbas, in his introduction to the anthology *Épica y colonia: Ensayos sobre el género épico en Iberoamérica (siglos XVI y XVII)*, pays special attention to colonial American epic poetry's specific features. While linked to imperial expansion, the poems still develop their own places and topics. Even within the limits of their poetic form, they reflect "una verdad histórica y ética" (a historical and ethical truth).[57] Firbas highlights the importance of looking at colonial epic poetry using "una lectura atenta de sus contextos de enunciación y recepción" (a reading attentive to their contexts of enunciation and reception), because this particular genre shows new forms of narrating local histories and "nuevas perspectivas o maneras de situarse ante la trama imperial" (new perspectives or ways of positioning themselves vis-à-vis the story of empire).[58] This is an essential point, because even though the imitation of classical epic poetry is cited more than once here, it is fundamental not to miss the American perspective in the two poems. Furthermore, because colonial epic poetry incorporates elements of other genres, including the chronicles of the Indies, it is "una suerte de termómetro literario de la época" (a kind of literary barometer of the period).[59]

Ercilla's poem is considered the pioneer of the American epic genre, and for that reason his model has been copied frequently in other poems inspired by the conquest of the Americas. Villagrá's *Historia de la Nueva México* is a clear example of such imitation, and examples are noted throughout this book (in some cases the lines copied from Ercilla are so obvious that they require no further explanation). A notable difference between the two poems is the theme of the Indians' relevance. While *La Araucana* gives a greater role to the presence and protagonism of the Indians (although not the central role), the *Historia* mostly follows the model of the colonial epic of New Spain in its exaltation of the heroic knight Oñate and his men.[60]

This book offers a unique format insofar as each chapter begins with quotations from the two poems that relate to the chapter's theme. Throughout the analysis, the reader will find a more extensive citation of lines from the texts than what is normally found in literary criticism. This format and the selection of verses enables readers to gain a clearer and more complete idea of the poets' styles and topics. In addition, because the epic poems are the main source material, examples from them are essential to support the arguments in each chapter.

It is hoped that the comparative study presented here, which includes historical events—human processes that took place in regions far removed from important political centers—results in an intellectual exercise that approaches universal themes important to us all. In other words, it is hoped that the south may know the north better, and the north may know the south better.

Part I

The Empire

CHAPTER 1

The Spanish Monarchy

Después que Carlos Quinto hubo
   triunfado
de tantos enemigos y naciones,
y como invicto príncipe hollado
las árticas y antárticas regiones,
triunfó de la fortuna y vano estado
y aseguró su fin y pretensiones
dejando la imperial investidura
en dicha sazón y coyuntura;

y movido del pío y santo celo
que del gobierno público tenía,
pareciéndole poco lo del suelo,
según lo que en el pecho concebía,
vuelta la mira y pretensión al cielo,
el peso que en los hombros sostenía
le puso en los del hijo, renunciados
todos sus reinos, títulos y estados.

After Carlos Fifth had triumphed
over so many enemies and nations,
as the unbeaten prince had trodden upon
the Arctic and Antarctic regions,
triumphed over fortune and vain state
and assured his end and claims
living the imperial investiture
on that blissful occasion and opportunity;

moved by piety and saintly zeal,
that for the public government he had,
seeming very little what was on earth,
according to what he conceived in his
   heart,
returning the look at heaven,
the weight that his shoulders sustained
placed it on his son, renouncing
all his kingdoms, titles, and estates.

(The goddess Bellona in Ercilla, *La Araucana*, 17.53, 1–8; 54, 1–8)

Y vista aquesta causa mal parada,
Al punto procuró el Marqués heroico,
Por ser del mar del Sur Adelantado,
Que por este derecho pretendía
Y alegaba ser suya la jornada,
Y assí por no perderla ni dexarla
Vino a tomar de España la derrota
Para tratar con la imperial persona
De vuestro bien aventurado Abuelo,
Carlos Quinto, de toda aquesta causa,
Cuio alto y prudentísimo gobierno
Tuvo de los imperios más notables,
Reynos y señoríos desta vida
La suprema y más alta primacía

And, deciding the matter will end ill,
Immediately the heroic Marquis claimed,
As Adelantado of the South Sea,
This right he claimed and alleged
To make the voyage was his in fact.
And so he might not lose or let it lapse
He took at once the way to Spain
To treat with the imperial person
Of your most fortunate grandfather,
Carlos the Fifth, on all that case,
Whose lofty and most prudent government
Did have of empires the most notable,
Of kingdoms and of lordships in this life
The highest and most lofty primacy

(Villagrá, *Historia*, 3, 197–210)

In the National Library of Madrid there is a document titled "Maxims for the Palace." It includes various sections with rules of comportment to be followed by any vassal who dealt with the king, as well as references to how the king should treat his vassals.[1] These maxims project an image of an almost omnipotent Spanish royal authority. Reading them conjures up the degree of intimidation a subject no doubt felt on encountering the king. The section titled "Gallantry or Grace" cites an anecdote pertinent to this book. According to the document, the poet Alonso de Ercilla was so intimidated by the presence of King Felipe II that he could not speak a single word.

> So austere was the prudent and great king, don Felipe II, that when don Alonso de Erzilla y Zuniga, who was a very discreet gentleman (who composed the poem *La Araucana*) was speaking to him, he got lost without making what he wanted to say clear such that the king, having heard that his unease stemmed from the respect with which he viewed his Majesty, said to him one day, *Don Alonso, tell me in writing.*[2]

By way of a lesson or moral, the document adds: "This is how princes should understand whence this respect of the vassals is born, and this is how the vassals should understand to thus respect princes."[3]

Access to the monarch was not generally easy. A few years before Felipe II's accession to the throne, his father, Carlos V, had imposed on the court of Castile the ceremonial protocol created by the Dukes of Burgundy in the fifteenth century, a strict formality that impeded easy access to see or speak with the king.[4] The sensation, less of respect than of fear, that King Felipe II's presence produced in his vassals is understandable, given his characteristic austerity, added to the authority he held as the most powerful monarch of his time.

In the middle of the sixteenth century, the Spanish monarchy was the strongest in the Western world, an empire "on which the sun never set." Spanish possessions in Europe included the Holy Roman Empire that Felipe's father governed as Carlos V (as king of Spain he held the title Carlos I). In 1556 Felipe II inherited the Spanish crown but not the title of emperor, for Carlos passed the possession of the Holy Roman Empire to his brother Fernando, Felipe II's uncle. Territories added during the reign of Felipe II included the first Spanish settlement in the Philippines in 1565. The empire was later strengthened with the union of the crowns of Spain and Portugal in 1580. Although Felipe did not himself exercise the title of emperor, he ruled such an enormous area, especially after the conquest of the Philippines, that he was occasionally called "emperor of the Indies." Today historians still use the word "empire" for the reign of Felipe II, and this book will use this term. Nevertheless, officially, Felipe II's authority was exercised as king of Spain and his rule was known as the Spanish monarchy.[5]

As for the two regions analyzed in this book, the first attempts to conquer New Mexico had begun during the imperial period of Carlos V, and the conquest of Chile also began during his rule. In the poetry cited at the beginning of this chapter, both Ercilla and Villagrá refer to events that occurred during the government of Carlos V. Nevertheless, it was during the reign of Felipe II that the most important events in the conquest of Chile and the start of the conquest of New Mexico took place. Historians generally agree that it was during the reign of Felipe II that the Americas began to form an active part of the Spanish monarchy.

The reign of Carlos I of Spain (r. 1516–56) is considered to be a continental empire: European possessions and the policy exercised in them constituted the bulk of Spanish empire. During the reign of Felipe II (r. 1556–98), especially because of the development of trade, the empire expanded to become part of the Atlantic economic framework. The apogee of Spanish imperialism during the reign of Felipe II was directly correlated with the growth of trade between Seville and the Spanish American colonies.[6] The mines of Zacatecas in Mexico (Viceroyalty of New Spain) and Potosí in Bolivia (Viceroyalty of Peru) began to be exploited in 1546, but their silver did not represent an important income for the Spanish crown until the end of the 1550s, around the time when the reign of Felipe II began. The region of Nueva Granada (modern-day Colombia and Venezuela) had been added to the Spanish empire in the 1530s.

This situation lasted until about the 1640s. Between 1621 and 1641 the Spanish Atlantic empire began to decline, principally because of a reduction in trade and a decrease in shipments of silver from the Spanish colonies. The reign of Felipe III (r. 1598–1621) was a period centered on similar imperial premises, since his father, Felipe II, had prepared him for duties comparable to those previously established by Carlos I.[7] According to British historian John Elliot, Felipe II's father had trained him to inherit the government with an education in which a "deep sense of duty" predominated.

> His father had listed his moral and political obligations in his famous series of Instructions, in which it could be read that "as the principal and firm basis of your good government, you must always recognize that all your being and goods come from God's infinite goodness and submit your desires and actions to his will."[8]

From this training came the feeling of duty to God, to his dynasty, and to "the many subjects whom God had entrusted to his care,"[9] which permeated Felipe II's government. From Castile, and between 1584 and 1598 from the monastery of El Escorial, Felipe II ruled his European and American dominions and the Philippines. Taken as a whole, his dominions were characterized by great diversity of terrain and peoples on whom unity was conferred by the "dynastic element" that, according to Elliot, is "crucial to understanding Felipe's mentality and his attitude with respect to the tasks of government."[10] Felipe had inherited the mission to preserve this dynastic inheritance, especially the defense of the Catholic faith. But in contrast to his father, Felipe decided to live in Spain (he also lived in the Low Countries for three years of his reign). His court resided permanently in Madrid after 1561. Carlos V had traveled tirelessly throughout his European dominions, but "Felipe preferred, in the words of an Aragonese memorial, 'to rule the world from a throne.'"[11]

It is important to underscore the length of Felipe II's reign: forty-two years in total, not to mention that for years before his ascension in 1556 he had already taken charge of many government functions as prince and heir to the throne. There were two stages to his reign: that of Renaissance prince in the first decades of his rule, and that of the tired and ill ruler of the decade of the 1590s. To this must be added the changes that had taken place after 1548 with respect to court ceremony, to reduce access to the king. During the years of his dotage, this etiquette contributed to the image of a "semi-hidden monarch," dressed in black as a result of his many years of mourning deceased wives and children.[12] While important events in the conquest of Chile developed during the stage of the "Renaissance prince," the conquest of New Mexico began precisely in 1598, the final year of Felipe II's life.

According to historian Henry Kamen, the creation of the Spanish empire can be placed in the mid-sixteenth century, when Spain was prepared not so much to conquer and expand but to solidify what it possessed.[13] In the second half of the sixteenth century, during the forty-two years of Felipe II's reign, lands that had been conquered during the first half of the century began to be secured. This period of consolidation of the colonized territories extended to the beginning of the seventeenth century and was marked in great part by the New Ordinances for Settlement and Discovery of 1573, the writing of which Felipe II entrusted to Juan de Ovando. These ordinances gave the colonization of the Indies a different character from that given in the New Laws of the period of Felipe's father, Carlos I (or Carlos V). During the reign of Felipe II, at least in theory, no one spoke of conquest; rather, of pacification and consolidation of what had been gained.[14]

The situation of the two frontier territories studied here sharply diverged from that of the rest of the imperial possessions. One could almost say that they did not completely coincide with the period of consolidation. Near the outset of Felipe II's rule, the death of the conquistador Pedro de Valdivia (1553) at the hands of the Araucanians was the beginning of the period of Spanish domination characterized by advances and retreats in Chilean territory, with a high degree of violence. On the northern frontier, the first Spanish settlement in New Mexico, carried out under the leadership of Juan de Oñate during the last year of Felipe II's life, could be considered late in the process of pacification and consolidation of the Spanish colonial dominions to which the New Ordinances for Settlement and

Spanish colonization in the Americas (1540–1599). *Map by Erin Greb. Copyright © 2016, University of Oklahoma Press.*

The administrative regions and cities depicted here are from the period covered in the poems *La Araucana* and *Historia de la Nueva México*. Brazil is also included—from 1580 to 1640 Portugal and all its colonies belonged to the Spanish monarchy.

Discovery of 1573 referred. While in other parts of the Spanish colonial Americas there already existed universities, on these two frontiers the situation was largely unstable and precarious. Nevertheless, Spanish bureaucracy arrived in the most remote places, and Chile and New Mexico were no exception; slowly but surely they were incorporated into Spain's administration and economy.

Those two faraway regions, like any other territory added to the Spanish colonial system, became integrated into the European and international administration of the Spanish monarchy.[15] Domination implied a centralization that attempted, at least in theory, to control all aspects of the administration of the Americas and the Philippines from Spain. As Felipe II's biographer Manuel Fernández Álvarez puts it, the monarch's stance on the Indies began to emerge when he was still a boy. Pride in a new system of empire such as Spain's must have influenced him as a youth, when news arrived of the Spanish conquest in the Indies. His teacher, Ginés de Sepúlveda, must have imparted the successes of the Spanish conquest to the prince. According to Fernández Álvarez,

> the prince liked to ask Pedro de Lagasca about matters of the Indies, when the peacemaker of Peru, on his return to Spain, went to the imperial court to report to Carlos V on the success of this mission and met him in Mantua.[16]

Pedro de Lagasca mentioned in his letters that "he had seen and comprehended what the ancients had not suspected" with respect to the extent of the Spanish empire.[17] Diego de Villalobos y Benavides, another contemporary of the reign of Felipe II, who was witness to and a participant in the European scene of the imperial wars of Felipe's latter years, echoed the importance of the empire at the end of the sixteenth century:

> because of its virtues the name Spaniard was almost immortal, from the most Antarctic regions to the Arctic [regions] of our poles, passing the torrid regions of the Equinox, following the rapid path of the sun, circling the ocean and the Earth, without leaving any place where Spanish crosses were unknown.[18]

Although the consolidation of what had been conquered, rather than expanding into new territories, was a main objective of Felipe's reign, his government's financial problems—in large part because of the need to maintain political and religious supremacy in Europe—meant that even at the end of his rule "the fever of gold and the fever of the faith" continued to rage. Thus, at the end of his monarchy Felipe II still saw gold and faith as intertwined concepts.[19]

The poems of Ercilla and Villagrá echo this mixed idea of the empire along with the view of Spanish people as capable of dominating almost the entire globe. Some lines, and in Ercilla's case entire cantos, are almost exact copies of the words of military men who were their contemporaries, such as Diego de Villalobos. The image of empire that functioned so well as a framework for epic poetry (ancient, medieval, or modern) became, in *La Araucana* and the *Historia*, not the product of fantasy or the poets' imagination but the depiction of a historical reality: the most extensive empire in Earth's history up to that time.

The monarchy of Felipe II, whose realms encompassed vast, distant regions, instilled radical change in the colonies, given its ambition of transforming core values, ways of life, and beliefs to remake them after the fashion of Spain and the "civilized West." But, as is well known, the process of Westernization was not completely successful, and although it is not the purpose of this book to analyze the result, it is important to record and recognize it. This process was referred to at the time as "Hispanization." Bernal Díaz del Castillo referred to it as the "good conduct of life."[20] But "to Hispanicize" is not an adequate concept to define this process; "Westernize" is more accurate. As historian Serge Gruzinski explains, it was more Westernization than Hispanization because the former "animates a deeper and more definitive process than "Hispanicize."[21]

According to Gruzinski, in the sixteenth century the Spanish Catholic monarchy could be defined as a "planetary conglomerate" that covered various continents and connected diverse forms of government, as well as economies, societies, and religious traditions. The phenomenon of "planetization" was seen also in the spread of Spanish urban models to the colonies, which Carlos V had already initiated. Printing presses and institutions of higher education were established in the Americas and Asia, with the concomitant importation of Spanish literary genres.[22] Questionnaires administered in colonial towns obtained sufficient geographic information to produce the *relaciones geográficas*, which numbered among many other texts that permitted the monarchy to achieve global knowledge of the conquered lands.[23]

In the realm of commerce, a transatlantic market that surpassed the borders of Europe was generated. In the financial realm, the constant arrival of American silver and gold in Spain, shipped from there to the rest of Europe, initiated a period of monetary speculation—and the growth of Spanish debt. In the social realm, the circulation and interchange of goods and people created an unusual phenomenon: societies that formed part of this global space projected a "mestizo" reality which, with its mixture of races and cultures, was difficult to explain or ignore from the European perspective.[24] In the realm of religion, however, the situation was more unified. The existence of the *Real Patronato*, or royal patronage, gave the king of Spain absolute powers over the Catholic Church and the ecclesiastical organization in his European and overseas possessions. The doctrine imposed by the Counter-Reformation made itself felt throughout the Spanish empire, and as historian John Elliot notes, it "dictated a certain degree of coherence and an ideology common to the dominions of the king of Spain that were in other ways very diverse."[25]

Through the Real Patronato, the Spanish crown had the "divine" right and the mission to Christianize the Indians of the Americas. The Spanish language and the Catholic religion were two key elements of Spanish colonial expansion and became essential parts of the construction of empire. This endeavor had begun on the Iberian Peninsula long before 1492, the year of the Christian Reconquest of the Iberian Peninsula, with the marriage of Isabel of Castile and Fernando of

Aragón, an event that had achieved the political and religious union of two large regions, and with it, the beginning of a concentration of royal power.

The Spanish empire of the sixteenth century, with its laws, its language, and its religion, whose development was based on the concept of *de facto* and *de jure* possession and control, has inspired writers and chroniclers from the beginning of Spanish colonial expansion.[26] The poetry of Ercilla and Villagrá was written with this "planetary" consolidation of Spanish power in the second half of the sixteenth century as the backdrop. Both poets, though they attempt to grant recognition and significance to Indian cultures (Ercilla more than Villagrá), cannot escape a Western, Christian, imperial perspective that the poets themselves—direct participants in conquest—represent. Fundamental aspects of the construction of empire appear in the poems, such as overseas trade (including commercial traffic by sea between west and east and the constant search for a passage between the Atlantic and Pacific oceans), the continual search for precious metals to sustain the power (and pay the debt) of Spain in Europe, and religion as a fundamental element backed with royal authority. Together with the idea of a "predestined" monarchy and the defense of a dynastic heritage wed to the Catholic faith—a legacy that Carlos had been so insistent on leaving to his son Felipe—these aspects of empire-building occur in both poems. Nevertheless, even with the poems' strong underlying theme of imperial Spain, they represent the topics and geographic space of the Americas.

Elizabeth Davis, in her study titled "The Epic of New Spain and Imperial Ideology," mentions the topic of imperial Spain as central to the epic poetry of New Spain of the seventeenth century, but the topic applies perfectly to the case of Chile and *La Araucana* in the sixteenth century. The epic of New Spain, and the Spanish American epic in general, reflected the image of an expanding empire with the special characteristics of the American scene, which, in Davis's words, created a paradox: "poetry that incorporated the American reality at the same time that it documented the inevitability of the conquest."[27] To this paradox is added that of the subject of this chapter: the contradictory idea of "the American reality" that, while it appeared to be unique and different from European reality, continued to be part of the same empire. For the Spanish monarchy, the colonies were but a small portion of their holdings and nothing more than a territory with subjects subordinated to the absolute power of a king.

Imperial space, including a monarchy that merged political and religious authority together, was a special subject in colonial literature. The idea of a global world has appeared in colonial texts since the first chronicles, in which the word "world" is frequently used. The authors of those texts began to see a larger context. This planetary view was inspired by the existence of an expansive empire as seen from a Western vantage point. The writers viewed themselves as citizens of the world. These chroniclers, born in Spain and its colonies, belonged to an extensive empire and moved, traveled, observed, and saw a diverse and complex "Spanish world," which they wrote about.[28] Ercilla and Villagrá belonged to this group of writers.[29] They composed their epic poems within the "universal context of the monarchy" and also from a Western point of view. This Westernization also implied using mechanisms, techniques, and topics that positioned the histories in verse in a larger framework of Western history without which no literary work of this period had legitimacy.

The second part of this book will discuss specific examples of this characteristic—echoes of classical tradition—in the two poems. Each poet turns to elements that make his poem parallel to the great poems that laud the greatness of another empire, the Roman Empire. There is no doubt that just as the Roman Empire inspired Virgil and Lucan, and the Carolingian Empire inspired Ariosto, the Spanish empire inspired Ercilla and Villagrá. Without abandoning the classical and Renaissance models, they gave their work its own Spanish American flavor.[30]

Against the backdrop of Spanish imperial expansion, both poems allude to the importance of Spanish royal authority over the new lands. Literary critic Rolena Adorno affirms that the "polemics of possession" is the central theme of most typical works in the Spanish-American colonial literary tradition. The writers debated Spain's right to the conquest and also the treatment of the indigenous population. The content of these narratives not only represents social values and political practices, but the colonial writers' words themselves can be considered elements of a state policy.[31] *La Araucana* and the *Historia de la Nueva México* fall into this category.

What makes American-themed epic poetry unique is the special characteristics it acquires in the context of this new geographic space. While imitating a preexisting epic formula, the poems reflect aspects of the history of an empire that was neither Roman nor Carolingian. It is, therefore, of great importance not to forget this factor when analyzing the poems. To try to explain the histories told or praised by Ercilla and Villagrá, using only a comparison with classical epic poets, is insufficient for understanding the perspective from which they wrote.

The idea of an enormous empire still in the process of expanding, together with the existence of a monarchy that combined political and religious authority, appears in the prologues of both poems, although with some differences. The poets dedicated their poems to their respective kings and directed themselves to their king as principal interlocutor (Felipe II in *La Araucana* and Felipe III in the *Historia*). The messages the poets chose to include in their prologues each had special meanings. Ercilla emphasizes the importance of writing about the bravery of the Araucanians, although it appears in the context of warfare that consolidated the Spanish empire in Europe. Villagrá, in his prologue and dedicatory to the king, highlights the importance of the religious mission of the Spanish monarchy. Each poem thus emphasizes the theme of empire but establishes, starting with the prologue, a different message about how each poet sees the indigenous presence in the framework of Spanish imperial expansion.

In the prologue to part 1 of *La Araucana*, published in 1569, Ercilla refers explicitly to the need for his history to be set down on paper so that the feats of Spaniards in distant lands are not forgotten.

> I have decided to print it, aided in this by the importuning of many witnesses to much of what is found therein and by the harm that was done to some Spaniards, with their feats in perpetual silence, lacking someone to write about them, and finally, because the Spaniards who have set foot in that part of Peru can scarcely get news of it.[32]

After mentioning the importance of recognizing Spanish deeds, Ercilla refers to the need to speak of the valor with which the Araucanians defended their territory and mentions that the reader may possibly find that the poem is on their side, "if in some way it seems that I appear to be someone inclined toward the Araucanians, dealing with their matters and their bravery more extensively than that which it appears that barbarians require." The poet later praises the Araucanians' bravery in defense of their territory: "for many have not given them [the Araucanians] the advantage, and there are a few who have with such great constancy and firmness defended their land against such ferocious enemies as are the Spaniards."[33] Note that the poet, after referring with admiration to the Araucanians' bearing, again underscores the intimidating bearing of the Spaniards as an enemy.

In part 2 of his poem, published in 1578, Ercilla anticipates in a second prologue directed "to the reader," the inclusion of the topic of the imperial Spanish presence in Europe, with the battles there of San Quintín and Lepanto, and adds that his poem also touches on the Araucanians' triumph in the city of Concepción. The two great European battles are presented in the same context as the battle in Chile because, the poet says,

> It is of no little daring to want to put two such great things in such a humble place; but the Araucanians deserve everything, because for more than thirty years they held to their opinion, without ever dropping their weapons from their hands.[34]

About the time of the publication of the first and second parts of *La Araucana*, the poet, then in Spain, witnessed major events in the reign of Felipe II. In the 1570s King Felipe II's authority was consolidated after years of important decisions and battles. He was, in other words, building what would be his home and empire and not that of his father.[35] The first edition of part 3 of *La Araucana* was

Alonso de Ercilla, age 45. *Biblioteca Nacional, Madrid, IH/2777/1.*

Engraving made for the 1578 edition of *La Araucana*, parts 1 and 2. Attributed to Juan de Arfe.

published in 1589, just nine years after the annexation of Portugal to the Spanish empire. No doubt this was why the "royal privilege," or authorization for its publication, was given not only in Spanish but also in Portuguese. The authorization's appearance in a language other than Spanish was a reminder to readers of the larger linguistic and political dimensions of the empire. In the year 1597 the three parts of *La Araucana* were published together for first time, just one year before the death of Felipe II and the end of his reign.

Villagrá, on his part, in his dedication of *Historia de la Nueva México* to King Felipe III, mentions the importance of royal authority, especially as it relates to the expansion of the empire and the Catholic faith,

PRIMERA,
SEGVNDA, Y
TERCERA PAR-
TES DE LA
ARAVCANA,

De don Alonſo de Ercilla y çuñiga,
Cauallero de la orden de Santiago,
Gentil hombre de la camara
de la Mageſtad del
Emperador.

DIRIGIDAS AL REY
don Felippe nueſtro Señor.

EN ANVERS,
En caſa de Pedro Bellero, *1597.*
Priuilegio Real.

Title page, first edition of *La Araucana*, parts 1–3, by Alonso de Ercilla y Zúñiga, 1597. *Biblioteca Nacional, Madrid, Cerv.Sedó/8743.*

The poem is dedicated to King Felipe II and bears the king's coat of arms. Ercilla died in 1594 and never saw his complete poem published.

knowing that with one voice the whole world confesses, that in so exalted a prince and his vast monarchy the title of preserver, defender, and amplifier of the Roman Church and of all those who like true sons seek to broaden its sacrosanct boundaries and size.[36]

Though he published his poem in 1610 and dedicated it to Felipe III, Villagrá makes constant reference to the importance of the reign of Felipe II, a historical period essential to the decision to conquer New Mexico and to the events of its conquest. Thus, he frequently addresses Felipe III as if it had been during his rule that the Spanish settlement of New Mexico took place. According to Villagrá, the conquest of New Mexico came about by "divine consent" and was destined to be carried out by "Your Majesty" (the poet does not say that the conquest was destined for his father, Felipe II).[37]

not without the admirable providence of the Tribunal of God that after so many years since the creation of the universe sought to destine the conquest of our New Mexico to Your Majesty's powerful arm alone, having hidden it from all the greatness and efforts of your fortunate ancestors, grandfathers, and great-grandfathers of laudable memory.[38]

Like Ercilla, Villagrá in his prologue emphasizes the need for the historical facts to be told in writing because it is the only way for the great feats to be recorded: "history not only makes those who are absent present, it also resuscitates and gives life to the dead." He also reiterates the need for there to be a written record of what the Spaniards did on their *entrada* into New Mexico: "so that the many travails and feats of those valiant men who entered New Mexico in the conversion of so many nations and peoples may not be lost, swallowed up, or extinguished."[39]

The prologues and dedications of the two epics demonstrate tendencies that in some way mark the main intention of each poet. It is true that both felt the need to mention the importance of the Spaniards' deeds and that the underlying theme of empire is present in both poems. Both poets followed a classical model, and the limitations of the censorship to which their works were exposed is also evident. Nevertheless, one must suppose that they also had a degree of freedom to decide which facet to emphasize. The prologues and dedications must be weighed in this light, even though this means passing them through the filter of the poets' subjectivity.

It may be useful to see how each poet chose to begin his poem and to what extent royal authority, empire, or the feats of Spanish conquistadors are protagonists at the beginning of each poem. As necessary as it was to begin with a dedication to the king and to address him specifically in their prologues, it was also *de rigueur* to specify, from the first canto, the geographic space in which the

Gaspar de Villagrá, age 55, in the first edition of *Historia de la Nueva México*, printed in Alcalá de Henares, Spain, 1610. *Center for Southwest Research, University Libraries, University of New Mexico.*

Villagrá would die at sea ten years later when he was returning to the Americas to occupy an administrative post in Guatemala.

conquest took place and the heroes or main protagonists in each case. In both poems, the first eight lines of the first canto allude to Spaniards ("valiant men" in *La Araucana*, "brave men" in the *Historia*) as the protagonists. Ercilla mentions the Spaniards and the conquest in the first stanza, followed by the other protagonists, the Indians of Chile, in the second stanza.

HISTORIA
DE LA NVEVA
MEXICO, DEL CAPITAN
GASPAR DE VILLAGRA.

DIRIGIDA AL REY D. FELIPE
nueſtro ſeñor Tercero deſte nombre.

Año   1610.

CON PRIVILEGIO.
En Alcala, por Luys Martinez Grande.
coſta de Baptiſta Lopez mercader de libros

Title page, first edition of *Historia de la Nueva México* by Captain Gaspar de Villagrá, 1610. *Fray Angélico Chávez History Library, New Mexico History Museum.*

The poem is dedicated to King Felipe III and bears the king's coat of arms. Villagrá was in Spain when the book was published. Meanwhile, the poem's protagonist, Juan de Oñate, was in Mexico awaiting the final verdict of the charges brought against him and other members of the 1598 expedition, including Villagrá.

No las damas, amor, no gentilezas
de caballeros canto enamorados,
ni las muestras, regalos y ternezas
de amorosos afectos y cuidados,
mas el valor, los hechos, las proezas
de aquellos españoles esforzados,
que a la cerviz de Arauco no domada
pusieron puro yugo por la espada.

Cosas diré también harto notables
de gente que a ningún rey obedecen,
temerarias empresas memorables
que celebrarse con razón merecen,
raras industrias, términos loables
que más los españoles engrandecen
pues no es el vencedor más estimado
de aquello en que el vencido es reputado.

Not of ladies; not of love; not of the
    gracious gestures
of gentlemen's love songs,
not demonstrations, presents, and
    tenderness
of loving affection and care;
but the deeds, the courage, the valor
of those strong Spaniards,
who, to the neck of untamed Arauco,
with their swords, placed the yoke of
    oppression.

Things I will also tell, notable Sir,
of people who obey no king,
rash memorable undertakings
that with reason should be celebrated,
praiseworthy terms to their rare talents
that more to enhance the Spanish;
for then, is not the conqueror more
    esteemed
for which the conquered is reputed.

(Ercilla, *La Araucana*, 1.1, 1–8; 2, 1–8)

These first two stanzas of *La Araucana* are directly inspired by the format Ariosto used in his *Orlando Furioso*. Charlemagne is replaced by King Felipe II, and Orlando is replaced by the Araucanians.[40] In the third stanza, Ercilla informs the reader that his story is based on real events and that his lines will only gain influence and authority if the king approves them.

Suplícoos, gran Felipe, que mirada
esta labor, de vos sea recebida,
que, de todo favor necesitada,
queda con darse a vos favorecida.
Es relación sin corromper sacada
de la verdad, cortada a su medida;
no despreciéis el don, aunque tan pobre,
para que autoridad mi verso cobre.

I beg of you, great Philip upon seeing
this work, be received by you,
which needed of all your grace,
is within your favor to receive it.
It is a narrative without alteration
of truth, fitted to its measure;
do not scorn the gift, however poor,
so my verse may gain acceptance.

(Ercilla, *La Araucana*, 1.3, 1–8)

Villagrá, on the other hand, introduces conquistador Juan de Oñate in the first lines of his *Historia* and subsequently cites the Spaniards as heroes in their armed conquest.[41] Note also in the first lines the mention of the expansion "beyond the known world" (*plus ultra*), which provides the motif for this portion of the poem.[42]

Las armas y el valor heroico canto,
El ser, valor, prudencia y alto esfuerzo

I sing of arms and the heroic man,
The being, courage, care, and high effort

De aquel cuya paciencia no rendida,	Of him whose unconquered patience,
Por un mar de disgustos ponzoñosa	Though cast upon a sea of cares,
Los hechos y proezas va encumbrando	In spite of envy slanderous,
De aquellos españoles valerosos	Is raising to new heights the fears,
Que en la Occidental India remontados,	The deeds, of those brave Spaniards who,
Descubriendo del mundo lo que esconde,	In the far India of the West,
'Plus Ultra' con braveza van diciendo	Discovering in the world that which was hid,
A fuerza de valor y brazos fuertes,	"Plus Ultra" go bravely saying
En armas y quebrantos tan sufridos	By force of valor and strong arms,
Quanto de tosca pluma celebrados.	In war and suffering as experienced
	As celebrated now by pen unskilled.

(Villagrá, *Historia*, 1, 1–13)

Villagrá finds direct inspiration in the first verses of Virgil's *Aeneid*, with Oñate as the Aeneas of the *Historia*.[43] Later, he finds inspiration in Ercilla when communicating with King Felipe III. Note the reference below to the American space, specifically to "the New Mexico," and to Spanish royal authority, which, in the words of the poet, ruled the whole planet.

Suplicoos, Christianísimo Filipo,	I beg of thee, most Christian Philip,
Que, pues de nueva México soys fénix,	Being the Phoenix of New Mexico
Nuevamente salido y producido	Now newly brought forth from the flames
De aquellas vivas llamas y cenizas	Of fire and new produced from ashes
De ardentísima fee, en cuyas brasas	Of the most ardent faith, in whose hot coals
A vuestro sacro Padre y señor nuestro	Sublime your sainted Father and our lord
Todo deshecho y abrasado vimos,	We saw all burned and quite undone,
Suspendáis algún tanto de los hombros	Suspend a moment from your back
El grande y grave peso que os impide	The great and heavy weight which bears you down
De aquese inmenso globo que en justicia	Of this enormous globe which, in all right,
Por sólo vuestro brazo se sustenta	Is by your arm alone upheld

(Villagrá, *Historia*, 1, 14–24)

In the next lines of the same canto, Villagrá again mentions the protagonism of Juan de Oñate, whom he calls the "Christian Achilles," an interesting comparison to the hero of Homer's *Iliad*.[44] From the beginning of the poem, the allusion to the Gospel and Christian religion signals the importance of the religious theme in the conquest of New Mexico. Villagrá addresses the king as his principal interlocutor, as did Ercilla. Nevertheless, it is important to note that the poet forgets he is addressing Felipe III when he says "you wished" Oñate to be the leader. Villagrá should have said "that your father (Felipe II) wished."

Y, prestando, gran Rey, atento oído,	And, lending, O great King, attentive ear.
Veréis aquí la fuerza de trabajos,	Thou here shalt see the load of toil,

Calumnia y aflicciones con que planta	Of calumny, affliction, under which
El evangelio santo y Fee de Christo	Did plant the evangel holy and the Faith
Aquel Christiano Achiles que quisistes	of Christ
Que en obra tan heroica se ocupase.	That Christian Achilles whom you wished
	To be employed in such heroic work.

    (Villagrá, *Historia*, 1, 25–30)

The theme of imperial expansion continues in the second canto of the *Historia*. Villagrá refers to the magnitude of the conquest of a "new world" that appears small from the point of view of the conquistadors' spirit.

Y porque vuestra gente Castellana,	And because your Castilian folk,
A quien parece corta la grandeza	To whom the grandeur of the Universe
De todo el universo que gozamos	entire
Para pisarla toda y descubrirla,	That we enjoy, to tread and to discover
Por sí misma alcanzó una grande parte	Seems small,
De aqueste Nuevo Mundo que inquirimos,	Did for themselves grasp a great part
Adelante diremos quáles fueron	Of this new world which we explore,
Y quiénes pretendieron la jornada	I shall say later who they were,
Sin verla en punto puesta y acabada.	Those who the journey undertook
	Not seeing it done and ended in a moment.

    Villagrá, *Historia*, 2, 300–305)

Turning again to *La Araucana*, the importance of empire appears with clarity in part 2 (specifically cantos 17 and 18), published in 1578, and in part 3 (canto 37), published in 1589. Two main concepts connected with the theme of empire appear in both Ercilla and Villagrá. One is that of *plus ultra* and *non plus ultra;* the other is the search for a passage between the Atlantic and Pacific oceans (known as the North and South seas). Ercilla employed a third concept (Villagrá does not do so explicitly), that of connecting battles on American soil with battles on European soil. Ercilla devotes a large part of *La Araucana* to the battle theme, with the aim of showing the Spanish fighting spirit in the expansion of empire on two different fronts in two parts of the known world.

Although the topic of empire appears in different forms in the two poems, Ercilla employs it with greater frequency and more extensively, which is something of a paradox considering the importance he gives the Araucanians in his prologue. Evidently there is a reason for this. During the period covered in *La Araucana*, the Spanish empire was constantly expanding in Europe, with major battles taking place during the reign of Felipe II (San Quintín and Lepanto) and the important annexation of Portugal in 1580. Ercilla takes advantage of the warfare in Europe as a subject that fits perfectly with the formula of epic poetry. The poet also links what was happening in Chile to what was happening in Europe.

It has been asserted from the beginning of this book that the Spanish monarchy in the sixteenth century acquired "planetary" characteristics in the context of "Westernization." Spain not only governed but also insisted on imposing a European political, cultural, and religious model. This idea of globalization, of the implantation of a uniform world, was represented geographically by the idea of plus ultra, going beyond the known world. Plus ultra was the motto of the conquest of America and part of Castile's coat of arms. Reference to the counterpart of this motto, non plus ultra or *nihil ultra*, not going beyond the known world, also occurs. The reference to the Pillars of Hercules in the Straits of Gibraltar at the mouth of the Mediterranean Sea, as the limit of the known world, was also frequent in Renaissance poetry, for example, in Dante and Ariosto.[45]

Both poems mention the Spanish challenge to the ancient idea of not going beyond the pillars that mark the portal to the unknown. The voyagers' boldness demonstrated once again the universality to which the Catholic monarchy was predestined. Ercilla introduces this theme in part 2, canto 23, and continues with it in subsequent cantos. An imaginary character, the Indian wizard Fitón, appears in order to introduce the idea of an expanding Spanish empire.[46] Looking into a magic ball in which the known world is visible, the wizard permits the poet to see the geographic extent of Spanish authority, making specific allusion to the Pillars of Hercules, the boundary of the ancient world.[47]

"Mira a Cádiz donde Hércules famoso
  sobre sus hados prósperos corriendo,
fijó las dos colunas vitorioso,
Nihil ultra en el mármol escribiendo;
mas Fernando católico glorioso,
los mojonados términos rompiendo,
del ancho y Nuevo Mundo abrió la vía,
porque en un mundo solo no cabía."

"Look at Cádiz where famous Hercules
running over his prosperous fate,
established the two pillars victorious,
writing Ultra Nihil in marble;
but glorious Catholic Fernando,
breaking landmarks,
of the width and new world opened the
    road,
because he did not fit in one world."

(Ercilla, *La Araucana*, 27.37, 1–8)

The question of "to go or not to go" beyond the known world appears in canto 2 of Villagrá's poem. Referring to the origin of the peoples who occupied New Mexico, he mentions that they were "foreign people" who came from lands to the north and who belonged to "different nations" with respect to languages, customs, and laws. According to the poet, this reality led to confirmation of the need to take down the pillars and their inscription of "not going beyond" (non plus ultra). The poet emphasizes that only valiant people dedicated to fighting are capable of going beyond the known world.

Entre los cuales cuentan Mexicanos
Y Tarascos, con gente de Guinea.
Y no parando aquí también afirman
Aber, como en Castilla, gente blanca,

Among which they do count the
    Mexicans,
Tarascans and the folk of Guinea.
Nor stopping here, they do affirm
That they have people white, as in Castile.

Que todas son grandezas que nos fuerzan
A derribar por tierra las columnas
Del *non Plus Ultra* infame que lebantan
Gentes más para rueca y el estrado,
Para tocas, vainicas y labores,
Que para gobernar la gruessa pica,
Generoso bastón y honrrada espada.

All these are grandeurs which do lead
    us on
To throw to earth the columns
Of that same *non plus ultra* which they
    raise,
Folk more for distaff and for parlor fit,
For coifs, for sewing and such labor,
Than for the wielding of the mighty pike,
The generous scepter, and the honored
    sword.

(Villagrá, *Historia*, 2, 219–29)

The discourse in both poems also acquires a greater geographic dimension when the poets mention the Atlantic and Pacific oceans navigated by Spaniards and the search for a passage between them. Europeans saw the Pacific (or South Sea) for the first time in 1513 from Panama with the expedition led by Vasco Núñez de Balboa. In 1520 Hernando de Magallanes, in his circumnavigation of the globe, found a passage between the two oceans in the far south (the future Strait of Magellan). In the beginning of the 1540s, in the early days of the conquest of Chile, which took place from the north, the exact distance between Peru and the far south of the continent was not yet clear to the Spaniards.

On the northern frontier, when Vázquez de Coronado explored the territory that would be called New Mexico (1540–42), the distance between the Gulf of Mexico and the west coast of the continent up to the Gulf of California was also not known with exactitude.[48] Moreover, one of the objectives of Oñate's 1598 expedition was not only to take possession of New Mexico but also to find the route to the Atlantic coast and there locate the best places for seaports. A century after the voyage of Columbus, Spaniards were still seeking a passage between the two oceans, this time north of New Spain. The "Columbian dream" continued unfulfilled, at least on the northern frontier of the Spanish empire.

Both poets refer to the two oceans in their respective poems. At the beginning of canto 1, Ercilla mentions the geographic location of Chile in the context of the two oceans and the passage between them.

Y estos dos anchos mares, que pretenden,
pasando de sus términos, juntarse,
baten las rocas, y sus olas tienden,
mas esles impedido allegarse;
por esta parte al fin la tierra hienden
y pueden por aquí comunicarse,
Magallanes, Señor, fue el primer hombre
que, abriendo este camino, le dio nombre.

These two wide oceans endeavor,
passing their boundaries, to join,
beat the rocks and their waves expand,
 but they are impeded of joining;
here, at last, the earth cracks
and they can communicate.
Magellan, Sir, was the first man
who, on opening this path gave it
    its name.

(Ercilla, *La Araucana*, 1.8, 1–8)

The idea of dominating as far as the south of Chile, and from there founding settlements reaching to the Atlantic, was among the most important objectives of the conquest of Chile. Pedro de Valdivia, first conqueror of Chile, stated in a 1545 letter to Carlos V that the founding of Santiago was the first step in continuing with settlement toward the south, to stretch as far as the Strait of Magellan and the Atlantic Ocean.[49] In December 1553—the same month as Valdivia's death at the hands of the Araucanians—a group of men sent by the governor arrived at the mouth of the Strait of Magellan on the Pacific side.[50] The lines cited above confirm the importance of Chile's geographic position on the way to the passage to the Atlantic.

Villagrá gives New Mexico the same degree of importance in his *Historia*. Closely following Ercilla's model, Villagrá mentions at the beginning of his poem the geographic location of New Mexico in relation to the Atlantic Ocean (North Sea), the Colorado River ("rough Californio"), and the Gulf of Mexico. The poet also makes reference to the "Sea of Pearls" southwest of New Mexico, which was none other than the Gulf of California.[51]

Del bravo Californio y mar de perlas
Casi otro tanto dista por el rumbo
Que sopla el sudueste la marina;

> Toward the rough Californio and Sea
>   of Pearls
> The distance in that direction is about
>   the same
> Toward where the southwest wind strikes
>   the coast;

(Villagrá, *Historia*, 1, 67–71)

Note that Villagrá does not explicitly mention the South Sea (Pacific) but only the "Sea of Pearls." It is possible that when the *Historia* was published, the poet knew that the "Sea of Pearls" was not the South Sea, but a gulf, although he does not mention it. What is apparent in the poem is that Oñate intended to seek the South Sea when he led an expedition to the west after having taken possession of New Mexico.[52]

Porque determinaba yrse breve
A ver el mar del Sur,

> As he had determined to go shortly
> To see the Ocean of the South

(Villagrá, *Historia*, 17, 342–43)

On this occasion, at the end of 1598, Oñate did not make it to the coast, but he succeeded on his second attempt in 1605, after the span of events Villagrá narrates in his poem. The instructions to Oñate from the viceroy of New Spain, Luis de Velasco, included a section about the search for seaports, which had to be kept secret from potential "enemies."[53] Curiously, the instructions mention the search for possible ports in the North Sea (Atlantic) but not in the South Sea. Oñate's 1601 expedition to the plains to the north and east of New Mexico doubtless had the aim of seeking an Atlantic port, as he had been instructed. This objective was not achieved, but the 1605 expedition resulted in success insofar as it reached the Gulf of California from New Mexico, crossing the present-day state of Arizona.

The importance for New Mexico of seeking a passage to a sea port went hand in hand with the search for resources to prop up the monarchy. Accounts of expeditions of the 1580s to New Mexico show that in addition to the goal of religious conversion there was the clear aim of finding gold and silver mines. This indicates that in the general context of the reign of Felipe II, there continued to be a marked interest in finding silver and gold in his dominions, and New Mexico was no exception. Likewise, the Spaniards' search for gold in Chile was in large part the central objective of their presence in the region. Other testimony from the period shows this to be the case. The chronicler Alonso de Góngora y Marmolejo, who was in Chile between 1549 and 1576, makes several mentions of events during the conquest of Chile related to the Spaniards' quest for gold.[54] Referring to Pedro de Valdivia, he mentions that on one occasion Valdivia kept gold that belonged to his men.[55]

Ercilla includes references to the presence of precious metals in Chile in various sections of his poem. In canto 2 he mentions the importance of gold mines in the vicinity of Concepción, previously the fortress of Penco.

Mientras esto en Arauco sucedía,	While this was happening in Arauco,
en el pueblo de Penco, más vecino	at Penco, the nearest town
que a la sazón en Chile florecía,	where at that time flourished
fértil de ricas minas de oro fino,	mines of fine gold,
el capitán Valdivia residía,	Captain Valdivia resided,
(Ercilla, *La Araucana*, 2.88, 1–5)	

In the stanzas at the end of canto 2, the poet links Valdivia with greed in the search for gold, a cause that according to Ercilla led the captain to his death and his deserved punishment.[56] According to the poet, Valdivia was careless with the Spanish defense, delaying his arrival at the fortress of Tucapel to stop and extract gold from a mine. Eventually the Spaniards were defeated at Tucapel, and Valdivia was decapitated.

Pero dejó el camino provechoso	But he left the advantageous road,
y, descuidado dél, torció la vía,	carelessly, took a turn in the route,
metiéndose con otro, codicioso,	placing himself on another road of avarice,
que era donde una mina de oro había;	where there was a gold mine;
y de ver el tributo y don hermoso	and on seeing the tribute and beautiful gift
que de sus ricas venas ofrecía,	its rich veins offered,
paró de la codicia embarazado,	full of greed he stopped,
cortando el hilo próspero del hado.	cutting the prosperous thread of destiny.
(Ercilla, *La Araucana*, 2.92, 1–8)	

Ercilla mentions the existence of gold in Chile in a geographic context, pinpointing the vicinity of Concepción as one of the richest. He also alludes to the thousands of Indians forced to labor in the gold mines, and the wealth accumulated by Spaniards because of gold. The poet refers to all three topics and the destruction of Concepción by the Araucanians in the following lines.

Piérdese la ciudad más fértil de oro	The city of fertile gold is lost
que estaba en lo poblado de la tierra,	it was where more population inhabited,
y adonde más riquezas y tesoro	where more wealth and treasures
según fama en sus términos se encierra.	according to its fame are enclosed within
	its boundaries

(Ercilla, *La Araucana*, 7.56, 1–4)

A quién diez a quién veinte y a quién treinta	To whom ten, and to whom twenty, and to whom thirty
mil ducados por año les rentara;	thousand ducats of revenues for a year;
el más pobre tuviera mil de renta,	the poorest would have a thousand,
de aquí ninguno de ellos abajara;	no one would get less;
la parte de Valdivia era sin cuenta	Valdivia's share was beyond counting
si la ciudad en paz se sustentara,	if peace in the city could be sustained,
que en torno la cercaban ricas venas	that it was surrounded by rich veins
fáciles de labrar y de oro llenas.	easy to work and filled with gold.

(Ercilla, *La Araucana*, 7.57, 1–8)

Cien mil súbditos servían	One hundred thousand subjects served
a los de la ciudad desamparada;	those of the abandoned city;
sacar tanto oro en cantidad podían,	they could take out so much gold,
que a tenerse viniera casi en nada.	that by having held back they came to have almost nothing

(Ercilla, *La Araucana*, 7.58, 1–4)

Ercilla's lines describe the Spanish loss of Concepción and at the same time present the economic dimension of that tragic attack. They exemplify the idea presented by scholar Julie Johnson, who says that the Araucanian attack on Concepción "not only brings about the devastation of a particular area of geographical space but also threatens the loss of the designation of space as an ideological and theological symbol."[57] Concepción, therefore, was a space full of imperial meaning, and at the same time, the poet uses the opportunity to criticize Spanish ambition. As Johnson puts it, he "transforms a Golden Age of wealth, influence, and power into an age of gold that encourages idleness and greed."[58]

The chronicler Gerónimo de Vivar, who was in Chile between approximately 1550 and 1558, also mentions forced Indian labor in the mines and the importance of gold and silver in the region, especially in the south near the cities of Villarrica and Valdivia (both founded in 1552).[59] In fact, Villarrica was so named because of the precious metals in the region. Ercilla mentions Villarrica and the volcano of the same name in his poem. Finally, there is another section in *La Araucana* in which Ercilla refers to the importance of precious metals as they relate to the commerce of the Indies and the arrival in Spain, specifically in Seville, of the riches originating in the Americas. The poet makes this allusion in the course of his encounter with the wizard Fitón and the vision of the known world that the wizard shows him.

"Mira a Sevilla, vees la realeza de templos, edificios y moradas, el concurso de gente y la grandeza del trato de las Indias apartadas, que de oro, plata, perlas y riqueza dos flotas en un año entran cargadas y salen otras dos de mercancía con gente, munición y artillería." (Ercilla, *La Araucana*, 27.36, 1–8)	"Look to Seville, do you see the royalty of temples, buildings and habitations, the gathering of people and the greatness of the commerce of the remote Indies, that of gold, silver, pearls and wealth two fleets in one year enter loaded and another two leave with merchandise, with people, ammunition and artillery."

These lines were first published in part 2 of *La Araucana* in 1578, when Felipe II had already been in power for twenty-two years as king of Spain and its overseas dominions. The Americas continued to be the most important source of gold for the Spanish crown. Most shipments of precious metals came from gold and silver mines in the viceroyalties of New Spain and Peru. During the reign of Carlos I, it was mostly gold, and during the reign of Felipe II, it was mostly silver. The initial search for gold in Chile, of which both Ercilla and the chroniclers of the period so often speak, belonged to the 1550s, still within the reign of Carlos I. These precious metals were, in the words of one of the biographers of Felipe II, "stained with the blood of the Indians forced to work in the mines."[60]

Except for the period of approximately five years at the beginning of the reign of Felipe II, shipments from the Americas constantly increased and translated into millions of pesos, particularly after 1561. As Manuel Fernández Álvarez affirms, the figures were "sufficiently important to aid us in understanding the miracle of the supremacy of the Catholic monarchy in sixteenth-century Europe." With this infusion of gold and silver, "the monarchy of Felipe II could raise armies and armadas and keep up war with half of Europe throughout his reign."[61] If the armed forces consumed two-thirds of the budget in peacetime, imagine the enormous increase of that quantity in times of war (recall that Spain was in constant war in Europe in the last three decades of the reign of Felipe II).

By 1598, the year of Felipe II's death, when the conquest of New Mexico was taking place under Oñate's command, the financial situation of the empire was catastrophic. By 1599, Spain's economy still depended in large measure on the shipments sent from the colonies, and the monarchy's debt continued to grow unceasingly.[62] Historians Bárbara Hadley Stein and Stanley Stein, in their classic study on American silver and the finances of the Spanish empire, refer in the following terms to the role silver played during the reigns of the Habsburg dynasty (1517–1700):

> The perception of silver as crop, or *fruto*, combined with the Habsburg conception of a dynastic patrimonial empire linking Central Europe, Germany, Burgundy, the Netherlands, and Spain in a kind of international division of labor transformed Castile into the financial core of the Catholic order in Europe.[63]

To cite an example related to the historical period covered by the poems, 70 percent of the military operations against France in 1557, including the aforementioned battle of San Quintín, were financed with Spanish colonial silver.

By contrast with Ercilla in *La Araucana*, Villagrá devotes little space in the *Historia* to the existence of mineral resources, except for salt flats. Mention in the *Historia* of the existence of precious metals in New Mexico is specifically related to an earlier expedition to the area led by Antonio de Espejo (1582–83).[64]

Y después de aber visto aquella tierra	And, after having seen that land,
Salió también diziendo maravillas,	He did return telling of marvels,
Loándola de muchas poblaciones	Praising it for many towns
Y minas caudalosas de metales	And mines of precious ores
Y gente buena toda y que tenía	And all good people who did have
Bezotes, brazaletes y oregeras	Lip rings and bracelets and earrings
De aquel rubio metal, dulze goloso,	Of that gold metal, toothsome sweet,
Tras que todos andamos desbalidos.	For which we all go wandering, destitute.
(Villagrá, *Historia*, 5, 127–34)	

The contrast between the content of these lines and the information left by Diego Pérez de Luxan, who kept the campaign diary of the Espejo expedition, demonstrates the obvious fact that the search for mines was one of the expedition's goals. Again and again the testimony mentions that the mines located were few and of poor quality, that is, not silver or gold but only copper.[65] Thus, the existence of any "mines of precious ores," which, according to Villagrá, the Espejo expedition had found, is difficult to prove, given that the written testimony about the expedition does not confirm it. Subsequently, the Oñate expedition demonstrated that there was no mineral wealth except for salt lakes and the possible existence of some silver mines, supposedly in Arizona, whose description in the documents is neither detailed nor clear.

The analysis of the stories of the expeditions prior to Oñate´s demonstrates what literary critic Maureen Ahern has called "the conflictive nature of those early encounters" that were "spurred by the obligatory alliance of evangelization and mining fever."[66] Oñate's 1598 expedition did not have, at least in the official instructions, the objective of seeking mines, but the testimony about his expedition—and his own familial background in the silver mining business—shows that he was following the trail of what the expeditions of the 1580s had reported.

Returning to what Villagrá wrote about the search for minerals between 1598 and 1599, he mentioned the salt lakes found by an exploratory group under the command of Captain Marcos Farfán de los Godos, whom Oñate sent out in November 1598. The salt lake was discovered eight leagues south of Zuni Pueblo (although the report of the expedition located it to the west of the pueblo).[67]

Y luego al Capitán Farfán mandaron	And then they did order Captain Farfán
Que fuesse a descubrir ciertas salinas	To go discover certain saline lakes
De que grande noticia se tenía,	Of which they had heard great reports.
Y poniendo por obra aquel mandato	And putting into practice that command
Con presta diligencia y buen cuidado,	With rapid diligence and goodly care,
En brebe dio la buelta y dixo dellas	He shortly did return and talk of them,
Que eran tan caudalosas y tan grandes	That they were so well-filled, so very large,
Que por espacio de una legua larga	That for the space of a long league
Mostraba toda aquélla sal de gruesso	All was covered with salt and to the depth
Una muy larga pica bien tendida.	Of a very long pike in full length.
(Villagrá, *Historia*, 18, 374–83)	

The testimonies left by this expedition mention the discovery thus:

> This saline is round and about twelve leagues in circumference. The whole deposit is made up of hard, crystallized salt, as fine as that from the sea, or even better. . . . This witness feels certain that nowhere in Christendom or elsewhere can such a marvelous thing be found. Nor does our king possess such salt.[68]

Salt was indeed a valuable mineral, but it was neither gold nor silver. The poet later mentions the discovery of mines by Captain Alonso de Quesada (also from the Farfán de los Godos group) who, according to Villagrá, described the land as "abundant in metals" and reported the existence of pearl-bearing shells near the "pearl coast," which the Spaniards had not yet been able to reach from New Mexico. Doubtless, this refers to the coast of the "Sea of Pearls" (the Gulf of California), which Oñate reached on his 1605 expedition.

Y después que anduvieron muchas leguas,	And after they had wandered many leagues,
Padeciendo grandíssimos trabajos,	Suffering very great trials,
La buelta dio Quesada, muy contento,	Quesada did return, very content,
Diziendo grandes vienes de la tierra	Saying much good about the land,
Y que era de metales abundosa	And that it was abundant in metals
(Villagrá, *Historia*, 18, 396–408)	

According to the testimony of the witnesses to the expedition, when they asked the Indians of the area where they had obtained the pearl-bearing shells they wore in their noses and on their foreheads, the natives stated that they got them from the sea, which was a thirty-day journey from their "rancherías."[69]

> And, making signs with their hands by placing one over the other in the shape of a shell, they opened it on one side, saying that the shells were to be found in that water, and that when they opened them they found some round, white beads inside, which they indicated by signs to be as large as kernels of maize.[70]

Villagrá does not provide any details about the metals that Quesada and his men found. This concords with the vague, although overly optimistic, description that the participants of the expedition give in their testimony. Quesada reports that he saw "many large veins with much ore," and not having adequate tools, only brought a small quantity that he and his men dug out with their daggers to show to the governor. In his testimony, Quesada said that he and other members of the expedition "had made assays of the ore with quicksilver, and that they had obtained a large quantity of silver, despite the fact that the amount of ore was small."[71] Quesada also affirmed that for these reasons he was sure that "the discovery is very rich and his Majesty will be well served by it in the royal fifths." Moreover, the Indians of the region had informed his men that there were more mines in the area.[72]

Years after the period that Villagrá dealt with in his poem, letters from the Marqués de Montesclaros, viceroy of New Spain, to King Felipe III dismissed the idea of significant metal deposits in the region.[73] In his letter of October 28, 1605, to the king, the viceroy spoke of the conquest of New Mexico in these terms:

> I cannot help but inform Your Majesty that this conquest is becoming a fairy tale. If those who write the reports imagine that they are believed by those who read them, they are greatly mistaken. Less substance is being revealed every day.[74]

In the signed letter, the viceroy affirmed that "the greatest benefit that could be hoped for is the discovery of the South Sea." He recommended the construction of ships to explore the coast and added that

> If a harbor is found that could be used for the Philippine ships, they should take possession of it and seek the best means of fortifying it. If it should prove to be an appropriate place, it might be possible to explore from there the interior or island of the Californias, which has always been so much sought.[75]

During the years that Villagrá wrote his poem, it was clear to the viceroy that the only potential economic wealth of New Mexico was the possibility of exploring the coast of the Gulf of California with the aim of establishing ports for commerce with the Orient. In his poem, Villagrá did not include a detailed description of precious metals found because, evidently, there were none, at least not in the quantity and of the quality hoped for by the viceroy. Oñate's expedition, therefore, only made one contribution of possible economic importance: having arrived at the South Sea from New Mexico. The short shrift Villagrá gives to the existence of precious metals in New Mexico in his poem is in agreement with what historians have been able to show from documents of the period.

The events presented in the *Historia* center on the first two years of the Spanish settlement in New Mexico (1598–99) with limited references to two previous expeditions (1540–42 and 1580–82). As far as the expansion and strengthening of the Spanish empire, the historical period about which Villagrá wrote was the beginning of the end of the empire's European hegemony. The lack of references in the *Historia* to warfare between Spain and other powers as determining factors in its imperial and Catholic supremacy contrasts with what Ercilla relates in *La Araucana*. The battles that made Spain the leading European power during the apogee of Felipe II's reign took place in the historical period Ercilla covered in his poem. Major defeats that presaged the beginning of the end of Felipe II, such as that of the invincible armada in 1588, correspond to a later period.

The European environment of warfare associated with imperial Spanish political and religious expansion stands out in *La Araucana*. Ercilla writes about two central battles for Spanish hegemony in Europe during the reign of Felipe II: San Quintín and Lepanto. The poet not only includes these battles, fought in European territory, but also connects them with Chilean territory and the Spanish victory against the Araucanians at the fortress of Penco. Relying on his knowledge of the ancient classical world as well as his imagination, Ercilla uses "the marvelous" or supernatural as a medium to present these events. Reference has already been made to the imaginary wizard character, Fitón. It is by means of this trope as well as an encounter in the poet's dreams with the goddess Bellona that Ercilla includes a geographical description of the known world and specific references to the theme of European warfare in the context of Spanish dominion.

According to literary critic Isaías Lerner, Ercilla turns to the marvelous apparition of the goddess Bellona not as part of the description of war—a feature typical of classical epic poetry—but "as a mechanism that permits the temporal and spatial unification of the events of the empire."[76] In fact, the poet uses the fantastic to foretell future historical events, which he includes in the midst of an account of the conquest in Chile. In a dream sequence, the goddess Bellona takes the poet to the top of a mountain from which she permits him to see the confrontation between the Spaniards and the French at the battle of San Quintín, which the army of Felipe II won on August 10, 1557.[77]

"Aquélla es Sanquintin que vees delante
que en vano contraviene a su ruina,
presidio principal, plaza importante,
y del furor del gran Felipe dina".
  (Ercilla, *La Araucana*, 17.56, 1–4)

"That is San Quintin you see ahead
that in vain contravenes its ruin,
main garrison, important site,
of the furor of the great Felipe worthy."

"Llegamos, pues, a tiempo que seguro
Podrás ver la contienda porfiada,
y sin escalas, por el roto muro
entrar los de Felipe a pura espada;
verás el fiero asalto y trance duro,
y al fin la fuerte Francia aportillada,
que al riguroso hado incontrastable
no hay defensa ni plaza inexpungable."

"We arrived, therefore, on time that surely
you will see the disputed war,
and without ladders, through the broken
  wall
you will see Philip's men enter with pure
  sword;
you will see the fierce assault and hard
  peril,
and finally the French fortress breached,
That to rigorous incomparable fate
there is no defense nor stronghold
  impregnable."

  (Ercilla, *La Araucana*, 17.58, 1–8)

The last ten stanzas of canto 16 and almost all of canto 18 are devoted to San Quintín and to a series of subsequent European events. Breaking from the traditional epic formula that he uses so well in recreating the environment of European warfare, Ercilla devotes many lines to recording military encounters and matrimonial alliances aimed at strengthening the political and religious authority of Felipe II. Ercilla mentions the division of territory in Europe (through the peace treaty of Cateau-Cambrésis in 1559); the marriage of Felipe II to Isabel de Valois (eldest daughter of King Henry of France); and upon the death of the latter, the last marriage of Felipe, to Anne of Austria (daughter of Emperor Maximilian II). He also mentions the religious wars in France around 1572 and a series of battles against the Turks between 1563 and 1565. In this struggle against the "infidel," Ercilla devotes lines to the rebellion of the *moriscos* in Granada (1568–70).

"También con intención de libertarse,
en el próspero reino de Granada
los moriscos vendrán a levantarse
y a negar la obediencia al Rey jurada"

"Also with pretense of being liberated,
in the prosperous Kingdom of Granada
the Christianzed Moors will come to lift
  themselves
and deny obedience to the sworn King"

  (Ercilla, *La Araucana*, 18.48, 1–4)

By including these events, the poet demonstrates the magnitude of the imperial domain of Felipe II in Europe that culminated in the battle of Lepanto and victory over the Ottoman Empire in 1571. As a device to include this last event in the poem, Ercilla uses the wizard Fitón, who in his cave shows the poet images of the naval battle in his crystal ball. One of the most interesting sections of the poem regarding the theme of empire is the speech that Ercilla places in the mouth of the Turkish general Alí Bajá, who encourages his soldiers by telling them,

"Abrid, pues, y romped por esa gente,
echad a fondo ya el poder cristiano
tomando posesión de un golpe solo
del Gange a Chile y de uno al otro polo."

"Open up, and attack that people,
throw down that Christian power
taking possession by one blow alone
from the Ganges to Chile and from one
    pole to the other."

(Ercilla, *La Araucana*, 24.36, 5–8)

Ninety stanzas (720 lines) of canto 24 are devoted entirely to Lepanto and the participation of Juan de Austria, Felipe II's half-brother, as the hero of the battle.

Ercilla presents the battle of San Quintín and the battle of Lepanto together with other European events, mingling them with events of the conquest of Chile, especially the Araucanian attack on the fortress of Penco and the battles of Lagunillas and Millarapué. In the description of these violent encounters, Ercilla devotes lines to the Indian leaders Rengo, Galvarino, and Caupolicán. The poet presents details of the cruelty experienced in the battles of Chile in a paradoxical context. The blood and violence, including the amputation of the hands of the Araucanian Galvarino, are juxtaposed with the exaltation of the empire through Spanish victories in Europe. For the reader, the bloody Araucanian defense of their territory appears to blend into the general framework of Spanish monarchical power: "seen from Europe, the peripheral American epic only acquires a real existence when it appears joined to events close to the central Spanish policy," as Lerner puts it.[78]

Imperial Spain's presence in *La Araucana* continues with the magical vision newly created by Fitón, which allows the poet to see the geography of the planet and of the places known up to that time in Asia, Europe, Africa, the Americas, and the cities and regions of Spain. Demonstrating his poetic ability and knowledge of geography, Ercilla devotes fifty-four stanzas (of a total of sixty-one) of canto 27 to this description. In this section of the poem, Ercilla is concerned with demonstrating the meaning of Spanish imperial power translated into specific material symbols of the Catholic monarchy, as in the case of Felipe II's construction of the monastery of El Escorial (1563–84).

"Será un famoso templo incomparable
de sumptuosa fábrica y grandeza,
la máquina del cual hará notable,
su religioso cello y gran riqueza.

"It will be a famous and incomparable
    temple
of sumptuous manufacture and greatness,
a representation that will highlight
its religious zeal and great wealth.

Será edificio eterno y memorable,
de inmensa majestad y gran belleza,
obra, al fin, de un tal rey, tan gran
   cristiano,
y de tan larga y poderosa mano.
	It will be an eternal and memorable
	   building,
	of immense majesty and great beauty,
	a work, finally, of a certain king, so great a
	   Christian,
	and of so great and powerful hand.

   (Ercilla, *La Araucana*, 27.34, 1–8)

Ercilla chose to end his poem with a canto dedicated to the empire. The lines of canto 37 of part 3, published in 1589, refer to the concept of just war that the poet uses to introduce the theme of Felipe II's legitimate right to the throne of Portugal, which justified the invasion of that kingdom. Ercilla wrote about the concept of just war not to refer to the Spanish war against the Araucanians, but to explain the legality of Spanish expansion in Europe.

Y pues del rey como cabeza pende el peso de la guerra y grave carga, y cuanto daño y mal della depende todo sobre sus hombros solo carga. Debe mucho mirar lo que pretende, y antes que dé al furor la rienda larga, justificar sus armas prevenidas, no por codicia y ambicion movidas.	From the King's head hangs the serious weight of war, and when the result is damage and evil the load is on his shoulders alone. He should look to what he seeks, and before he gives free rein to rage, he has to justify the use of arms not moved by greed and ambition.

   (Ercilla, *La Araucana*, 37.13, 1–8)

The poet includes further lines that illustrate the idea of a monarch who did not take up arms out of ambition to conquer more territory but to obey the law and in defense of what was just. According to Ercilla, greed did not motivate a king whose dominions extended "to the point where the sun sets."

Como Felipe en la ocasión presente, que de precisa obligación forzado, a favor de las leyes justamente las permitidas armas ha tomado; no fundando el derecho en ser potente ni de codicia de reinar llevado, pues se estiende su cetro y monarquía hasta donde remata el sol su vía.	As Felipe in the present occasion, forced by an obligation, exactly in favor of the laws has taken the arms permitted; not founded by the right on being powerful not taken by an ambition to reign, for his throne and monarchy extends to the point where the sun sets.

   (Ercilla, *La Araucana*, 37.14, 1–8)

In 1582, one year after Felipe's coronation as king of Portugal, Ercilla was in that country and there joined the armada that sailed to the conquest of the Azores. According to the Chilean historian José Toribio Medina, if Ercilla did not participate in the naval battle between the Spanish armada and the French fleet on July 22, 1582, at the very least he witnessed it, because he described the battle in detail in a *romance* he authored, published in Lisbon in 1586. According to Medina, if Ercilla had published another epic poem after *La Araucana*, it would have been about the Portuguese campaign because he had been a witness.

> From that moment, perhaps, wishing to expand the horizons of his lyre, he proposed to write a poem about the whole campaign in Portugal, a country about which he had shown himself to be interested, and in the history of its conquest by the monarch to whom he had devoted his efforts, which would permit him to extol his name even more.[79]

In summary, there is no doubt about the presence of the imperial theme in *La Araucana*, nor is there any doubt about Ercilla's intention to elevate the figure of Felipe II as the absolute leader of the empire. The exaltation of imperial power may have been exaggerated—after all, it is an epic—but the events Ercilla related offer a panorama sufficiently accurate as to the absolute power of the monarch, the size of his empire, and the central elements of the construction of empire. Moreover, it must not be forgotten how close Ercilla was to the king from the time the poet was very young, and that as an adult he also participated in campaigns in Europe as a soldier in the army of Felipe II. The words cited above from the biographer José Toribio Medina are not exaggerated with respect to Ercilla's loyalty to his monarch.

Elizabeth Davis supports the thesis that Ercilla's purpose was to show a bond with the king and create a "sustained dialogue" with his monarch throughout the poem. Davis concludes that the many "instances of apostrophe to the monarch" make it possible to characterize Ercilla's lines as a "discourse of service as the dominant one in the epic."[80] As a result, there is a bias in the poem that "places the text into a default pro-Habsburg position, and this partially makes up for the lack of a clearly defined Spanish hero in the epic."[81] The existence of this bias also suggests that the thesis of the poet's sympathy for the Araucanian struggle is not completely supported. As a vassal at the service of the crown, Ercilla takes a position that shows what Davis has characterized as his "fractured subjectivity,"[82] an idea that has also been presented indirectly by Paul Firbas. Firbas arrives at similar conclusions through the analysis of the poet as a direct participant in the colonial war. According to Firbas, in moments of narrating details of unjust violence, the poet often chooses to escape from a scene of cruelty to one that is imaginary.[83] A similar perspective is presented by scholar Raúl Marrero-Fente, who analyzes Ercilla's use of native voices raised against the conquest as a literary element that creates a dual position of the poet.[84]

Classifying Ercilla as an "imperial poet" is not new. Numerous historical and literary studies assert it. One example is a statement by Lerner in his introduction to an edition of *La Araucana*: "Ercilla decides to be fully conscious of the intention, the official cantor of the empire and devotes to it a great part of his political life and his literary life."[85] Thus, the Spanish conquest of Chile and the Araucanians' defense of their territory are presented in the poem in an overarching imperial context without which the poet could not have conceived of his work. The poem is a text that exalts the empire: "the testimonial value might come from the most remote place in the conquered lands, but the poetic voice rises from such latitudes as a symbol of the universal unity of power."[86]

The discussion of Ercilla as imperial poet cannot be complete without citing scholar David Quint and his book *Epic and Empire.* He bases his analysis on the fact that the epic of *La Araucana* follows two models: Lucan's *Pharsalia* and Virgil's *Aeneid.* Following the first model, Ercilla highlights Araucanian resistance. Following the second model, he emphasizes the success of empire over the "barbarian" Araucanians. Quint states,

> The choice between the two models determines whether the subject matter of the Araucana is imperial conquest or freedom fighting, whether its heroes are the Spanish conquistadors or the leaders of the Araucanian resistance, whether it takes the side of the winners or the losers.[87]

The use of both models allows Ercilla to avoid tilting one way or the other and in this way celebrates both Spanish imperialism and the Araucanian defense. Nevertheless, according to Quint, Ercilla's tilt toward the poetic model of Lucan "corresponds to what has made the Araucana perennially surprising to its readers: the tilting of its sympathies to the Araucanian chiefs and their desperate struggle."[88] Lucan's model shows Pompey's resistance to the power of Julius Caesar, that is, the defense of one who does not allow himself to be conquered easily. This conclusion comes, then, from Ercilla's use of a specific literary model.

Even though this analysis is correct, particularly with respect to its logic, if one looks at the poetic and historical aspects separately, it is possible to offer another reading as a conclusion to the topic of the Spanish monarchy and empire in *La Araucana*. Ercilla indeed follows the canons of epic poetry, including specific models (Lucano, Virgil, Juan de Mena, among others). Also, in this context, there are the typical formulae: the dedicatory to the king, addressing the king as his interlocutor throughout the poem, descriptions of battles on both Chilean and European soil, and other events that add drama and entertainment, such as descriptions of storms, love stories, and encounters with fantastic characters. The poet narrates historical events, many of which he participated in as a witness and protagonist. Also relevant in this context is the life of Ercilla, his childhood, his relationship to the monarchy and to the monarch, and his active participation in fundamental events that marked Spanish imperial expansion, such as being a king's soldier in Spanish-American and European territories. One must also include parallel events that took place in Spain. One such example is the legal aspect of the conquest as dictated from Spain. And certain decisions that Ercilla made had a real intentionality, such as the selection of which group to include first in his poetry; which events to use to conclude his poem; and whether to describe historical characters in a derogatory or admiring way.

The reader must consider all of these points, interpreting both the poetic and the historical elements. Ercilla is a poet of empire, or at least a writer whose subjectivity (using Davis's concept) makes him tend more toward the side of monarchy than toward that of the natives. Other literary critics have analyzed this question from different perspectives and coincide in their conclusions, which is that Ercilla's contradictions and inconsistencies make it difficult to define his position.[89]

The presence of certain imperial symbols in *La Araucana*, already noted, no doubt moves the balance to seeing Ercilla as an imperial poet. Their existence helps us understand the characteristics of a reign such as that of Felipe II. One of these symbols was the monastery of El Escorial. Toward the end of his reign, Felipe ordered its design and construction. It was more monastery than palace, more church than home. The biographers of Felipe II have written extensively about the importance of this building in the monarchy of the Felipes. Here it is also necessary to emphasize that all royal decisions made about the conquest of New Mexico originated in this place. In fact, in 1595 Felipe signed the royal cédula at El Escorial that approved the conquest and Spanish settlement of New Mexico. At the time, his physical condition had completely deteriorated, and he was in his final years of life (he died on September 13, 1598).

Villagrá, in his *Historia de la Nueva Mexico*, recounts a conquest that took place in 1598–99. Had Felipe II had the opportunity to hear and read about it, he would have been pleased that his power and particularly his religion had arrived in such distant lands. With the reign of Felipe II as the general historical framework of the *Historia*, it is logical that the imperial theme would be present, directly and indirectly, in the poem. Villagrá did not represent the same type of imperial poet that Ercilla was because the empire of the 1590s was not that of the 1550s. Nevertheless, the *Historia* has many attributes of an imperial poem. Villagrá's poem seeks to vindicate an imperial presence even though it was becoming debilitated. As in the case of *La Araucana*, Villagrá could not have written the poem without that frame of reference, even with a diminishing empire such as it was in 1598. Villagrá's verses perpetuate imperial practices that had survived a century and more, if one counts the conquest of the Americas and the Christian reconquest on Spanish soil.

The interpretation Jill Lane offers in her article "On Colonial Forgetting: The Conquest of New Mexico and its *Historia*" provides keys drawn from literary criticism to understand the theme of empire in Villagrá's poem. According to

Lane, the existence of "performative acts and rhetorical postures, both warlike and writerly" that occurred in the conquest of New Mexico and which the poet includes in his poetry, "make up a complex economy of inscription that circulates the performative force through which empire is produced, maintained, articulated, and enacted."[90] Ceremonies such as taking of possession of the land following the ritual of the famous *requerimiento*, and the acts of vassalage and obedience to the king and the Catholic religion, in which the natives were forced to participate, were but two of the various imperial rituals to which Villagrá devotes his poetry.

Directly or indirectly, the *Historia* includes words and events that remind readers of the importance of the Spanish presence in regions as remote as New Mexico, although the empire was in decline and Villagrá did not have (as Ercilla did) important Spanish European victories to narrate in his poem. However, the poet repeatedly emphasizes an imperial image such as the one that Felipe II represented fifty years earlier but that no longer existed as such: "The conquest of New Mexico is haunted everywhere by ghosts of conquest past,"[91] as Lane puts it. Here was a new context and a new land, a "new" Mexico, where the participation of the conquistador, in this case Juan de Oñate, was constantly limited by new laws such as the New Ordinances for Settlement and Discovery of 1573 and especially by the profound religious imprint on the conquest of that region. Precisely because Villagrá is giving an account of a late conquest, he reiterates the imperial theme to give it the same importance as previous conquests: "the soldier enacts the 'new' conquest by performing history, by restoring and restaging the behaviors of those who produced conquest when it was still named and valued as such."[92] Because of the historical moment in which his conquest took place, Ercilla may not have felt the same need as Villagrá to emphasize the imperial theme. After all, *La Araucana* was the product of the same historical circumstances that were ongoing in the Americas and especially in Europe.

Davis expresses some of the reasons that the epic poetry of New Spain, including Villagrá's *Historia*, reflects the "aspirations of imperial Spain." Referring specifically to the Spanish victory in putting down the rebellion of the Acoma Indians, Davis argues that "Villagrá's poem manipulates history and omits details that could enhance the image of the inhabitants of Acoma," all in the interest of exalting the image of the victorious Spaniards.[93] Villagrá's *Historia* is considered an example of the epic of colonial New Spain as a type "that translates a historic moment and its ideal: the apogee of Spanish hegemony in American territory."[94] There is, however, a difference of opinion among literary critics about the poet's message or intention in presenting the events at Acoma and whether or not the poem is imperialist in character.

Genaro Padilla, in his book *The Daring Flight of My Pen*, claims that Villagrá's poetry includes "an embryonic mestizo subjectivity."[95] Padilla uses examples from the poem to show what he considers to be the poet's contradictions: for example, idealizing native cultures at the same time as he represents himself as a soldier who fought against the Indians of New Mexico. In Padilla's words, "Villagrá the poet discloses a more complex understanding of native life and culture than he is usually credited for."[96] Another aspect Padilla underscores is Villagrá's so-called lack of loyalty to Oñate, which would prove that the intention of the poem was not to justify the actions of its hero and of Villagrá himself, and therefore, the poem's political message is not the exaltation of the conquest. Moreover, the *Historia*,

> while [it is] commemorative verse dedicated to the King and to memorializing a colonial entrada, it does indeed summon competing social and ideological positions over the course of its narration that call royal authority into question, however obliquely.[97]

According to Padilla, the poem illustrates the ambiguity that exists in Villagrá's thinking since his identity as a criollo on one hand and that one of the imperial Spaniard on the other appear in competition.[98] Following the same model of analysis as Quint, Padilla turns to the comparison with the classical model in the analysis of the last cantos of the poem that refer to the battle of Acoma. With Virgil and his *Aeneid* as his model, Villagrá's message in this part of his poem is to show "an act of senseless cruelty." Thus, the poet "turned to the *Aeneid* as a way of thinking through the moral cost of empire."[99] In spite of the contradictions in Villagrá's message with respect to the imperial theme, there is sufficient material in the poem to demonstrate that the *Historia* may still be considered part of the literature of empire. Moreover, while the hypothesis of Villagrá's ambiguous reality—being criollo and at the same time feeling Spanish—can be supported through his own lines, the argument of a lack of loyalty to Oñate cannot be supported, if the historical evidence is considered. As a result, the argument of Villagrá's anti-imperialist position falls short.

Although the *Historia* has been considered by some critics as a late poem in the history of the Western epic, painstaking analysis by scholar Manuel Martín Rodríguez has shown that the *Historia* reflects the traditional characteristics of the classical epic. For any reader interested in the dual literary and historical function of the poem, Martín Rodríguez's study is essential. He makes it possible to understand the line between the literary and the historical more easily, as well as the occasions when both perspectives come together or influence each other.[100]

A historical reading of Villagrá's poem tells us that we are dealing with an imperial poem that recounts the vicissitudes of an empire in decline. The poem provides sufficient information to demonstrate that the central theme is the conquest and that joined with this topic is that of the construction of empire. It is late and weakened, but it is an empire nonetheless.

Some conclusions can be drawn from the poetic and historical perspectives to bring to a close the analysis of the central theme of this first chapter. Villagrá uses the model of the classical epic, and as a result, historical events and real people are sometimes endowed with fictional characteristics. Nevertheless, this does not mean that true historical aspects cannot be salvaged from the *Historia*. It relates directly to what was actually happening on the northern frontier of the Spanish American empire, and at a higher political level, in the Spanish empire in general at the end of the sixteenth century.

The first part of this chapter provided an analysis of some themes present in the *Historia* that pertained to the construction of the Spanish empire of Felipe II: the idea of the Spanish mission to extend the empire beyond the known world (plus ultra), the search for maritime passages between the two oceans with commercial goals on a planetary scale, and the search for mineral wealth. Political and religious unity as a central element of the Spanish monarchy of the sixteenth century also impinges on the poem, starting with the dedication to the king.

There is no criticism of the empire or questioning of the king's authority in the *Historia*, at least not explicitly. If one is attentive to the poet's words, there is criticism of the authority of some bureaucrats such as governors and viceroys. The poet praises the effort of soldiers in the conquest, at the same time as he repeatedly reminds us that his only and most important interlocutor is the king himself.[101] The dedication to King Felipe III and the fact that the poet constantly addresses him in the poem can be considered part of the poetic formula. So too are the references to fantastic elements and characters, to the supernatural, to auguries and prophecies, to the inspiration of classical heroes (Ulysses, Achilles, and Aeneas), and to the graphic description of battle and of destruction and death as a result of it (even though it is only one, the battle of Acoma). The influence of the classical epic is clear, as Martín Rodríguez has shown. Martín Rodríguez's analysis has made it possible to determine that the figure of Oñate in the *Historia*, following the model of various classical heroes, shows himself to be close to what he may have been in reality: an individual full of nuances and ambiguity, "poorly defined and to a certain extent poorly drawn."[102]

In its literary, historical, and geographical content, the poem also represents the land of the Americas. In parts of the poem, Villagrá turns to the theme of the Indians, and one detects in the poet a clear ethnographic interest. Villagrá's poem may be thought of as "an early example of Creole letters in New Spain."[103] His birth origin in Puebla, New Spain, must have influenced how he saw and experienced the American landscape. Although Villagrá does not overtly discuss his, or anyone else's, seventeenth-century criollo identity, his complaints about the lack of recognition for the conquistadors and their descendants (criollos) can be interpreted as implying a distinction between the criollo and the peninsular-born Spaniard.

It is thus possible to assume that we are looking at an example of early *crio-llismo*. Scholar Francisco Lomelí has also proposed looking at the poet and his poem as a reflection of a space and its peoples with a clear, non-Spanish identity.[104] Scholar Sandra M. Pérez-Linggi, in her article "Gaspar Pérez de Villagrá: *Criollo* or Chicano in the Southwest?," proposes looking at Villagrá as "a marginalized *Criollo* who understands the injustice of his position and fights within the system to gain access to the same power others enjoy."[105] These scholars' contributions are a good starting-place to debate Villagrá's criollo identity, a theme that still needs to be studied in greater depth, since some interpretations can be considered erroneous due to mistaken historical facts.[106]

That Villagrá was a conqueror cannot be denied, and he does not hide that aspect in his poem. In relation to the participation of the poet as witness and protagonist of several of the events he recounts, it is debatable whether his direct participation made his *Historia* more valid. Literary critics have expressed doubts about the matter.[107] Still, what cannot be ignored is that, as in the case of Ercilla, Villagrá attempts to link his life and work to the presence of his monarch; whether to Felipe III or in allusions to his father, Felipe II. In fact, Villagrá mentions the image of a Felipe II prepared to listen to his subjects. Whether this was true or not is another matter; what is asserted here is that the poet wished to highlight his good standing with the court of Castile and possibly with the king, as is presented in the following lines.[108]

Siete años continuos me detuve	Seven years continuous was I
En vuestra illustre y levantada corte	In your illustrious and lofty court
Y no vi pobre capa ni mendigo	And saw no poor gentleman or beggar
Que con facilidad no se llegase	That did not come, and with great ease,
A vuestro caro Padre y señor nuestro	To your beloved father and our lord
A contalle sus cuitas y fatigas	To tell him of his troubles and fatigues
Con esperanza cierta y verdadera	With certain and most genuine hope.
De bellas remediadas y amparadas.	
(Villagrá, *Historia*, 20, 281–89)	

The allusion the poet makes to his service to the king as a writer of the history he witnessed crops up at least five times in the poem.[109] Using the allegory of the sword and pen, he refers to his dual service to the king as soldier and writer. In this connection, it is worth citing the final lines of the poem, wherein Villagrá mentions the possibility of continuing the story.

Y por si vuestra Majestad insigne	And if your famous Majesty
El fin de aquesta historia ver quisiere,	Should wish to see the end of this story
De rodillas suplico que me aguarde	I beg upon my knees that you will wait
Y también me perdone si tardare,	And pardon me, also, if I delay,
Porque es difícil cosa que la pluma,	For 'tis a thing difficult for the pen

Abiendo de serviros con la lanza,
Pueda desempacharse sin tardanza.
    (Villagrá, *Historia*, 34, 383–89)

To lose all shyness instantly,
Having to serve you with the lance.

To conclude, it is also important to mention similar lines in Ercilla's poem. In the final canto, he connects his own life and "labors" to the kingdom and his monarch. Ercilla also asserts how much he gave in support of the expansion of the empire of Felipe II.

Cuantas tierras corrí, cuantas naciones
hacia al helado norte atravesando,
y en las bajas antárticas regiones
el antípoda ignoto conquistando!
Climas pasé, mudé constelaciones
Golfos innavegables navegando,
estendiendo, Señor, vuestra corona
hasta casi la austral frígida zona.

How many lands have I passed through,
    how many nations
traversing towards the icy north,
and in the lower Antarctica regions
conquering the unknown antipodes!
I went through climes, changed
    constellations
Navigating unnavigable gulfs,
extending, Lord, your crown
almost to the austral frigid zone.

    (Ercilla, *La Araucana*, 37.66, 1–8)

What is said and what is left unsaid in the last lines of both Ercilla's and Villagrá's poems relay the poets' intentions. Though in Villagrá's last canto the central theme is the battle of Acoma and the dramatic Indian defeat, in which the lines accentuate the Spanish victory, the poet makes no mention of the cruel and controversial measures his leader, Oñate, took to punish the rebel Indians. Therefore, what Villagrá does not say is as important as what he does say. And if he does not say it, is it because of censorship, to avoid any controversy that might bring about the censure of his poem? Or because of a personal issue, given that he was accused of being part of the group that repressed the Acomas? When the poem was published, what was the poet's situation with respect to the accusations against him? What was it best to say, and what was best to leave unsaid in his poem when it was published in 1610? This topic is covered in greater depth in chapter 2.

In his final canto, Ercilla, meanwhile, underscores the importance of Felipe II's empire, directly linking the poet's own participation with the task of expanding the king's imperial authority. The poet leaves nothing to speculation. Ercilla includes himself as part of the enormous enterprise of extending Spanish authority to the southernmost region of South America. Ercilla neither selects an ambiguous ending nor chooses to make a final mention of the Araucanian defense in Chile, except in the final lines in which he refers to fighting against the Araucanians. Ercilla concludes his poem talking about the empire and about himself as an important part of its expansion. This is in contrast with Villagrá, who maintains the suspense almost to the end: Acoma destroyed and a possible continuation of the story in a future poem. But the empire, the power of the king, and above all the results of a more than controversial Spanish victory were not part of the end of Villagrá's poem.[110] Perhaps the following chapter can answer or explain some of these questions.

CHAPTER 2

The Law

¡Cuán buena es la justicia y qué importante!	How good justice is and how important!
Por ella son mil males atajados;	Thanks to her a thousand wrongs are parried
que si el rebelde Arauco está pujante	if the rebellious Arauco pushes ahead,
con todos sus vecinos alterados	with all its neighbors aroused,
y pasa su furor tan adelante,	and its furor passes so far ahead,
fue por no ser a tiempo castigados;	it is because of not disciplining them on time;
la llaga que al principio no se cura,	a wound not cured at the beginning,
requiere al fin más áspera la cura.	in the end requires the most difficult of cures
(Ercilla, *La Araucana*, 4.1, 1–8)	

Quando con huena y presta diligencia	When with a good and rapid diligence
La braveza del cáncer no se ataja,	The spreading of a cancer is not stopped,
No es posible que el mísero paciente	'Tis not possible that the sad patient
Escape con la vida, porque es cierto	Escape with his life, for 'tis certain
Que la aya de rendir a tal dolencia.	That he must give it up to such disease.
Y si la atrocidad de los delictos	And if justice does not strictly
Justicia con rigor no los reprime,	Repress the wickedness of crime,
También es imposible que gozemos	It is impossible that we enjoy
De la gustosa paz en que vivimos.	The pleasant peace in which we live.
Desto dechado grande nos han dado	Of this those rude barbarians of Arauco
Aquellos bravos bárbaros de Arauco,	Have given us a notable standard,
Pues por no más de aberles dilatado	Since, for no more than delaying
El debido castigo a tales culpas	The punishment due to such crimes,
Sincuenta largos años son pasados	Fifty long years have gone by
Que en efusión de sangre Castellana	When in effusion of Castilian blood
Sus omicidas armas no se han visto	Their homicidal arms have not been seen
Enjutas ni cansadas de verterla	Or dry or tired of shedding it.
(Villagrá, *Historia*, 27, 1–17)	

According to a legend of the Spanish conquest in Chile, before killing the conquistador Pedro de Valdivia, the Araucanians forced him to drink molten gold. Beyond the question of the veracity of this event, the story illustrates the reality of gold fever, which characterized the first decades of the conquest of the Americas. The lust for gold had devastating consequences for both sides on the southern frontier of the empire, but particularly for the Indians. Such a legend could have arisen only in a context of violence and conflicting world views.

> If the story that Valdivia was made to drink gold at the moment of his death is true, it merely speaks to an inability to understand an invader who was judged not by what he was but by what he sought.[1]

Valdivia died at the hands of the Araucanians on December 25, 1553, in the fortress of Tucapel, which he had founded that same year. He was decapitated, and his head was suspended from a pole.

The Spaniards who participated in the conquest of Chile during the decades of 1540 and 1550, beginning with the adelantado Valdivia himself, were seeking nothing more than recompense—especially in the form of precious metals—for the material investment and personal effort they had made. The consolidation and maintenance of the Spanish empire required private capital and concessions that the crown had to make to the conquistadors. Immediately after the founding of Santiago de la Nueva Extremadura on February 24, 1541, Valdivia began to do what every conquistador did: discover the secrets of the land, which amounted to nothing more than finding out everything he could about gold and silver. The period between 1541 and 1553 was characterized by the constant hunt for treasure, the use of Indian labor, and the search for native knowledge about the places where there was gold, whether in the mountains or in watercourses. Many abuses were committed in these years, although in theory there was a legal framework to control excesses in the treatment of the Indians, the use of their labor, and the occupation of their land.

From the beginning of the conquest and colonization of the Americas, the Spanish crown saw the need to create legislation to avoid the unavoidable. This legislation had two key periods in the sixteenth century that to some degree correspond to the legal framework of the historical period covered in the two poems. Ercilla wrote about an early period of the reign of Felipe II that had a particular set of laws, while Villagrá wrote about a second period of that reign, which was characterized by different laws with respect to the treatment of Indians. This provokes the question of what material from each poem can be identified with the legal system of each period. To what extent can the poems—and events immediately after their publication—help to understand the application of imperial law to the conquest of each frontier? More difficult to answer, but no less important to reflect upon, is how what is said—and not said—in these two epic literary poems reflects a political and legal reality.

The first period of the conquest in Chile took place in the legal framework of the New Laws of 1542, which, in theory, attempted to protect the Indians.

Nevertheless, the characteristics of the war on the Chilean frontier did not reflect the existence of or fulfillment of these laws. Ercilla's discourse in verse appears to reproduce a feeling of guilt for abuses committed and reflects an attitude of sympathy and admiration for the Indians. He presents the theme of justification of the war from both the Araucanian and Spanish sides. In doing so, the poet moves from one side of the fight to the other in a display of inevitable contradictions. Villagrá's poem, by contrast, has as its legal backdrop the New Ordinances for Settlement and Discovery of 1573, which attempted to correct the errors of previous laws that had not completely managed to eliminate abuses. In this effort, the word "conquest" was replaced with "pacification." Villagrá's poetry partially reflects this legal context and appears, in some sections of the poem, to show empathy for the Indians. Above all, though, the poet seeks to justify war against the natives, specifically in regard to the incident at Acoma.

From a legal standpoint, from the time the Americas were incorporated into the crown of Castile, Castilian law governed them. Once the conquest began on the North and South American continents and especially when facing cultures with complex organization, such as the Aztecs and Incas, the crown established the standard that Indian customs and organizations should be utilized whenever possible, as long as they did "not contradict the supreme interests of the colonizing State."[2] But soon it became apparent that even with the incorporation of some native customs, the application of the old Castilian law was not efficient enough for so different a geographic, social, and economic reality. The decision was made to create more specific norms, which came to constitute Indian law. The laws had the following characteristics: First, specific cases were legislated and then the law tried to generalize from there. Second, proliferating instructions on how to govern led to the phenomenon of "bureaucratic thoroughness." Third, the Laws of the Indies included the conversion of the Indians to the Catholic faith.[3] This last element meant that laws were frequently dictated by theologians and moralists rather than jurists. The laws' failure to consider such essential elements as social and economic matters led to a separation between "the law and the facts."

> One was a doctrine declared in law, and the other was the reality of social life. It sought to go too far in the noble desire to defend for the Indian a standard of living that was elevated in the social order and spiritual order and in dictating, in order to protect him, norms that were difficult or impossible to comply with, giving rise to, unintentionally, the fact that arbitrariness would prevail, leaving the Indian at the mercy of the Spanish encomenderos and the authorities of the colony.[4]

This last, the abuse of authority, characterized the first stage of the conquest of Chile. Among other obligations and privileges that the adelantado Pedro de

Valdivia took on because of his *capitulación*, or contract, of October 10, 1539, was the authority to distribute encomiendas to the members of his expedition. They, like him, had invested their own resources in the enterprise of conquest. The capitulación was "the primary source" of new Indian law in the first decades of the Spanish American conquest, becoming the principal law to apply in conquered territory as a sort of municipal right. The theme of the treatment of the Indian had been included in the capitulaciones texts as least as early as 1526.[5] This concern was surely the result of years of insistence on the part of Bartolomé de Las Casas and others about the need for a policy to protect the Indians.[6]

As early as 1515, Las Casas's allegations about abuses committed in Cuba led to his recommendation in 1516 to import white and black slaves (Berbers from North Africa) for certain jobs, such as mining, thus to alleviate the burden on the Indians. Las Casas was not questioning Castile's right to govern the Indies, but the lack of a policy for just treatment of the Indian.[7] In his "Memorial for the Relief of the Indies" of 1518, Las Casas asked that the Indians of the Caribbean and of the American mainland be removed from private hands, that their freedom be given back, and that their lands that the colonizers had usurped be returned to them. In 1540 his allegations were even more energetic because the abuses had continued during the conquest of New Spain and Peru. This time he insisted on the end of the encomienda as a system of Indian slavery and recommended placing the Indians directly under the jurisdiction of the crown. The conquistadors and lower members of the expeditions of conquest, having become encomenderos, had committed abuses and had legally claimed all sorts of liberties for themselves. The crown could arrest this situation by retaking control through its American bureaucrats: the viceroy, the high court judge (*oidor*), the royal officer (*oficial real*), and so forth, and by promulgating laws limiting the power of local encomenderos: "America had to be reconquered when it had scarcely been discovered."[8]

Emperor Carlos V did not turn a deaf ear to these protests, and as a result the New Laws of 1542 were proclaimed, which established as the most important measure the elimination of the encomienda—understood as personal service by the Indians.[9] When Valdivia founded the city of Santiago in Chile in February 1541, the original form of encomienda still existed. Moreover, by royal cédula issued in 1536, certain military obligations for encomenderos were established, which Valdivia put into practice immediately because he needed military assistance.[10] The process that led to the promulgation of the New Laws of 1542 came about when Valdivia began his conquest and during the first Indian rebellions. In September 1541 the town of Santiago was attacked and destroyed.

With the New Laws, Carlos V had ruled in favor of Las Casas's argument, but the reaction from the colonies was the rebellion of the encomenderos and civil war in Peru, while in New Spain application of the new legal code was suspended.[11] As a result, the encomienda was reinstated in 1545, although this time, at least in theory, payment of tribute replaced service or forced labor. In Chile in 1546, Valdivia was still using the system of distribution of Indians in encomiendas. In order to continue the conquest to the south, in Arauco (the land of the Araucanians), he had to take measures such as reducing the number of encomenderos in Santiago, offering as compensation encomiendas in the territories to be conquered. Thus, the self-titled "governor" Valdivia could count on the military assistance of the encomenderos (from men to horses) in exchange for "the promise made to the dispossessed that Indian draft laborers would be designated for them in the first city settled in the land farther beyond."[12] Valdivia gave the authority to each conquistador-encomendero to found cities and distribute Indians among his men. Although by 1557 this system had proved a failure, in those first years characterized by a founding fever, the excesses and abuses were constant with respect to the treatment of the Indians, who were distributed by force and obliged to work for the founders (including Valdivia).

Ercilla echoes this early part of the conquest. His first cantos present the founding of cities and the consequences of granting land and Indians to those who had contributed financially to their establishment.

Dejando allí el seguro suficiente
adelante los nuestros caminaron;
pero todas las tierras llanamente,
viendo Arauco sujeta se entregaron,
y reduciendo a su opinión gran gente,
siete ciudades prósperas fundaron:
Coquimbo, Penco, Angol y Santiago,
la Imperial, Villarrica, y la del Lago.

El felice suceso, la vitoria,
la fama y posesiones que adquirían
los trujo a tal soberbia y vanagloria,
que en mil leguas diez hombres no cabían,
sin pasarles jamás por la memoria
que en siete pies de tierra al fin habían
de venir a caber sus hinchazones,
su gloria vana y vanas pretensiones.

Leaving a secure force,
our men walked on ahead;
but all the lands clearly,
seeing the Arauco subjugated, surrendered,
and, having reduced such great people to
   their way of thinking,
founded seven prosperous cities:
Coquimbo, Penco, Angol and Santiago,
La Imperial, Villarrica and the one of the
   lake.

The happy event, the victory,
the fame and possession they acquired,
brought them to such pride and vainglory,
that in thousand leagues ten men could
   not fit,
without passing through your memory
that in seven feet of earth, in the end
they had to fit their arrogance,
their vainglory and vain pretenses.

(Ercilla, *La Araucana*, 1.66, 1–8; 67, 1–8)

By way of example of the magnitude of the Indian labor each founder obtained, there is the case of Pedro de Villagrá, who received fifteen thousand Indians in encomienda as a citizen of La Imperial, and Gerónimo de Alderete, who received six thousand Indians in encomienda in the land south of the Río Toltén, inside the boundaries of La Imperial. The same happened with the rest of the Spaniards who participated in the establishment of those towns.[13]

When the speed with which the founding of villas and fortresses such as Arauco, Purén, and Tucapel took place is analyzed, it must be remembered that Valdivia was also promoting the development of new towns because of his need to compensate his men by granting encomiendas to those who had loaned him money or other types of aid, such as men and horses. The adelantado needed economic assistance to continue the occupation and especially the search for gold. To obtain the money, he granted permission to found towns, which included license to distribute Indians. Although he was in debt, Valdivia always came out ahead and as a last resort sought recourse from the state, using some of the accumulated funds that belonged to the king. Whenever a distribution was made, the adelantado always received land and Indian labor to extract gold.[14]

The resource most needed and sought after by the Spaniards in Chile was not land but Indian labor. The conquest of the Americas and European colonization in general in the sixteenth century was characterized not by an interest in controlling territories but men. As Chilean historian Jorge Pinto Rodríguez expresses, the Spanish wanted "men who could produce what was needed to connect the local economy with the European economy, that is, precious metals."[15] Land in itself had little value if it had no gold. It was worth still less if it did not have nearby Indian labor to extract the ore. Therefore, first in order of importance was land with gold and an Indian population. Then, if there was no gold, the Indian population was a guarantee of labor, and as a consequence, production and payment of tribute in kind. Spaniards, therefore, had no interest in land without either gold or natives or both. For the natives, by contrast, gold was not their most precious resource. Therefore, Spanish greed for the precious metal received special attention from those who denounced abuses against the Indians.

Ercilla described the extent of this ambition in the case of Valdivia, who, according to the poet, arrived too late to aid the fortress of Tucapel, which was under Araucanian attack, because he had made a detour to search for gold. The poet also describes Valdivia's attitude toward the law. His character had devolved to that of a true tyrant:

Crecían los intereses y malicia
a costa del sudor y daño anejo,
y la hambrienta y mísera codicia,
con libertad paciendo iba sin freno.
La ley, derecho, el fuero y la justicia
era lo que Valdivia había por bueno:
remiso en graves culpas y piadoso,
y en los casos livianos riguroso.
    (Ercilla, *La Araucana*, 1.68, 1–8)

Self interest and evil grew
at the cost of sweat and foreign harm,
and the hungry and miserable greed
grazing freely went out of control.
The law, rights, judicial power and justice
was what Valdivia had as a right:
remiss in grave situations and pious
and in simple cases rigorous.

These lines coincide with the historical period, in which the main goal with respect to the conquest was the search for gold. This motive continued to exist after Valdivia died, during the administration of his successor, García Hurtado de Mendoza, Ercilla being witness to part of his period as governor. The poet ascribes to the Indian leader Galvarino a speech about gold in a sequence in which he addresses the council of caciques.

"Volved, volved en vos, no deis oído
a sus embustes, tratos y marañas,
pues todas se enderezan a un partido
que viene a deslustrar vuestras hazañas;
que la ocasión que aquí los ha traído
por mares y por tierras tan extrañas
es el oro goloso que se encierra
en las fértiles venas de esta tierra."

Ercilla, *La Araucana*, 23.12, 1–8)

"Return, return to yourselves, do not give ear
to their lies, treatments and frauds,
for all will straighten out to one party
that it comes to tarnish your feats;
that the occasion that has brought them here
by sea and lands so alien
is the sweet taste of gold that is held
in the fertile veins of this land."

In 1550–51, while Valdivia was promoting the founding of settlements and the distribution of Indians for the search for gold in Chile, one of the most important debates in the history of human rights—specifically the rights of the Indians—was taking place in Valladolid, Spain. Emperor Carlos V gathered a royal council in that city to debate the arguments of Las Casas and Juan Ginés de Sepúlveda, the latter in defense of Indian slavery.[16] Sepúlveda was known at court as the tutor of Prince Felipe, and in 1545 he began to express publicly his position in opposition to Las Casas. In his writing titled *Demócrates segundo*, he explained why war against the natives of the Americas was just. Felipe, however, had received visits from Las Casas, who had dedicated to the prince his *Brief Account of the Destruction of the Indies* (1552), a publication in which he depicted with vehement passion the abuses against the indigenous population in the Americas in the first decades of the conquest.[17]

Evidently, the New Laws of 1542, which had been dictated as a result of Las Casas's charges, had not been effective (as noted, the encomienda was reinstated in Peru in 1545). Therefore, the debates of the 1550s, which were contemporaneous with Ercilla's preparation for his voyage to the Americas, continued to address the same points of Las Casas's defense of the Indians four decades earlier. The royal authorities were at least trying to do something.

In 1549 the Council of the Indies recommended to Carlos V that he suspend all conquests, and it called for a panel of experts—jurists and theologians—to be formed to debate the problems of the conquest and recommend how to proceed with it in the future. As a result, in April 1550 the emperor sent secret instructions to the authorities of New Spain and Peru ordering the suspension of the conquest, while he ordered the creation of a council of specialists. The debate in Valladolid was the result of these measures, and it centered specifically on the arguments of Las Casas and Sepúlveda, with each defending his position. The former, following the Aristotelian-Thomist school of natural law, adapted concepts of canon law to the political arena. Las Casas grounded his defense of the right of the Indians to their dominions in law, while Sepúlveda based his defense on philosophy, not law.[18]

As a result, the council of experts ruled in April 1551 that military conquests should be suspended, except those directed by missionaries with the aim of conversion to Christianity. Nevertheless, in the face of constant pressures, especially from the viceroy of Peru (Andrés Hurtado de Mendoza, Marqués de Cañete), the emperor authorized new conquests in Peru in December 1555. In 1556 new instructions on how to proceed with the conquest were issued.[19] The legal context of the conquest of Chile in the years that Ercilla was there and that inform his poem was, therefore, that of these instructions. The outcome of the Valladolid debate was met with local pressures from the encomenderos of Peru. In addition, in 1556 Felipe II became king of Spain, and from that time on, Las Casas's influence began to wane.[20]

Doubtless Ercilla knew about this debate because in those years he was in Valladolid at the court of Prince Felipe. Las Casas lived in the convento of San Gregorio, located near the prince's residence. Other influences to the poet's education could have come from his father, Fortún García de Ercilla, who was a jurist and author of writings about just war,[21] and from his teacher in Valladolid, Juan Cristóbal Calvete de Estrella, who was also in charge of teaching Prince Felipe's pages. Calvete was the author of a chronicle titled "Historia de Chile" and another about Peru, "Rebelión de Pizarro en el Perú y vida de Pedro de Lagasca."[22] Between his experience in Valladolid and seven months of residence in Lima (1556–57) before arriving in Chile, Ercilla must have become familiar with the debate about the treatment of the Indians and certainly the details of the latest rebellions of encomenderos in Peru.[23]

Another factor may have added to Ercilla's knowledge of the ideas put forth by Las Casas and could have influenced the defense of the Araucanians in his poem. In Chile the poet met the Dominican priest fray Gil González de San Nicolás, a friend of Las Casas and a disciple of Francisco de Vitoria.[24] In 1552 fray Gil was in Lima and had been named protector of Indians and vicar general of Chile by the provincial of the Dominicans in Peru. He departed for Chile in 1557. Once there he dedicated himself to promoting his idea of defensive war. In his opinion, the Indians had a right to make war if their freedoms and properties were usurped. He dedicated himself to preaching these principles to the soldiers. According to the chronicler Góngora Marmolejo, fray Gil's words "were said with such power, that they made a strong impression on the spirits of the captains and soldiers."[25] Ercilla was in Chile the same two years that fray Gil was there (1557–59). There can be no doubt that the poet knew him. Moreover, the friar sailed from Chile to Lima on the same ship that Ercilla took in 1559. It is more than possible that during the voyage and while in Lima, fray Gil spoke with Ercilla about the unjust war against the Araucanians.[26]

The major arguments about abuses in the Americas exposed by Bartolomé de Las Casas, Dominican father Francisco de Vitoria, and fray Gil González de San Nicolás, which could have influenced Ercilla, are the following:

1. The merits of the Indians' intelligence, reflected among other things in their social organization and capacity for self-government and their exercise of free will;
2. Their right to free will and to own their land, and as a consequence, to defend themselves if their rights were threatened;
3. The Spanish attitude of arrogance and greed compared to an initial Indian attitude of fear and submission as defensive tools;
4. The hypocritical Spanish attitude of proclaiming Christian principles but in practice doing the opposite. Related to this point was the use of physical violence—from indiscriminate slaughter, to the amputation of hands, to forced labor in mines, to being obliged to transport burdens.
5. Identification with the king but not with the colonists, because the friars did not question the right of the crown to domination in the Americas or mass conversion to Christianity; rather, they questioned the abusive treatment of the Indians.[27]

Ercilla's poetry does not subscribe wholly to these notions; there are differences. For example, he does not necessarily reflect Las Casas's vision with exactitude. Moreover, the poet's contradictions and his tendency to switch sides on an issue cannot be overlooked. Whether it was a need to adhere to the format of the epic, because of the direct influence of classical authors such as Virgil, because deep down he continued to be an imperial poet, or because it was in his interest to leave his posture ambiguous, only in certain lines of the poem can the reader clearly discern the poet's position.

From the beginning of *La Araucana*, in the prologue to part 1, Ercilla shows his intentions by depicting the Araucanians admiringly. He mentions their capacity for self-government and organization, and he establishes a comparison with other indigenous peoples, with the Araucanians being one of the few to have resisted the Spaniards. As noted previously, Ercilla tends to judge Araucanian bravery by their capacity to resist a people as brave as the Spaniards.

> If to some it appears that I seem inclined to the side of the Araucanians, speaking of their things and bravery at greater length than what is required for barbarians, if we want to see their upbringing, customs, methods of war and the exercise of them, we will see that many have not given them an advantage,

and that there are a few who with such great steadfastness and firmness have defended their land against such fierce enemies as the Spaniards.[28]

Ercilla appears to use the word "barbarian" in a sense similar to that of Las Casas. He does not relate the term to Sepúlveda's concept, in the sense of an ignorant people who lack the ability to reason. The use of "barbarian" in the poem is more closely related to the idea of opposition to Christianity.[29] Thus, the term appears in the prologue and also in the following lines.

Como toros que van a salir lidiados, cuando aquellos que cerca lo desean, con silbos y rumor de los tablados seguros del peligro los torean, y en su daño los hierros amolados sin miedo amenazándolos blandean: así la gente bárbara araucana del muro amenazaba a la cristiana.	Like bulls that are going to be fought, when those that encircle them desire with whistles and murmurs, from platforms safe from danger to fight the bulls, in harming them with sharpened iron without fear threatening them, so it was with the barbarian Araucanian people, who from the wall threatened the Christians.

(Ercilla, *La Araucana*, 11.58, 1–8)

Ercilla mentions the basis of political and military organization, represented by the authority of those leaders the Spaniards called "caciques."

De diez y seis caciques y señores es el soberbio Estado poseído, en militar estudio los mejores que de bárbaras madres han nacido; reparo de su patria y defensores, ninguno en el gobierno preferido. Otros caciques hay, mas por valientes son éstos en mandar los preeminentes.	By sixteen Indian Chiefs and princes is this superb State held, the best of those born to these barbarian mothers are selected for a military education; restorers and defenders of their homeland, none favored in Government. There are other chiefs who because of their bravery are the superior ones selected to govern.

(Ercilla, *La Araucana*, 1.13, 1–8)

The poet also refers to the upper level of Araucanian political organization upon mentioning events related to the gathering of Indians in a council or senate to make decisions democratically.

Juntos, pues, los caciques del senado, propóneles el caso nuevamente, el cual por ellos visto y ponderado,	Together, then, the Indian chiefs of the Senate, propose the case again, which is reviewed and pondered,

se trata del remedio conveniente;	discussing the convenient remedy;
y resuelto en uno y decretado,	and resolved and decided,
si alguno de opinión es diferente,	if there is someone whose opinion is
no puede en cuanto al débito eximirse,	different,
que allí la mayor voz ha de seguirse.	it can not as far as duty be excused,
	here the greater voice is to be followed.

(Ercilla, *La Araucana*, 1.35, 1–8)

These lines also demonstrate the exercise of the freedom of self-determination. The Araucanians were able to make their own laws and decisions as an independent people. This right was what gave the Araucanians the reputation of being "indomitable," in the sense that they refused to submit to laws that were not their own (obviously the matter of being "indomitable" is a classification from the point of view of the conquistador).

No ha habido rey jamás que sujetase	There has not been a King who ever bound
esta soberbia gente libertada,	this arrogant liberated people,
ni extranjera nación que se jatase	nor a foreign nation that can boast
de haber dado en sus términos pisada,	of having stepped within their boundaries;
ni comarcana tierra que se osase	nor neighboring land which dared
mover en contra y levantar espada.	move against it and lift sword.
Siempre fue esenta, indómita, temida,	They were always exempt, unconquered,
de leyes libre y de cerviz erguida.	feared,
	free of laws and proud of themselves.

(Ercilla, *La Araucana*, 1.47, 1–8)

The Incas had not been able to subjugate the Araucanians. When the Spaniards arrived, the Araucanians apparently believed the Incas had returned. Eventually they began to call the Spaniards "huinca," which means "new Inca."

The theme of free will appears throughout the poem and provides the context for various episodes, all related to the democratic discussions and decisions the Araucanians eventually made, as was their custom. In several instances, the references are spoken by the elderly Colocolo, thus demonstrating the Araucanian respect for the opinion of an authority with the experience that age confers. After the death of Pedro de Valdivia in 1553, the Araucanians challenged themselves: continue the war as they had up to that time, with open resistance and without hiding their desire to defend their land at all costs, or continue to face the Spaniards with some other type of strategy. At the beginning of part 2 of *La Araucana*, Ercilla depicts two simultaneous events: the arrival in Concepción of the new governor, García Hurtado de Mendoza, and the meeting of the Araucanian senate to decide which strategy to follow. Internal squabbles were evident, particularly between the leaders Tucapel and Rengo, and the voice of the aged Colocolo was heard, calming tempers with his discourse on the importance of unity.

"Volved sobre vosotros, que sin tiento
corréis a toda priesa a despeñaros;
refrenad esa furia y movimiento,
que es la que puede en esto más dañaros.
¿Sufrís al enemigo en vuestro asiento,
que quiere como a brutos conquistaros,
y no podéis sufrir aquí impacientes
los consejos y avisos convenientes?"

(Ercilla, *La Araucana*, 16.69, 1–8)

"Go back amongst yourselves, without a
  halter
you run in all haste to throw yourselves
  headlong;
restrain that fury and movement,
that is what can most harm you.
You endure the enemy where you choose,
who as brutes want to conquer you,
and you can not endure here impatient
advice and expedient warnings?"

"cese, cese el furor y civil guerra
y por el bien común tened por bueno
no romper la hermandad con torpes
  modos
pues que miembros de un cuerpo somos
  todos."

(Ercilla, *La Araucana*, 16.71, 5–8)

"cease, cease the furor and civil war
and for the very common good hold as
  proper
not to break up the brotherhood in stupid
  ways
because we all are members of one body."

A similar example appears in the verses that mention the election of the successor to Caupolicán, whom the Spaniards had executed.

Pero el cacique Colocolo, viendo
el daño de los muchos pretendientes,
como prudente y sabio conociendo
pocos para el gran cargo suficientes,
su anciana gravedad interponiendo
les hizo mensajeros diligentes
para que se juntasen a consulta
en lugar apartado y parte oculta.

(Ercilla, *La Araucana*, 34.38, 1–8)

But the cacique Colocolo, seeing
the damage of many pretenders,
as wise man and sage recognizing
few great enough for the position,
his old authority interposing
sent diligent messengers
so they could join in consultation
in a remote and hidden place.

The theme of free will also appears in the poem through the voice of Milla-lauco, who addresses García Hurtado de Mendoza, communicating the decision of the senate with respect to accepting the peace (an untruthful position because the secret Araucanian strategy was to attack).

"Que el ínclito senado, habiendo oído
de vuestra parte algunas relaciones
con sabio acuerdo y parecer, movido
por legítimas causas y razones,
quiere acetar la paz, quiere partido
de lícitas y honestas condiciones,
para que no padezca tanta gente
del pueblo simple y género inocente."

(Ercilla, *La Araucana*, 17.9, 1–8)

"The renowned Senate, having heard
on your behalf some discourses
by sage agreement and opinion, moved
by legitimate causes and reasons,
wants to accept peace, wants a resolution
of licit and honest conditions,
so there is not so much suffering by people
who are of simple and innocent kind."

Ercilla's lines in this section come close to describing the actual historical event that other authors have confirmed.[30]

One might speculate that the poet mentions events or traditions having to do with free will because of what he saw and heard, that is, reflecting a true tradition. It is not known whether Ercilla had read the writings of University of Salamanca theologian Francisco de Vitoria on the theme of free will. But it is possible that he learned about the subject indirectly from Las Casas, who was influenced by Vitoria's ideas. The point here is that it is difficult to determine at times when Ercilla is manifesting the direct influence of thinkers such as Las Casas or Vitoria—directly, or indirectly through Las Casas. Of course, if he wanted, the poet could have elected not to mention the Araucanians' ability to govern themselves. He could have omitted references to positive aspects of Indian organization. Instead, he evidently chose to include events and mention traditions that showed the Indians' capacity for independent government.

Elizabeth Davis has analyzed Vitoria's influence on *La Araucana* by examining the poet's discourse of vassalage and service to the king. If the natives of Chile are subject to the same laws as other vassals of the king, then "the rules that govern sociopolitical life in Arauco should be the same ones that obtain in the home country."[31] Some lines in the poem suggest that Ercilla coincides with Vitoria and Las Casas in the idea of considering Indians from the Americas to be "civilized societies" by virtue of having a social hierarchy with a ruling and warrior elite at the top.[32] Davis, however, concedes that the poet also includes lines that highlight the Araucanian lack of willingness to submit to one king. This characteristic, plus the lack of virtue implied by the Araucanian leaders' disunity, betrayal, dissension, and discord, is a sign of imperfection that could mean Ercilla agrees with the practice of the encomienda, although not of enslavement.[33]

To add to the complexity of the analysis, Gilberto Triviños in his article "El mito del tiempo de los héroes en Valdivia, Vivar y Ercilla" states that regarding the discourse of the "invention of Chile" and the discovery of the "other," the poet cites events and descriptions that can be traced back to letters Valdivia wrote to the king as well as to Gerónimo de Vivar's *Crónica y relación copiosa y verdadera de los Reinos de Chile* (1558). According to Triviños, Ercilla relied more than has been previously thought on the vision and information presented by Vivar, whose text was published before part 1 of *La Araucana* came out. Triviños suggests that the portrayal of the Araucanians, their social organization, and events related to their leaders as they appear in *La Araucana* have their origin in Vivar's story more than in Ercilla's imagination or knowledge.[34]

From a historical perspective, it has been argued that the Araucanian type of social organization eventually made it possible for their resistance in Chile to succeed. At the same time, particularly in the first decade of the conquest with Pedro de Valdivia, when the natives were surprised and still in shock, that social organization initially facilitated the Spanish entrada and the subjugation of the

Indians to the encomienda system. As has been noted by those who have studied the Mapuches (from Mapuche, the name scholars use for the language spoken in Arauco) in depth, this nation demonstrated throughout the invasion that it was dynamic rather than static. As a way of adapting to the circumstances and to avoid losing their identity, the Mapuches had to modify their structure with the arrival of the Incas, and they did the same with the Spaniards. In the latter case, they also changed through the course of three centuries of living under Spanish domination. Thus, the concept of territorial identity evolved from the beginning of the Spanish conquest.[35]

For the historical period that Ecrilla covers in his poem—the first decades of Spanish occupation—the existing organization was still the same used during the Inca expansion. The Indian term *lof* ("lebo" for the Spaniards) was the basis of the social structure of Araucanía and constituted a type of tribe with its own territory and *longko* ("cacique"). Each lof could have between fifteen hundred and three thousand Indians united by family ties, whether collateral or closely related, and were in turn divided into smaller units. Several communities or lof made up the *rewe* and several rewe made up the *aillarehue*. Each lof acted and governed itself with considerable independence. When the longkos had to make decisions about the defense of territory on a large scale, as was the case of the Spanish invasion, the longkos gathered in a council or senate. In these meetings the eldest longkos were of particular importance, and their advice was respectfully followed. In addition, there was the position of *werkén* (ambassador), who was designated to make agreements with the enemy.[36] Ercilla mentions the function of the councils and that of the eldest longko, as well as that of the ambassador, in the context of native organization and decision making. Although the poet does not provide details about the use of native organization for the benefit of the Spaniards, other sources from the period are very clear on the subject.

The first laws promulgated by the crown addressed the need to respect Indian organization and customs. Accordingly, when Pedro de Valdivia began his conquest of Araucanía, he took advantage of the existing lebo system and superimposed on it the encomienda system of personal service. In a letter to Carlos V (Carlos I of Spain), dated September 25, 1551, in Concepción, Valdivia stated:

> I distributed all the caciques from the river to here [from the Biobío to Concepción], without giving one to the other side, by their *levos*, each with its own name, which are like surnames, and where the Indians recognize subjugation to their superiors, among a hundred and a hundred and fifty conquistadors, and I distributed the *levos* of Indians to those from two leagues all around for service in the home.[37]

This way of distributing encomiendas based on the original Indian organization must have made the Indian communities feel dominated, exploited, and out of control of their own decision making. Initially, the lebo did not disappear as a unit. It was simply placed under Spanish control, and its members were obligated to perform personal service. All the members of the lebo had to work for their encomendero, except for the principal cacique, his family, and his servants. However, control over the principal authority implied the entire unit was controlled.[38]

The strategy of imposing the encomienda on top of the lebo system, together with the fear provoked by firearms and horses, doubtless led to an initial state of surrender to Spanish domination, particularly in the region where Valdivia and his men first arrived (north of the Biobío River). The Araucanians responded with fear and did not offer immediate resistance.[39] The response was similar everywhere Spaniards went in the Americas. In part II of this book, the concept of "entrada" and the Spanish ritual of taking possession of the land will be examined in more detail. In general, if the Indians offered no opposition, Spaniards understood that they had the right to occupy the land.

Ayudó mucho el inorante engaño	A great deal helped the falsehood
de ver en animales corregidos	of seeing in admonished animals
hombres que por milagro y caso extraño	men who, by fortune and odd coincidence,
de la región celeste eran venidos;	had come from the celestial region;
y del súbito estruendo y grave daño	and the sudden noise and serious harm
de los tiros de pólvora sentidos,	of the sound of shooting of gunpowder,
como a inmortales dioses los temían	made them fear they were immortal gods,
que con ardientes rayos combatían.	who fought with burning rays.
Los españoles hechos hazañosos	The Spaniards' heroic achievements
el error confirmaban de inmortales,	confirmed the error of their immortality
afirmando los más supersticiosos	and the most superstitious affirming
por los presentes los futuros males;	from the present they could see the future evils;
y así tibios, suspensos y dudosos,	and so, unenthusiastic, bewildered and doubting,
viendo de su opresión claras señales,	seeing clear signs of their oppression,
debajo de hermandad y fe jurada	under signs of brotherhood and sworn word
dio Arauco la obediencia jamás dada.	Arauco gave obedience it never gave before.

(Ercilla, *La Araucana*, 1.64, 1–8; 65, 1–8)

Faced with the Spanish attitude toward occupying the land, dividing it among the colonists, and especially, distributing Indians to make them work in the search for gold, the initial Indian response was transformed into resistance. Las Casas had denounced Spanish arrogance and greed, and Ercilla also referred to them. The poet began his third canto with a reflection on greed, which he characterizes as:

del provecho y bien público enemiga,
sedienta bestia, hidrópica, hinchada,
principio y fin de todos nuestros males!
¡oh insaciable codicia de mortales!
    (Ercilla, *La Araucana*, 3.1, 1–8)

enemy of progress and public good;
thirsty beast, hydrophobic, inflated,
beginning and end of all our wrongs!
Oh insatiable greed of mortals!

He goes on to cite Valdivia as an example of greed. Here the poet projects the idea of just war on the part of the Indians in response to Spanish greed.

A Valdivia mirad, de pobre infante
si era poco el estado que tenía,
cincuenta mil vasallos que delante
le ofrecen doce marcos de oro al día;
esto y aun mucho más no era bastante,
y así el hambre allí lo detenía.
Codicia fue ocasión de tanta guerra
y perdición total de aquesta tierra.
    (Ercilla, *La Araucana*, 3.3, 1–8)

Look at Valdivia, from a poor child
if the estate he had was small,
fifty thousand vassals up front
offer him twelve weights of gold daily:
this and even much more was not enough,
so hunger detained him there;
greed is the reason for so much war
and the total loss of that land.

In the next stanza, the poet makes an overt reference to the Araucanians' right to defend themselves from the abuses committed in the name of greed.

Esta fue quien halló los apartados
indios de las antárticas regiones;
por ésta eran sin orden trabajados
con dura imposición y vejaciones,
pero rotas las cinchas, de apretados,
buscaron modo y nuevas invenciones
de libertad, con áspera venganza,
levantando el trabajo la esperanza.

    (Ercilla, *La Araucana*, 3.4, 1–8)

That greed was who found the remote
Indians of the Antarctic regions;
because of that greed they were forced to
   work without order
with hard imposition and abuse;
but their girths broken, taking risks,
they sought ways and new inventions
for liberty with rough vengeance,
raising work to hope.

Further testimony from the period that refers to the theme of greed and resistance is that of Captain Alonso de Góngora Marmolejo.

> At that time the Indians, seeing how they forced them to build houses and in the fields, and extract gold, things that they were not accustomed to there, considering these great labors insufferable, secretly plotted to rebel.[40]

The abuses included being forced to carry burdens, something to which Ercilla also alludes in the poem.

    The theme of greed and war in epic poetry has been studied by literary critics and is considered one of the most common aspects of any Renaissance epic poem. Ercilla follows this conventional formula, but in *La Araucana* he ascribes the vice of greed to both groups, Spanish and Araucanian, "whether there is historical basis for this or not,"[41] showing ambiguity as to which ones are the truly greedy.

The theme of violence in the poem is presented with the same ambiguity as in the case of greed. Ercilla presents in his lines a "rationalization of the violence," and though disturbed by the unjustified violence against the Indians, he employs fiction "para asimilar la violencia de la colonización" [to assimilate the violence of colonization].[42] This ambiguity is especially clear in his use of love stories about the Indian female characters of Gualcolda, Tegualda, and Glaura.[43] In key moments in which the poet must refer to violence in the war of conquest, he does not take a political and ideological position, but an ambiguous one through the use of native women's stories. These characters denounce the Spaniards' excessive use of force and other instances of violence, which represents criticism against the invaders' cruelty. His technique is what Kallendorf and other scholars have called the use of "further voices," a conventional element of Renaissance epic poetry used by Ercilla.[44] The poet included fictional stories, visions in dreams, and magic to distance himself from the violence that he, in part, helped cause through his personal experience as invader.

The sections of the poem in which Ercilla recounts events of violence and physical torture, including executions, are related to real historical facts and the poet does not use fiction to present them. One example has to do with Galvarino, an Araucanian who was taken prisoner at the end of the battle known as Lagunillas, November 7, 1557. His hands were cut off as exemplary punishment.

Nuestro campo por orden recogido,
retirado del todo el enemigo,
fue entre algunos un bárbaro cogido,
que mucho se alargó del bando amigo.
El cual a caso a mi cuartel traído
hubo de ser, para ejemplar castigo
de los rebeldes pueblos comarcanos,
mandándole cortar ambas las manos.

Our field as ordered gathered,
the enemy completely retired,
among some a barbarian was captured,
who had wandered too far from the
   friendly band.
 By chance he was brought to my barracks
 and for exemplary punishment
to show the neighboring rebellious towns,
it was ordered for both of his hands to be
   cut off.

(Ercilla, *La Araucana*, 22.45, 1–8)

The amputation of hands was one of the punishments Spaniards used on the Araucanians as well as on indigenous groups in other parts of the Americas. Las Casas denounced this method, which Spaniards had used in the Caribbean. This cruel custom was also common in Europe at the time as punishment for an opposing warrior hero who had been taken prisoner.[45]

After the Araucanian defeat in the battle of Millarapué (November 30, 1557) many Araucanians were captured, and those who appeared to be leaders were condemned to the gallows. These events are included in the poem.

Fueron entre estos presos escogidos	There were among those chosen prisoners
doce, los más dispuestos y valientes,	twelve, the most willing and valiant,
que en las nobles insignias y vestidos	who in their noble badges and dress
mostraban ser personas preeminentes;	showed themselves to be people of prominence;
éstos fueron allí constituidos	there they were constituted
para amenaza y miedo de las gentes,	as a threat and to people's fears,
quedando por ejemplo y escarmiento	and as example and lesson
colgados de los árboles al viento.	they were hanged from the trees in the wind.

(Ercilla, *La Araucana*, 26.22, 1–8)

Ercilla demonstrates that he was not in agreement with the sentence and even attempts to save one of the condemned, Galvarino, who after his hands were amputated had been freed to go back to his people as a warning.

me opuse contra algunos, procurando	I opposed to some, trying
dar la vida a quien ya la aborrecía;	to give life to he who already hated it;
pero al fin los ministros, porfiando	but finally the officers, insisting
que a la salud de todos convenía,	it was for the good of all,
forzado me aparté y él fue llevado	I was forced to leave and he was taken
a ser con los caciques justiciado.	to be put to death with the caciques.

(Ercilla, *La Araucana*, 26.29, 1–8)

Ercilla's opposition to execution also appears in the context of Caupolicán's death.

Paréceme que siento enternecido	It seems to me it will soften
al mas cruel y endurecido oyente	even the cruelest and hardened listener
deste bárbaro caso referido,	when referred to this barbarous case
al cual, Señor, no estuve yo presente,	to which, My Lord, I was not present,
que a la nueva conquista había partido	I had left for a new conquest
de la remota y nunca vista gente;	to a remote and never before seen people;
que si yo a la sazón allí estuviera,	if I had been there for the occasion,
la cruda ejecución se suspendiera.	the raw execution would have been suspended.

(Ercilla, *La Araucana*, 34.31, 1–8)

Paul Firbas has noted that immediately after relating the episodes of execution of Araucanian leaders, Ercilla moves in the next stanza to describe his encounter with the magician Fitón, which initiates a scene focused on the greatness of the Spanish empire.[46]

The execution of caciques was common in the conquests of New Spain and Peru (one recalls the case of the Inca leader Atahualpa). In Chile, though many caciques were taken prisoner or executed, and though the Spaniards exerted control through the imposition of the encomienda system on the lebo, it was still difficult for the Spaniards to eliminate caciques altogether. That was easier to do in the large empires where, once the emperor was captured, the nation collapsed in the absence of the highest authority.[47]

In the incident of the Indian attack on Tucapel, in which the Spaniards were defeated and Valdivia was executed, the poet has Lautaro give a speech to inspire his companions not to wane in battle. The leader's words project the idea of the right to the defense of their independence as a nation.

¡Oh ciega gente, del temor guiada!
¿A dó volvéis los temerosos pechos?
que la fama en mil años alcanzada
aquí perece y todos vuestros hechos.
La fuerza pierden hoy, jamás violada,
vuestras leyes, los fueros y derechos
de señores, de libres, de temidos
quedáis siervos, sujetos y abatidos.

Oh, blinded people guided by fear!
To where do you turn those feared chests?
Fame that took a thousand years to
  achieve
here perishes as well as all your
  accomplishments.
Today you lose the strength, never once
  violated,
your laws, privileges and rights
as masters, as free and feared people,
you become subservient, subdued and
  discouraged.

(Ercilla, *La Araucana*, 3.35, 1–8)

Fijad esto que digo en la memoria,
que el ciego y torpe miedo os va turbando.
Dejad de vos al mundo eterna historia,
vuestra sujeta patria libertando.

Fix in your memory what I say
that blind and stupid fear is fretting you;
leave to the world an eternal history,
liberating your conquered home.

(Ercilla, *La Araucana*, 3.38, 1–4)

Declaring war in self-defense as a response to excesses committed was a principle proclaimed by fray Gil González de San Nicolás. In a letter to Las Casas, he spoke of the Indians of Chile and the encomienda system used there, saying it was a true case of slavery: "they suffer so much harm, that, seeing it, one cannot tell about it without feeling pain."[48] In addition to what Ercilla may have personally observed in Chile, fray Gil doubtless shared this information with Ercilla, either in Chile or when they traveled in the same ship from Chile to Peru in 1559. As a result, in some lines the poet argues for the legitimacy of violent Spanish action against the Araucanians while agreeing with the natives' right to defend themselves. At times in first person and at times speaking through Indian leaders, Ercilla recognizes that the Indians had the right to self-defense for patriotic reasons, that is, because their freedoms as a nation were being attacked, so Spanish violence was unjustified. At other times, however, the poet seems to move to a position of legitimizing Spanish action and projecting a different message. If the Indians broke a sworn promise, the war against them was justified and their right to defend themselves was not legitimate.

A clear example is at the beginning of part 2 of the poem, where Ercilla tells of the arrival of the ship carrying the poet and the new governor (Garcia Hurtado de Mendoza) to Chile, landing at the port of Concepción and Talcahuano Island. The lines of the poem convey the idea that the Indians should convert to Christianity. Ercilla mentions this in the context of the illegitimacy of the Indian rebellion: they had violated a "sworn oath" not to fight. In other words, because the Indians had previously accepted conversion during the first period of the conquest with Valdivia, and later rebelled, they must accept that they had broken a promise to the new religion, and therefore had to recognize it anew (and, obviously, accept Spanish dominion).[49]

dándoles a entender que nuestro intento	letting them know our intent
y causa principal de la jornada	and main reason for the journey
era la religión y el salvamento	was religion and the salvation
de la rebelde gente bautizada	of rebellious baptized people
que en desprecio del Santo Sacramento,	who in scorn of the Sacred Sacrament,
la recebida ley y fe jurada	the law and sworn faith they had
habían pérfidamente quebrantado	accepted,
y las armas ilícitas tomado;	they perfidiously have broken
	illegally taken up arms;

(Ercilla, *La Araucana*,16.29, 1–8)

Ercilla uses the first person ("our intent") when mentioning that the Spanish motivation was to save native souls. On their arrival Spaniards were expecting, or at least hoping for, a submissive attitude on the part of the Araucanians. In the following canto (17) the poet confirms that the Spanish suspicions were correct, in light of the duplicitous message of the natives, in this case sending Millalauco as ambassador to propose peace while at the same time the Araucanians were preparing to attack.

Nunca negarse deben los oídos	Never should you deny your ears
a enemigos ni amigos sospechosos,	to enemies nor suspicious friends,
que tanto os dejan más apercebidos	so much they leave you the more warned
cuanto vos los tenéis por cautelosos.	as much as you have them guarded.

(Ercilla, *La Araucana*, 17.1, 1–4)

Cuando piensan que más os desatinan	When they think the more they confuse you
con su máscara falsa y trato estraño,	with their false mask and strange treatment
os despiertan, avisan, encaminan	they waken, they warn, they guide
y encubriendo, descubren el engaño;	under cover, they discover deceit;

veis el blanco y el fin a donde atinan,	you see the target and the end to where they aim,
el pro y el contra, el interés y el daño;	pro and against, interest and hurt;
no hay plática tan doble y cautelosa	there is no talk so double and guarded
que della no se infiera alguna cosa.	that something from it may not be inferred.

(Ercilla, *La Araucana*, 17.2, 1–8)

Ercilla continues to show ambiguity in treating the topic of legitimacy of war against the Araucanians. While many lines in the poem refer to Spanish greed and the injustices committed against the natives, other lines, such as those previously mentioned, seem to indicate that the poet wants to show no tolerance for natives' deceit.

When the European context is considered, the lines show a clear position about the justice of war. The previous chapter explained the importance that empire acquires in the poem with the introduction of themes such as the battles of San Quintín and Lepanto and the invasion of Portugal. Here the poet introduces the concept of just war applied to the European scene. It is possible that in the period between his American experience and finishing the poem, Ercilla reflected on the origins of the war and that there "was maturing in the poet a skeptical opinion on the conditions of just war."[50] In the opinion of scholar Jaime Concha, Ercilla is able to talk about a just war in the case of Europe because "the warrior energy of his [Spanish] people met its just cause against the Ottoman infidels more than against American Indians."[51] In the case of the war with Portugal, the poet expounds on the right to make war. He expresses the idea that the right of Felipe II to the throne of Portugal was legitimate, and the war was therefore just. As in the case of Lepanto, here the poet finally appears to find a context that determines that Spain can exercise its right to war for a just cause, something that in the Araucanian war is less clear. In canto 37, the poem's last, several concepts of just war are presented: war is part of the human condition and has a divine origin (because of original sin), war allows peace to exist in contrast to the excess of authority and ambition, and war is unjust if it is caused by greed or hate.

La guerra fue del cielo derivada	The war is derived from heaven
y en el linaje humano transferida,	and transferred onto human lineage,
cuando fue por la fruta reservada	when the forbidden fruit
nuestra naturaleza corrompida.	corrupted our nature.
Por la guerra la paz es conservada	Through war peace is conserved
y la insolencia humana reprimida,	and human insolence repressed;
por ella a veces Dios el mundo aflige,	through it sometimes God the world afflicts,
le castiga, le enmienda y le corrige;	punishes it, amends it and corrects it.

(Ercilla, *La Araucana*, 37.2, 1–8)

la guerra es derecho de las gentes	war is the people's right,
y el orden militar y diciplina	and military order and discipline
conserva la república y sostiene,	conserves the republic and sustains it,
y las leyes políticas mantiene.	and political law maintains.
(Ercilla, *La Araucana*, 37.3, 5–8)	

Pero será la guerra injusta luego	But war will then be unjust
que del fin de la paz se desviare,	if from the result of peace it deviates,
o cuando por venganza o furor ciego,	or when for vengeance, or blind furor;
o fin particular se comenzare;	or a private goal it commences;
(Ercilla, *La Araucana*, 37.4, 1–4)	

Por donde es justa guerra permitida	Where just war is permitted,
puede la airada vencedora gente	angry victorious people can
herir, prender, matar en la rendida	injure, seize, kill in a surrender,
y hacer al libre, esclavo y obediente	and make the free, slave and obedient
(Ercilla, *La Araucana*, 37.7, 1–4)	

After making his arguments about when war is just and when it is not, Ercilla includes Felipe II and the war with Portugal, and he devotes his poetry to exposing the causes for which war was justified in that case. The poet affirms that Felipe II had legitimate reasons to go to war and was not moved by greed or ambition. He adds that the king,

llamado del derecho y la justicia	called by right and justice
contra el rebelde reino va en persona	against the rebel Kingdom, goes in person
(Ercilla, *La Araucana*, 37.15, 3–4)	

The concept of just war cropped up in the 1550–51 debate between Las Casas and Sepúlveda over Indian rights, with consequences for Peru and Chile. The poet alludes to events that took place in Peru because of the Spanish crown's decision to modify the encomienda system. By 1552 when the new viceroy, Andrés Hurtado de Mendoza, arrived in Peru, the rebellion that had begun as early as 1544 had not been suffocated completely. As noted, Ercilla must have witnessed in Lima the final measures taken by Hurtado de Mendoza to put down the Spanish encomenderos' rebellion of 1552. The crown's position obviously triumphed, as did the viceroy over the encomenderos. Ercilla includes lines about the rebellion that show his position against the rebels and his support for the justice meted out by the new viceroy. Las Casas also held this position, supporting the king but not the colonists.

Oliendo el Virrey nuevo las pasiones	The new viceroy sensing the passions
y maldades por uso introducidas,	and wickedness introduced by use,
el ánimo dispuesto a alteraciones	the spirit disposed to disturbances

en leal apariencia entretejidas,	with loyal appearance interwoven,
los agravios, insultos y traiciones	the grievances, abuses and betrayals
con tanta desvergüenza cometidas,	committed with so much shamelessness,
viendo que aun el tirano no hedía,	seeing that the tyrant did not yet smell,
que, aunque muerto, de fresco se bullía,	although dead rouses itself,
entró como sagaz y receloso,	he entered as sagacious and suspicious,
no mostrando el cuchillo y duro hierro,	not showing a knife nor hard steel,
que fuera en aquel tiempo peligroso	that at that time it would be dangerous
y dar con hierro en un notable yerro,	to meet with steel in a notable error,
mostrándose benigno y amoroso	showing himself benign and loving
trayéndoles la mano por el cerro,	takes them by the hand through the mountain,
hasta tomar el paso a la malicia	until taking the pass to the evil
y dar más fuerza y mano a la justicia.	to give more strength and hand to justice.

(Ercilla, *La Araucana*, 12.77, 1–8; 78, 1–8)

Nevertheless, the poet claims a few lines later that he does not condemn the rebels because before dying they were pardoned and that it was in the hands of the king alone to judge them. Viceroy Hurtado de Mendoza had to deal with the last part of the rebellion and the execution of the encomendero leaders. Demonstrating what appears to be an objective and balanced view, the poet mentions not taking a position and alludes to the force with which the viceroy punished the rebels.[52]

Dar mi decreto en esto yo no puedo,	To give an opinion on this I can not do,
que siempre en casos de honra lo rehuso;	always in cases of honor I decline;
sólo digo el terror y estraño miedo	I only speak of the terror and strange fear
que en la gente soberbia el Marqués puso	the marquis placed on these arrogant people
con el castigo, a la sazón acedo,	with the punishment, at the time sour,
dejando el reino atónito y confuso,	leaving the reign amazed and confused,
del temerario hecho tan dudoso	by so rash and so doubtful an act
que aun era imaginarlo peligroso.	that was even dangerous to imagine.

(Ercilla, *La Araucana*, 12.83, 1–8)

When the new governor of Chile, García Hurtado de Mendoza, son of the viceroy of Peru, arrived in 1556, three years after the death of Valdivia, with the precedent of the civil war occasioned by the encomenderos, the legal context of the encomienda was not the same as in Valdivia's day. In various lines of the poem, Ercilla presents a reformist position that had begun with the government of García Hurtado—measures that coincided with the Ercilla's time in Chile.

Puso el Gobernador luego en llegando	reforming justice and customs
en libertad las leyes oprimidas,	corrupted during the times of disorder,

la justicia y costumbre reformando	the Governor on arriving put
por los turbados tiempos corrompidas,	freedom from the oppressive laws ,
y el exceso y desórdenes quitando	removing excesses and disorders
de la nueva codicia introducidas	introduced by new greed
en todo lo demás por buen camino	for all of the rest in good order
dio la traza y asiento que convino.	he gave the appearance and place that to it belonged.

(Ercilla, *La Araucana*, 30.31, 1–8)

In the response García Hurtado gave to Millalauco, when the latter, as ambassador, offered to make peace, the governor demonstrated a tendency to attempt to correct the abuses.

Oída la embajada, don García,	After hearing the embassy, Don García,
haciéndole gracioso acogimiento,	giving a gracious welcome,
en suma respondió que agradecía	responded that he was thankful
la propuesta amistad y ofrecimiento,	for the offer and proposal of friendship,
y que en nombre del Rey satisfaría	and on behalf of the King would satisfy
su buena voluntad con tratamiento	their good will with treatment
que no sólo no fuesen agraviados,	that not only would not offend them,
mas de muchos trabajos relevados.	but with much work they would be exonerated.

(Ercilla, *La Araucana*, 17.14, 1–8)

In the speech to his soldiers before the battle of Lagunillas, García Hurtado called for moderation, according to Ercilla.

"Lo que yo pido de mi parte y digo	"What I request of you on my behalf and say
es que en estas batallas y revueltas,	is that in these battles and turns,
aunque os haya ofendido el enemigo,	although the enemy has offended you,
jamás vos le ofendáis a espaldas vueltas;	you never will offer turned backs;
antes le defended como al amigo	to the contrary you will defend him like a friend
si, volviéndose a vos las armas sueltas,	if, turning to you loose weapons,
rehuyere el morir en la batalla,	withdraw dying in the battle,
pues es más dar la vida que quitalla."	because it is better to give life than to take it."

(Ercilla, *La Araucana*, 21.55, 1–8)

All this seems to indicate that *La Araucana* reflects the debates in Spain, and it depicts the consequences in the Viceroyalty of Peru in general and Chile in particular of the measures taken after the debates of 1550–51.

A further example of Ercilla's awareness of the Indian rights debate in Spain is his denunciation, through poetic characters, of the hypocritical Spaniards.

Ercilla lets the Indian leaders Galvarino and Caupolicán give voice to the idea that Spanish actions were the opposite of the Christian principles that Spaniards so often preached.

"Y es un color, es apariencia vana
querer mostrar que el principal intento
fue el estender la religión cristiana,
siendo el puro interés su fundamento;
su pretensión de la codicia mana,
que todo lo demás es fingimiento,
pues los vemos que son más que otras gentes
adúlteros, ladrones, insolentes."
  (Ercilla, *La Araucana*, 23.13, 1–8)

"It is a pretext, it is a vain appearance
to want to show the main intent
is to extend the Christian religion,
being its foundation their sole interest;
their pretense flows from greed,
everything else is feigning,
we see them as more than other people
adulterers, thieves, insolent ones."

This is one of the clearest examples in the poem of the possible influence that Las Casas and especially fray Gil González de San Nicolás may have had on Ercilla. Both the theme of greed for gold and the manner of conquest and treatment of the Indians were against Christian dogma. One of the most vivid passages in the poem is in canto 32, which describes the confrontation between the Indians and Spaniards in the fortress of Cañete. In this episode, the poet depicts the events as though he had been an eyewitness, denouncing the slaughter as Las Casas had regarding the Caribbean and Mexico.

Unos vieran de claro atravesados,
otros llevados la cabeza y brazos,
otros sin forma alguna machucados,
y muchos barrenados de picazos;
miembros sin cuerpos, cuerpos desmembrados,
lloviendo lejos trozos y pedazos,
hígados, intestinos, rotos huesos,
entrañas vivas y bullentes sesos.

  (Ercilla, *La Araucana*, 32.8, 1–8)

Some were thrust through from one
    extreme to the other,
others heads and arms taken,
others without shape crushed,
and many chopped to pieces;
members without bodies, dismembered
    bodies,
raining afar pieces and chunks,
livers, bowels, broken bones,
living entrails and bubbling brains.

La mudable sin ley cruda fortuna
despedazó el ejército araucano,
no habiendo un solo tiro ni arma alguna
que errase el golpe ni cayese en vano.
Nunca se vio morir tantos a una
y así, aunque yo apresure más la mano,
no puedo proseguir, que me divierte
tanto golpe, herida, tanta muerte.
  (Ercilla, *La Araucana*, 32.10, 1–8)

The changeable raw fortune without law
destroyed the Araucanian army,
without there being a single shot nor arms
that missed its blow or fell in vain.
Never were so many seen to die at once
thus, although I accelerate my hand,
I can not continue, I am diverted by
so many blows, wounds, so much death.

The moderation that Governor García Hurtado de Mendoza had called for did not appear to obtain in this battle, and the poet, even with his contradictions, cannot hide his disgust: "Questions about ideological justification and about the status of the Indians are superseded by the poet's revulsion at the killing, which he goes on to describe in horrific detail."[53] Before relating the details of the battle, Ercilla begins with a reflection that, in the opinion of literary critics, is perhaps one of the passages most identifiable "as a high moral moment in the epic."[54]

La mucha sangre derramada ha sido	Much blood spilled has been
(si mi juicio y parecer no yerra)	(if my judgement and view is not faulty)
la que de todo en todo ha destruido	that it has destroyed
el esperado fruto desta tierra;	the prospective fruits of this land;
pues con modo inhumano han excedido	in an inhuman way it has exceeded
de las leyes y términos de guerra,	the laws and terms of war,
haciendo en las entradas y conquistas	making of the entries and conquests
crueldades inormes nunca vistas.	enormous cruelties never before seen.
(Ercilla, *La Araucana*, 32.4, 1–8)	

In the next stanza, Ercilla reinforces two ideas: first, his own view notwithstanding, that the general opinion is that justice is on the side of the final victor; and second, that cruel slaughter is in some ways just, even though painful.

Y aunque ésta en mi opinión dellas es una,	Although this is my opinion,
la voz común en contra me convence	the common voice convinces me
que al fin en ley de mundo y de fortuna	that finally in law and the fortunes of war
todo le es justo y lícito al que vence.	everything is exact and licit to the one who conquers.
Mas dejada esta plática importuna,	But leaving this importune talk,
me parece ya tiempo que comience	it is time it seems to me that I begin
el crudo estrago y excesivo modo,	the cruel havoc and excessive ways,
en parte justo, y lastimoso en todo.	partly fair, and pitiful in everything.
(Ercilla, *La Araucana*, 32.5, 1–8)	

This passage, as with so many others in the poem, reminds the reader that this is an epic, and "epic, like everyone, loves a winner, and the poet's rapid switches in allegiance depend on fortunes of war that can turn from one canto to the next."[55] As Ercilla voices the idea that everything is legal for the victor in the context of the confrontation between Spaniards and Indians, he also returns to this theme at the end of the poem in the context of justifying the war with Portugal. Ercilla states that if the war is considered just, the victor has all the rights.

que el que es señor y dueño de la vida,	who is the master and owner of life,
lo es ya de la persona y justamente	is also owner of the person and justly

hará lo que quisiere del vencido,	will do with the conquered as he will,
que todo al vencedor le es concedido.	that everything to the conqueror is conceded.

(Ercilla, *La Araucana*, 37.7, 5–8)

On the theme of the right of the victor in just war, the poet makes no distinction with respect to context, whether it is the Americas or Europe. It may simply be that Ercilla was responding to the canons of the epic, in which case it is difficult to know his exact position. What can be inferred is that Ercilla's position on the justification of the conquest was not exactly the same as that of Las Casas. The Dominican friar declared during the debates of 1550–51 that although according to the Scriptures, God called for war against certain nations, he referred to the Canaanites and other tribes, not idolaters in general. Las Casas argued that the rude nature of the Indians (who in his opinion were not primitive because they were capable of self-government) was not a motive for war against them. Their engagement in human sacrifice should not subject them to war, either. Between indiscriminate war and human sacrifice, the latter was the lesser evil: "Of two evils, choose the least."[56] Las Casas believed that royal law over the Indians of the Americas embraced only the Christianization of the natives and that all conquest was illegal.[57]

La Araucana expresses the idea of the legitimacy of the Indians' fighting in self-defense because of abuses committed against them. Still, the illegality of the conquest is never introduced, whether directly or indirectly, in the poem. Ercilla passes over the unjust execution of Caupolicán without comment and mentions only his own absence on that occasion because he "had departed on a new conquest."

From a legal standpoint, *La Araucana* contains instances that indeed reflect the ideas of Las Casas and the spirit of the New Laws of 1542. The poet presents the conflict that arose when the colonizers violated those laws, and his support for the authority of the king and viceroy in opposition to the Spanish encomenderos. The "further voices" that denounce violence in the poem are included in fictional stories. The clear presence of the poet's subjectivity, his contradictions, and ambivalent position fit perfectly with an imperial project that had its own problems. Ercilla's poetry expresses no doubt that Spain was in the right. The war was just, "but the estimation of the necessary degree of 'justice'—that is, of punishment—was in error."[58] In the Americas the law was accepted but not obeyed, as the saying went, and the local officers were in charge of punishment. It is as though the poet and his text represent all the fractures and weaknesses of a government that could not keep up with the task of governing such a vast and complex empire. During the period when Ercilla's American experience

Signature of Alonso de Ercilla, in his position as state censor of books. Here Ercilla approves the epic poem *Elegías de varones ilustres de Indias* by Juan de Castellanos, Madrid, 1588. *Biblioteca de la Real Academia de la Historia, Madrid, Manuscritos, 9/4831, folio 3v.*

The *Elegía* is the longest poem written in Spanish about the conquest and colonization of the Americas. Castellanos was a soldier and priest who worked in the Spanish colonies. His poem deals with the Caribbean and what are today Colombia and Venezuela. The text reads:

Yo he visto este libro y en el no hallo cosa mal sonante ni contra buenas costumbres y en lo que toca a la Historia la tengo por verdadera por ver fielmente escritas muchas cossas y particularidades que yo vi y entendi en aquella tierra al tiempo que pase y estube en ella por donde infiero que va el autor muy arrimado a la verdad, y son guerras y acaecimientos que hasta aora no las e visto escritas por otro autor y que algunos olgaran de saberlas.
       Don Alonso de Ercilla.

I have seen this book and I find in it nothing offensive or against good morals, and insofar as it bears on history, I know it to be true because it faithfully records many things and particularities that I saw and understood in that land in the time I spent and was in it, for which reason I conclude that the author is very close to the truth, and there are wars and events that I have not seen written by any other author until now and that some will enjoy knowing about.
       Don Alonso de Ercilla.

took place, the Spanish empire was going through a contradictory stage. On one hand, the crown supposedly wanted to act in defense of the Indians, and on the other, Spanish colonization in the Americas had but one objective: income.

The historical period about which Gaspar de Villagrá writes in *Historia de la Nueva México*, by contrast, had different characteristics. The conquest of New Mexico was late when compared to Chile and other regions of the Americas. The 1590s were characterized not only by a different imperial reality but also by different legislation. As in Chile, the particular features of the frontier—its geography and its native population—gave another nuance to the conquest of New Mexico and its consequences. The personal history, education, and experiences of Gaspar de Villagrá prior to his participation in the conquest marked his poetry but also his behavior in the short time he was in New Mexico.

Gaspar Pérez (later known as Gaspar de Villagrá) was born in 1555 in Puebla de los Ángeles, in the Viceroyalty of New Spain. That same year, his poetic counterpart, Alonso de Ercilla, was already twenty years old and embarking for Chile

by way of Panama and Peru. People in Peru were still living with the conse-
quences of the civil war between the viceregal authority and the encomenderos
while they prepared for a new expedition to Chile that would be directed by the
new governor, García Hurtado de Mendoza.

Meanwhile, Gaspar Pérez began his infancy in Puebla, New Spain, a city that
had been expressly founded without granting encomiendas to the founding citi-
zens. Hernán Pérez and Catalina Ramírez, Gaspar's parents, had come to New
Spain in 1546.[59] Hernán was a curer of hides at the time.[60] In the following years
he dedicated himself to intense commercial activity in New Spain that took him
to Spain on business with relative frequency, at least after the year 1562.[61] Pos-
sibly by 1566 the family moved from Puebla to Mexico City.[62] The father's eco-
nomic position evidently permitted him to send his son Gaspar to study at the
prestigious University of Salamanca.

In 1569, when father and son embarked for Spain, Gaspar was fourteen years
old. It is logical to suppose that at such a young age, Gaspar had neither contact
nor experience related to debates ongoing in Spain about the treatment of the
Indians and the encomenderos' abuses. Thus, in Salamanca, Gaspar Pérez, which
is how his name appeared in the student registries, was surely exposed for the
first time to the world of laws and probably also to debates over the law applied
to the Indians of the Americas. The education he received in Salamanca marked
his personal and professional life later in New Spain and New Mexico.

The importance of Gaspar's studies in Salamanca vis-à-vis his later poetry have
been demonstrated in large part by his biographer, Manuel Martín Rodríguez.
His coursework ranged from knowledge of classical sources to studies of gram-
mar (between 1569 and 1571, before enrolling as a university student) to courses
in ecclesiastical law, sources of law, private law, penal law, and administrative
law taken at the university, to training in the use of arguments in dialectic con-
frontations.[63] Although the book of graduates with bachelor's degrees in law for
1576 has not survived, it is possible to follow Gaspar Pérez's academic career in
civil law through the books of enrollment preserved in the Archive of the Uni-
versity of Salamanca, which prove that he enrolled as a "law student" each year
between 1572 and 1575. All indications are that he concluded his law studies in
1576 because the last registration as a student corresponds to December 1575.[64]
Although it was not rare for wealthy criollo and mestizo families to send their
sons to a Spanish university such as Salamanca, it is notable that between 1572
and 1576 Gaspar Pérez was the only civil law student born in New Spain, or any-
where else in the Americas, listed in the registries.[65]

Martín Rodríguez has provided important details on Gaspar Pérez's studies in
Salamanca, to which the reader can turn. The poet appears to have completed
his studies in a reasonable time and to have belonged to the third of students in
the second half of the sixteenth century who finished their course of studies.[66]

Whether by his own decision or that of his parents, or both, it does not appear to be by chance that Gaspar chose to study civil law. That branch of the law was the most attractive for those who planned to fill administrative posts in the Americas or in Spain. Such individuals could become members of *audiencias* or be named governors, *corregidores*, or *alcaldes*, or practice law or become legal advisors.[67] In other words, to be a government employee with the possibility of advancement, civil law was the appropriate course of study.

While Gaspar was studying at the University of Salamanca, the New Ordinances for Settlement and Discovery of 1573 were decreed. They constituted the legal basis of the future conquest of New Mexico. A question that is almost impossible to answer is whether as a student Villagrá had the opportunity to hear his professors debate the content of the laws that had just been decreed and that would define the conquest of New Mexico. It is, however, possible to give a clear, affirmative answer to the question of whether his studies in Salamanca influenced the vision of the future Gaspar de Villagrá in the use of Salamancan pedagogy, the application of the law, and his religious formation.

A scholar of the education provided by the University of Salamanca has summarized its values in this way:

> a university representative of the values of aristocratic unity characteristic of the Crown of Castile: Tridentine Catholic religiosity, imperial politics (the dream of imperial Rome and its law), logic and deduction, a class-stratified society, with a noble-aristocratic mentality, criteria of unity, obedience and hierarchy. . . . Old humanistic programs, carved from the stone of the cloister, stairway, and façade, cried out for rationality and virtue as opposed to vice and desires.[68]

It should also be recalled that the Tribunal of the Inquisition was keeping watch over intellectuals who taught in Salamanca in case they might transmit any progressive vision to their students. Precisely in the years when Villagrá was studying in Salamanca, fray Luis de León, a professor at the university, was condemned to prison in Valladolid, where he remained from February 1572 to December 1576.[69]

Villagrá's poem evidences a truly orthodox religious vision, verging on fanatical in the opinion of some scholars. Its overt religiosity echoes the fact that the ordinances of 1573 insisted on "pacification" and subsequently, on the fundamental goal of religious conversion in the specific case of New Mexico. The strong religious theme also indicates that the poet was an extremely devout Apostolic Roman Catholic, proud of his religion and the purity of his blood (elements that went hand in hand). With respect to the influence of Salamancan pedagogy, Martín Rodríguez has synthesized the characteristics that might have influenced the future poet, both in the poem and in the subsequent arguments he had to make to defend his actions in New Mexico.

[To win] the support of the authorities, which unfolds as the principal strategy in his Memorial of Justification, for example, Villagrá had to have based himself on the model learned from the Salamancan lectures and from the rereadings and repetitions that dealt in an exhaustive way with a theme with reference to an ample body of relevant texts. . . . Finally, it is likely that the treatment in his poem of certain themes, such as just war, have echoes of how those same themes (or another similar one) could have been dealt with in the Salamancan classrooms.[70]

Doubtless, the poet's legal studies influenced his predilection for inserting documents into the poem. As Martín Rodríguez puts it so well, this "discursive and ideological device" also serves to "justify the legality of the conquest."[71]

Villagrá's poem, *Historia de la Nueva México*, includes references to six matters that fit the historic-legal context of his day:

1. Oñate's capitulación, or contract, to be leader of the expedition to New Mexico with titles of governor and adelantado; the inspections and orders to delay his departure, including a transcription of the viceroy's order and reference to a letter containing complaints by Oñate

2. Taking possession of the land using the *requerimiento* and act of obedience and vassalage

3. The missionary nature of the expedition, as in pueblos given to the Franciscans

4. A request for goods from the Indians without specific mention of tribute payment

5. Oñate's request for application of the law in the case of treason or rebellion on the part of the Spanish participants in the enterprise

6. A discussion about the concept of just war against the Acoma Indians.

As noted, the poet includes prose in his poem in the form of documents relative to the events he is narrating. The legal context of the conquest toward the end of the sixteenth century required following a painstaking bureaucratic process, with the need to document, revise, and annotate every instruction: "while Oñate is theoretically embarking on a 'new' discovery into the great 'unknown,' his every move there is allowed to be neither new nor unknown; each is already written and sealed by legislative authority."[72] Villagrá not only presents this legal context in his poem but also appears to affirm, with the transcription of documents as metatext, that Oñate's enterprise followed the letter of the law.

Yet, the poem is lacking in certain details. In some cases, the previously mentioned legal points appear in a very general way, making it an incomplete and unreliable source for the historian to verify some specific facts in detail. Still,

Villagrá does not completely avoid mentioning some of the facts. Instead, he elects to include and expound on themes such as the choice of Oñate as leader (throughout canto 6) and the rivalry that arose with other competitors. He also mentions that the crown provided Oñate with aid or a loan and the obstacles with which Oñate struggled during preparations for the expedition. References to the complications that caused the expedition to be delayed continue in several of the ensuing cantos.

Villagrá uses the beginning of canto 6 to assert that Oñate is the perfect leader. He adduces the noble heritage of Oñate's wife (Isabel de Tolosa Cortés Moctezuma), as great-granddaughter of Moctezuma and granddaughter of Hernán Cortés, and that Oñate is a good choice of leader because he offered everything needed for such an enterprise. The poet mentions the viceroy's order, as well as the acceptance and signing of the capitulación, or contract, naming Oñate governor and adelantado. This section of the poem depicts actual events and proves the poet's interest in mentioning everything that might lend legitimacy to Oñate's enterprise. Thus, Villagrá refers to the viceroy's decision to accept Oñate's request to command the expedition, the fact that Oñate gave his patrimony to this enterprise, and the appointment, one by one, of the principal members of the expedition.

En que el Virrey resuelto, sin estorbo,	In which the Viceroy, free from hindrance,
Tuvo por bien de darle y encargarle	Found it good to give him and deliver him
Aquesta impressa en veinte y quatro días	That enterprise. 'Twas four-and-twenty days
Del mes de Agosto y año que contamos,	Into the month of August, and the year we count
Mil y quinientos y noventa y cinco.	One thousand and five hundred ninety-five.

(Villagrá, *Historia*, 6, 136–40)

Don Juan sin detenerse ni tardarse	Don Juan, without delay or lingering,
Obedeció la carta, y esto hizo	Obeyed the order and did this
Ante escribano público, rindiendo	Before notary public, there surrendering,
Su vida, su persona y su hazienda	His life, his person, and his whole estate
A vuestro Real servicio, . . .	Unto your Royal Service, . . .

(Villagrá, *Historia*, 6, 186–90)

The poem does not mention some of Oñate's demands that were not granted. For example, he asked for authorization for himself and his successors to establish (to add to or reduce) the tribute the natives had to pay in "fruits of the earth" both to the king and to other principal members of the expedition. This request was denied as well as another request for the enterprise to be under the sole jurisdiction of the Council of the Indies and not the viceroy or the Audiencia of Mexico.[73] According to the instructions that followed the signing of the contract, Indians could not be obligated to perform forced labor, and Oñate was to strictly follow the New Ordinances for Settlement and Discovery of 1573 for colonization and pacification.[74] Moreover, a subsequent revision to the capitulación and instructions established in greater detail the treatment of the Indians and of tribute, stipulating that

> there be moderation in imposing personal services on the Indians, and, if possible, that none be required on them now in the beginning in order not to exasperate and disturb them or to arouse some hatred against the Christians, as the natives are not accustomed to such forced services.[75]

Oñate was prohibited from requiring Indians to work, at least at first, and from sending them to perform forced labor in the mines. Moreover, the treatment of the Indian in New Mexico was not to repeat, at least initially, what was done in the rest of New Spain. With respect to tribute payment, the burden was to be as light as possible.

> It is asked that at present no tribute be levied on the Indians, unless it be light and moderate, in recognition of the obedience which they owe to his majesty, and that this should not be levied on each individual Indian directly but on the pueblo and council in common.[76]

The revision made specific reference to the ordinances of 1573, enjoining Oñate to try "only to predispose the Indians and persuade them in kindly manner to pay tribute by way of acknowledgment. Observe great circumspection and moderation in this in the beginning."[77]

The poem neither includes the topic of the distribution of Indian pueblos as encomiendas nor the obligation of Indians to pay a tribute in goods. At least for the first two years of Spanish settlement (1598–99), the period that Villagrá covers, no documents exist that show that Oñate distributed Indians among the colonists, at least not until 1601. By 1606 there is a record of the granting of pueblos to Spaniards.[78] We can assume that at the beginning of the settlement, Oñate tried to follow the instructions of not forcing Indians to work or taking their land, but a few years later that was not the case. During the seventeenth century, pueblos were distributed in encomiendas and in some cases the colonizers lived on the Indian lands. Furthermore, Diego de Vargas, as governor of New Mexico (1691–97), requested an encomienda. He also reintroduced the requerimiento, a practice considered obsolete elsewhere in the Spanish American empire by the end of the seventeenth century.[79]

According to the instructions to Oñate, the payment of tribute in goods should have been done only at first by asking peacefully and by the Indians' willingness to give them to the Spaniards with no pressure. Those goods would normally be maize, blankets, and animal skins.[80] Once in New Mexico, Oñate's men asked the Indians for those, but desperation at times led to violence. As the historian John L. Kessell writes, "to keep from starving, Oñate and his men had collected tribute from the beginning, sometimes by violent means."[81] This was the case with Juan de Zaldívar and his men at Acoma Pueblo, which set in motion a violent response by the natives, who killed Zaldívar and several of his men.

Villagrá does not include much information in his poem about how much pressure Zaldívar put on the Indians. On the contrary, he mentions the Acoma Indians' strategy to divide Zaldívar's group in order to attack them. This event and its consequences will be expounded later in this chapter. For now, it is important to reflect on whether the poet's omission of Zaldívar's aggressive behavior was to avoid boring the reader with details, or because he did not consider it important. The suspicious reader may speculate that the poet preferred to avoid including anything that might provide too much detail about what the Spaniards were not permitted to do with respect to punishment, forced labor, or payment of Indian tribute. If the poet had been interested in including documents in his poem, as he did in other sections, he could have done so in the description of relations with the natives.

By contrast, Villagrá alludes directly to one of Governor Oñate's demands when he negotiated his contract: authority over the Spaniards who participated in the enterprise.

Assí don Juan pidió que sólo un punto	So Don Juan asked that but one point
Pidiesen de su parte y no otra cosa,	be for himself demanded and no other thing,
Y fue que se le diese mano abierta	And 'twas that he be given a free hand
Para poder hazer castigo entero	And power to give the whole of punishment
O para perdonar si conviniese	Or pardon, if it should seem best,
Aquéllos que se fueron contra vando,	To those who had entered 'gainst command;

(Villagrá, *Historia*, 6, 229–34)

Keeping in mind that these lines were written after settlement had taken place and Oñate had made some controversial decisions in New Mexico, it is understandable why the poet elected to include this clause. An example of his questionable judgment as leader was his decision to send Villagrá to pursue and carry out the execution of four deserters.

One brief note regarding the issue of criollo identity that was introduced in the previous chapter: The question is whether or not there were limits on the power wielded by Oñate, the Zaldívar brothers (Maese de Campo Juan de Zaldívar and Sargento Mayor Vicente de Zaldívar), and Villagrá because they were criollos.

Scholar Sandra M. Pérez-Linggi mentions the importance of "resistance and search for equality"[82] in the poem in reference to these criollos and their expectation of being rewarded for their service.[83] This argument seems logical; it makes sense for Villagrá to include in his poem lines about deserving rewards like any other conqueror for his service to the crown. But it is also important to recall the legal context of the time, specifically that the ordinances of 1573 played an important role in the limitations of power; the actions of these late conquerors were more regulated and limited by law than any other sixteenth-century conquerors.

Some lines in the poem reflect another part of the custom and practice at the time, making reference to the possible rewards for those willing to participate in the armed enterprise. Town criers of the day advertised the expedition, touting the rights of those who signed up for it. The list of merits to be won was most attractive to those interested in signing up, from the title of hidalgo to the right to be a landowner.

Echaron luego bandos y contentos
Por las calles más públicas y plazas
Pregonaron aquellas libertades
Que concedéis, señor, a los que os sirven
En el oficio duro de las armas.

They then read proclamations and gaily
Through all the plazas and the public streets
Heralded well the liberties
That you, O lord, concede to those who serve you in
The hard employ of arms.

(Villagrá, *Historia*, 6, 298–302)

The personal monetary stake that Oñate invested in the military effort, to which the poem alludes, is no exaggeration. As was true with most colonizing enterprises of the sixteenth century in Spanish America, the expedition to New Mexico was first and foremost a financial and material effort on the part of the participants, especially the leader, Oñate. The crown contributed some specific aid, such as the loan of six thousand pesos to ready the expedition between 1596 and 1598; the gift of four thousand pesos with the goal of seeking out and arresting members of an earlier, unauthorized expedition; and the expenses of the eight missionaries and two Franciscan brothers who accompanied the expedition. Oñate received an annual salary of six thousand ducados, to be collected from future income from the province to be conquered, but this salary never materialized because the colony of New Mexico did not produce sufficient income.[84] The crown also provided gunpowder and lead. The greatest increase in royal expenses came from the required inspections that were ordered between 1596 and 1598. The delays resulting from the dispute over the leadership of the expedition increased the costs. Oñate had to keep the army together and feed it at his expense. Studies have shown, however, that the crown's financial burden to equip an expedition of two hundred men and their families, plus servants and Indian auxiliaries, was less than that incurred by Oñate, his family, and his friends.[85]

The poet devoted three cantos to describe the process of revisions, changes of mind by viceregal authorities, and inspections that resulted in almost three years of delay, from September 21, 1595, when the then viceroy of New Spain, Luis de Velasco, issued the contract, to January 26, 1598, when Oñate and his expedition finally departed.[86] Some of the clauses of the contract Velasco signed were rejected by his successor, the Conde de Monterrey. Particularly worthy of mention are those clauses that refer to who would have jurisdiction over Oñate and to the matter of personal service of the Indians, two questions that clearly had to do with controlling Oñate, especially with respect to possible abuses of authority.

The poem refers to the importance Oñate gave to the inclusion of dedicated friars on the expedition. In accordance with the contract, Oñate requested six Franciscan friars, which the viceroy agreed to provide. But a subsequent change to the contract raised the number of friars to twelve, although eventually there were eight missionaries and two lay brothers.[87]

Villagrá foregrounds the relevance of religion for the entrada. He addresses the king, and indirectly, his role as the leader of the Catholic Church.

Pidió le diesen Religiosos graves,	He asked that serious monks be sent,
De buena vida y fama, pues con ellos,	Men of good life and fame, because with
Más que con fuerza de armas, pretendía	them,
Serviros, gran señor, en esta entrada	More than by force of arms, he might
Y aliviaros la carga de los hombros	Attempt to serve you, lord, upon this
Que es fuerza sustentéis mientras el	expedition
mundo	And ease from off your shoulder that
Nuestra ley sacrosanta no guardare.	burden
	Which needs must be you bear while this
	our world
	Still doth not keep our law most
	sacrosanct.

(Villagrá, *Historia*, 7, 63–69)

The poem includes a reference to the appointment of Luis de Velasco y Castilla to the Viceroyalty of Peru. His replacement in the post he vacated as viceroy of New Spain was Gonzalo de Zúñiga y Acevedo, Conde de Monterrey. The latter ordered the suspension of all plans related to the expedition to New Mexico and a delay until he could familiarize himself with the matter. Villagrá uses the following lines to highlight his own belief that Oñate and no one else should lead the enterprise.[88]

Del don Juan que ninguno en nueva
   España
Pudo con más justicia competirle
Aquesta noble impressa que le dieron.

    (Villagrá, *Historia*, 6, 371–73)

Of our Don Juan, to prove that no one in
   New Spain
Could, with a better right, compete with
   him
That noble enterprise they'd given him.

In canto 7 Villagrá includes two complete documents: the royal cédula of May 1596 by which the king suspended the expedition until further notice, and the order from the new viceroy of New Spain, the Conde de Monterrey, putting the cédula into effect. The poet refers to this fact in canto 8, underscoring Oñate's patience and respect for viceregal authority and his submission to the viceroy, who had asked the conquistador to continue to obey the law.

Mando segunda vez que le intimasen
La cédula Real y mandamiento
Para que con más fuerza se abstuviesse
Y aquella noble entrada no intentase,
De que podía estar bien descuidado
Por el grande respecto y reverencia
Con que don Juan guardaba y acataba
Las cosas de justicia y sus ministros.
    (Villagrá, *Historia*, 8, 170–77)

Ordered a second time he be informed
About the Royal order and command
So that he might abstain more certainly
And not attempt the noble expedition,
Though he might well be free from care
Because of the respect and reverence
With which Don Juan kept and observed
The things of justice and its ministers.

In canto 9 Villagrá refers to the second inspection the expedition had to undergo.[89] In canto 10 the final *visita*, or inspection, is mentioned.[90] The expedition had moved north to the Conchas or Conchos River, and Oñate awaited this final inspection to officially begin the entrada. The poet uses the occasion to point out the indifference of the inspector and lack of any help he had rendered. These observations coincide with a message the poet conveys in more than one section of his poem, about the deficiencies of the bureaucrats in contrast to the will and dedication of the soldiers.

Allí el Visitador, con gran tibieza,
Al General le dijo prosiguiesse
Aquesta larga entrada y que marchase.
Y assí se despedió, sin más palabras
Y sin darle papel ni cosa alguna
Que fuesse de importancia ni provecho;
Cuio fin pobre y dexo desabrido
Causó suma tristeza y desconsuelo

    (Villagrá, *Historia*, 10, 271–78)

The Inspector with great frigidity,
Did tell the General he might pursue
That mighty entry and might march
Thus he took leave, without more words,
Not given him a paper nor any other
   thing
That might be of importance or of use.
Which sorry end and impolite departure
Caused mighty sadness and affliction

The great frustration of Oñate and his men apparently also stemmed from the fact that the inspector not only did not leave a final document of approval, but also did not do what was normally done in such cases, which was to give a speech in support of the leader and his men. Villagrá makes explicit the anger of the governor, who immediately sent the viceroy a letter complaining of all the difficulties the inspector had created, which had had a detrimental effect on the resources of his expedition and caused its long delay in departing.[91] At the beginning of canto 11, as with the start of each canto, the poet begins with a reflection. Here, the thought refers to the feelings Oñate expressed in his letter to the viceroy.

Como quiera que el alma lastimada	Since of the suffering and tormented soul
Es cierto que descansa quando cuenta	'Tis certain it doth rest when it doth tell
La fuerza del dolor que la fatiga,	The power of the pain that wearies it,
Por sólo descansar de sus trabajos,	Only as rest from his labors,
Cercado de dolor y desconsuelo,	Borne down with pain, disconsolate,
Aqueste molestado caballero	That sorely troubled gentleman
Tomó papel y tinta y una carta	Took paper and took ink and sent at once
Despachó luego al Conde, en que dezía	A letter to the Count in which he told
Las grandes aflicciones y congojas,	The great afflictions and anxieties,
Las pérdidas, los gastos y trabajos,	The losses, the expenses, and the work,
Persecuciones, cargas y disgustos	The persecutions, burdens,
Que esta larga jornada había tenido,	disappointments
Y aquel ardiente celo y buen desseo	That this long entry had endured,
Que de servir a Dios y a vuestro Padre	And too, that ardent zeal and good desire
En él estuvo siempre y aquel ansia	Of serving God and your father
De ver la conversión de tantas gentes	Which he had always had, and his fervent
Al gremio de la Iglesia reduzidas	desire
	To see conversion of so many folk
	Brought to the bosom of the Church

(Villagrá, *Historia*, 11, 1–17)

Once again the poet stresses the importance of religion as the objective of Oñate's enterprise and to Oñate himself, whom Villagrá represents as an extremely religious man. The constant references to this theme in the poem confirm the thesis that Villagrá has no interest in denigrating or criticizing the governor. This principle is constant in the poem from beginning to end.

Even a casual reading reveals the poet's respect for the great financial risk to which Oñate and his men were subject. While evangelical conversion was a main goal of this enterprise, the private individuals involved would not have invested so much without another important objective in mind, which was to locate mines, of silver at a minimum, and obtain Indian tribute. The successful mining enterprise of Oñate's father, Cristóbal de Oñate, and his companions in Zacatecas continued to be an inspiration and fed the hope that New Mexico would become another Zacatecas. Finally, the stakeholders hoped to find a water passage to the ocean, a discovery that would translate into many diverse economic benefits.

Villagrá alludes to New Mexico's potential as a place for converting people to the Catholic faith and as a source of resources, and insists that if Vásquez de Coronado's expedition was not successful in finding riches it was because they did not persist in their search. He adds that if they had not given up, another great world would have been discovered such as that of Mexico.

Y si los deste campo no volvieran	And if those of the camp had not turned
Las espaldas tan presto como vimos,	round
Fuera posible aberse descubierto	Their backs so quickly as we saw them do,
Otro mundo tan grande y poderoso	'Twere possible then to have found
Qual éste que tenemos y gozamos.	Another world as great and powerful
	As this we have here and enjoy.

(Villagrá, *Historia*, 4, 382–86)

Canto 11 presents the topic that the enterprise tried to appear from the outset as though it had suffered no setbacks. Oñate's express orders to the leaders under his command emphasized that everything be shown in a framework of success and optimism. Therefore, the poem refers to the leaders in the vanguard reporting good news about the journey when they returned to the main body of the expedition, even when this was not entirely true.[92]

Mandó el sargento que los tres Pilotos,	The Sergeant ordered the three guides
Con algunos amigos, se bolviessen,	To go back with some friends of his,
Y por cumplir el orden que tenía	And, to fulfill the order that he had
Del noble General, mandó callasen	From the noble General, he ordered they
Y cosa de trabajos no dixessen	be still
A nadie del Real, mas que contasen	And say nothing about their sufferings
Alegres nuevas todos, publicando	To any in the camp, but that they say
Dexaban buen camino descubierto,	Nothing but good news unto all
De buenos pastos, aguas y buen monte	That they had left a fine road they had
	found,
	With pasture excellent and waters and
	good woods

(Villagrá, *Historia*, 11, 236–44)

According to Martín Rodríguez, the admission of having exaggerated his claims produces doubt about Villagrá's authority as an eyewitness.[93] It is possible that Oñate saw the need to lie to keep up the morale of the people who had already begun to complain. Nevertheless, it must also be noted that the poet could have withheld this admission of lying, which, after all, also implicated him. It seems a little naive, keeping in mind that both Villagrá and Oñate were subsequently accused of exaggerating the riches of the land.

There were obviously great hopes of finding gold and silver in New Mexico when Oñate finally took possession of the land. In Canto 14, Villagrá describes the process of claiming the land, including prose and transcribing the document of taking possession. Once more the poem serves as a useful tool to demonstrate fulfillment of the law, specifically the ordinances of 1573. One of the characteristics that differentiated the conquest of New Mexico from others in the Americas was that the new legal context demanded that everything be documented, and the poem reflects this environment. As Martín Rodríguez has noted, from a literary perspective, there are three distinct parts to the *Historia*: "the first part is historical, the second is anthropological, and the third is epic."[94] Documents that Villagrá includes "adapt themselves to the structural function" of the poem:

> the orders of the king and viceroy are key for the preparation of the expedition ("first part"), the act of taking possession was a requisite *sine qua non* for the conquests of new territories ("second part"), and the legitimacy or not of the war against the natives of those new lands depended on the authorization of the priests ("third part").[95]

The *Historia*, of course, touches at many points on the topic of conversion of the Indians of New Mexico to the Catholic faith. The ordinances of 1573 specified that the main goal of the new discoveries and settlements was preaching the gospel. In this regard, historian Tamar Herzog analyzes the true meaning of the ordinances. Once the natives were baptized and presumably converted, the ordinances "allowed Spaniards to remain in the territory even until the conclusion or failure of this mission," and beyond the results of conversion, "the Spaniards had the right to settle, defend themselves, and make use of the Indians."[96] This principle was contained in the ordinances, and when the documents of the Oñate expedition and Villagrá's poem are analyzed, everything accords with the spirit of the ordinances: conversion, yes, but also settlement and the use of Indians as a source of economic benefit. Thus, by 1598 the situation in New Mexico was no different from that of the earlier Chilean conquest. The number of Indians to be subjected to empire, including their conversion, was what really had value: more subjects, more tribute, and in many cases more labor. The ordinances stipulated that such work was only permitted if it was voluntary, but in practice the situation was often quite different.

The defense of the right of the Indians to their property and liberty does not appear in the *Historia de la Nueva México* as clearly as in *La Araucana*. So, is Villagrá really a defender of the rights of the Indian? Is there any indication of these rights in the poem? Villagrá puts speeches in the mouths of Indians denouncing Spanish greed and calling for the defense of the right to be free. But such utterances appear to be balanced by other Indian voices that cry out for peaceful relations with the Spaniards. Therefore, Villagrá never clamors for freedom in a single Indian voice without another Indian voice that seeks conciliation. The poem thus presents, from canto 18 onward, the suspicious attitude of the Acoma leader Zutacapán, in contrast with other Acoma leaders who accepted the Spanish presence from the beginning—for example, Zutancalpo, son of Zutacapán, and Chumpo, the elderly leader.[97] Zutacapán speaks for rebellion, and the poet describes it this way:

Pues siendo aquéste de ambición cautivo,	But this man, being captive of his ambition,
Invidioso, soberbio y alevoso,	Envious, proud, and treacherous,
Amigo de mandar y ser tenido,	Eager for power and to be considered great
Pareciole ser ya llegada la hora	It seemed to him that now the hour had come
De que libertad fuesse medianera	To be able to mount and raise himself.
Para poder subirse y levantarse.	

    (Villagrá, *Historia*, 18, 25–29)

In the subsequent lines Zutacapán speaks to the Acomas, inciting them to take up arms. Here the theme of the defense of Indian freedom appears clearly.

"¿Será bien que perdamos todos juntos	Will it be well we all, together, lose
La dulce libertad que nos dexaron	The sweet freedom that was left us
Nuestros difuntos padres ya pasados?	By our dead fathers, now gone on?

    (Villagrá, *Historia*, 18, 40–42)

Zutancalpo's young voice, in contrast, clamors for moderation and defends the good intentions of the Spaniards.

"Bien os consta que entraron los Castillas,	"'Tis evident enough to you that the Spaniards
Según grandes guerreros, en la tierra	Entered into the land like great warriors,
Bien prevenidos todos, con cuidado,	All well on guard, very careful,
La noche toda en peso, con sus velas,	All the entire night with their guards out,
Sabemos duermen juntos bien armados,	And in the towns that they have entered we know
Y en pueblos que han entrado conozemos	That they have left all men in pleasant peace."
Que en paz gustosa a todos los dexaron."	

    (Villagrá, *Historia*, 18, 114–21)

Then, the elder Chumpo gives his opinion.

"Yo soy de parecer que luego, auna,	"I am of the opinion that, unanimous,
Las armas se sosieguen y descansen,	You should lay down and set aside your arms,
Que, como os tiene dicho Zutancalpo,	For, as Zutancalpo has said to you,
Si en otros pueblos guerras no han tenido	If these Spaniards whom we await

Aquellos Españoles que esperamos,	Have in the other pueblos had no war,
Hijos, ¿qué causa puede aber bastante	My children, what cause can there be
Para que aquí nosotros los temamos?”	That we should have fear of them?
(Villagrá, *Historia*, 18, 156–62)	

In the next lines, the poet describes Zutacapán's fury at not being able to convince the Acoma people, because the peaceful posture of the other two leaders, one young and the other old, had won out. To describe Zutacapán's angry reaction, Villagrá uses the simile of the bull.

Y qual furioso toro que, bramando,	And, like a furious bull which, bellowing,
La escarba de la tierra vemos saca	We see tear up the surface of the earth
Y sobre el espacioso lomo arroja,	And throw it over his broad sides,
Y firme en los robustos pies ligeros	And, firm in his robust, swift feet,
El ayre en vano azota, hiere y rompe	In vain lash at the air, wound and tear it
Con uno y otro cuerno corajoso,	With both his formidable horns,
Assí salió este bárbaro sañudo,	Thus this barbarian, enraged,
Al hijo maldiciendo y blasfemando	Cursing, blaspheming, at his son
(Villagrá, *Historia*, 18, 172–79)	

The poet uses this fictitious drama of the leaders arguing to introduce the next episode to the reader. When Governor Oñate arrived at Acoma to announce and carry out the act of vassalage as he had done in other pueblos, the Acoma leader Zutacapán tried to persuade Oñate to go down with him into one of the kivas, with the secret intention of attacking him.[98] The governor suspected such an attack and refused to go into the kiva. The poet adds that he did not learn about this episode involving Oñate "until a great deal of time had passed."[99] The poet uses a fictional dramatization to introduce the origin of discord among the Acoma leaders and especially the reaction of Zutacapán, who will be the subsequent instigator of the attack on Maese de Campo Juan de Zaldívar and his men.

The inspiration provided by *La Araucana* is evident here. The lines cited above signal the reader that Villagrá is copying Ercilla's model in the use of Indian voices. Ercilla's Colocolo is Villagrá's Chumpo. Literary critics have found other similarities between the Indian characters of *La Araucana* and the *Historia*. Ercilla's Tucapel is Villagrá's Zutacapán and Caupolicán is Zutancalpo,[100] although the latter has also been compared to Ercilla's Gicombo.[101] A parallel can also be drawn regarding the meaning of those voices as a vehicle for the poet to critique Spanish violence and greed, in the same way as Ercilla did in his poem.

As mentioned earlier, the *Historia* claims that the Pueblo Indians' acceptance of the Spanish presence in New Mexico, including at Acoma Pueblo, had been entirely voluntary. In the Spaniards' view, the natives had participated without pressure in the act of obedience and vassalage, accepting the authority of the king of Spain and the Christian religion. They believed that the Indians knew what they were doing because a translator had correctly informed them. Villagrá mentions having achieved the pacification of the territory "without a drop of blood being shed."[102] But the incident in Acoma in which Maese de Campo Juan de Zaldívar and several of his men were killed changed the course of events. From the Spanish point of view—Villagrá included—the Indians broke their promise of accepting Spanish authority, and punishment was necessary to preserve the peace. Of course, up to that moment the peace was fictitious. Pacification "without a drop of blood" had been achieved simply because the Indians had no choice but to accept it. In reality, they hoped that at some time the Spaniards would simply leave.

From canto 21 to canto 34 (the last), Villagrá devoted himself to describing the events that led to the final battle of Acoma. From a literary standpoint, the poet found the inspiration for an epic poem in the events, including a battle and a victor. From a historical standpoint, Villagrá described events in which he had actively participated as both witness and protagonist. From a legal point of view, the poet, sticking rather closely to the original documents, presented the process that Governor Oñate and his advisors—including Villagrá—followed to determine whether to declare war on Acoma. The poetry combines with prose in this section, in the same way as Villagrá had done in previous sections of the poem to lend legitimacy to his words.

In general, the poem presents, although in summary, more or less the same history that appears in the extant witness statements about what happened between December 1 and 4, 1598. The maese de campo and his men arrived at Acoma seeking supplies. This action was equivalent to a request for Indian tribute, which, according to law, should have been left up to the Indians to decide at the beginning of the conquest, so that delivering goods would be voluntary. According to Villagrá, Zaldívar "pidióles que le diesen por rescates/ algunos bastimentos que tuviesen" (he asked them to give him in barter/ such provisions as they might have). The poet continues on to the rest of the episode without providing more details about what type of goods the Spaniards requested. According to witnesses, Zaldívar traded some objects the Spaniards had in exchange for some goods from the pueblo, but because what they needed most was maize flour, and the Indians said they did not have any, the Spaniards camped not far from the pueblo waiting for the Acoma people to gather the amount they requested. When they returned to the pueblo, apparently without the slightest suspicion of an ambush, the natives' attitude was different. They made the Spaniards go individually to the houses to look for flour, and in this way the group was divided. That seems to have been the Indian strategy for attacking the Spaniards, killing Maese de Campo Zaldívar and several of his men.

Villagrá titled canto 22 "Donde se declara la derrota del Maese de Campo y muerte de sus compañeros, causada por la traición de los indios Acomeses" (Where is told the destruction of the Army Master and the death of his companions, caused by the treachery of the Acoma Indians). The poet uses this canto and the next one to describe for the first time a violent encounter between Indians and Spaniards. This is where episodes of the Spanish attack on Acoma (which is presented in six cantos, from 29 to 34), begin to unfold. This violent denouement was without doubt what the ordinances of 1573 had tried to avoid, as had the specific instructions given to Oñate about the treatment of the Indians and the request for voluntary tribute. But the reality of the frontier trumped any law emanating from Spain or Mexico City. As is to be expected, Villagrá tries in this last part to show that Governor Oñate's decision to declare war was legal.

Thus, the *Historia* goes on to include, in verse and prose, everything Villagrá considered necessary to legalize and justify the attack on Acoma. Just as Ercilla devoted part of his poem to the theme of just war, so too did Villagrá. The justification of war during the conquest of New Mexico at the end of the sixteenth century thus had the same meaning it had for the conquest of Chile fifty years earlier and for Felipe II's invasion of Portugal back in Europe: war is "just and necessary" to preserve the peace. Such was the final conclusion arrived at by the Franciscan priests whom Oñate consulted about the punishment of the Acoma people.

Villagrá included a prose transcription of a large portion of the reply that the Franciscan commissary, fray Alonso Martínez, and the other priests made to Oñate. The answer was based on two points or questions: What is required for war to be just? And what can be done with the vanquished and their goods by the person who wages just war?[103] In their response, the Franciscan fathers stated that just war required:

1. The authority of a king or his equivalent, or someone to whom the king had delegated power
2. Defense of the innocents who suffer unjustly
3. Recovery of stolen property and punishment of delinquents
4. Most of all, to achieve and preserve peace

Their reply added that "el acto de la guerra no es acto de elección y voluntad, sino de justa ocasión y necesidad" (the act of war is not an act of choice and free will but of just occasion and necessity).[104]

Immediately after hearing the Franciscan priests' response, Oñate convoked a general assembly whose edicts reflected the priests' point of view about the necessity of war to preserve the peace:

> the punishment should under no circumstances be postponed . . . unless it was executed immediately the land could not be colonized and no one could live there, as the natives from all districts were on the alert . . . If these Indians were not punished this time, they would form a league, rebel, and destroy us easily.[105]

Villagrá summarizes Oñate's decision in the poem.

Con cuios pareceres bien fundados	With whose opinions, well-founded
En muchos textos, leyes y lugares	On many texts, laws and places
De la Escriptura santa, luego quiso,	In holy Scripture, then the Governor,
Viendo el Gobernador que concurrían	Seeing how all these things agreed
Todas aquestas cosas en el caso	Upon the case and doubts that he had
Y dudas que assí quiso proponerles,	wished
Cerrar aquesta causa y sentenciarla,	To be proposed to them, he wished
Mandando pregonar, a sangre y fuego,	To close that case and give sentence,
Contra la fuerza de Acoma, la guerra.	Ordering war, with fire and blood,
	Proclaimed against the fort of Acoma.

(Villagrá, *Historia*, 25, 18–26)

Villagrá's intention to show the legality of the decision and the need to punish the rebel natives is evident in the poem. The official position of the poet, included in the "Memorial of Justification" prepared for his defense and that of Oñate and printed in 1614, is consistent with what he says in the poem. In the memorial, Villagrá writes that

> when the case demands it, it is something very ordinary, holy, and very much permitted in war, to burn towns, put them to the knife, and without hearing any argument from them, stab them, and kill them, in the same way that against all truth the evildoers say, that the adelantado Juan de Oñate did.[106]

To this he added

> And this is the truth, many famous soldiers, captains, and generals, maeses de campo, and viceroys, kings, and emperors, very Catholic sons of our holy Mother Church Militant, by their own hands carried out the same justice, that the adelantado is said to have carried out with his.[107]

Later, the same document lists European examples, citing among others the emperor Carlos V himself and his approval of the punishment given to rioters in Sicily and other parts of the empire.[108] At the end of a long list of examples, Villagrá reaffirms his position in defense of Oñate's decision.

> "I bring all this to excuse the Adelantado, and I refer to all those famous men who carried out the above punishments, because in carrying them out they did nothing new in war, but what was much used and ancient, and more so during uprisings."[109]

The punitive mission to Acoma was entrusted to Vicente de Zaldívar (Juan's brother and Oñate's nephew). Juan de Oñate designated individuals from among the members of the expedition who would form a war council to make the necessary decisions on the field of battle. The six members of this council, as an extension of their responsibility, would be included as advisors to the governor in the subsequent decision about punishment following the engagement.[110] Villagrá refers in the poem to his appointment to this council.

Y porque bien en todo se acertase,	That he might succeed well in all,
Del consejo de guerra mandó fuesen,	He ordered out from the council of war
Y al Sargento mayor acompañasen,	To go in company with the Sergeant Major
El Contador y Provehedor Zubía,	The paymaster and the purveyor Zubía
Y Pablo de Aguilar, Farfán y Márquez,	And Pablo de Aguilar, Farfán y Márquez,
Y yo también con ellos quiso fuesse	And wished me, too, to go with them
Porque con tales guías me adestrase	As with such guides I might gain skill
En vuestro Real servicio y no estuviesse	In your Royal service and might not be
Tan torpe como siempre me mostraba	So stupid as I always showed myself
En cosas de momento y de importancia.	In things of moment and of importance.
(Villagrá, *Historia*, 25, 121–30)	

Curiously, even though Oñate confirmed Villagrá's appointment as a member of the council in writing because of "the experience in cases of war that he has,"[111] the poet demonstrated humility with respect to how much he had to learn from his companions. Oñate probably was referring more to Villagrá's legal experience than his experience as a soldier on the field of battle.

Some details of the Spanish attack on Acoma and the Indians' defense, as well as Villagrá's participation in the battle, are provided in the second part of this book. Perhaps the only aspect pertinent here is their parallels with *La Araucana*. First, Villagrá chooses to end his poem with an episode similar to those Ercilla describes when depicting battles in his poem. Second, Villagrá brings up the same Indian struggle in Chile that Ercilla presents in *La Araucana*. Villagrá uses it as an example to show that if the Acoma rebellion had not been put down by force, Spanish domination would have failed in New Mexico as it did in Chile.

Villagrá ends his poem with the description of the battle of Acoma, which took place between January 22 and 24, 1599. The battle ended with the Indians' defeat, the burning of the pueblo, and the death of hundreds of Acoma people, many of whom leaped off the mesa to kill themselves rather than surrender. According to Villagrá's own testimony, on the final day of the battle, he

> saw that Indians began to break jail, which was an estufa [kiva] that seemed very strong. They had entrenched themselves so that no Spaniard dared go down into it, and a large number of Indians escaped. In view of this fact, the sargento mayor ordered the fighting continued without quarter. So it was done, and they set fire to houses and provisions and killed many of the natives.[112]

According to this testimony, around six hundred people—men, women, and children—were taken prisoner. The poem coincides in general with the number of prisoners mentioned in Villagrá's separate declaration.

Más de seycientos dieron en rendirse	More than six hundred surrendered
Y dentro de una plaza con sus hijos,	And in one plaza, with all their children
Y todas sus mujeres, se postraron	And all their women, they did put themselves
Y como presos, juntos se pusieron	Into the Sergeant's hands and were at peace
En manos del Sargento y sossegaron.	

(Villagrá, *Historia*, 34, 97–100)

Although there is not a description in the poem regarding the incident mentioned above about the Indians hiding in a kiva, the poet does mention the flight and subsequent capture and imprisonment in a kiva of the Indians Tempal and Cotumbo. According to Villagrá, they were taken prisoner after a frustrated attempt to escape. They refused to convert to Christianity and insisted on wanting to take their own lives rather than surrender, for which reason they asked for knives to kill themselves. As told in the poem, the governor refused this request and instead ordered that they be given two nooses so that they might hang themselves.[113]

Las dos sogas tomaron y al pescuezo	Took the two nooses and, setting
Ceñidas por sus manos y añudadas,	The same upon their necks and knotting them,
Salieron de la estufa y esparciendo	They came out of the kiva, and casting
La vista por el campo, que admirado	Their glance over the camp, which wondered much
Estaba de su esfuerzo y condolido,	At their courage and sympathized with them,
Juntos la detuvieron y pararon	They halted it and centered it upon
En unos altos álamos crecidos	Some lofty poplar trees that were well grown
Que cerca, por su mal, acaso estaban.	And were, by some evil chance, near.
Y no bien los notaron cuando luego	And hardly had they noted them when they
Dellos, sin más acuerdo nos dijeron	Informed us instantly they wished
Querían suspenderse y ahorcarse.	To hang themselves and die upon those trees.

(Villagrá, *Historia*, 34, 314–24)

Later the poet continues narrating this event, which is related in the final verses of the poem in which the two Indians put a curse on the Spaniards.

"Gustosos quedaréis que ya cerramos	You will remain joyful for we now close
Las puertas al vivir y nos partimos	The doors of life and take our leave,
Y libres nuestras tierras os dexamos.	And freely leave to you our lands.
Dormid a sueño suelto, pues ninguno	Sleep sure and safe because no one
Volvió jamás con nueva del camino	Uncertain and laborious, we now take,

Incierto y trabajoso que llevamos.	Ever returned with news about the road,
Mas de una cosa ciertos os hazemos,	But yet of one thing we do assure you:
Que si volver podemos a vengarnos	That if we can return for our vengeance,
Que no parieron madres Castellanas,	Castilian mothers shall not bear,
Ni bárbaras tampoco, en todo el mundo	Barbarian either, throughout all the world,
Más desdichados hijos que a vosotros."	Sons more unfortunate than all of you.

(Villagrá, *Historia*, 34, 354–64)

In *La Araucana*, Ercilla depicts a similar episode when, after the battle of Millarapué, twelve caciques, among them Galvarino, are condemned to hang themselves. In *La Araucana* the event can be corroborated through other historical sources, as scholar David Quint concludes,[114] while in the *Historia* there is no evidence, even in Villagrá's later testimony, that the hanging took place. Suicide by hanging is considered in literary criticism "a well-known epic topos,"[115] but in the *Historia*, as Martín Rodríguez suggests, it "is charged with original meanings."[116] Yet, one should not overlook the possibility that Villagrá, even with his knowledge of classical epic poetry, might have copied Ercilla, finding in that episode of *La Araucana* the perfect way to end his own epic poem.

A comparison between the episode that Villagrá uses to conclude his poem and what he stated as a witness under oath show a contradiction. The native voice of suffering and loss acquires a greater dimension and meaning in Villagrá's lines cited above, unmatched in his previous cantos. But his own historical testimony as a witness after the battle, by contrast, does not speak of the natives with such admiration or eloquence. He gave the last part of his testimony on February 11, 1599, in Santo Domingo Pueblo, summarizing what he had witnessed.

> This is all the witness knows, other than that he considers these Indians evil and perverse because they lived in such a stronghold. Besides being such a strong place, the whole pueblo had been undermined with tunnels passing from house to house, which will indicate that they were bold fighters and robbers. That is why the witness thinks they were emboldened to kill the maese de campo and the others who died with him.[117]

From a standpoint of literary criticism, the end of the poem has two meanings, particularly the Indians' curse. Quint points to diametrically opposite readings and ideologically conflicting messages. The lines do not offer, therefore, "a single official viewpoint."[118] According to Quint, in the context of the canons of epic poetry fortune usually favors the victorious (the Spaniards at Acoma). The fortune of the loser (Acoma Pueblo) is left to fate, thus leaving open the possibility that their destiny will change in the future.[119] Moreover, the theme of mothers who repent having given birth to their sons (as Villagrá mentions, in the case of the Castilian mothers) is a constant in classical literature (Hannibal, for example, against Rome).[120]

Villagrá draws on themes of the traditional epic, such as the role of fortune and that of the curse, but he presents the episode at the end of the *Historia*. Quint suggests that through this choice the poet is adding a specific meaning: "the form both determines and constitutes part of the ideological content itself."[121] In other words, the poet seems to project the idea that not everything has been said or decided, and that the defeat of the Indians is not the end of the story. Thus, the conclusion of the poem shows that everything can change. The possibility of another insurrection remains open (*Que si volver podemos a vengarnos*/ That if we can return for our vengeance).

With the previous argument Villagrá identifies, to a degree, with the loser. Nevertheless, such Indian resistance might perhaps be contained. In Quint's words: "The pose of stoic autonomy that the cornered Indians adopt as they hang themselves cannot disguise the fact that they are doing the Spaniards' work for them."[122] Therefore, their suicide can be interpreted to mean that the Indians are condemned after all "to a future of scattered suicidal gestures, ultimately without aim or direction.[123] Even though the topic is more complex (as is Quint's analysis), the aim of citing this interpretation here is to show the meaning of Villagrá's poem: to display a reality, even with historical distortion. According to Quint, "it suggests that behind the fictions of epic poetry lie other similar events: episodes of political struggle and colonialist violence."[124] Quint's explanation confirms the true value of Villagrá's poem, which, despite having been characterized as being of poor quality by some critics, sets forth serious themes that go beyond a simple tale of events, themes that form part of a complex historical reality, as was that of colonization.

Martín Rodríguez, on the other hand, compares the hanging of Tempal and Cotumbo to other dramatic events in the poem, such as the death of Juan de Zaldívar, whose body was never found; the foundational legend of Tenochtitlán; and the Indian murals of Puarai depicting the killing of several friars whose bodies were never found. Through the inclusion of these three examples, the author suggests that the native voice persists throughout the poem: "The physical absence of the Spanish bodies is thus filled by the embedded presence of the native American discourse which, in a sense, takes their place."[125]

The interpretations by Quint and Martín Rodríguez add to the richness of the *Historia*'s meaning. The attention that literary critics are now paying to the poem and its author is in itself an important step toward giving both the recognition they deserve. Villagrá and his poem are now being included in the corpus of Native American discourse in the literature of empire. One aspect of Villagrá's work that makes him of interest to modern literary critics is his novel use of original documents that he incorporates into the poem. Returning to the legal theme of this chapter, this poetic strategy supports the argument that he used the poem as a tool in his own defense. At the same time, as Martín Rodríguez has stated, the documents give the *Historia* relevance in the eyes of the critic and present-day reader.

> From a context such as ours, much more interested in questions of intertextuality, textuality, and metaliterature, the *Historia de la Nueva México* stands out for its modernity in the treatment of questions such as the limits between invention and reality, the capacity of the discourse to represent or not the text as a reference to previous texts and conditionings associated inevitably with each of those discourses.[126]

From a legal and historical point of view, Villagrá's motive for transcribing documents in his poem was understandable. His education as a law student influenced his grasp of the need to use those original texts. Also, his interest in making clear the legality of the actions and decisions of Oñate and his men (including himself) helps explain why the poet interposed the documents.

This chapter has emphasized what the poet chose to say or not to say in his poem. To conclude, then, with the analysis of the law it is necessary to look again at what happened after the battle of Acoma, specifically the punishment given to the Acoma Indians, an episode that the poet decided not to include in his work. There is sufficient documentation to provide the historian with some clues about Villagrá's position with respect to the punishment of Acoma, and, as a consequence, his position with respect to the decisions Oñate made. The documents provide a greater understanding of the poem and delineate their meaning, as well as projecting an idea of the application of the law then in force.

First, the reader must return to the citation from the *Historia* that opens this chapter. At the beginning of canto 27, Villagrá presents the reader with the Spanish departure for Acoma to punish the rebel Indians. The poet mentions that a punishment must be harsh and that justice must be applied with rigor to redress crimes so as to "enjoy the pleasing peace." Villagrá overtly cites the precedent of the "brave barbarians of Arauco" of Chile, where, because the "necessary punishment" was not applied, it led to fifty years of continuous war in which the "homicidal weapons" caused the spilling of so much "Castilian blood." Villagrá chose to refer to *La Araucana* and the Indians of Chile at the beginning of the first of several cantos in his poem dedicated to the Acoma rebellion and its punishment.

It is notable that he cites the same example of the Chilean case in his "Memorial of Justification" in 1614 as he defended Oñate's decision to act immediately and attack Acoma,

> because if they killed our maese de campo and with him two captains and seven companions and friends, was it right to wait for them to come for us all, as they came in Chile and carried off entire pueblos.[127]

Villagrá argues in the memorial that it was because of the decision to punish Acoma that there was not another uprising for fourteen years.

> There has been no barbarian who has rebelled or caused any damage whatsoever because more than a hundred pueblos, which were peaceful and subject to the crown of Castile, all had their encomenderos, to whom they paid tribute and gave their mantas and maize.[128]

The document adds that had it not been for the success of the punishment, "the war would have lasted for a great many years as it lasted in Chile because the punishment was deferred, as Alonso de Ercilla stated."[129]

In his justification of Oñate's decision, Villagrá compares the "poor fortune" of the governor of New Mexico with that of the Marqués del Valle (Hernán Cortés) during the conquest of Mexico and Pizarro during the conquest of Peru. He reiterates that Oñate did "on his expedition" as much as they did on theirs.[130]

There is one more curious and important point that Villagrá includes in the "Memorial of Justification." Continuing with the comparison to Hernán Cortés, he insists that if New Mexico had been a "rich land," everything Oñate did would have been justified, as it was with the Marqués del Valle, who, after the episodes denounced by Las Casas' book, did not receive any punishment, and

> who we know laid waste to New Spain by pure fire and blood, an event, if not done well, what punishment did he receive for it or what did the kings tell him with the Bishop of Chiapas having written and printed a book in which he wrote so many things, that he cautioned him against.[131]

This is the only reference to Bartolomé de Las Casas that Villagrá makes in his writings. The poet cites Las Casas and his *Brief Account of the Destruction of the Indies*, in which the writer denounced atrocities committed against the Indians during the conquest of Mexico by Hernán Cortés. Indirectly, the poet is also accepting Las Casas as an authoritative source. In the examples cited above, the poet uses his memorial in an attempt to justify Oñate's actions, supporting his leader's position with the comparison to other famous conquistadors who relied on similar methods of punishment.

The course that Villagrá followed immediately after the battle of Acoma demonstrates that at no time did the poet decide to take a position in defense of Indian freedom. Instead, he confirmed the need for war or punishment to keep the peace. Villagrá's role as "guarantor of the defender of the Indians of Acoma" during the trial was surely decided upon by Oñate because of the poet's legal education; he was, after all, the expedition's legal counsel.[132] In addition, there is a documentary reference, a letter from Oñate dated January 30, 1599, in which the governor addresses Villagrá as "captain, procurador general, member of the

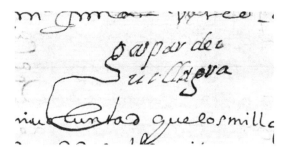

Signature of Gaspar de Villagrá on a fragment of his will that he dictated at sea on his way back to Mexico, September 1620. *Archivo General de Indias (Seville), Contratación 573, N. 15, R. 1/14, 7v.*

The text is a continuation of a previous page, where Villagrá had mentioned the division of his estate in equal parts between his wife Catalina de Soto and his two legitimate sons, José and Gaspar. He requests a pension for them due to his service to the king, including the position he was given of *alcalde mayor* of Zapotitlán, Guatemala, which he would not be able to occupy because of illness: "I ask, very humbly, Your Majesty as a Very Christian Prince give them whatever pension possible due to their poverty and need." For a Spanish transcription of the entire will, see Manuel Martín Rodríguez, *Gaspar de Villagrá: Legista, soldado y poet* (León, Spain: Universidad de León, 2009), 278–88.

council of war of New Mexico, and governor of Acoma."[133] There are no other references to this point, although the possibility exists that after the battle, Villagrá and others could have remained in Acoma for a few days.[134]

In a further demonstration of Villagrá's loyalty to Oñate and Oñate's confidence in the poet, the governor named him leader of the expedition that departed in 1599 for Mexico City to seek reinforcements. On this mission, Villagrá was also entrusted with taking a group of young girls from Acoma who were to be placed as novices in convents in Mexico City. As for Villagrá's reasons for not returning to New Mexico, there has been speculation about possible enmity between the poet and Oñate as the main reason for not joining the return expedition. The facts seem to indicate, however, that there were disagreements about the leadership of the expedition in which Villagrá was going to participate, which provoked his decision not to return, seeking "sacred refuge" in the church of San Francisco, in Santa Bárbara, on September 4, 1600.[135]

On May 14, 1614, the condemnation of Juan de Oñate, Gaspar de Villagrá, Vicente de Zaldívar, and other members of the expedition for Spanish settlement in New Mexico was handed down. Villagrá was accused of beheading two of the four deserters who escaped New Mexico (Oñate had given him the order) and lying about the riches of New Mexico. He was condemned to exile from New Mexico for six years and from Mexico City, its court, and five leagues around the city for two years without being able to hold any public office or position for the same period. Oñate, on his part, was accused of excesses and transgressions committed during the entrada and his administration of New Mexico. The list was long and included among other charges having punished the pueblo of Acoma in a very severe manner, wounding and killing many natives, and later inflicting severe punishment on the survivors.[136] Punishments such as cutting off the foot of males over the age of twenty-five and cutting off the right hand of two Hopi Indians recalled the punishment used by the Spaniards in the conquest of Chile. But Oñate lived in other times and under another type of law, the ordinances of 1573, and could not escape the charges of abuse as easily as the conquistadors of fifty years earlier.

Throughout all of these events, the relationship between Oñate and Villagrá was not one of enmity but the complete opposite. The facts and extant documentation are consistent with the perspective Villagrá employed in his poem with respect to Oñate. The communication between them continued throughout the years. In Spain Villagrá took charge of the legal matter of Oñate's appeal of his sentence and other related matters between 1615 and 1620. In Villagrá's will, signed on the high seas en route from Spain to New Spain on September 8, 1620, Villagrá declared that

> with this will is a closed and sealed paper, signed by my hand inside and out, which is a record of the expenses that I have incurred in the lawsuits I have pursued in His Majesty's court for don Juan de Oñate, adelantado of the provinces of New Mexico.[137]

The legislation that shaped the colonization of New Mexico is full of references to the importance of evangelical conversion, from the ordinances of 1573 to Oñate's contract and instructions. Villagrá's poem repeatedly stresses Oñate's preoccupation with obeying the law, and that intention is further reflected in the lines where he mentions the consultation with the friars and discussion that Oñate followed to decide on the punishment of Acoma. The poet renders in prose the arguments made by the Franciscan commissary, the head of the group of Franciscans who participated in New Mexico's settlement. Through the inclusion of this text Villagrá does not necessarily want to place responsibility for the punishment on the priests, but to show that a legal procedure was followed in which the opinion of the church was extremely important. It is evident that the consultation with the priests can be seen as yet another way of obeying the law— and for Oñate to avoid being accused of breaking it. Because evangelical conversion was one of the principal objectives of the ordinances of 1573, the figure of the priest was fundamental and necessary in New Mexico. Villagrá decided to include in his poem all the arguments made by the Franciscan commissary with respect to the concept of just war. Thus, the *Historia* demonstrates the importance of the Church and its mission in the conquest of New Mexico.

Scrutinizing the poet's life, we can understand the predominance of religion in the poem. There is no doubt about Villagrá's deep religiosity.[138] Martín

Rodríguez has explored this topic, and the reader should refer to his biography of Villagrá for more details. There are, however, a couple of aspects to cite here. One is the influence on Villagrá of his studies at the University of Salamanca. The other is his deep faith and religious conviction, which some events in the poet's life confirm. This aspect of Villagrá's character has led some literary critics to consider the poet's position as bordering on religious fanaticism. Thus, he has been characterized as a "voluntary inquisitor,"[139] as "scrupulous in matters of purity of blood and obsessed with hunting heretics," and as a "typical example of intolerance."[140] It is debatable whether Villagrá was really a religious fanatic, but what cannot be ignored is that his attitude, even before his participation in Oñate's campaign, showed signs of his deep devoutness and of his "sustained defense" of the Franciscans.[141]

If the reader turns to what the poem says about purity of blood and conversion, it indeed reflects a somewhat intolerant vision, although one common in its time.

Sólo una terrible falta hallo,	I find one fault, and that one terrible,
Christianissimo Rey, en vuestras Indias,	O King most Christian, in this your Indies,
Y es que están muy pobladas y ocupadas	And it is that they are too much filled and settled
De gente vil, manchada y sospechosa.	By a people base, corrupted, untrustworthy.
Y no siendo en España permitido	And since it's not allowed in Spain
Que passen esos tales a estas partes,	That such do come into these parts,
No sé qué causa puede haber bastante	I know not what cause could suffice
Para que no los hechen de la tierra	To keep us from ejecting them
Que les es por justicia prohibida;	From out this land that justice would deny them,
Pues la oveja roñosa es cosa llana	Since it is evident the scabby sheep
Que suele inficionar todo un rebaño.	Infect all the flock

(Villagrá, *Historia*, 4, 387–97)

Por cuia justa causa es bien se arranque	'Tis well, for this just cause, to root
Aquesta mala hierba . . .	Out this bad weed

(Villagrá, *Historia*, 4, 405–406)

Principalmente con tan buena ayuda	And do it chiefly with such goodly aid
Qual la del tribunal santo famoso	As of that holy, famous tribunal
Que gobiernan aquellos eminentes,	That those most eminent and famed
Insignes y doctísimos varones	And learned men do rule

(Villagrá, *Historia*, 4, 410–13)

Todos vigilantísimos guerreros	All warriors most watchful
Contra la peste y cáncer contagioso	'Gainst cancer and contagious plague

Que, por algunos miembros de la Iglesia,	That, through some members of the
Los del vil campo herético de Ramán,	Church,
En cuia siembra vemos que descubren	Those of the vile heretic camp propagate,
Pestilenciales nidos y veneros	In whose vile seed we see discovered
De perversos errores contagiosos	Most pestilential nests and source
	Of errors contagious and perverse

(Villagrá, *Historia*, 4, 420–26)

Que todas vuestras Indias se despojen	That all your Indies be quite freed
Desta bestial canalla y que se pueblen	Of that evil crew, and populated
De sólos Hijosdalgo y Caballeros	Only by knights and noble men
Y de Christianos Viejos muy ranciosos,	And very strong old Christians,
Que con éstos y no con otra gente	For with them, nor with other folk,
Podéis bien descubrir el universo	You well can all the universe discover
Y conquistarlo todo y reduzirlo	And conquer and reduce it all
Al suave yugo de la Iglesia santa.	To gentle yoke of Holy Church.

(Villagrá, *Historia*, 4, 444–51)

Villagrá could have elected not to include these verses, or he might have used more tempered language, and the same message would have been transmitted. Villagrá's characterization gives the reader the impression of reading a medieval or fifteenth-century author, not one from the beginning of the seventeenth century.

To conclude the analysis of Villagrá's poem from the perspective of law, it is worth looking at some characteristics of Ercilla's discourse that can be applied to Villagrá and his poem. As mentioned, Elizabeth Davis analyzed Ercilla's subjectivity as a vassal of the king. The link to the king shows Ercilla's commitment to the condition of servant, as reflected in his poem.[142] In Villagrá's case there is also a discourse of service characterized by a need to prove his loyalty to the crown and to Oñate, the leader of the conquest of New Mexico. As demonstrated in this chapter, there is enough documentation to conclude that Villagrá wished to establish a record to justify his actions during the conquest as well as those of Oñate: "the poem reads as an act of political desperation to set the historical record of what took place."[143]

⌒

Alonso de Ercilla died at home in Madrid on November 27, 1594. At the end of the previous year he had shown symptoms of illness. In a pair of letters written in December 1593 to Commander Diego Sarmiento y Acuña, Ercilla told him that "in my house the doctors have ordered me to eat a diet that is good for my chest ailment" and added in the other letter that "I have not been well and have stayed in bed and in the house to my great sorrow."[144] Ercilla was buried at the Discalced

Carmelite convent of Las Baronesas and in 1595 was transferred to a Discalced Carmelite monastery in Ocaña, Toledo (for the founding of which the poet had left money to his wife, María de Bazán).[145] Ercilla did not include references to the religious theme in *La Araucana* as frequently as Villagrá did later in the *Historia*. Ironically, Ercilla's remains were given Christian burial in a Carmelite convent, but Villagrá's body was never placed in a religious institution. The author of the *Historia* died on September 9, 1620, aboard the ship *Nuestra Señora de los Reyes*, which was carrying him back to his native land, New Spain. His body was cast into the sea, as was the custom in such cases.[146]

Ercilla died at the age of sixty-one, and although there is speculation about the possibility that before he died he was preparing a fourth part of *La Araucana*, what is certain is that his adventure in Chile, in whose conquest he had been so proud to participate, had been left behind, even though the fame of his poem would continue during his lifetime and beyond. By the time of Ercilla's death in Madrid, Juan de Oñate had begun to negotiate the clauses of the contract for the New Mexico enterprise with the viceroy of New Spain, and in 1596 Oñate named Gaspar de Villagrá as his *procurador general*. In the meantime, on the southern frontier of the Spanish empire, Chile in the 1590s offered a devastating panorama for Spanish interests as a consequence of an Araucanian counteroffensive. For a long time, the Spanish crown could not rely on a strong Spanish presence in the south. The northern frontier appeared to offer for that same decade a more hopeful future.

The process of Spanish settlement in the frontier zone of the north began fifty years after that of the southern frontier. The legislation under which each enterprise operated had different characteristics, which gave different perspectives to each settlement. Both poems reflect these distinctions in a general way as documents of their respective times. Each poet uses a discourse about vassalage that implies subservience in favor of the Spanish king and empire. Villagrá was more interested in justifying his actions through the use of prose and of a strong historical component in the poem, since there was a trial awaiting him. Ercilla's discourse, on the other hand, reflects the expectation of material compensation or reward.

There is, however, an important aspect in which the two poems coincide: both cover frontier spaces. It is impossible to understand the historical context of the poems without looking closely at the two regional spaces. Their isolation and distance from their respective colonial capitals, together with the need to subjugate Indians whom the Spaniards knew little to nothing about, and the challenge of establishing permanent Spanish settlements in those vast and isolated regions, are some of the characteristics common to both frontiers. Part II of this book explores the theme of geographic frontier space, which gives each poem a specifically American perspective.

Part II

The Frontier

CHAPTER 3

The Geography of War

Digo de norte a sur corre la tierra,
y báñala del oeste la marina;
a la banda de leste va una sierra
que el mismo rumbo mil leguas camina;
en medio es donde el punto de la guerra
por uso y ejercicio más se afina.
Venus y Amán aquí no alcanzan parte,
sólo domina el iracundo Marte.

Pues en este distrito demarcado,
por donde su grandeza es manifiesta,
está a treinta y seis grados el Estado
que tanta sangre ajena y propia cuesta;
éste es el fiero pueblo no domado
que tuvo a Chile en tan estrecho puesta,
y aquel que por valor y pura guerra
hace en torno temblar toda la tierra.

From South to North runs the land
the sea bathes it from the West;
to the East a strip of mountain range
runs for a thousand leagues in the same
direction;
in the center is where the point of the war
by custom and practice mostly is carried
on.
Here Venus and Amán do not have
influence,
only the passionate wrathful Mars
endures.

Then in this district as laid out,
where its grandeur is manifest,
at thirty-six degrees the state is located
that cost as much alien blood as well as its
own;
these are the fierce people, never subdued
that held Chile in such a rigorous setting,
whose courage and unsullied war
in turn makes the earth tremble all
around.

(Ercilla, *La Araucana*, 1.10, 1–8; 11, 1–8)

Y de la zona elada dista y tiene
Quinientas leguas largas bien tendidas;
Y en círculo redondo vemos ciñe
Debajo el paralelo, si tomamos
Los treinta y siete grados levantados,
Cinco mil leguas buenas Españolas,
Cuya grandeza es lástima la ocupen
Tanta suma de gentes ignorantes
De la sangre de Cristo, cuya alteza

And from the frozen zone its distance is
About five hundred full long leagues;
And in a circle round we see it hold,
Beneath the parallel, if we should take
The height of thirty-seven degrees,
Five thousand goodly Spanish leagues,
Whose greatness it is a shame it should be
held
By so great sum of people ignorant
About the blood of Christ, whose holiness

Causa dolor la ignoren tantas almas.
Destas nuevas Regiones es notorio,
Pública voz y fama que decienden
Aquellos más antiguos Mexicanos

It causes pain to think so many souls know
   not.
From these new regions 'tis notorious,
Of poet voice and fame, that there
   descended
Those oldest folk of Mexico

(Villagrá, *Historia*, 1.75–84)

As can be seen in the lines above, both Ercilla and Villagrá introduce the physical space in which their histories will unfold in the very first cantos of their poems. The poets also portray the idea of frontier by providing the latitude of each region: thirty-six degrees south and thirty-seven degrees north.[1] From the European point of view, the two zones represented the extremes of Spanish presence in American territory in the northern and southern hemispheres during the middle of the sixteenth century. Besides locating the space, both poets mention the central feature of Spanish conquest in each of the two frontier zones: for Chile, the presence of the "indomitable" Araucanians; and for New Mexico, the role that religion will play in the conquest of the Indian peoples.

In the 1540s, the historical period in which the two poems begin, the objective of Spanish expeditions in the Americas was to secure spaces that offered a sufficiently large indigenous population, or gold and silver, or both. Such places were also attractive from a commercial standpoint: potential land bridges which one could traverse between the two oceans. At that time Spaniards were exploring the thirtieth and fortieth parallels in both the northern and southern hemispheres, reaching areas as distinct geographically as those bathed by the Colorado River basin in North America and the Río de la Plata in South America. The Spanish presence in such remote regions did not necessarily mean the success of the colonizing enterprise, as will be seen in Chile and New Mexico.

In most cases, the Spaniards encountered geography that was difficult for European minds and eyes to comprehend. Those who wrote down notes about their journeys, sent letters to the king or other officials of the Spanish crown, or wrote long accounts of the expeditions in which they participated, project through their words the image of a natural American space, with a Western— and therefore Christian—view of the geography they encountered. Moreover, their purpose in describing what they saw was framed by economic reasons and not by a sense of admiration for the landscape.[2]

The direct participation of writers in the exploration, conquest, and colonization meant that many could add a dramatic tone to their works, plus that pride of presence that can only be achieved by firsthand experience. Because of the particular characteristics of conquest in the frontier zones, the description of the geography acquired a unique nuance. If the writer dealt with the encounter with great civilizations such as the Aztecs or Incas, with populous capital cities of grandiose, imperial stone architecture, a description of nature was unnecessary and not even remarked on. But in regions far removed from the great cities, natural space—as well as human resources and materials—were not only crucial to describe, they were also essential to the success or failure of the colonizing enterprise.

In September 1540 a small group led by Captain García López de Cárdenas arrived at one of the southern rims of what is today known as the Grand Canyon of the Colorado River. The handful of Spaniards belonged to the expedition of Vázquez de Coronado that was searching in North America for the famous and supposedly rich seven cities of Cíbola. This was just one year after Álvar Núñez Cabeza de Vaca began his exploration and colonization in South America that would lead him to reconnoiter the tributaries of the Río de la Plata and find a natural marvel comparable to the Grand Canyon: Iguazú Falls. Accounts written by the participants in these expeditions do not reflect an attitude of admiration for the beauty of the geography through which they passed; rather, they indicate frustration and disappointment. Those natural wonders were nothing more than geographic impediments to the Spanish advance.

The first description of the Grand Canyon based on witness accounts was noted by Pedro de Castañeda y Nájera, chronicler of the expedition of Vázquez de Coronado, as follows:

> They spent three days on this bank looking for a passage down to the river, which looked from above as if the water was six feet across, although the Indians said it was half a league wide. . . . Those who stayed above had estimated that some huge rocks on the sides of the cliffs seemed to be about as tall as a man, but those who went down swore that when they reached these rocks they were bigger than the great tower of Seville.[3]

To determine the size of a geographic landmark, there was no better way than to compare it with some known reference, and Seville tended to be the city to which explorers alluded. Such was the case in the account of the expedition of Álvar Núñez in South America, wherein he compared the Iguazú River with the Guadalquivir River in Spain. Referring to the falls formed by the Iguazú, he said that

> the current was very strong going down the Río Iguazú, and the canoes shot along furiously. Very close to where the party had launched itself into the river, it plunged in a fall over some high rocks with a great crashing noise that you could hear from quite a distance. The mist where the water dropped off with such force rose up for two or more *lanzas*. Because of this it was necessary to get out of the canoes, lift them from the water, and haul them overland past the falls.[4]

For Spaniards of the first half of the sixteenth century, exploration meant the search for people and resources, especially gold and silver, with the aim of conquest. The entradas had no other purpose than to find great centers of population, the more prosperous the better.[5] The aesthetic appearance of the landscape was neither a priority nor of interest when it came to describing the geography in reports and accounts.[6] In Western thought of the sixteenth century, unknown land was considered "uncivilized," and the conquest of the Americas confirmed it.[7] The "savage" nature of indigenous Americans was consistent with the "savage" land they inhabited, from a European point of view. Moreover, to their way of thinking, human beings were not part of nature; rather, they were a foreign presence in it, and therefore they reserved the right to impose themselves on nature and control it.[8]

This manner of observing and describing changed with the centuries, although it never abandoned that colonialist position. For the second half of the eighteenth century, the European attitude was more open to the idea of exploring in order to learn, but exploration was always linked to empire-building. Such was the case with the scientific expeditions organized to find an exact way to measure longitude and the circumference of the earth, for example, or to search for and study new species of animals and plants, or to find the much sought-after passage in North America from the South Sea (Pacific Ocean), as was the case with the Malaspina expedition sent by the Spanish crown in 1789. Also included in this list is Alexander von Humboldt's trip through what were still Spanish American colonies, a trip supported by the Spanish crown. It was necessary to wait until 1845 and the publication of the first volume of Humboldt's *Cosmos* for the image of an interrelated natural world, including the human species, in Western thought.[9] The preoccupation with environmental themes, including the relationship of human beings to other species, with greater sensitivity to the description and knowledge of animals, plants, and landscape, began to grow considerably just as the nineteenth century came to a close.[10]

The descriptions of the Grand Canyon or Iguazú Falls in the sixteenth century reflected the tendency of the times to see and explain something "new" in relation to something "old" or already known. Thus, a large rocky formation was compared to the Giralda, an Arabic tower in Seville. This method of observation prevented Spaniards from making other types of comparisons: "They saw the islands and mainland of the western ocean, therefore, largely through transference, through the exchange of verbal and visual images from an Old World context to a New."[11] The American landscape was neither beautiful nor immense in and of itself but in relation to what was known and to the goals of the conquest—and especially to the survival of Spaniards in those distant lands. What they saw was important only in relation to what they sought, mixed on occasion with some aspects of myth and fantasy: "the natural scenery in a land where

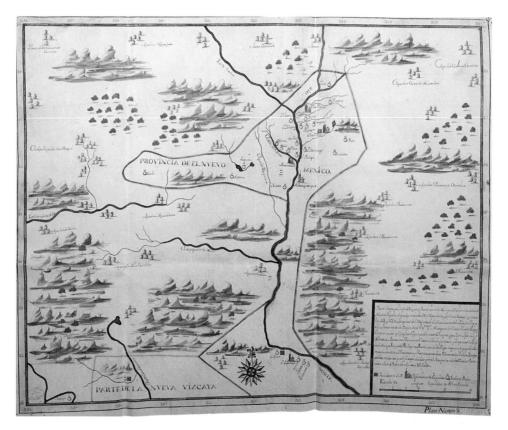

Plano Corographico del Reyno y Provincia de el Nuevo Mexico una de las de Nueva Espana situada entre los 31 y 38 grados de Latitud Boreal y los 258 y 264 de Longitud a el respecto de el Meridiano de la Isla de Tenerife (Orographic Map of the Kingdom and Province of New Mexico, one of those of New Spain, situated between thirty-one and thirty-eight degrees of Boreal Latitude and two hundred fifty-eight and two hundred sixty-four degrees of Longitude in relation to the Meridian of the Island of Tenerife.) *Archivo General de Indias (Seville), Mapas y Planos, México, 122.*

This map originated in the Presidio de Sinaloa in 1727. It shows in rich detail geographic features similar to what the Spanish encountered in 1598. Latitude marked is 31°–39° N and longitude 236°–266° E (the measurement was done in decreasing numbers from Tenerife to the east, instead of east to west).

The map shows that by 1727 the Province of New Mexico (no longer "Kingdom") covered approximately the same territory that Gaspar de Villagrá describes in his poem. The native pueblos mentioned by the poet were still in the same locations as at the end of the sixteenth century, when Oñate's expedition arrived in the area. In the south are Socorro, Isleta, and Senecu Pueblos. In the central area is a second Isleta Pueblo. In the west are Laguna, Acoma, and Zuñi Pueblos. East of the Río del Norte are Santo Domingo, Galisteo, and Pecos Pueblos. West of the Río del Norte are Santa Ana, Zía, Jemez, and Cochiti Pueblos. The map also shows other pueblos not on the poet's route. Finally, the map shows Spanish villages that were founded later, such as Santa Fe, Bernalillo, Albuquerque, and Santa Cruz de la Cañada.

The province boundaries are marked in red. They show that in the 128 years between 1599, when Villagrá left New Mexico, and 1727, when this map was made, the breadth of Spanish presence in the area was little changed. Major events of the seventeenth century, such as the Pueblo Revolt of 1680 and the return of the Spanish to govern the area in 1693 hardly changed the political-administrative map of the colony. Although there were no official boundaries, population was settled in two areas: the territory occupied by the Spanish and the Pueblo Indians, and the regions occupied by their common enemy in the eighteenth century, the Apaches.

The orography, or topographic relief, though incomplete and not very sophisticated, accurately shows the location of the Río del Norte, Spanish villages, and native pueblos, as well as mesas and rocky elevations. Not shown are the Malpaís and El Morro (or Peñol), which Villagrá traversed in his dramatic winter journey of 1599, located between Acoma and Zuñi.

125

Medallion with King Felipe II's coat of arms that was part of a larger banner carried by Juan de Oñate upon his entry into New Mexico in 1598. *Collections of the Archdiocese of Santa Fe on permanent loan to the New Mexico History Museum.*

The medallion is constructed in eight layers (red silk, paper, and linen) held together by two separate bindings. It was preserved at San Miguel Mission. Diego de Vargas mentions in his journals that a banner of Oñate was saved from the 1680 revolt and that Vargas returned it to Santa Fe. The reverse side of the medallion has an image of the Our Lady of Remedies (Nuestra Señora de los Remedios), holding the Christ child.

El Morro, viewed from the direction of Gaspar de Villagrá's approach. *Photo by Joel Mills. Creative Commons License.*

The poet arrived at El Morro in the winter of 1599, while trying to catch up with Oñate's group at the Hopi Pueblos. After Villagra's horse was killed in a trap, he crossed the lava fields on foot in a blizzard, and according to his poem, had to get rid of his breastplate and helmet to survive. Almost dying of exposure, hunger, and thirst, he made it to El Morro (he calls it *la peña* or *peñol*) where two of Oñate's soldiers found him.

Spanish colonial breastplate and helmet, mid- to late sixteenth century. *New Mexico History Museum Collections, Santa Fe (11447.45).*

The helmet is engraved with religious depictions: a kneeling figure (possibly Saint John) before Christ on the cross, and the Virgin Mary with the Christ child. Breastplate and helmet were found in the twentieth century in a cave in the Malpaís near Grants, New Mexico. The area is located between Acoma Pueblo and El Morro.

Acoma Mesa (*center-right foreground*), on the top of which Acoma Pueblo was located in the sixteenth century, still exists today. *Photo by Scott Catron. Creative Commons License.*

Villagrá participated in the 1599 Spanish attack on Acoma, which he vividly describes in his poem.

The Rio Grande, in the north valley of today's city of Albuquerque, looking south. *Photo by Alan Gross. Creative Commons License.*

Oñate's expedition traveled parallel to the east bank of the river.

Biobío River in central Chile, looking west from the city of Concepción. *Photo by the author.*

The Biobío River runs east to west from the Andes Mountains to the Pacific Ocean. In the sixteenth century the river was the natural dividing line between the main Spanish settlements and the land defended by the Araucanians. Concepción was founded in 1550 by Pedro de Valdivia, next to the estuary of the Biobío.

Villarrica volcano and lake, Chile. *Photo by Edosanra. Creative Commons License.*

In his poem Ercilla describes the Villarrica volcano as "a forge of Vulcan belching continuous fire." In 1552, on Valdivia's orders, Gerónimo de Alderete founded Santa María Magdalena de Villarrica beside the lake of the same name and at the mouth of the present-day Toltén River, north of the volcano. Two years later the town was abandoned. García Hurtado de Mendoza ordered it resettled in 1559, but in 1602 the Araucanians captured it definitively.

Partial view of the beach of Penco, Talcahuano Bay, central coast of Chile. *Photo by the author.*

Ercilla mentions "el morro de Penco" in *La Araucana* to identify the hill or group of hills located next to the beach in Talcahuano Bay. In 1550 Pedro de Valdivia founded Concepción beside the cerro de Penco. The geographic aspects of the bay Ercilla described in the sixteenth century are the same today. The city and port of Penco are located on the eastern side of Talcahuano Bay.

everything was very unusual seemed of interest not so much for how it looked, but, more than anything, for what it could reveal and hide."[12]

In 1540, the same year when, in September, Vázquez de Coronado's men arrived at the Grand Canyon, Pedro de Valdivia departed from Peru headed south, to make his entrada into Chile at the end of that year. In February 1541, in the valley of the Mapocho River, Valdivia founded the city of Santiago del Nuevo Extremo.[13] Vázquez de Coronado returned to Mexico City in 1542 with news that he had found no rich cities but had found indigenous peoples congregated in pueblos. For the next four decades, the New Mexico region ceased to be of interest for the Viceroyalty of New Spain.[14]

Meanwhile, Valdivia tried to convince King Carlos I (Carlos V of the Holy Roman Empire) of the riches and possibilities of Chile, especially of the need to establish settlements in the south as far as the Strait of Magellan. In a letter of September 4, 1545, Valdivia stated, referring to the resources of the land of Chile: "It is most abundant in pastures and sown fields, and for raising all classes of livestock and plants as can be described; abundant and very beautiful wood to make houses, an infinite amount of firewood for household use, and mines that are very rich in gold, and the entire land is filled with it."[15] He added that the founding of Santiago had been "the first step on which to build the rest and to go on settling all this land of Your Majesty clear to the Strait of Magellan and the North Sea."[16]

By the middle of the sixteenth century, cartographic production in Europe showed greater knowledge of the edges of the Spanish American empire on the southern frontier than on the northern frontier. A look at the 1540–42 atlas by the Genoan Battista Agnese shows the Strait of Magellan at the southern end of South America and the route Magellan followed in circumnavigating the globe. Carlos V, who had given the only copy of the map to his son Felipe, could perfectly visualize what Valdivia commented on in his letter. In 1540, Sebastian Münster published what soon became the most popular map of American lands of the period. The map does not show a clear outline of North America. A northern waterway to the South Sea had not yet been found, and it was believed that the land to the north of New Spain was much narrower than it really was. For this reason, expeditions sent to the north from New Spain in the second half of the sixteenth century expected to find the South Sea much closer than it really was.[17]

Chile and the poorly explored northern reaches of the Viceroyalty of New Spain were remote from Lima and Mexico City, the great capitals of the colonial empire. In both cases, the connection between the South Sea (the Pacific) and the North Sea (the Atlantic) was essential to the commercial and political interests of the Spanish empire. The two frontiers, north and south, were becoming vital to the plans of Spanish conquest during the entire first century of occupation. Thus, the description of human and natural resources, especially minerals and spices, but also soils for planting and suitable places for ports, filled the letters written to the king and viceroys by the conquistadors of the sixteenth century. Detailed accounts, maps, and illustrations frequently accompanied the letters.[18]

Reports that contain observations about natural resources, including some ethnographic notes, began to appear after 1505. Accounts in the form of letters, or *cartas de relación*, describing natural resources of the lands and the economic and social systems of their inhabitants existed from the moment of contact, such as that of Christopher Columbus, dated February 15, 1493. Often, the veracity and exactitude of what was described was doubtful. The letters written by explorers and conquerors constituted what has been termed an imperial literature in which describing implied conquering. As writer Ileana Rodríguez has explained, "describing practically assured taking possession of what was discovered."[19]

A strong interest in providing detailed geographic description doubtless existed in these first reports in letter form, but clearly with a utilitarian purpose of providing information about the land's potential for minerals, agriculture, and Indian labor. Valdivia's letter to the king about the conquest of Chile is one example of that approach. From the beginning, these letters also expressed discontent, heartache, and internal squabbles among members of the conquistador group. They also represent an attempt to establish in writing something that could be used later as a legal instrument to claim political and economic rights and even noble titles from the crown. A good example of this type of report in letter form, with a utilitarian objective as well as the goal of establishing the internal policy of the conquest in writing, is that of Hernán Cortés and his letters to King Carlos V (I of Spain) between 1519 and 1525.

Histories and chronicles written between 1520 and 1550, which ran to many more pages than the letters, had the same objectives. The emphasis in some cases was on the feats and achievements during the military conquest, such as the example of Bernal Díaz del Castillo and his *Historia verdadera de la conquista de la Nueva España*, written almost thirty years after the conquest and published for the first time a century later.[20] In other instances, the work was a description of nature, towns, and politics, as in the case of *Historia general y natural de las Indias, islas y Tierra Firme del Mar Océano*, by Gonzalo Fernández de Oviedo, written between approximately 1526 and 1527. This last example is perhaps the earliest case of a history of American lands with the deliberate aim of paying attention to natural features and urban geography.[21]

Even so, Fernández de Oviedo's *Historia* has been described as a natural history with a strong utilitarian component. What he chose to include, in what may be called a geographic perspective, anticipates some aspects of the two epic poems being considered in this book. The contents of his book include a physical description of the countryside, demonstrating admiration for the topographic features and the magnitude of the formations; plus the mention of animals, trees, plants, and fruits and their nutritional, medicinal, and industrial qualities; and agricultural life (for example, details of cultivation and the use of maize and cacao). References to the efficiency of the indigenous agricultural system compared with the emphasis on productivity of the Spanish system are also mentioned.

Fernández de Oviedo recognized the natives' knowledge of their land and what nature had taught them, and acknowledged that the Spaniards were dealing with well-organized agricultural societies. The writer pays attention to nature and indigenous customs. Through his descriptions, he allows a certain critique of the European model and the negative impact of the conquest to shine through. This implied criticism was also apparent in his commentaries on indigenous depopulation as a result of the conquest, although he did not go so far as to become a denouncer like Las Casas.[22]

Fernández de Oviedo's work relates to what Ileana Rodríguez has called "a subordinate harmonious coexistence," that is, the chronicler, from his Western viewpoint, shows an interest and even admiration in describing the nature and indigenous habits and organization in the Americas. The coexistence of the two systems and peoples is acknowledged within a universe that is still Eurocentric. He takes European history as his point of reference to explain that which is American. "The citations of Virgil, Pliny, Isidore, the comparisons of indigenous people with the ancient Greeks, Latins and Jews [are] a reinforcement of the authority of his text and imposition of the European Western world on the American world."[23]

Fernández de Oviedo's presentation of the topic of Christianization warrants separate mention. His posture is oriented to "finding confluences and coincidences, agreements between the two world views, and between the two religions." He is critical with respect to the "farce" of Christian rites, and he recommends baptizing fewer Indians but with the precaution that those who were baptized should be "whole Christians."[24]

Still, one cannot deny Fernández de Oviedo credit for having dedicated his voluminous work to describing the natural world and indigenous population of the Americas, topics only superficially dealt with before that time. His position has been correctly classified as "that of a businessman and a settler":

> The attitude of conquerors, bureaucrats, and clergy led him, early in his career, to a pessimistic view of human history. Natural history became an escape from an empire increasingly ruled by absurd and grotesque policies."[25]

However, albeit with subtle differences, Fernández de Oviedo's work belongs to the continuum of imperialist literature of the first half of the sixteenth century.

Decades later, the Spanish American epic followed this same model. The two poems analyzed here coincide with a type of discourse that includes the description of nature—with a utilitarian objective—and elements that serve not only as documentary proof of the specific facts of the conquest but also for legal recourse. In addition, in the epic, indigenous customs and admiration for the efficiency of certain indigenous practices and customs continue to be subordinate to that which is European.

All these characteristics speak of a literature that, to be recognized by the European reader and considered of use to the Spanish crown, had to fit into Western history. Thus, giving that which is indigenous a predominant place in the discourse does not imply a vindication of that which is indigenous. On the other hand, while the epic can rightly be seen as a historical source, there is a point at which poetry, including that of Ercilla and Villagrá, ceases to be a reference work, which is when the need arises for it to conform to the canons of the epic. This means that myth, fantasy, exaggeration, and obedience to meter trump some of the veracity that the poems might have from a historical point of view. This subject will be touched on again in this and subsequent chapters.

In 1571 one of the ordinances of the Council of the Indies signed by councilor José de Ovando established the position of chronicler cosmographer. The purpose of this position was to compile information about the western Indies, from geography and climate to demographics, economy, and more.[26] In 1573 Felipe II signed the *Ordenanzas de Descripciones*, which, at Ovando's initiative, ordered all the descriptions of American lands to be included in a *Libro de las Descripciones*.[27] Possibly connected with this initiative was the history of Chile written by Alonso de Góngora y Marmolejo, finalized in 1557 and dedicated to Ovando, president of the Council of the Indies.[28] The chronicler Góngora lived in Chile, where he arrived in 1549. At the beginning of his history he mentions Alonso de Ercilla and his *La Araucana*, saying that the poet was only in Chile for a little while and that his work was not "as copious as necessary to take notice of everything in the kingdom."[29] Therefore, it was necessary for Góngora to write a history that would include more information than Ercilla had provided.

The *relaciones geográficas* were prepared based on fifty questions, officially called "instruction and memorial," sent to Spanish-American colonial authorities in 1577.[30] The entire corpus of *relaciones geográficas* has been defined as literature "of commercial necessity and imperial expansion."[31] The lands encountered were described based on their mining and commercial potential, an essential condition "that the economic policy of mercantilism imposed on this literature."[32] In summary, as Raquel Álvarez Peláez wrote, the Spanish interest in knowing the natural resources of the American lands came from "the organization of a policy intended to obtain the maximum control and the maximum benefits from the American lands. . . . Reality demanded, for a better exercise of power, developing the study and, in many cases—such as medicinal plants, geographic maps, mining, etc.—scientific knowledge of the new world."[33]

These *relaciones* were created with the idea of obtaining geographical as well as historical and ethnographic information. Clearly, they were a continuation of the imperial literature of the first half of the sixteenth century, although this time with markedly bureaucratic overtones: "The *relaciones* can be seen as the epitome of Philip II´s bureaucratic machinery in an effort to keep control over the empire."[34] This objective is understandable, keeping in mind the legal framework of the time: "It is not inconsequential that this cognitive preoccupation corresponded to a policy shift from conquest to pacification."[35] In fact, as stated in part I of this book, the 1570s saw the enactment of a new type of legislation under Felipe II. Concretely, the new ordinances issued in 1573 referred to the administration and settling of the Spanish American colonies, with the word "conquest" now replaced by the word "pacification."[36]

Spanish-American epic poetry, in its own way and with its own format, was included in that imperial literature. As explained earlier, one of the important themes in *La Araucana* and the *Historia de la Nueva México* is that of the construction of the Spanish empire.[37] Geographical description played an important role in empire-building. From Columbus to Cortés to Fernández de Oviedo and the reports in letter form, this imperial literature of the sixteenth century constituted a model for describing the Americas and its natural environment. Obviously, there are differences in the way each author interpreted what he observed, depending on the region and decade in which he wrote.[38] However, in general, the poems of Ercilla and Villagrá continued a preexisting tendency and can be included as part of the spectrum of imperial literature. Both authors also followed the Renaissance model. It is therefore important to consider these geographic descriptions because they provide antecedents for the manner in which Ercilla and then Villagrá used landscape in their poems.

The inclusion of geography or the observation of nature on the part of both poets coincides with the European attitude of the sixteenth century explained at the beginning of this chapter. The two poets pictured the landscape as "savage" and the land as "remote" and "inhospitable." As a result of living in such a landscape, natives were classified as "fierce" (although also as "brave" and "noble"). Nevertheless, both poets also elected to describe pleasant, restful, green landscapes beside water and with sufficient food—with the aim of showing the importance of the deserved prize after so much suffering. Presenting this type of nature is also related to the participation of the respective heroes of each poem, who are often linked with a natural environment that is benign and harmonious.

Specifically, both poets used the description of geography to represent frontier warfare, invasion, subsequent occupation, and domination. Politically speaking, it suited the authors to present their central topic of warfare as entradas into a geography unknown to them and therefore perceived as hostile. The theme of geography obviously had a fundamental role in Roman classical epic poetry.

What is new here is that the geographic context is different from the European one, and as a result, the two poets use it in a novel way. One example is that they describe entering into territory "upon which no Christian has set foot." This expression is used by both poets, and perhaps Villagrá copied it from Ercilla, since the latter became such an important point of reference for epics about the Americas.[39]

Even though the sixteenth-century Spanish American epic copied a previous classical formula, it took on American characteristics through the deeds that its authors described, in many cases as protagonists or contemporary witnesses to what had occurred. In referring to these particular aspects of the Spanish American epic, Pedro Piñero Ramírez states:

> The adventure of discovery, the temerity of conquering vast and unknown territories, the wonder at seeing a new landscape, with flora and fauna never dreamed of, and the awareness that they were participating in the birth of a new world contributed to the development of a very literalized genre, but one that in those particular circumstances took on new life.[40]

For a poem to be considered epic, the history it relates must include war, feats of one or more heroes, verbal and military confrontations, and antagonism. In *La Araucana* and the *Historia*, the two poets make the description of the landscape an important element to heighten the central theme of violent confrontation. Moreover, the scenery of the armed struggle is a frontier space, which, because of its nature, is converted into imperial space. Therefore, the way the poets describe the landscape of the frontier is closely linked to the particular aspects of the story that they wish to emphasize.

In *La Araucana*, the landscape is linked to the presence of the central heroes (Araucanians and Spaniards). Landscape is also connected to the figure of the poet as a soldier and to the development of the war itself (entrada, settlement, and military confrontations). In the *Historia*, the landscape is linked to the presence of the central hero Juan de Oñate and the Spanish soldiers on the one hand, and the Indians on the other. Obviously, Villagrá also mentions features of natural space in the context of his participation as soldier and the development of the war itself (entrada, settlement, and military confrontation) and also in the conversion of the indigenous people to Christianity.

To explain the role of the landscape in *La Araucana*, it is helpful to turn to literary criticism. Its contributions in numerous analyses of this topic shed light on the importance of geographical description as an essential part of the epic genre, present in both poems. The Spanish writer Marcelino Menéndez y Pelayo argues that Ercilla does not transmit either an exciting or descriptively rich view of Chilean nature. In his now classic study of Spanish American poetry, Menéndez y Pelayo states, referring to *La Araucana*, that "nature is sometimes described, almost never felt, except in the idyll of the southern land and of the archipelago of Chiloé."[41] According to the literary critic, whose work was published in 1913, Chilean historians and geographers agreed that the topographic indications in *La Araucana* were very precise. But he considers that "they are neither graphic nor represent anything to the imagination" and adds that "Ercilla's inferiority in this does not proceed, in my opinion, from his lack of ability as a landscape artist but from the little imagination that in his time was given to what was later called 'local color.'" Menéndez y Pelayo saw the presence of nature in the poem only as linked to the central theme of war.

> It is certain that Ercilla's geographic descriptions lack analytical curiosity . . . But what is ingenious and reveals a privileged poetic organization, is the instinct to associate nature with human life, not as a mute spectator, but intervening, so to speak, in the epic conflict.[42]

Giuseppe Bellini adds that the special feature of Ercilla's description of the landscape is not the abundance of details but the impression he gives of "facing a world different from the Hispanic one."[43] For Bellini, one of the original aspects in *La Araucana* is "the fact that it is born in America, and reflects this, not only in the armed struggle but also in the characteristics of the landscape."[44] Ercilla saw nature and described it, although without abandoning what the Renaissance model imposed upon him.

> The descriptions of storms, of landfalls, of islands, of plains, rivers, and mountains reveal in Ercilla an attentive observer, an enthusiast for the geography in which he moves, who also remained linked to European Renaissance characteristics present in model epic poems without knowing or wanting to move away from them.[45]

Following this line of analysis, other literary critics have debated whether the description of nature in *La Araucana* is conventional (the typical Renaissance pastoral description), realistic, or a mixture of both; or whether what dominates is an idealized description of Chilean nature. Fernando Alegría believes that the way Ercilla describes the landscape is mostly conventional, but more realistic in the scenes in which the poet was physically present in the events he narrates.[46]

Literary critic Beatriz Pastor, in her classification of geography present in the poem, mentions three elements: conventional, realistic, and mythological. According to Pastor, the poet strategically chooses to be conventional when he associates Araucanian civilization with European civilization by means of Renaissance-style description. She notes, however, that the mythological form is present in the personification of the elements of nature (sea, sun, dawn, wind, and so forth), which is another characteristic of the Renaissance epic poem and a further association with the European cultural context.[47] According to Pastor,

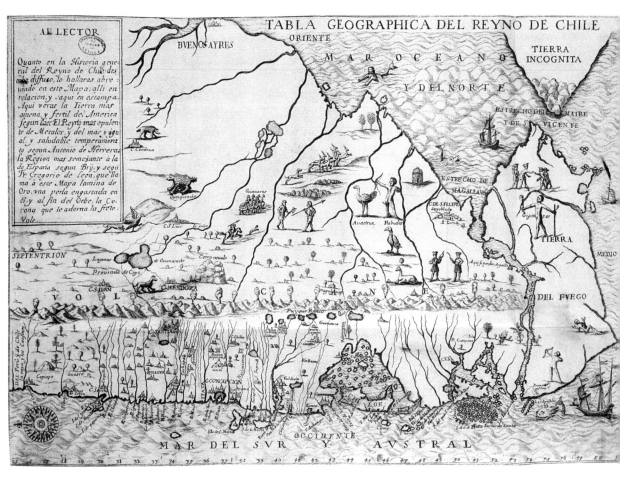

Tabla Geographica del Reyno de Chile (Geographic Map of the Kingdom of Chile), circa 1646.
Archivo General de Indias (Seville), Mapas y Planos, Perú-Chile, 271.

The map shows lands that are today Chile and Argentina, with the Spanish colonies that existed there by the 1640s. The map includes the Tierra del Fuego and the Strait of Magellan. Near the latter is the settlement of San Felipe, founded in 1580 by Pedro Sarmiento de Gamboa and depopulated a few years later. Geographic features shown include the Mar del Sur y Austral (Pacific Ocean) and Mar Océano y del Norte (Atlantic Ocean), populated volcanoes in the Andes, and the latitude (25–59).

Although this map was drawn a century after Alonso de Ercilla's stay in Chile, it shows some of the cities and forts mentioned in *La Araucana*, such as Santiago (inland, near the mountains), Concepción, Chillán, Arauco, Imperial, Villarrica, and Valdivia. These sites had been rebuilt on the original sites where they were founded in the sixteenth century. Rivers such as the Itata and the Biobío are also included, as well as the Canal de Chacao, which probably was the farthest south that the poet went.

140

Ercilla's choice creates the (fictitious) integration of the Araucanian people into Western history, which gives legitimacy to Araucanian history. "By inserting the Araucanian and his feats into Western history, Ercilla symbolically restores to American man a history that, within the poem, substitutes fictitiously and transitorily for the history and indigenous past that the conquest had taken from him."[48]

Rosa Perelmuter-Pérez points out that the lack of description of nature in *La Araucana* is owing, in part, to the fact that "the landscape is subordinated to fighting." The author labels as "idealized" the landscape that Ercilla describes in the conventional manner. This landscape is represented by an Araucanian camp and its Indians. She adds that Ercilla's description serves to create a parenthesis in the poem "where the reader and the characters can rest from the vicissitudes of war."[49] In employing an idealistic form, the description, according to that author, "has little or nothing to do with the real contemplation of nature."[50] Thus Ercilla continues a practice common for the period.

Synthesizing what the literary critics have observed about *La Araucana*, its description of the landscape is produced in three different contexts:

1. Events that happen during frontier war, alluding to the landscape and the Indian presence and also to the landscape and the Spanish presence
2. The poet directly participates in the conquest that he narrates
3. Narration is from a European perspective, evident in such things as a lack of sensitivity to the aesthetics of the landscape (nature is described with a specific purpose and closely linked to the theme of war) and the typical poetic-epic practice of idealized description.

Overarching all three concepts is the use of a literary form that permits the integration of Araucanian history into Western history.

Ercilla, from his perspective as a sixteenth-century conquistador and narrator, invented a geography that can only be understood and accepted as real if it is included in the historical and literary context to which it belongs. In this sense, Ercilla's epic has even been classified as "primitive" and not "cultured" because the poet, with his lack of aesthetic sensibility, "disparages the landscape."[51] Thus, the Andes mountain range is a "range of hills" and the Chacao Channel is a "drainage ditch."[52] Nevertheless, these seemingly limited, if inaccurate, descriptions were common in the literature of the period. The use of substantives such as "drainage ditch" was characteristic of such literature, in which "the lack of knowledge of the terrain creates a confused view that adheres more to the rules of the game of fiction than to those of scientific cartography."[53]

As for Villagrá's description of nature in his *Historia de la Nueva México*, what little has been written about it to date reaffirms the thesis explained for *La Araucana*. Even though Villagrá wrote his poem decades later, the Renaissance influence continues in his descriptions of the landscape. Proof of this is, for example, that he follows a linear succession, tracing a group of people back to their place of origin,[54] a characteristic feature framed in a geographic context. This device stemmed from a fully developed medieval tradition that still persisted in Spain.[55] Literary critics contend that if there is a real element in the description of landscape in Villagrá's *Historia*, this realism derives from the poet's involvement in many of the events he narrates.[56] But with Villagrá following the classical and Renaissance models so closely, and especially the example of Ercilla, the description of landscape in his poem adopts the same characteristics: "a tangled and unknown nature but precisely for this reason, fascinating."[57] However, depending on the context, Villagrá's apparent sensitivity to the landscape is notable, at times with a description more invented than real, at other times with a hostile landscape (for the Spaniards). In this last case,

Map of New Mexico by Enrico Martínez, 1602. Transcription of the original using modern lettering. *George P. Hammond and Agapito Rey, The Rediscovery of New Mexico, 1580–1594 (Albuquerque: University of New Mexico Press, 1966). Original in Archivo General de Indias (Seville), Mapas y Planos, México, 49.*

Martínez drew the map based on the account given by Juan Rodríguez Marinero, who went to New Mexico with Juan de Oñate. This is the first map that shows the Camino Real de Tierra Adentro linking Mexico City with New Mexico. A line with arrows shows the route followed by the 1598 expedition of Juan de Oñate, in which Gaspar de Villagrá participated. The expedition of 1601 is also depicted. The map shows rivers mentioned in Villagrá's poem, such as the Conchos and the Río del Norte (today the Rio Grande).

Places that Villagrá saw and included in his poem include, from south to north: the native villages of Socorro (4), San Cristóbal (12), San Felipe (13), Santo Domingo (14), and Galisteo (15); and the Spanish villages of Nueva Sevilla (6) and San Gabriel (25). This last is marked with a circle and, according to the map, is "where the governor resides." San Gabriel was still the main Spanish settlement in 1602 when the map was drawn.

A line of arrows shows the northeast route that Oñate followed to the plains in 1601. Villagrá himself had by then left New Mexico. The map offers important information about the location of rivers such as the Río Salado (Pecos River), Río de la Magdalena (Canadian River), and Río del Robledal (Arkansas River). The map legend mentions the *pueblo del nuevo descubrimiento* ("village of the new discovery"), north of today's Arkansas River. It was the settlement the natives called Quivira, probably near today's Wichita, Kansas.

The writing on the upper left of the map says that from that point (A): "up to the village of the new discovery all is plains with many cows that they call *civola*" (the native name for buffalo). Villagrá describes buffalo in his poem, as well as the vast plains.

The map includes the latitude (31°–38° N) and longitude (268°) in relation to the Island of Tenerife, Canary Islands). The Mar del Sur (Pacific Ocean) is shown, and in the lower right corner the mapmaker included the Gulf of Mexico, Río de las Palmas, and the important coastal city of Veracruz, with the fort of San Juan de Ulúa.

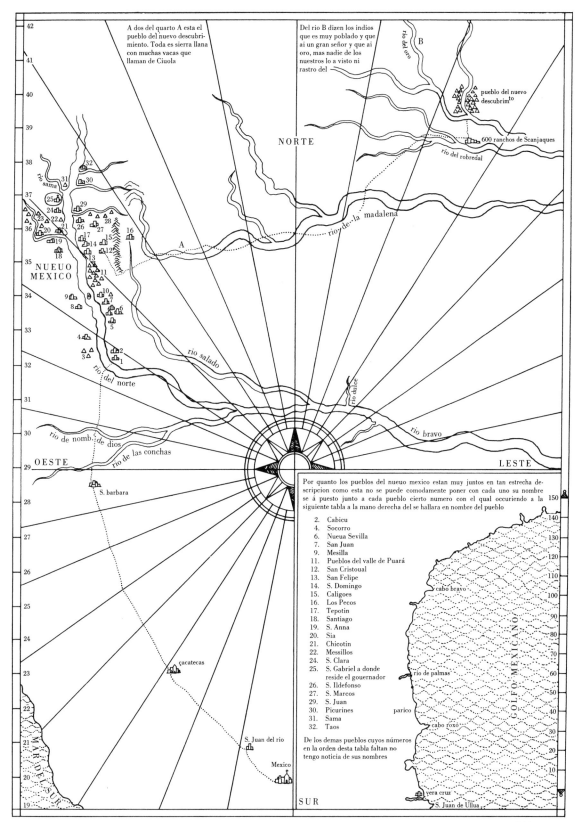

the similarity to Ercilla's descriptions in *La Araucana* is striking, especially the dramatic scenes in which the Spaniards must confront exhaustion, hunger, and thirst in the midst of what appears to them to be a defiant nature.

In general, the geographic context in the *Historia* appears to be closely tied to the central theme and subthemes of the poem. Descriptions of the landscape do not abound, and when they appear and move to the forefront through the detail and drama of the story, it is because they tend to be connected with the Spanish presence. Only on certain occasions are they linked to the indigenous presence, in contrast to *La Araucana*. Even the description of fauna, specifically the episode of the buffalo hunt, culminates in a demonstration of Spanish superiority when they kill the animals with firearms. The poet sees a landscape delimited or framed by the specific objectives of the conquest of New Mexico: the domination of a frontier land with a sedentary indigenous population, and the conversion of the people to Catholicism. Even though his *Historia* was published in 1610, Villagrá described nature—within the framework of Spanish presence—through the eyes of a conquistador of the first half of the sixteenth century.

In the following chapters, specific examples of the thesis presented here will be examined, but it seems appropriate to conclude this chapter with at least a few concrete cases, by way of a preview. At the same time, these examples will help illustrate both concepts: the American epic and the frontier epic, and the reasons why Ercilla and Villagrá followed a common model when it came to including geography in their poetry.

The practice of pinpointing the exact location of the conquered region was common among colonial chroniclers of the first half of the sixteenth century. Almost all began by describing the surroundings of the territory they saw and set foot in for the first time. References to east and west, north and south abound. To the cardinal points are joined the longitude and latitude traversed. "This first circulating view is therefore essential to the notion and conceptualization that after the sixteenth century, the European makes of the *Novo Orbe*. Primitivism, exoticism, racism would have their roots there."[58]

Thus, the geographic location of each frontier appears in the first canto of both poems. Villagrá's style is very similar to Ercilla's, and both, in turn, follow an existing model; imitation in the field of epic poetry was nothing new. Each poet presents the respective frontier, projecting the idea of the remote land in which the Spaniards had arrived. Ercilla states:

Es Chile norte sur de gran longura, costa del nuevo mar, del Sur llamado, tendrá del leste a oeste de angostura	From North to South, Chile is of great length, called the coast of the new Sea of the South, from east to west it narrows to

cien millas,[59] por lo más ancho tomado;   one hundred miles at its widest point;
bajo del polo Antártico en altura   under the South Pole in height
de veinte y siete grados, prolongado   extends twenty-seven degrees
hasta do el mar Océano y chileno   to where the Ocean and Chile
mezclan sus aguas por angosto seno.   mix their waters in a narrow gulf.
    (Ercilla, *La Araucana*, 1.7, 1–8)

Villagrá locates New Mexico geographically in this way:

Debajo el polo Artico en altura   Beneath the Arctic Pole, in height
De los treinta y tres grados que a la santa   Some thirty-three degrees, which the same
Ierusalem sabemos que responden,   Are, we know, of sainted Jerusalem,
No sin grande misterio y maravilla,   Not without mystery and marvel great,
Se esparcen, tienden, siembran y   Are spread, extended, sown, and overflow
  derraman   Some nations barbarous, remote
Unas naciones bárbaras, remotas
    (Villagrá, *Historia*, 1, 49–54)

Y en longitud nos muestran su districto,   And shows to us its location in longitude,
Según que nos enseña y nos pratica   According as most modern fixed meridian
El meridiano fixo más moderno,   Doth teach us and we practice,
Dozientos y setenta grados justos   Two hundred just degrees and seventy
En la templada zona y cuarto clima   Into the temperate zone and the fourth
                                           clime

    (Villagrá, *Historia*, 1, 63–67)

The coincidence between the latitude of New Mexico and Jerusalem is an example of the importance of the religious theme in Villagrá's poem. According to modern editors of the *Historia*, the comparison "is meant to underscore the then widely held idea that the former, with great significance for Spain's missionary goals, had been especially preserved by God."[60] In addition, an analysis by scholar Francisco Lomelí links geographic space and mythic allusion in the *Historia* through the sites between Central México and New Mexico: "placing New Mexico as the protagonist of the story as both a place and a mythic text."[61] According to Lomelí, "the narrative emphasizes a south to north axis as the story moves away from central México to New Mexico, the latter serving as the main geographical destination, except that the move is filtered through the imagination rather than a physical space."[62] Villagrá's tendency to look at space as imbued with myth provides Lomelí with his main argument to prove that, although Villagrá tries to highlight the greatness of the Spanish conquest, when including the land in his poem, he "dwells on a vertical, in-depth view of the indigenous inhabitants."[63] This conclusion from the perspective of literary criticism offers a good point to begin an analysis of the indigenous theme in both poems.

Is *La Araucana* a poem that extols indigenous greatness, and the *Historia de la Nueva México* a poem that praises Spanish valor? Or are the two aspects equally important in both poems? Is there a clear intent in the two poems to present a view of the Americas that is more European than American? Is war on the frontier—the entrada and its violent aftermath—the concept that most unifies the two poems? How can an element such as the description of nature, so often used in epic poetry, assist in answering these questions? The next chapters are dedicated to discussing these topics.

The Indians and Their Natural Space

Un paso peligroso, agrio y estrecho de la banda del norte está a la entrada, por un monte asperísimo y derecho, la cumbre hasta los cielos levantada; está tras éste un llano, poco trecho, y luego otra menor cuesta tajada que divide el distrito andalicano del fértil valle y límite araucano.	A dangerous pass, rough and narrow to the north lies the entrance, through a rugged and erect mountain the summit raised to the sky; behind is a plain, at a short distance, followed by another slope which divides the Andalican district of the fertile valley and the Araucano boundary.
Esta cuesta Lautaro había elegido para dar la batalla, y por concierto tenía todo su ejército tendido en lo más alto della y descubierto;	This slope Lautaro had selected to do battle, and by agreement he had his entire army laid out at the highest and most exposed point;

   (Ercilla, *La Araucana*, 4.90, 1–8; 91, 1–4)

Y assí, marchando en orden, nos llegamos, Al poderoso fuerte, el cual constaba De dos grandes peñoles levantados, Mas de trecientos passos devididos Los terribles asientos no domados, Y estaba un passamán del uno al otro, De riscos tan soberbios que igualaban Con las disformes cumbres nunca vistas, Desde cuyos asientos fue contando Zutacapán la gente que venía En orden dando vuelta a sus murallas.	Thus, marching in order, we did arrive Before the mighty fort, which consisted Of two great, lofty rocks upraised, The terrible, unconquered sites Divided by more than three hundred feet, And from one to the other was a neck Of rocks so lofty they equaled The outside peaks, such as were never seen. From these summits Zutacapán Was counting the people who came, In order marching round those walls.

   (Villagrá, *Historia*, 27, 117–27)

The images projected by the two poets in the previous lines are those of two indigenous leaders, the Araucanian Lautaro and Acoma's Zutacapán (a fictitious name given by Villagrá), preparing themselves to face the Spanish enemy in their land. The view the reader imagines is that of natives who knew their territory and its topography, but the description in no way conveys what the Indians thought and felt about their natural space. Nor do these lines reflect what the Indians felt as they prepared themselves to defend their ancestral space.

It can be argued—and in large measure this is what this second part of the volume deals with—that neither Ercilla nor Villagrá attempted to interpret what the natural space represented physically and spiritually for the Indians. That was not the main goal of their poems. Chapter 3 previewed some examples of how nature was described in the imperial literature of the Renaissance and well into the eighteenth century. The difference in meaning of space, nature, and cosmology for Europeans and Indians is best explained by examining the core concepts of indigenous world views; in particular, that of the indigenous peoples of New Mexico. For indigenous peoples, the idea of interdependence between person, community, and world was central. According to scholar Gregory Cajete:

> The geographical and structural orientations of indigenous communities to their natural place and the cosmos reflected a communal consciousness that extended to and included the natural world in an intimate and mutually reciprocal relationship. Through clan and societal symbolism, ritual, art, and visionary tradition, members connected themselves to the plants, animals, waters, mountains, sun, moon, stars, and planets of their world.[1]

The concept of connectedness is pivotal to the experiences of the members of an indigenous community from birth to death.[2] That interdependence is as ancient as the very origin of the individual: "Tribal people share in a deep and abiding relationship to place."[3] Thus, natural geography is crucial to the identification of one's place, and the "spirit of place" is considered sacred. For the Indian people, in contrast with the Europeans, "the land was full of spirit, full of life energy" from a rock or a tree, to a mountain or an insect. "The land and the place in which they lived were in a perfect state. The real test of living was to be able to establish a harmonious relationship with that perfect nature."[4] Furthermore, the "spirit of place" is an inseparable part of a natural landscape.

Allegories and metaphors are commonly used to explain the orientation of four directions in space according to indigenous tradition. The cardinal points are associated with plants, animals, and natural phenomena: "And each of the plants and animals represents a perspective, a way of looking at something in the center that humans are trying to know."[5] Landscape, understood as natural space, has a spiritual and mythic meaning. Histories, experiences, and rituals are associated with the physical elements of the landscape.[6] An example is found in the lines the Acoma poet Simón Ortiz uses to describe "the Acoma story of place," which are in stark contradiction to Villagrá's lines cited in the epigraph of this chapter.

> And they came to a Place That Was Prepared,
> the tall, massive stone they know as Aacqu.

Like all the other Pueblo people, the Acoma
have always known where the center is.[7]

Similarly, other lines written by Ortiz show the contrast between the Acoma cosmological vision and that of the Spaniards. In his poem "Land and Stars, the Only Knowledge," he writes:

North, West, South, and East.
Above and Below and All around.
Within knowledge of the land,
We are existent.
Within knowledge of the stars,
We are existent.
Coldness and wind and the snow, northward.
Mildness and mountain and the rain, westward
Hotness and desert and the hail, southward.
Warmness and mesa and the sun, eastward.
Starshine and sky and the darkness, upward.
Earthsource and stone and the light, downward.[8]

Ortiz wrote these lines at the end of the twentieth century, but they convey the beliefs of the natives of New Mexico four centuries earlier. The importance that "the knowledge of the land and the stars" has for natives is evident, as well as the meaning of the four directions.

Villagrá's mode of presenting the New Mexican geography follows the model set by the chroniclers and adheres to a general rule of the times, for early in his poem he pinpoints the location about which he is writing. The lines of the first canto cited in the epigraph to chapter 3 of this book are a good example of what information the poet wants to highlight. He mentions that New Mexico is at 37 degrees latitude. In the lines following this fact, he mentions that the land was inhabited by "people ignorant of the blood of Christ." Thus in the first canto, at the same time as he presents the location of New Mexico, he establishes the religious theme that would prevail in the rest of the poem. Moreover, in this first presentation of the native population, it does not seem important to the poet to describe the Indians in any more appropriate way. Ercilla followed the same canon of location, precisely stating the geographical area that is the scene of the war. He fuses together natural characteristics of the region (fertility of the Chilean soil) with those of the Araucanians (proud and warlike people).

Chile, fértil provincia y señalada	Chile, fertile and eminent province
en la región antártica famosa,	in the famous Antarctic region,
de remotas naciones respetada	by remote nations respected
por fuerte, principal y poderosa;	as strong, principal and powerful;
la gente que produce es tan granada,	the people it produces are so great,

tan soberbia, gallarda y belicosa,	so arrogant, gallant, and warlike,
que no ha sido por rey jamás regida	they have never been ruled by a king
ni a estranjero dominio sometida.	nor submitted to the reign of a foreigner.
(Ercilla, *La Araucana*, 1.6, 1–8)	

The lines cited from *La Araucana* and the *Historia* are examples that show, from the first canto of both poems, the particular perspective from which each poet handles the theme of the Indians and their spaces. Both Ercilla and Villagrá include a description of nature, which they associate with the presence of the Indians. It is Ercilla who gives the Indian the greater role, nonetheless, whether in the context of natural space or through allegory.

Literary critics have debated Ercilla's manner of portraying Chilean nature and the physical characteristics of the Araucanians, particularly in regard to the physical strength that made them good warriors. Ercilla considers their bellicose quality to be a reflection of the geographical location of Chile (the climate) and also of destiny (fate).[9]

En fin, el hado y clima desta tierra,	In short, the fate and the climate of this country,
si su estrella y pronósticos se miran,	if its stars and fortune are examined,
es contienda, furor, discordia, guerra	is conflict, fury, discord, war
y a solo esto los ánimos aspiran.	and only to this do the spirits aspire.
Todo su bien y mal aquí se encierra,	All the good and bad are enclosed here,
son hombres que de súbito se aíran,	they are men that easily become irritated,
de condiciones feroces, impacientes,	of fierce and impatient condition,
amigos de domar extrañas gentes.	inclined to dominate foreign people.
(Ercilla, *La Araucana*, 1.45, 1–8)	

Thus, nature is represented in the physical characteristics of the Araucanians, a demonstration of the consonance between humans and their environment.[10] The physical appearance and ferocity of the Araucanian people, as the poet sees it, are related to the harsh geographical conditions of their land.[11] In this case, the metaphor of the rough natural environment is used to support one of the subthemes of the poem: the Indian as hero. A further example (in canto 15) is the uncontrollable winds—an analogy for the Araucanian character—that greet the arrival of the Spanish fleet in Chile and its new leader, García Hurtado de Mendoza: "the native resistance is refigured in the natural forces of the storm."[12]

Ercilla's use of the trope of consonance between the humans and their landscape functions perfectly in an epic poem. It should therefore not be assumed that Ercilla's poetry corresponds to historical reality. As the Chilean historian Sergio Villalobos has observed, the poet's use of this method should not be construed to mean that the Araucanian race was warlike by nature, or that this "military race" passed its characteristics on to its mestizo descendants, the Chileans.[13] Villalobos adds:

> The Araucanians were not a warrior race, because there are no warrior races, rather each pueblo develops fighting abilities or those of any other type, impelled by the necessities of the moment. For several centuries before the arrival of the Spaniards, the Araucanian tribes had lived at war among themselves for various reasons.[14]

According to Villalobos, the myth of "the militaristic character, of a warlike and patriotic nature, repeated without criticism in the country, is the consequence of racism at the beginning of the century that has been maintained by the inertia of prejudice."[15]

Elsewhere in *La Araucana*, the description of nature veers in a different direction and Ercilla portrays an idealized and paradisiacal landscape. It is worth noting, however, that in the prologue to part 2, Ercilla chooses to connect the Araucanians with a more or less infertile nature: "some dry terrain" and "uncultivated and stony fields."[16] The poet is trying to demonstrate how the Araucanians' struggle in defense of their territory is even more praiseworthy because it concerns land without material value. Ercilla wishes to convey qualities of valor, fortitude, and pride on the part of the natives, who are prepared to defend their land at all costs. The poet appears contradictory with respect to his assessment of geography, unless one takes into account that Ercilla was intentionally drawing on certain literary techniques to make his epic history more effective.

That the author devotes most of the first canto of *La Araucana* to describing the Araucanians, their customs, their natural space, and their great knowledge of nature says much about one of the objectives of the poem, which is to emphasize the Indians as protagonists. Of these first stanzas, the ones devoted to presenting the Araucanians' thorough knowledge of their physical space, especially in the context of warfare, are worth highlighting here.

De pantanos procuran guarnecerse	With the swamps they protect themselves
por el daño y temor de los caballos,	from the damage and dread of horses,
donde suelen a veces acogerse	where they, at times, shelter themselves
si viene a suceder desbaratallos;	if it happens they are routed;
allí pueden seguro rehacerse,	there they can safely regroup,
ofenden sin que puedan enojallos,	insulting without angering,
que el falso sitio y gran inconveniente	that the treacherous and highly unsuitable site
impide la llegada a nuestra gente.	impedes the approach of our people.

(Ercilla, *La Araucana*, 1.25, 1–8)

Ercilla's description in this part of his poem is especially significant because it anticipates the connection between military tactics and terrain that he will mention later in the context of battle against the Spaniards. Ercilla continues,

Hacen fuerzas o fuertes cuando entienden	They build fortresses when they recognize
ser el lugar y sitio en su provecho,	it is the place and location of advantage,
o si ocupar un término pretenden,	or if they claim to occupy a boundary,
o por algún aprieto y grande estrecho;	or some risky and long narrow passageway;
de do más a su salvo se defienden	where, without injury, they can defend themselves
y salen de rebato a caso hecho,	and attack suddenly,
recogiéndose a tiempo al sitio fuerte.	retiring quickly to the fortified site.

       (Ercilla, *La Araucana*, 1.28, 1–7)

There are, however, other lines in this first canto where Ercilla associates a gentle nature with the indigenous presence, specifically with activities related to the Araucanian custom of gathering in councils. These were meetings in which the principal caciques made decisions or resolved situations that affected the entire tribe.

Hácese este concilio en un gracioso	The loveliest nook in the woods is chosen
asiento de mil florestas escogido,	for the assembled council's setting,
donde se muestra el campo más hermoso	where the most beautiful countryside is
de infinidad de flores guarnecido;	garnished with a world of flora;
allí de un viento fresco y amoroso	there by fresh and amorous breezes
los árboles se mueven con ruido,	trees are rocked with rustling,
cruzando muchas veces por el prado	and a tranquil and limpid brook
un claro arroyo limpio y sosegado,	crosses many times the meadow,[17]

        (Ercilla, *La Araucana*, 1.38, 1–8)

La Araucana here represents a type of early colonial literature that sought to connect the land with the idea of paradise or a utopia in which everything was perfect and harmonious because of the isolation in which the people lived. Hence, Ercilla's description of nature has been linked to the concept of idealized landscape. Ercilla's description of the archipelagos of southern Chile and its inhabitants is one such example of an idyllic landscape.

Al fin una mañana descubrimos	Finally one morning we discovered
de Ancud el espacioso y fértil raso,	the fertile and spacious plain Ancud,
y al pie del monte y áspera ladera	and at the foot of the mountain and sharp hill
un estendido lago y gran ribera.	a large lake and great coast.
Era un ancho archipiélago, poblado	It was a wide archipelago, filled
de innumerables islas deleitosas,	with countless delightful islands,

cruzando por el uno y otro lado	crossing by one side and other
góndolas y piraguas presurosas.	rapid gondolas and canoes;
(Ercilla, *La Araucana*, 35.40, 5–8; 41, 1–4)	

The lake described by Ercilla is called Llauquihue. Traveling around its coast toward the south, the Spanish group came to the bay of Reloncaví, which in the Mapudungún language means "reunion of valleys" or where the valleys meet. This is where they saw the small islands that the poet refers to. The use of terms such as "gondolas and piraguas" is worthy of note: the first is of European origin and the second an indigenous word from the Caribbean. According to Isaías Lerner, Ercilla was the first to use the term "gondola" in a literary piece.[17]

Ercilla subsequently mentions having been well received by the Indians of the place. His description of the behavior of the Indian leader who received them links the geographic theme of climate to the physical aspect of the Indians and their clothing.

Mucho agradó la suerte, el garbo, el traje	We were pleased by the garb, the dress
del gallardo mancebo floreciente,	of the gallant flourishing young man,
el expedido término y lenguaje	the expedient term and language
con que así nos habló bizarramente;	with which he gallantly spoke to us;
el franco ofrecimiento y hospedaje,	the frank offer and lodging,
la buena traza y talle de la gente,	the good appearance and shape of the
blanca, dispuesta, en proporción fornida,	people,
de mano y floja túnica vestida;	white, willing, of hefty proportion,
	dressed with cloak and slack tunic;
la cabeza cubierta y adornada	
con un capelo en punta rematado	head covered and adorned
pendiente atrás la punta y derribada,	with an embroidered cardinal's hat
a las ceñidas sienes ajustado,	a sloping tip pulled down in back,
de fina lana de vellón rizada	adjusted tight to the temples,
y el rizo de colores variados,	made of fine curly fleece wool
que lozano y vistoso parecía	and the swirl of varied colors,
señal de ser el clima y tierra fría.	that it seemed luxuriant and showy
	a sign of a cold climate and land.
(Ercilla, *La Araucana*, 36.7, 1–8; 8, 1–8)	

The poet's message is that the lack of contact with Europeans allowed these paradises to persist. In the words of Beatriz Pastor: "The corrupting and destructive effects of the conquest are announced here in an explicit way."[18]

La sincera bondad y la caricia	The sincere kindness and caring
de la sencilla gente destas tierras	of the simple people of these lands
daban bien a entender que la cudicia	truly gave to understand that greed
aún no había penetrado aquellas sierras;	had not yet penetrated those mountains;
(Ercilla, *La Araucana*, 36.13, 1–4)	

Salían muchos caciques al camino	Many caciques came to the road
a vernos como a cosa milagrosa,	to look at us as a miraculous thing,
pero ninguno tan escaso vino	but none scarcely came
que no trujese en don alguna cosa:	who did not bring a gift of some kind:
(Ercilla, *La Araucana*, 36.18, 1–4)	

In sum, Chilean geography in *La Araucana* appears to be especially linked to the Indian presence, with emphasis on the natives' knowledge of their geography. The severe natural environment of Chile, matched by its brave indigenous people, intersect in the central theme of war. These similes contrast with interludes of idyllic landscapes inhabited by gentle people.

In the *Historia de la Nueva México*, Villagrá uses the description of nature more often when discussing the Spaniards than when discussing the Indians. Nevertheless, it is worth analyzing the occasions when Villagrá avails himself of the poetic identification of the Indians with the geographic environment they inhabit. Such references generally appear in situations where geography collaborates in some way to highlight the epic characteristics of the poem. This is the case in the account of the origin of the Indians, including allusions to legend, and the reference to the Indians' geographical knowledge of their physical space and the use of its natural resources. It is remarkable how often Villagrá alludes to classical mythology and looks to the authors of the classical epic and Ercilla's poem for inspiration. The theme of nature linked to the indigenous presence in the *Historia* is a reminder of Villagrá's knowledge of the techniques of epic poetry and his ability to adapt them to the context of the northern frontier of the Spanish American empire.[19]

In the first canto, Villagrá opts for the typical use of legend in the epic, in this case that of the ancient Mexicans, the Aztecs, who, led by two brothers, wandered southward looking for the legendary place where they would found Tenochtitlan. In telling the story, Villagrá makes constant reference to geographic locations to show the journey the Aztecs made from north to south. The poet refers here to the mythological name of the north wind and to the legend of its capture in a cave.

Dixeron, pues, aquellos naturales,	They told us then, those native folk,
Unánimes, conformes y de un voto,	Unanimous, agreed, and with one voice,
Que de la tierra adentro, señalando	That from that land beyond, and pointing out
Aquella parte donde el norte esconde	That section where the North doth hide
Del presuroso Boreas esforzado	The hollow cavern, craggy,
La cóncava caverna desabrida,	Of vigorous and hasty Boreas,
Salieron dos briosíssimos hermanos	There came two courageous brethren,
De altos y nobles Reyes descendientes,	Of high and noble Kings descended,

(Villlagrá, *Historia*, 1, 117–23)

In the midst of details of a supernatural world and with many allusions to European mythology, Villagrá uses the character of the devil, who appears dressed as a "fierce old woman" who tells the two brothers that one of them should go back north and the other one continue south. Thus, the poet presents the story of the Aztec (or Mexica) migration from the north to the south to end at the place in central Mexico that would become the Aztec capital of Mexico-Tenochtitlan. Along with the Nahua legend, the poet relates important geographic information on native origins. Danna Levin Rojo, in her book *Return to Aztlán: Indians, Spaniards, and the Invention of Nuevo México*, offers a detailed analysis of Villagrá's use of Nahua mythology in his poem, which includes "the central elements of the Aztec/Mexica migration as recounted in Nahua tradition,"[20] specifically in the poem's section on the Aztecs' settlement in central Mexico. In the legend, as recounted by Villagrá, the old woman anticipates how to locate the exact spot for establishing the city.

Mas donde en duro y sólido peñasco,	But where on a hard and solid rock
De christalinas aguas bien cercado,	Girded by waters crystalline
Viéredeis una Tuna estar plantada,	A cactus planted you shall see
Y sobre cuias gruessas y anchas hojas	Upon whose thick and spreading leaves
Una Aguila caudal bella, disforme,	A beautiful red-tailed eagle sits, quite enormous,
Con braveza cebando se estuviere	And it be eating greedily
En una gran culebra que a sus garras	On a great snake that in his claws,
Veréys que está rebuelta y bien assida,	As you shall see, is twisting, but well gripped.
Que allí quiere se funde y se lebante	Here it is willed that you shall found and raise
La metrópoli alta y generosa	The lofty, generous metropolis
Del poderoso estado señalado,	Of the strong state indicated.
Al qual expresamente manda	For which 'tis ordered most express
Que México Tenuchtitlán se ponga.	It Mexico Tenochtitlan be named.

(Villagrá, *Historia*, 2, 97–109)

Villagrá goes on to describe the division of the land between the two brothers and their people.

Será bien señalaros los linderos,	It will be well to mark the limits down,
Términos y mojones de las tierras	The borders and the boundaries of the lands
Que cada cual por sólo su gobierno	That each for his sole governance
Ha de reconocer sin que pretenda	Will accept, nor pretend
Ninguno otro dominio más ni menos	To any other rule, not more nor less
De lo que aquí quedare señalado.	Than that which shall be there assigned to him.

(Villagrá, *Historia*, 2, 117–22)

La retaguardia toda dio la vuelta	All the rear guard did turn again
Para la dulce patria que dexaban	Toward that sweet fatherland they'd left
Por la parte del Norte riguroso,	In regions of the hardy North,
Y para el Sur fue luego prosiguiendo,	And toward the South there still kept on
La vanguardia, contenta, le da, ufana,	The vanguard, marching proudly and content,

(Villagrá, *Historia*, 2, 153–57)

The poem's reference to the Aztec migration deserves some attention. The Spaniards learned the story from the natives and then used it in regard to the physical space they themselves were trying to conquer. Levin Rojo's analysis helps us understand that Mesoamerican indigenous views came into play as "part of the conqueror's cognitive repertoire, molding their expectations and inform- ing their interpretation of the landscape and people they subsequently came across."[21] The author develops her thesis concerning the great "impact that local indigenous knowledge and cosmology had on the conqueror's understanding of America's geographic and cultural reality."[22] She touches on the argument that native sources influenced the Spaniards by making them aware of "an empirical reality that would support the idea of extending the colonization to the north."[23] Levin Rojo incorporates the role of Villagrá and his poem in her study in the context of what she terms the "invention of Nuevo México."

Certain lines in the *Historia* offer evidence of what the poet had learned from indigenous sources in Mexico. He makes direct reference to New Mexico and the origins of its native population as part of the story of Aztec migration.

Y aquesta misma historia que he contado	And this same story which I here have told
Sabemos, gran señor, que se pratica	We know, great lord, is oft related
En lo que nueva México llamamos,	In that same place we call New Mexico,
Donde así mismo fuimos informados	Where, we ourselves were told,
Ser todos forasteros, y apuntando	They all were strangers, and in so narrating
Al pasar dan indicio se quedaron	The long journey of those two brethren,
Sus padres y mayores, y señalan	In passing, they do say, their forefathers and ancestors
Al levantado norte, donde dizen	Remained, and they point out
Y afirman ser de allá su descendencia.	The far off Northland, whence they say
	And do affirm themselves to be descended.

(Villagrá, *Historia*, 2, 204–13)

Villagrá mentions the example of the ruins, known today as Casas Grandes, in Chihuahua, Mexico, as an indication of the former Mexican presence in the region.

Y haber salido destas nuevas tierras	And having come from these new lands,
Los finos Mexicanos nos lo muestra	The fine Mexicans, is proved to us by
Aquella gran Ciudad desbaratada	The ruins of that great city
Que en la Nueva Galicia todos vemos,	Which we all see in New Galicia,
De gruessos edificios derribados	Of mighty buildings, all laid waste, if
Donde los naturales de la tierra	Where they, the natives of the land,
Dizen que la plantaron y fundaron	Say it was made and founded there
Los nuevo Mexicanos que salieron	By those New Mexicans who came
De aquesta nueva tierra que buscamos.	Out of the new land that we seek.
(Villagrá, *Historia*, 2, 229–38)	

It is noteworthy that in his account of the geographic origin of the Indians, Villagrá mentions that he is of the opinion that they all came from Asia. He makes no mention, however, of native accounts about the provenience of the Indians found in their creation stories.

Que para mí yo tengo que salieron	Who, for myself, I think that they did come
De la gran China todos los que habitan	From the great China, all who live,
Lo que llamamos Indias.	In what we call the Indies.
(Villagrá, *Historia*, 2, 296–98)	

After having made use of legend as a technique of the epic, and of offering through it the explanation of the origin of the Mexicans and of the Indians of the Americas in general, Villagrá mentions that this information was an indication to the Spaniards that they were on the right path to New Mexico.

Y assí como por brújula descubre	And thus, just as the skillful gambler discovers
El buen tahur la carta desseada,	The much desired card as with compass,
Asegurando el resto que ha metido,	Saving the money he has bet,
Assí, con estas pintas y señales	E'en so, by these same traces and these signs
Seguros, assentamos todo el campo	Assured we set up the whole camp
En el gustoso albergue descubierto.	Within this pleasing refuge we'd discovered
(Villagrá, *Historia*, 2, 265–70)	

A relevant connection can be made here with Villagrá's cultural identity and personal history. The recourse to indigenous knowledge indicates that he, like many other Spaniards in Mexico, not only had learned about indigenous cultures but was interested in demonstrating that aspect of his heritage with pride. Of course, he frequently cites cultural information originating from his European heritage, for example, the references to ancient European history, poetry, and mythology. It seems that in this aspect of the geographic space, he found a way to unite, as a criollo, his two backgrounds.

Manuel Martín Rodríguez likewise discusses the use of indigenous sources in the *Historia*. He points out the poet's ability to combine "classic tradition and prehispanic inheritance." He also notes the importance the *Historia* gives to the Aztec tradition when "the only omen regarding a 'promised land' is in reference to the already distant Aztecs and not to the contemporary soldiers of Oñate."[24] However, perhaps we can see an example of something close to an omen, but one that might more aptly be called predestination, when Villagrá refers to New Mexico as being geographically at the same latitude as Jerusalem, as in the lines cited in chapter 3 of this book. In that instance the poet is looking at his Hispanic inheritance as an important point of reference. Geographic location again becomes relevant to Villagrá's presentation of the story.

Villagrá credits the Indians for their geographical knowledge in the sections that mention the use of Indian guides. One in particular stands out. The section is devoted to the Indian Villagrá calls Mómpil, who gives the Spaniards a geography lesson by using an arrowhead to draw a complete map on the ground.

Y assí, como si bien cursado fuera	As though he had been educated
En nuestra mathemática más cierta,	In our most accurate mathematics,
Casi que quiso a todos figurarnos	As if he wished to draw for us
La línea y el Zodíaco y los signos,	The line, the Zodiac, and the signs,
En largo cada qual de treinta grados,	Each one thirty degrees in length,
Los dos remotos Polos milagrosos,	The two remote, miraculous, Poles,
El Artico y Antártico cumplidos,	The Arctic and the Antarctic entire,
Los poderosos círculos y el exe.	The mighty circles, the axle.
(Villagrá, *Historia*, 12, 431–38)	

Puso del Sur y Norte los dos mares,	He put the two Seas of the North and South,
Con Islas, fuentes, montes y lagunas	With islands, springs, mountains, and lakes,
Y otros asientos, puestos y estalajes.	And other features, places, parts.
(Villagrá, *Historia*, 12, 441–43)	

The native cartographer also located the Río del Norte that the Spaniards so eagerly sought, as well as the final objective of their route, a sedentary Indian population.

Pintonos la circunvezina tierra	He painted for us the neighboring lands
Y el asiento del caudaloso Río	And the location of the mighty stream
Por quien tantos trabajos se sufrieron	For which so many toils were borne,

Y todos los aguages y jornadas	And all the water holes and day's marches
Que era fuerza tener en el camino	That one must needs make on the way
Por aber de beber sus turbias aguas	To have their turbid waters to drink in.
(Villagrá, *Historia*, 12, 445–50)	

Allí pintó también las poblaciones	There he drew, too, the villages
De nuestra nueva México y sus tierras,	Of our New Mexico, its lands,
Poniendo y dándose a entender en todo	Making us understand it all
Como si muy sagaz piloto fuera.	As he were a most learned guide.
(Villagrá, *Historia*, 12, 458–61)	

Villagrá refers to himself as a witness to what he writes. The positive impression that Mómpil made on him inspired him to dedicate the quite eloquent lines at the end of the canto to the guide. This is one of only a handful of occasions on which Villagrá speaks of the Indians with such admiration.

Y por la mucha parte que me cupo,	And for the great part that I had in it,
Será bien que celebre la grandeza	'Tis well I celebrate the grandeur
De la más alta bárbara, gallarda	Of that most elevated, spirited barbarian,
De pecho y corazón el más rendido	In spirit and in heart the most obsequious
Que en bárbara nación se a conocido.	That in a barbarous nation was ever known.
(Villagrá, *Historia*, 12, 465–69)	

Scholar Francisco Lomelí adduces the encounter with Mómpil as proof of how Villagrá's story "is overwhelmed by the mystique of the region for its unabashed independence and autonomy, its brave Pueblo natives and their pride." The poet's plan of glorifying the Spanish conquest falters as "Spaniards find themselves at the mercy of the indigenous people." Lomelí mentions an important aspect of the poet's encounter with the adversary and ties it to a similar view by Ercilla in his *La Araucana*. In the Mómpil episode, Villagrá "reaches the point of admiring their [the Indians'] personal and community makeup in the same manner that Ercilla praised the leader Colo and other indigenous protagonists for their larger-than-life qualities."[25]

Another allusion to the Indians' knowledge of the region occurs when the Spanish ask them for a guide to go to the plains to hunt buffalo.

Con esto, le pidieron que una guía	At this, they asked him if he would
Fuesse servido darles y que fuesse	Be pleased to furnish them a guide who would
Tal que a todos juntos los llevase	Be such as could conduct them all
A los llanos que todos pretendían.	To those plains which they all were searching for.
(Villagrá, *Historia*, 16, 255–58)	

And, specifically in the context of warfare, Villagrá notes the Indian leaders' knowledge of their land, demonstrated by their use of caves and hiding places during the battle of Acoma.[26]

Villagrá's presentation of the Indians, whether in the context of geographic location or in the description of nature, was inspired by the classical authors he favored. A concrete example is the idea of nature in a dream, an artifice that originated with Virgil and that is included in the *Historia* in the midst of a love story between the Indians Polca and Milco. Polca arrives at the Spanish camp searching for his beloved Milco, but he eventually escapes from the Spanish camp without her. Night falls and everyone goes to sleep, and then the Indian cosmographer Mómpil also escapes. Villagrá describes the night thus:[27]

Y luego que en mitad del alto Polo,	And when in the midst of the lofty Pole,
Según aquel varón heroico canta,	As that heroic man doth sing,
Los Astros levantados demediaron	The lofty stars were 'minishing
El poderoso curso bien tendido,	Their mighty, wide-extended course,
En el mayor silencio de la noche,	In the great silence of the night,
Quando las bravas bestias en el campo	When the brave beasts throughout the fields
Y los más razionales en sus lechos	And those more rational in their beds,
Y los pezes en su alto mar profundo	The fish in their great, profound deep,
Y las parleras aves en sus breñas	The chattering birds upon their boughs,
En agradable sueño amodorrido	All sunk in agreeable sleep
Reposan con descuido sus cuidados,	Repose in freedom from their cares,

(Villagrá, *Historia*, 13, 270–80)

Allusions to the Indians' use of natural resources appear on occasions in which the poet introduces the topic of the different lives of nomadic versus sedentary Indians. Arriving on the banks of the Río del Norte, the advance party of Spaniards encountered nomadic Indians whose "simple" habits and use of resources Villagrá describes.

Saliendo el Aguilar con este orden,	Aguilar then departing with these orders,
El campo fue marchando las riberas	The camp did march along the banks
Deste copado Río caudaloso	Of this well-forested and rich river,
Cuyos incultos bárbaros grosseros,	Whose unlearned, rude barbarians
En la pasada edad y en la presente,	In ages past, and in the present, too,
Siempre fueron de bronco entendimiento,	Were always of crude comprehension,
De simple vida bruta, no enseñada	Of simple lives, brutish, untaught
A cultivar la tierra ni romperla	To cultivate the earth or break it up,
Y en adquirir hazienda y en guardarla	And in acquiring farms and keeping them
También de todo punto descuidados.	Completely unaccustomed, too.
Sólo sabemos viven de la caza,	We know they live only by the chase,
De pezca y de raízes que conocen,	By fishing and by roots they know,

Tras cuia vida todos muy contentos,
De las grandes Ciudades olvidados,
Bullicio de palacio y altas Cortes
Pasan sin más zozobra sus cuidados.
    (Villagrá, *Historia*, 15, 53–68)

In which life, all very content,
Unknowing of the great cities,
The noise of the palace and the high courts,
They pass over their cares without anxiety.

The previous lines contrast with the customs and natural environment inhabited by the sedentary Indians whom the Spaniards called Pueblos, after the villages in which they lived.

Son lindos labradores por extremo.
Ellos hilan y tejen y ellas guisan.
Edifican y cuidan de la casa,
Y visten de algodón vistosas mantas
De diversos colores matizados.
Son todos gente llana y apazible,
De buenos rostros, bien proporcionados,
    (Villagrá, *Historia*, 15, 315–21)

They are extremely skillful laborers.
They spin and weave, the women cook
And build and take care of the house,
And wear seemly cotton mantles
Of divers colors, many-hued.
They are all simple, peaceful folk,
Of good faces and all well-formed,

Son lindos nadadores por extremo
Los hombres y mugeres, y son dados
Al arte de pintura y noble pesca.
    (Villagrá, *Historia*, 15, 336–38)

They are extremely graceful in swimming,
Both men and women, and are given
To the art of painting, noble fishing, too

Y son supersticiosos hechizeros,
Idólatras perdidos. Inclinados
A cultivar la tierra y a labrarla,
Cogen frisol, maíz y calabaza,
Melón y endrina rica de Castilla,
Y ubas en cantidad por los desiertos.
    (Villagrá, *Historia*, 15, 343–48)

And they are superstitious enchanters,
Damned idolaters. Much inclined
To cultívate the earth and work the same,
They harvest beans, corn, and squashes,
Melons and rich sloes of Castile,
And grapes in quantity through the desert.

Another significant reference to geography involves the desert climate and the desperation the Indians demonstrated because of a lack of rain.

Confussos, preguntamos a las lenguas
La causa de aquel llanto y nos dixeron
Que lloraba la gente por el agua
Que mucho tiempo ya pasado abía
O las nubes jamás abían regado
La tierra, que de seca por mil partes
Estaba tan hendida y tan sedienta
Que no le era posible que criase
Ninguna de las siembras que tuviesse.
    (Villagrá, *Historia*, 16, 29–37)

Confused, we asked the translators
The cause of that wailing, and they replied
That 'twas for water all the people wept,
For much time now has passed away
In which the clouds had never watered
The earth, which, in a thousand places dry,
Was so cracked and so burnt with thirst
That 'twas impossible to raise
As much as one of the crops they had sown.

Because his objective was to give religious conversion a prominent place in his account, Villagrá moves here from describing the Indian's sadness to introducing the topic of religion and the Spaniards' paternal Christian attitude.

Que no llorasen más ni se cansasen	That they should weep no more nor be
Porque ellos rogarían a su Padre	downcast,
Que estaba hallá en el Cielo se doliesse	Because they would ask their Father,
De toda aquella tierra, y que esperaban	Who there in Heaven was, to have pity
Que, aunque inobedientes hijos eran,	On all that land, and that they hoped,
Que a todos muchas aguas les daría	Though these were disobedient children,
Y que éstas que vendrían de manera	He yet would give much water to them all
Que todos los sembrados se cogiesen.	And they would come in such good time
	That all the planting might be saved.

    (Villagrá, *Historia*, 16, 42–49)

There are references to species of animals in contexts such as the hunt carried out by the Indians, in which Villagrá shows his admiration for their hunting skill.

En esta alegre caza vimos muertas	In this joyous hunt we saw killed
Largas ochenta liebres muy hermosas,	Some eighty large, beautiful hares,
Treinta y quatro conejos, y no cuento	Rabbits some thirty four, nor do I count
Los raposos que allí también juntaron	The foxes that were also gathered there.
Y no sé yo que tenga todo el mundo	And I do not know that the whole world
Liebres de más buen gusto y más sabrosas,	has
Más crecidas, más bellas ni más tiernas	Hares of a better taste, more savory,
Que esta tierra produze y sus contornos.	Larger, more beautiful, or more tender
	Than this land and its neighborhood
	produce.

    (Villagrá, *Historia*, 18, 365–72)

Based on the evidence presented in these examples, it is clear that both Ercilla and Villagrá are using elements of the literary Renaissance epic in their poems when they include the geographic context or description of nature in treating the theme of the Indians. Though Villagrá imitates the Ercillian model to a great degree in the *Historia*, he also finds inspiration in classical authors of the epic, especially Virgil and Ariosto. Much of what the two poems reveal about the Indians and their natural space has to do with the poets' desire to follow the canons of the epic. Thus, it is necessary to proceed with caution when declaring details to be historical.

Inherent in their handling of the Indian theme is the poets' attempt to give an original story from the Americas legitimacy as well as to inscribe it within Western history. This subject has already been examined in the case of Ercilla, and in the case of Villagrá, given that he follows the Ercillian model, the same holds true. We are obliged to consider carefully how much historical truth the two poems reflect, because it is the intent of both poets to emulate European history. Therefore, one must consider all these factors to avoid mere speculation.

About 40 percent of the lines in Villagrá's *Historia* are devoted to the Indians,[28] in stories that take place in one of four contexts:

1. The encounter with and description of what was new to the Spaniards—customs, indigenous use of natural resources, Indian knowledge of geography
2. The use of techniques borrowed entirely from epic poetry, such as military speeches by the leaders of Acoma
3. Direct references to the indigenous reaction to the Spanish entrada, and the stance taken by the Indians toward adopting a new religion, language, and so forth; in other words, to Spanish settlement
4. The attitude of resistance, including military confrontation, represented by the battle of Acoma

The calculation of 40 percent supports the argument that the Indians should be considered an important topic in the *Historia*. On the other hand, the poet opted to devote most of his poem, some 60 percent, to the theme of the Spaniards.

Villagrá selected, from various possibilities with an Indian theme, those which served him for the epic: legend, love story, conquest, speeches, antagonism, and the encounter with the exotic. He chose to describe nature in association with the Indians to aid the epic. The inclusion of the legend of the ancient Mexicans and their geographical location, the descriptions of customs and use of natural resources by the Indians of New Mexico, and the references to their geographic knowledge of their region are examples of what Villagrá wished to highlight. He relied on those elements not only to inform but also to present what was exotic and different about the people encountered. He did not go any further with respect to the theme of the Indians. Nor did he choose to delve deeper into the topic, or to include a single word of an indigenous language, or give any details about Indian religion, or record the cruel punishment meted out to the Indians who survived the battle of Acoma. These points, plus the fact that references to the Indian theme account for fewer than half of the lines of the poem, demonstrate that Villagrá did not choose a complete identification with the Indians as a message of his poem.

To conclude the analysis of the central theme of this chapter, it is important to reiterate that although *La Araucana* is a poem with a Spanish American theme, it must be included in the genre of literary Renaissance epics. The *Historia* adheres to this model and becomes a Spanish-American epic poem that also draws on *La Araucana* for inspiration, relying on the same classical models Ercilla used.

As regards the description of nature, it has been shown that each poem uses this method to mirror the character of the Indians.

If there is one single element that unites the geography of both poems, it is the common theme of the frontier. In both cases, conquest took place in an unfamiliar—to the Spanish—frontier. In New Mexico, the region and its inhabitants were poorly known, and in the Chilean Araucanía, they were completely unknown. Moreover, the two frontiers were geographically far from colonial cities or even towns. The encounter with an unknown culture, which had yet to feel the influence of European culture, is common to both poems. The description of geography is marked by the frontier location and by the canons of the Renaissance epic with a Spanish American theme.

Finally, there is the aspect of legitimization of Indian history by making it Western through reference to classical authors and the use of a European literary model. This has already been discussed for *La Araucana*. For Villagrá's *Historia*, the same conclusion is possible because the poet uses the same concepts. By means of this Westernization in narratives in general and in the epic in particular, the Spanish American world was presented to Europeans. This process occurred in literature through the insertion of an American story into the European mold. French historian Serge Gruzinski calls this process "Westernization" rather than "Hispanicization," because the former

> cannot be reduced to the whims of Christianization and to the imposition of the colonial system; it activates deeper and more determinant processes: the evolution of the representation of the person and of the relations between beings, the transformation of figurative and graphic codes, often means of expression, and of transmission of knowledge, . . . that is, the redefinition of the imaginary and of the real in which the Indians were destined to express themselves and to subsist, forced or fascinated.[29]

Both poets were participants in this process of Westernization of the Americas, not only through their writing but also through their very presence as part of the conquering group.

In this apparently uniform process of Westernization, there were regional peculiarities. As noted, the frontier space lent special characteristics to both poems. Both frontiers offered a unique reality that was ideal for use as the scene of the epic. In both cases the frontiers were spaces in which an encounter took place, sometimes peaceful, sometimes violent, but always complex. The two poems evoke the start of a period of advances and retreats in the process of Spanish colonization. Ercilla's description of the impossibility of conquering the Araucanian territory and Villagrá's presentation of the tragic encounter at Acoma Pueblo are merely previews of what will happen on both frontiers during the seventeenth century. What the two poems present is, in short, the beginning of a period that has come to be called the "first America," in which nothing is simple or easy to explain, and events take place that establish the foundations of a society whose problems still exist today. Historians Carmen Bernard and Serge Gruzinski could not have said it better.

> Within the confines of this new continent, in which the Spaniards began to reconstruct the world from which they had departed, stretched rebellious and poorly controlled frontier regions—Florida, the north of Mexico, Yucatan, Chile, and the River Plate. . . . In those *no man's lands*, true *Far Wests* (before the term existed), there arose embryos of societies whose anarchy and violence anticipated a view of America with which we are familiar. In spite of their distance the soldiers of New Mexico and Florida, the first emigrants to Buenos Aires and São Paulo, pursued ways of life that resemble one another for their precariousness and for their isolation.[30]

Both poems analyzed here project a historical reality that continued for several decades after their publication. Although they present historical facts, Ercilla and Villagrá take liberties by including fantasy, allegory, and other elements typical of the epic genre. Nevertheless, history has shown that the message of the two poems coincided with the phases of Spanish domination in the two frontier spaces over the course of the seventeenth century. One has only to recall the successful Indian revolt of 1680 in New Mexico and the constant Araucanian resistance up to the middle of the same century.

CHAPTER 5

Spanish Entrada, Landscape, and Battle

Y pues es la sazón tan oportuna
y poco necesarias las razones,
no quiero detener vuestra fortuna,
ni gastar más el tiempo en oraciones.
Sús, tomad posesión todos a una
desas nuevas provincias y regiones,
donde os tienen los hados a la entrada
tanta gloria y riqueza aparejada.
    (Ercilla, 35.8, 1–8)

Since the occasion is so opportune
and reasons not very necessary,
I do not want to halt your fortune,
nor spend more time in speeches.
Go ahead, all take possession at once
of these new provinces and regions,
where fate has you, at the entrance
of so much harnessed glory and wealth.

Por escabrosas tierras anduvimos
De Alárabes y barbaros incultos
Y otros, desiertos broncos, peligrosos,
Cuio tendido y espacioso suelo
Nunca jamás Christianos pies pisaron.
    (Villagrá, *Historia*, 14, 43–47)

We went through rough and craggy lands
Of Arabs and of rude barbarians,
And other deserts, wild and perilous,
Upon whose wide and spacious soil
No Christian foot has ever trod.

Se tomó posesión de aquella tierra
En vuestro insigne, heroico y alto nombre
Haciendo en esta causa cierto escrito
Que aqueste será bien que aquí lo ponga
    (Villagrá, *Historia*, 14, 343–46)

[We] took possession of the land
In your famous, heroic, lofty name,
Making some record of the case,
Which it is well I give to you

In the second volume of his work *Cosmos*, naturalist Alexander von Humboldt devotes a section to the description of nature in literature. He mentions Ercilla and *La Araucana* among examples of the literature of Western civilization and other regions. According to Humboldt, it was not Ercilla's intention to describe the natural environment: "the aspect of volcanoes covered with eternal snow, of torrid sylvan valleys, and of arms of the sea extending far into the land, has not been productive of any descriptions which may be regarded as graphical."[1] Here we might recall the importance for the German naturalist of embracing nature in literature. He saw the natural world as an interrelated whole in which a synthesis of different disciplines is required to understand it.[2] For Humboldt, Ercilla's poem instead reflects a sense of nationality, although presented without "poetic enthusiasm,"[3] and Humboldt relates the poem's deficient geographic context to Ercilla's lack of means.

> Ercilla is unaffected and true-hearted, especially in those parts of his composition which he wrote in the field, mostly on the bark of trees and the skins of animals, for want of paper. The description of his poverty, and of the ingratitude which he, like others, experienced at the court of King Philip, is extremely touching.[4]

The naturalist illustrates this affirmation with the following lines from *La Araucana*:

Climas pasé, mudé constelaciones	I passed climates, moved constellations
golfos innavegables navegando,	navigating unnavigable gulfs,
estendiendo, Señor, vuestra corona	extending, lord, your crown
hasta casi la austral frígida zona.	almost to the austral frigid zone.[5]

Humboldt continues in this vein, citing further examples of geographic description in the poem, which he characterizes as "lacking life and animation."[6]

The naturalist's assessment is not far from that which this chapter seeks to demonstrate. The example Humboldt proffers happens to include the lines where Ercilla tells King Felipe II of the large expanse conquered by Spain in the southern zone. Taking possession of the land in the name of the king of Spain with the aim of expanding his empire and converting the indigenous population to Christianity is presented in Ercilla's poem with a view of nature that seems secondary to a larger theme. The same is true of Villagrá and his *Historia de la Nueva México*. The description of the landscape is almost always subordinate to the action of the two groups, Indians and Spaniards. This can be attributed to the poets' adherence to the rules of epic poetry, but also to the challenge of dealing with a geographic space different from the European one. The American space must be presented and described to a European audience in the context of the encounter between Spaniards and Indians. In other words, it appears that in the American epic, specifically in these two poems, geographic space is recognized and interpreted as a function of what has been conquered.

Whereas in the preceding chapter the poets' interpretation of the Indians in their natural space was analyzed, this chapter seeks to analyze the theme of taking possession of the land, the resulting subjugation of the indigenous population—and its connection with geographical description—and the Spanish goal of occupying frontier spaces. The Spaniards enacted what can be termed a "dichotomy of possession," the repeated assertion of the peaceful aim of the conquest, confronted with the fact that the Indians were given no choice. In situations in which the Indians resisted Spanish domination, the response was armed retaliation, and the natural setting became the scene of fighting. In both

La Araucana and the *Historia de la Nueva México*, battles were an important focus of the poems (more so in *La Araucana*). In fact, they could not be called epic poems if they did not depict armed and hand-to-hand struggle between enemies.

In both poems, taking possession of the land is associated with the concept of "entrada." The terms "entrada," "entrar," and "entrando," which appear in several cantos in both poems, refer to the act of taking possession of the land, an act that, depending on the Indians' reaction, could be peaceful or by force. Both Ercilla and Villagrá refer to the entrada into land where "foreigners" or "Christians" had never before set foot. The entrada and the geographic context of advance toward unknown land necessarily have a military connotation. The *Diccionario de la Real Academia de la Lengua Española* defines *entrada* as: "action of entering;" "invasion the enemy makes in a country, city, and so forth." The word *entrar* is defined as: "invading or occupying something by force of arms; entering land, city, castle."[7] Therefore the concept of entrada implies taking possession by force, whether of an Arab castle during the Spanish Reconquista or of indigenous land in the Americas.

The two poems contain references throughout to the suffering and anguish of the Spanish soldiers in their entrada into isolated and remote lands. The mention of the Spanish effort and sacrifice is always framed by a hostile natural environment, but one that, finally, they manage to dominate, at least in the view of the two poets. In the prologue to part 1 of *La Araucana*, for example, Ercilla mentions that the goal of his work is to publicize the Spaniards' feats, primarily because they involve land about which almost nothing is known, being "so remote and distant."[8]

Thus, it is established from the beginning of the poem that the Spaniards are, in part, the heroes. The other half of the heroic role in *La Araucana* belongs to the Araucanian Indians whom the poet also mentions in the prologue, highlighting the valor with which they defended their territory "against such ferocious enemies as the Spaniards."[9] Noteworthy here is that Araucanian bravery, according to Ercilla, is measured as a function of the bravery of the Spanish enemy. The topic of Spanish valor has such importance that it appears in the first two stanzas of the poem (see chapter 1).

The Spanish entrada into Chile is also presented in the first canto. The poet devotes various stanzas to describing the dangers and suffering that Pedro de Valdivia and his men experienced in initiating the taking of the land. The adelantado Diego de Almagro had only explored the region, but Valdivia led the entrada into Chile.

Tuvo a la entrada con aquellas gentes batallas y recuentros peligrosos	In the entrada with those people he had battles and dangerous encounters

en tiempos y lugares diferentes	at different times and places,
que estuvieron los fines bien dudosos;	and the results were very doubtful;
pero al cabo por fuerza los valientes	but, in the end, by force the brave
españoles con brazos valerosos,	Spaniards
siguiendo el hado y con rigor la guerra	with valiant arms,
ocuparon gran parte de la tierra.	following the fate and rigor of war
	occupied a great part of the land.

    (Ercilla, *La Araucana*, 1.58, 1–8)

The next lines continue with Valdivia crossing rivers, penetrating into Araucanian territory, and taking possession.

The Spanish advance into Indian land was accompanied by a ritual that merits being presented in detail here. During the first decades of the Spanish conquest, the taking of land was accomplished through an official act by which the adelantado or governor took possession in the name of the king. Between 1514 and 1573 this act was called the "requerimiento." The ritual was followed by the supposed submission of the Indians to both political and religious authority. According to Patricia Seed in her study of ceremonies of possession in the New World, the requerimiento was a military and political ritual that had no parallel in any other European culture. She adds: "Read aloud to New World natives from a written text, the Requirement was an ultimatum for Indians to acknowledge the superiority of Christianity or be warred upon."[10]

The use of this legal instrument served, in the Spanish view, to legitimize and regulate the conquest. It was necessary to "inform" the Indians of what they did not know: that Jesus's power was transmitted to Saint Peter and from him to the popes who came after him, one of whom had granted to Spain the rights to America (and Portugal).[11] Tzvetan Todorov elucidates the meaning of this document.

> The juridical reasons for the Spanish domination being thus posited, it remains only to establish one thing: that the Indians were informed of the situation, for they may have been unaware of these successive gifts which the popes and emperors were making to one another. This unawareness will be remedied by the reading of the *Requerimiento*, in the presence of an officer of the king (though no interpreter is mentioned).[12]

If the Indians accepted Spanish authority without showing signs of resistance, they could not be reduced to slavery (and they would be protected even if in a state of servitude). If, however, they did not accept, they were punished. This process therefore demonstrated neither legality nor equality because the Spaniards established the rules and the Indians could "choose only between two positions of inferiority." Spanish superiority was "already contained in the fact that it is they who are speaking, while the Indians listen."[13]

The period of the conquest of Chile that Ercilla recounts was ruled by the use of the requerimiento, which Pedro de Valdivia employed on various occasions. Its efficacy was doubtful, because the Indians did not cease their hostilities. In *La Araucana*, Ercilla mentions the founding of settlements and fortresses in the endeavor to make the Araucanians submit to Spanish authority.[14]

The ritual of requerimiento was also put into practice by García Hurtado de Mendoza during his term as governor.[15] At the end of part 1 of the poem, Ercilla refers to the appointment of Hurtado de Mendoza as the new adelantado of Chile, replacing Valdivia following his death at the hands of the Araucanians. The poet refers to the mission that awaited the Spaniards under the leadership of the new governor (the group the poet himself joined) and the great expanse of land to conquer. Once again, mention of the remote land is coupled with the idea of the bravery of the participants in the struggle, both Araucanians and Spaniards. After the unfortunate experience of Pedro de Valdivia and his men in Chilean territory, the poet anticipates the violent reception that awaited Hurtado de Mendoza.

Oh valientes soldados araucanos,	Oh brave Araucano soldiers,
las armas prevenid y corazones,	prepare weapons and hearts,
y el usado valor de vuestras manos	and the experienced courage of your hands
temido en las antárticas regiones,	feared in the Antarctic regions,
que gran copia de jóvenes lozanos	because a great number of lusty youth
descoge en vuestro daño sus pendones,	unfurl their banners to harm you,
pensando entrar por toda vuestra tierra	planning to enter your land from everywhere
haciendo fiero estrago y cruda guerra!	making fierce havoc and crude war.

(Ercilla, *La Araucana*, 13.17, 1–8)

The meaning of the entrada is clear in these lines: taking possession by force of arms.

One of the most meaningful episodes under the rubric of taking possession of the land occurs in canto 35 of *La Araucana*, one of the last cantos of the poem. In February 1558 the new governor departed with a group of soldiers toward the area south of the town of Valdivia, the southernmost region touched by the Spaniards up to that time. Ercilla, who later joined the group, includes an account of the entrada. He describes the remote lands the Spaniards had reached, spurred by the self-interest that had motivated the conquest. The poem refers to a hostile nature that made the Spanish march arduous. The desire to conquer, which in the course of the canto Ercilla ends up calling "greed," is presented as the reason that led the Spaniards to travel to inhospitable and distant regions.

Así por mil peligros y derrotas,
golfos profundos, mares no sulcados,
hasta las partes últimas ignotas
trujo sin descansar tantos soldados,
y por vías estériles remotas
del interés incitador llevados,
piensan escudriñar cuanto se encierra
en el círculo inmenso de la tierra.

   (Ercilla, *La Araucana*, 35.3, 1–8)

Dije que don García había arribado
con prática y lucida compañía
al término de Chile señalado
de do nadie jamás pasado había
   (Ercilla, *La Araucana*, 35.4, 1–4)

Thus for a thousand dangers and defeats,
deep gulfs, seas non-plied,
until the last parts unknown
brought without rest so many soldiers,
and by remote and sterile roads
taken by their urgent interest,
they plan to examine as much as is
 contained
in the immense circle of the land.

I said that Don García had arrived
with a practical and exemplary company
to the end of Chile
which nobody in the past had reached.

"Don García" refers to García Hurtado de Mendoza. The words that follow the above lines in the poem are those included in the epigraph at the beginning of this chapter. In them Ercilla mentions the governor's exhortation to his soldiers to take possession of the land upon which they were stepping, and stressing the fact that no foreigners had ever gone there before.

Luego pues de tropel toda la gente
a la plática apenas detenida,
pisó la nueva tierra libremente,
jamás del estranjero pie batida;
   (Ercilla, *La Araucana*, 35.9, 1–4)

Then all the people in a rush
when the talk had hardly stopped,
step freely on the new land,
never stirred by alien foot;

  The next lines describe a landscape difficult to traverse. Because Ercilla was part of the group of soldiers under the command of Hurtado de Mendoza, the poet describes the crossing in the first person, granting himself the title "discoverer."

Pasamos adelante descubriendo
siempre más arcabucos y breñales,
la cerrada espesura y paso abriendo
con hachas, con machetes y destrales;
otros con pico y azadón rompiendo
las peñas y arraigadas matorrales,
do el caballo hostigado y receloso
afirmarse seguro el pie medroso.

   (Ercilla, *La Araucana*, 35.31, 1–8)

We went ahead, discovering
always more craggy areas of brambles
 and bushes,
opening up closed thickets and paths
with axes, with machetes and hatchets;
others with pick and hoe breaking up
rocks and ingrained heaths,
to which a harassed and suspicious horse
could set forth the timid foot.

According to Ercilla, their Indian guide had tricked the expeditionaries. The coastal mountain range closed off the route to the west, and the tall northern banks of the Río Maullín blocked the way. The expedition had to go back through the impenetrable vegetation and suffer the high humidity of the region.[16] In fact, even today the local ecosystem as one approaches those mountains presents a humid climate (90 percent humidity) owing to the drop in temperature and the increase in precipitation. As a result, the soils are thick, rich in organic matter, and the vegetation becomes much denser and more varied.[17] Ercilla describes how difficult it was for soldiers and horses to traverse that region.

Era lástima oír los alaridos,	It was pitiful to hear the cries,
ver los impedimentos y embarazos,	to see the impediments and
los caballos sin ánimo caídos,	encumbrances,
destroncados los pies, rotos los brazos;	the horses without spirit fallen,
nuestros sencillos débiles vestidos	men with feet maimed, and arms broken;
quedaban por las zarzas a pedazos;	our simple weak clothes
descalzos y desnudos, sólo armados,	torn to pieces by the brambles;
en sangre, lodo y en sudor bañados.	barefoot and naked, armed only,
	with blood, mud and bathed in
	perspiration.

(Ercilla, *La Araucana*, 35.35, 1–8)

The poet continues to describe the difficult journey that lasted a week.

Siete días perdidos anduvimos	Lost for seven days we marched
abriendo a hierro el impedido paso,	opening with iron an impeded path
que en todo aquel discurso no tuvimos	and in all that time we did not have
do poder recliner el cuerpo laso.	anywhere to rest our tired body.

(Ercilla, *La Araucana*, 35.40, 1–4)

Regarding Ercilla's true motive for describing the aforementioned scenes in such detail, Ángel Álvarez Vilela in his article "La expedición a Ancud en *La Araucana*, o la recuperación del mérito por parte de Ercilla," argues that the poet used "certain narrative resources and organized the historical matter to discredit Governor García Hurtado de Mendoza."[18] While Ercilla alludes to the extreme difficulties the expedition went through, he does not mention achievements such as the founding of the town of Osorno, an event in which the poet was present. The tricks of the native guide who abandoned the expedition did not really happen as Ercilla presents it, according to Álvarez Vilela. Nor were the Spaniards lost for seven days.[19]

The description in the poem of the arrival at a fertile plain—Ancud—and a lake and beautiful bay, today the site of the coastal city of Puerto Montt, does not include any specific reference to Hurtado de Mendoza. In this section "the figure of don García dissipates and disappears." Instead, Ercilla—the soldier and discoverer—becomes the most relevant figure.[20] The lines describing this region evoke an almost paradisiacal landscape (see chapter 4). In summary, the description of the geography for the expedition to southern Chile is directly tied to personal experience and becomes political when the poet deliberately uses it to show Hurtado de Mendoza's mistakes and lack of leadership and to silence the governor's achievements. As Álvarez Vilela affirms, Ercilla imposed a "punishment of silence on don García" in the second and third parts of *La Araucana*,[21] and, when all is said and done, this had a lot to do with the governor's punishment of Ercilla later on in the story.

Returning to the description of geography at that idyllic place described by the poet, there is a mention of a fruit theretofore unknown to the Spaniards but that helped them satisfy their hunger. Ercilla called it *frutilla de Chile* (Chilean strawberry). In his *Historia natural y moral de las Indias* (1590), fray José de Acosta described this wild fruit as "appetizing to eat, which almost tends to the flavor of sour cherries, but it is completely different, because it is not a tree but a plant that grows little and spreads over the earth."[22]

Mas con todo este esfuerzo, a la bajada	With all this effort, at the descent
de la ribera, en partes montuosa,	to the riverside, in part hilly,
hallamos la frutilla coronada	we found the crowned strawberry,
que produce la murta virtuosa;	produced by the virtuous myrtle;
y aunque agreste, montés, no sazonada,	although rural, wild, not mellow,
fue a tan buena sazón y tan sabrosa,	it was so good at that occasion and so
que el celeste maná y ollas de Egito	flavorful,
no movieran mejor nuestro apetito.	that the celestial manna and pots of Egypt
	did not move our appetite any better.

      (Ercilla, *La Araucana*, 35.44, 1–8)

As noted in chapter 4 of this book, the paradisiacal islands that Ercilla describes were the home of a peaceful indigenous population that gave the group of Spaniards a warm welcome. The Spaniards interpreted the Indians' demonstrations of friendship as a voluntary choice to submit to Spanish authority. The lines about this beautiful setting and its people are followed by others in which the poet returns to the theme of possession of the land. Ercilla and a group of soldiers, in a small boat, crossed to one of the islands in the area of the *desaguadero* (drainage ditch), the present Canal de Chacao, which separates the Chilean mainland from the big island of Chiloé. Once he landed on one of the small islands, the poet decided to leave a sign of his presence there by carving his name on the trunk of a tree.

Pero yo por cumplir el apetito	But I to satisfy my appetite
que era poner el pie más adelante,	which is to place my foot forward,
fingiendo que marcaba aquel distrito,	feigning that I was marking that district,
cosa al descubridor siempre importante,	something always important to a discoverer,
corrí una media milla do un escrito	I ran a half mile where a writing
quise dejar para señal bastante,	I wanted to leave as a sure sign,
y en el tronco que vi de más grandeza	and on a tree trunk of the largest tree I saw
escribí con un cuchillo en la corteza	I wrote on its bark with a knife
Aquí llegó, donde otro no ha llegado,	Here arrived, where no one else has,
don Alonso de Ercilla, que el primero	Don Alonso de Ercilla, the first one
en un pequeño barco deslastrado,	with a small unballasted ship,
con solo diez pasó el desaguadero	with only ten men passed the channel
el año de cincuenta y ocho entrado	in the year of fifty eight
sobre mil y quinientos, por hebrero,	one thousand and five hundred, in February,
a las dos de la tarde, el postrer día,	at two in the afternoon, of the last day,
volviendo a la dejada compañía.	returning to the company left behind.

(Ercilla, *La Araucana*, 36.28, 1–8; 29, 1–8)

Ercilla did not hide the pride he took in his status as discoverer or the significance he attached to marking his presence on the land. After relating this experience, the poet devotes the rest of the penultimate canto of his poem to mentioning, with no further details, the events that led to his exile from Chile and his return to Peru and later to Spain.

These lines narrate the return of his group, headed by García Hurtado de Mendoza, to the fortress of La Imperial, where they held a fiesta of celebration and welcome. An altercation took place in which Ercilla was the protagonist. The situation was so grave that the governor condemned those involved to the gallows, including the poet, a sentence that was later transmuted to exile. Ercilla describes his departure from Chile, betraying signs of indignation and resentment. In these lines it is noteworthy that he categorizes as "ingrate" that land for which he had struggled, in this way transferring his frustration to the physical space itself and indirectly to its people, about whom he had written with such admiration.

Y en un grueso barcón, bajel de trato,	In a thick barge, commercial ship,
que velas altas de partida estaba,	whose sails were high for departure,
salí de aquella tierra y reino ingrato	I left that land and ingrate kingdom
que tanto afán y sangre me costaba;	that cost me so much toil and blood;
y sin contraste alguno ni rebato,	and without any mishap or rebuttal ,
con el austro que en popa nos soplaba,	with the wind that blows on our stern,
costa a costa y a veces engolfado	coast to coast and sometimes lost sight of land
llegué al Callao de Lima celebrado.	I arrived at the celebrated Callao of Lima.

(Ercilla, *La Araucana*, 36.37, 1–8)

These are not the only lines in which the poet mentions his frustration as a soldier whose efforts had not been recognized or appreciated. In other parts of the poem there are references to the soldiers' labor in difficult circumstances, in remote and inhospitable zones where they risked their lives for the imperial cause.[23]

In canto 20 of his *Historia de la Nueva México*, Villagrá also devotes numerous lines to the lack of recognition of the soldiers' valor and hardships, with constant references to the inhospitable land and the rigors of the climate. The type of landscape that Villagrá describes has different characteristics from the landscape Ercilla describes. Nevertheless, the portrayal of the Spanish presence in a frontier geographic context is similar in the two poems. It is noteworthy how close to Ercilla's style Villagrá's is when describing the entrada and subsequent taking possession of the land.

In *La Araucana*, Ercilla presents the Spanish conquest as framed by a geographical setting at times hostile and at times idyllic. Villagrá does the same in the *Historia*. His description of nature is frequently tied to the concept of entrada, and therefore, of taking possession of and occupying the territory that in the specific case of New Mexico, was linked to the conversion of the sedentary indigenous population to Christianity. In addition, both poets devote a large portion of their poems to describing the history of the entrada on both frontiers before their own arrival. Just as *La Araucana* refers to Pedro de Valdivia's earlier conquest, the *Historia* refers to expeditions to the north that preceded Oñate's entrada.

Villagrá devotes three entire cantos to the expeditions before 1598. Worthy of special mention are the lines about Vázquez de Coronado's exploration between the years 1540 and 1542. Canto 4 recounts the events and circumstances related to the frustrated search for rich cities and Coronado's resulting decision to return to Mexico City, after failing in his hopes. Coronado had to confront the complaints of some men who considered that two years was not enough and that it was too early to leave without having seen "de aquel estado la grandeza" (the grandeur of that state). On the other hand, in recording the differences of opinion among the expedition's members about the decision to suspend their search and return to Mexico City, Villagrá mentions the complaints of those who did not continue on, and especially the laments of their suffering as a consequence of the harshness of the land and its natural phenomena.

Otros, por el contrario, se afligían,	Others, on contrary, were much cast down,
Llorando hambre, desnudez, cansancio,	And wept their hunger, nakedness, fatigue,
Terribles yelos, nieves y ventiscos,	The fearful cold, the snow, and blizzards,
Pesados soles, aguas y granizo,	The burning sun, the rain, and hail,
Gran pobreza y trabajos de la tierra,	Great poverty and labor of the land,
Miserias del camino trabajoso,	The miseries of toilsome road,
Postas y centinelas peligrosas,	Dangerous watches and sentry posts,

El peso de las armas desabridas,	The overwhelming weight of arms,
Inclemencia del cielo riguroso,	Inclemency of the rigorous skies,
Y riesgos de la vida no pensados,	Most unconsidered risks of life,
Enfermedades y otros disparates,	Sickness and other bits of nonsense,
(Villagrá, *Historia*, 4, 84–94)	

Although Villagrá's purpose was to demonstrate the lack of perseverance of Vázquez de Coronado's expedition, which is the central theme of canto 4, the lines cited above were not fictitious. The contemporaneous account of the events written by the chronicler Pedro de Castañeda confirms what Villagrá wrote in presenting the difficulties that the Spaniards of that expedition faced in exploring such vast expanses.[24]

Perhaps the most representative lines that describe nature linked to Spanish ordeals in the *Historia* are those of canto 14. They refer to the road followed by the advance party that Juan de Oñate sent out to look for the shortest and most appropriate route to the Río del Norte (today the Rio Grande). Villagrá was in this group, which crossed the sand dunes that today constitute part of the Chihuahua Desert in northern Mexico. The poem recounts the travails the group underwent in crossing the desert.[25]

Contra el rigor del hado prohejando,	Driving against the hardness of our fate
Nuestra derrota siempre proseguimos,	We ever held unto our course,
Ya por espesas breñas y quebradas,	Now through thick briars and ravines,
Por cuios bravos bosques enrredados	Entangled in whose harsh forests
Las fuertes escarcelas se rasgaban,	Even our strong cuisses were torn,
Ya por ásperas cumbres lebantadas,	Now over high and rugged peaks,
Por cuias zimas los caballos lasos	Over whose summits we did drive
Por delante llevabamos, rendidos,	Our tired horses on before,
Hijadeando, cansados y afligidos,	Panting and tired and quite worn out,
A pie y de todas armas molestados,	On foot and hindered by all our arms,
Y las hinchadas plantas ya desnudas,	Our swollen feet, now quite naked
Descalzas, sin calzado, se assentaban	And shoeless, without shoes we still did set
Por riscos y peñascos escabrosos,	On cliffs and ragged looming rocks,
Ya por muy altos médanos de arena,	Now over lofty dunes of sand,
Tan ardiente, encendida y tan fogosa	So ardent, burning, and fervent
Que de su fuerte reflexión heridos	That, wounded by their strong reflection,
Los miserables ojos, abrasados,	Our miserable eyes, burnt up
Dentro del duro casco se quebraban.	'Neath our hard helmets, failed us quite.
(Villagrá, *Historia*, 14, 53–70)	

These lines recall those of Ercilla when he describes García Hurtado de Mendoza and his men crossing through the impenetrable vegetation in Chile, before arriving at Lake Llanquiue. Obviously, the geography was different, but Villagrá's style is similar.

As in the south of Chile, the environmental factors of the far north of New Spain limited the conditions of the journey in regard to such things as the choice of campsites. The Chihuahuan Desert is a vast, high desert with sparse vegetation and only occasional springs and rare perennial streams. Four hundred years ago, it was, as today, a region of climatic extremes with a wide range of annual temperatures, low and erratic rates of precipitation, high winds, low humidity, high evaporation rates, and intense solar radiation.[26]

That Villagrá's lines coincide with the geographic characteristics of the region demonstrates that the poet was not exaggerating. His way of presenting the Spaniards' suffering in the geographic context on their search for the Río del Norte is quite effective at transmitting the drama of the circumstances to the reader. The account culminates with the poet feeling close to death.

Quatro días naturales se passaron	Four complete days did pass away
Que gota de agua todos no bebimos,	In which we drank no drop of water
Y tanto, que ya ciegos los caballos	there,
Crueles testaradas y encontrones	And now the horses, being blind,
Se daban por los árboles sin verlos,	Did give themselves most cruel blows
Y nosotros, qual ellos fatigados,	And bumps against the unseen trees,
Vivo fuego exalando y escupiendo	And we, as tired as they,
Saliva más que liga pegajosa,	Exhaling living fire and spitting forth
Desahuziados ya y ya perdidos,	Saliva more viscous than pitch,
La muerte casi todos desseamos.	Our hope given up, entirely lost,
	Were almost all wishing for death.

(Villagrá, *Historia*, 14, 90–99)

Villagrá's lines, "Four complete days did pass away/ in which we drank no drop of water there" recall Ercilla's lines cited above: "Lost for seven days we marched/ opening with iron an impeded path." Villagrá later describes the party's arrival at the river:

Alegres, arribando el bravo Río	And we all, happily did come upon the
Del Norte, por quien todos padezimos	roaring River
Cuidado y trabajos tan pesados.	Of the North, for which we all had
En cuias aguas los caballos, flacos,	undergone
Dando tras pies, se fueron acercando	Such care and such enormous toil.
	Unto whose waters the weak horses
	Creeping, staggering much, approached

(Villagrá, *Historia*, 14, 104–108)

Here the poet again turns to the Ercillian (also Renaissance) model when he describes arriving at the fertile fields beside the river, like the arrival at the fertile zone of Ancud described by Ercilla.

Y qual si en los Eliseos campos frescos	And as if in the fresh Elysian Fields
Ubiéramos llegado a refrescarnos,	We had arrived, there to refresh ourselves,
Assi, señor, nos fueron pareciendo	Such, lord, there did appear to us
Todas aquellas playas y riberas,	All those beaches and banks,
Por cuios bellos pastos los caballos,	Among whose goodly pasture the horses
Repastándose alegres, descansaban	Were gladly grazing and resting
Los fatigados güessos quebrantados	Their tired and exhausted bones
Del pesado camino trabajoso.	From the laborious, weary road.
(Villagrá, *Historia*, 14, 124–31)	

Villagrá continues to describe the landscape, making reference to birds, plants, and species to hunt. The account is overly idyllic, even naive.

Assí por estas altas arboledas,	Likewise among those lofty trunks,
Con entonado canto regalado,	With dainty, sweet-intoned song,
Cruzaban un millón de pajaricos,	There flew a million little birds,
Cuyos graciosos picos desembueltos,	Whose graceful, unembarrassed throats
Con sus arpadas lenguas, alababan	And lyric tongues did sing the praise
Al inmenso señor que los compuso.	Of that All-powerful Lord who had made them.
Y aunque las aguas del gallardo Río,	And even the waters of the harsh river,
En raudal muy furiosas y corrientes,	At flood, a furious, roaring stream,
Se yban todas vertiendo y derramando	Were all flowing and pouring down
Tan mansas, suabes, blandas y amorosas,	As peaceful, pleasing, and mild
Como si un sossegado estanque fueran,	As though they were a quiet pool
Por anchas tablas, todas bien tendidas,	Over wide flats and well spread out,
(Villagrá, *Historia*, 14, 144–55)	

Villagrá and the other members of the vanguard returned to meet the rest of the army led by Oñate and showed them the way to the river.

Villagrá's account generally agrees with the itinerary found in contemporaneous documents of the expedition. Of course, the poet adds a great deal of drama to the lines devoted to crossing the desert; likewise, to the profuse happiness he describes at reaching the fertile zone beside the river. These embellishments are no doubt owing to the poetic license of the epic, in contrast with the brief register of events in the documents.[27] Subsequently, the poet relates that when the whole expedition finally reached the river, he and four members were named by Oñate to seek a ford to cross. Villagrá includes himself in the poem as protagonist or "discoverer," just as Ercilla had. Worthy of note is that Villagrá directly addresses the king when he refers to the army ("your camp").

Mandó el Gobernador que sin tardanza	The Governor ordered that without delay
El Sargento saliesse y se aprestase	The Sergeant should set out at once
Con cinco compañeros escogidos	With five chosen companions,
Y diestros en nadar, porque buscasen	All skillful in swimming, to seek

Algún seguro vado al bravo Río	Some safe ford through the swift river
Para que por él todo vuestro campo	So that by it all this your camp
Seguro y sin zozobra le passase.	Might pass safely and without fear.
Y poniendo por obra aquel mandato	And carrying that order out
Salió Carbajal y Alonso Sánchez	There went Carvajal, Antonio Sánchez,
Y el gran Christóbal Sánchez y Araujo	The great Christóbal Sánchez and Araujo,
Y yo también con ellos porque fuesse	And I, too, with them, that I might
El número cumplido de los cinco.	Complete the number of the five.

(Villagrá, *Historia*, 14, 274–85)

Here, as did Ercilla in the south of Chile, Villagrá mentions the encounter with peaceful Indians who helped the Spaniards find the ford to cross the river. The poem transmits the paternalistic Spanish attitude, highlighting that the Spanish group gave the natives some clothes, prompting them to respond generously.

De súbito nos fuimos acercando	We suddenly did come upon
A unos pagizos ranchos, do salieron	Some thatched huts from whence there
Gran cantidad de bárbaros guerreros.	came out
Y por ser todo aquello pantanoso	Great numbers of barbarian warriors.
Y no poder valernos de las armas,	And as that place was all marshy
Assí para los bárbaros nos fuimos	And we could not well use our arms,
Mostrándonos amigos agradables	We went ahead toward the barbarians
Y como el dar al fin quebranta peñas,	Showing ourselves agreeable friends.
Dándoles de la ropa que tuvimos	And as giving even breaks rocks,
Tan mansos los volvimos y amorosos,	Giving them of the clothes we had
Tanto que quatro dellos se vinieron	We made them so peaceful, friendly, to us
Y un lindo vado a todos nos mostraron.	That four of them did come with us
	And showed to us a goodly ford.

(Villagrá, *Historia*, 14, 288–99)

Oñate chose that place, on the bank of the Río del Norte, on April 30, 1598, to take possession of the land in the name of King Felipe II of Spain.[28] In order not to "corrupt," as the poet puts it, what was said during the ceremony of taking possession, lines of verse are replaced with prose in this part of the poem. The poet titled this part "Of how we took and seized upon possession of the new land." He mentions the importance of having opened a road to be traversed. Saying "I have left a road made open for wagons" indicates an attitude of taking control of space; but in fact, the road had already existed for the Indians thousands of years before the arrival of the Spaniards. Villagrá makes a textual transcription of the original document.[29] The ritual included saying Mass and presenting a play written especially for the occasion by Captain Farfán.[30]

The weight that Villagrá gives to the act of possession, a theme not mentioned in detail in Ercilla's *La Araucana*, is noteworthy. It is significant that in the *Historia*, the author transcribed the speech word for word. At the end of the sixteenth century, the ritual of taking possession on the northern frontier of the Spanish American empire followed the same steps as at the beginning of the century. The ritual included the speech of taking possession of the space and its resources, as well as its Indians, under Spanish law (civil and criminal) using expressions such as "a horca y cuchillo" (right and jurisdiction to punish with the death penalty).[31]

Villagrá provides few details about the day-to-day itinerary during the journey to the north, but he selects certain themes to expand upon in the poem. For example, there are no specific references to the expedition's traversing of what is today known as the Jornada del Muerto. Following this route, the Spaniards left the river to follow a shortcut without water, which finally took them back to the river.[32] Villagrá omits a discovery in which he was the protagonist and which could have been used effectively in his poem. He had found a water hole in the middle of the desert after noticing that a dog that accompanied them had come back with muddy paws.[33] The site kept the name of "paraje del perrillo" (campsite of the little dog) for the two centuries that followed, and by the year 1766 it was called just "perrillo" (little dog). This is how it appears on Bernardo Miera y Pacheco's 1779 map.

At the end of today's Jornada del Muerto the group caught sight of the first of the long string of sedentary pueblos, which were the ones Oñate and his men sought. At this point in the itinerary, Villagrá presents a quasi-allegory of religion and climate. He refers to a great storm that appeared to be a "sign from heaven."

Y estando a vista de los pueblos	And being well within sight of the towns
Parece que la tierra, estremecida,	It seemed the earth did tremble there,
Sintiendo la gran fuerza de la Iglesia,	Feeling the great force of the Church
Sacudiendo los ídolos furiosa,	Shaking the idols furiously,
Con violencia horrible arrebatada	With horrible, impetuous violence
Y tempestad furiosa y terremoto,	And furious tempest and earthquake.
Estremecida toda y alterada,	All trembled and altered,
Assí, turbada fue con bravo asombro,	It thus was troubled with fearsome shadow
Cubriendo todo el cielo de entricadas	Covering all the heaven with intricate
Nubes tan densas, negras y espantosas	Clouds, and so dense, black and fearful
Que pavoroso pasmo nos causaban	They caused us an awesome amazement
(Villagrá, *Historia*, 15, 95–105)	

In the Indian pueblo that the Spaniards named Santo Domingo, on July 7, 1598, the first of many "acts of obedience and vassalage" was held in the New Mexican territory. This ceremony was nothing more than putting the famous requerimiento into practice. As noted, this ritual still existed in 1598, although it was not called thus. With the New Ordinances for Settlement and Discovery of 1573, the Spanish crown had attempted to put an end to abuses and initiate a new phase in which—at least in theory—pacification and evangelization, not war, were the goals. After 1573 the act, by which Indians were placed under Spanish authority and the Catholic religion, began to be called an "instrument of obedience and vassalage."[34] This was nothing more than a name change; as can be deduced from the documents and from the poem itself, it was practically the same requerimiento implemented in the 1550s in Chile. Villagrá omits mention of the first pueblo where this act of obedience and vassalage was carried out, the Indian pueblo Khe-wa, the one the Spaniards called Santo Domingo. The poet only describes a later ceremony held in the Indian pueblo Okeh, which Oñate named San Juan de los Caballeros. Its natives, according to Villagrá, received the Spaniards in a friendly manner.[35]

Aquí, los indios muy gustosos	Here all the Indians with pleasure
Con nosotros sus casas dividieron.	Did share their houses with our folk.
(Villagrá, *Historia*, 16, 18–19)	

Spaniards interpreted the Indians' demonstration of friendship as consent to and acceptance of Spanish occupation. For the Indians, it probably meant having the Spaniards as guests for a time and nothing more.

Villagrá mentions the importance that the "memory book" had in the act of submission on the part of the Indians. He was referring to the diary of the expedition that apparently was used as a symbol in the ritual of obedience.[36]

Por cuia causa luego despacharon	Wherefore they then did send about
El libro de memoria, que era el sello	The Book of Memory, which was the seal
Con que era el General obedezido	By which the General was obeyed
De toda aquella tierra, porque en viendo	In all that land, for, on seeing
Los bárbaros el libro se rendían	The Book, the barbarians obeyed
A todo lo que aquél que le llevaba	All that the one who carried it
De parte el General les proponía.	Proposed to them on the General's part.
(Villagrá, *Historia*, 17, 179–85)	

In the next lines Villagrá mentions how Indian obedience to the king was demanded. The wording represents clearly the true meaning of the conquest: the Indians must submit voluntarily, giving their obedience to the king, and they would be rewarded.

Que era fuerza que todos libremente	That it was necessary that all should freely
Diessen la libertad y la obediencia	Resign their liberty and obedience
A vuestra Real corona y que entendiesen	Unto your Royal Crown, and understand
Que a los que bien viviesen les daría,	That to those who lived well he would offer,
En vuestro nombre, premios muy honrrosos.	In your name, most honorable rewards.
(Villagrá, *Historia*. 17, 269–73)	

Subsequently, Villagrá clarifies that those who did not submit would be punished, and those who were at first obedient but later rescinded their submission to the laws would pay with their lives.

Y que asimismo que era bien supiesen	And it was also well they know
Que a los que hiziessen mal que sin escusa	That those who should do ill, without excuse
Abían de ser todos castigados	Should all be punished according to
Según que los delitos cometiesen,	What crime they might commit,
Y que los que una vez se sujetasen	And that the ones who once had submitted
Y diessen la obediencia a vuestras leyes	And given obedience to your laws
Que en ninguna manera no podían	Could never in any manner
Con pena de la vida, hacerse afuera.	Release themselves upon the pain of death.

(Villagrá, *Historia*, 17, 279–86)

The act of obedience and vassalage obviously included religious conversion.

Con esto, alegre, el noble Comissario	Happy at this the noble Commissary
Allí también a todos les propuso	There also did propose to all
Que dexasen su vil idolatría	That they should leave their vile idolatry
Y adorasen a Christo, Dios y hombre,	And adore Christ, the God and man,
Cruzificado, muerto y sepultado	Crucified, dead, buried,
Por la salud de todo el universo.	For the salvation of all the universe.

(Villagrá, *Historia*, 17, 299–304)

Villagrá then puts words in the mouth of the Indians, apparently to demonstrate that their conversion was not coerced.

A lo qual juntos todos replicaron	To which they, all together, did reply
Que quisiessen primero doctrinarlos	That they wished first that he would instruct them
En aquello que assí les proponían	In that which he thus had set forth to them
De aquel hombre mortal, passible y muerto	About this mortal man, suffering and dead

(Villagrá, *Historia*, 17, 305–15)

The poet subsequently mentions the list of Indian pueblos assigned to each priest who accompanied the conquistadors.[37] Even though Villagrá does not mention it, it is known that he was present when the acts of obedience and vassalage were carried out in the pueblos of Zuni and Hopi, because he signed the acts as a witness.[38]

The *Historia* conveys a view of space in which the Spanish appear to occupy every corner, although the reader does not perceive the immensity of the geographic space in which the pueblos were distributed. The poet also appears to show the Indians' total acceptance of both the foreign occupation and the new religion. But the reality was different, and Villagrá, who when he wrote the poem already knew the tragic denouement of Oñate's methods, decided to present in canto 17 an overly optimistic view of the conquest of New Mexico. Thus, the reader is surprised when in subsequent cantos the poet describes a revealing fact: the Indians of Acoma were prepared to resist.

Villagrá himself would directly experience the distrustful attitude of the natives of Acoma when he stopped at the pueblo to ask for provisions. He was returning from the mission that Oñate had entrusted to him, to search for and punish four deserters. Not seeing signs of friendship, he immediately bade farewell without getting off his horse and began what he described as a very difficult march, noting the geographic and climatic features of the region he had to traverse. Alone, hungry, and frozen, he and his horse fell into a trap apparently placed there by the natives to catch animals. After losing his horse, he continued on foot, and three Spaniards from Oñate's group found him near the site known today as El Morro, which at the close of the sixteenth century was an Indian campsite well-known to the Spaniards, who called it *el estanque*, or "the water hole of the rock."[39]

After Villagrá's stop at Acoma, the pueblo was next visited by Maese de Campo Juan de Zaldívar and his group of men, demanding provisions. The Indians' distrustful attitude that the poet had noted led to violence in the face of the aggressive Spanish demand. The Acoma Indians killed Zaldívar and at least nine of his men. This event produced an even more tragic denouement with the Spanish decision to attack Acoma (a description of which, as mentioned, is included at the end of the poem).

The Spanish occupation on the northern frontier initially seemed to be received with signs of peace, order, and acceptance on the part of the Indians, but events demonstrated that violence and fighting occurred as often on the northern frontier as on the southern frontier. Both poems reflect their particular circumstances. Ercilla demonstrates that from the outset there was Indian resistance; Villagrá, by contrast, speaks of the peaceful acceptance of Spanish occupation but ends the poem with an exceedingly tragic battle. For the reader who does not know how the *Historia* ends, it is easy to come away with the impression that in *La Araucana* the inclusion of violent acts is foreseen, but in the *Historia* the first cantos in no way foreshadow a violent denouement. Villagrá could have given his poem a different focus from the beginning. Nevertheless, the themes of Spanish occupation by peaceful means and conversion to Christianity appear to have been what the poet was most interested in emphasizing.

Both poets use geographical description to frame episodes of fighting. The lines devoted to fighting not only follow the well-known model of the epic, but also show the natural context of each frontier when they portray a violent encounter. From a description of land and sea as trembling from the beating of drums and other sounds of war, to specific descriptions of the natural space of the battles, both poets deploy all the resources of the classical epic as well as their firsthand knowledge as witnesses or participants in the violent scenes. In addition, Ercilla demonstrates his poetic ability by describing in detail battles at which he was not present and landscapes that it is questionable if he saw. However, this does not take away from the fact that he, on horseback and on foot, crossed the region and was familiar with its natural environment.

In *La Araucana*, Ercilla's object is to incorporate the description of the landscape into the unfolding of the battles with the aim of demonstrating both Indian and Spanish bravery. He depicts a savage geography, identifying it with Indian rebelliousness, while he uses elements of the landscape as challenges to Spanish power. His purpose, in part, is to demonstrate the Araucanians' profound knowledge of their territory. Another objective is to show Spanish bravery in confronting not only the Chilean environment but also the deep Araucanian knowledge of their region. The landscape becomes a protagonist in the battles. In some cases Ercilla's descriptions of the natural surroundings are meant to show why the Araucanians chose certain places to fight. For example, the stanza that follows tells of the battle waged by the Araucanian leader Lautaro against Francisco de Villagrá and his troops in the so-called Cuesta de Andalicán on February 26, 1554. This is a hearsay description of the battle, for Ercilla had not yet arrived on Chilean soil, but the description of the terrain makes the reader think he was at the site at some point.[40]

Un paso peligroso, agrio y estrecho
de la banda del norte está a la entrada,
por un monte asperísimo y derecho,
la cumbre hasta los cielos levantada;
está tras éste un llano, poco trecho,
y luego otra menor cuesta tajada
que divide el distrito andalicano
del fértil valle y límite araucano.

(Ercilla, *La Araucana*, 4.90, 1–8)

A dangerous pass, rough and narrow
to the north lies the entrance,
through a ragged and erect mountain,
the summit raised to the sky;
behind is a plain, at a short distance,
followed by another slope
which divides the Andalican district.
of the fertile valley and Araucanian
    boundary.

Esta cuesta Lautaro había elegido
para dar la batalla, y por concierto
tenía todo su ejército tendido
en lo más alto della y descubierto;
viendo que a pie en lo llano es mal
    partido
seguir a los caballos campo abierto,
el alto y primer cerro deja esento,
pensando allí alcanzarlos por aliento.

(Ercilla, *La Araucana*, 4.91, 1–8)

This slope Lautaro had selected
to do battle and by agreement
had his entire army laid out
at the highest and most exposed point;
seeing that being on foot on the plain gives
    poor advantage
following horses in an open field,
the tall and first mountain leaves clear,
thinking to reach them there without
    stopping.

Ercilla's next lines continue to show his concern for locating geographical features with precision.

Porque se tome bien del sitio el tino	So as best to understand the site
quiero aquí figurarle por entero.	I want here to describe it entirely.
La subida no es mala del camino,	The climb from the path is not bad,
mas todo es lo demás despeñadero;	but all the rest is precipitous;
tiene al poniente al bravo mar vecino	to the west lies the savage sea
que bate al pie de un gran derrumbadero	which beats at the foot of a great precipice
y en la cumbre y más alto de la cuesta	and at the summit and highest point of
se allana cuanto un tiro de balleta.	the hill
	the land levels off.

(Ercilla, *La Araucana*, 4.92, 1–8)

The battle ends with a disastrous Spanish defeat. Ercilla devotes two entire cantos to it, emphasizing that geography and the Araucanians' close familiarity with the territory aided Lautaro in his ambush of the Spaniards. The poet makes many references to the character of the terrain. On top of the hill, the Araucanians had built a sort of stone wall behind which they defended themselves and which the Spaniards reached only with considerable effort.

Aunque la cuesta es áspera y derecha,	Although the hill is tough and precipitous,
muchos a la alta cumbre han arribado,	many reached the high summit,
adonde una albarrada hallaron hecha	where they found a dry stone wall
y el paso con maderos ocupado.	completed,
No tiene aquel camino otra deshecha,	and the pass full of timbers.
que el cerro casi en torno era tajado:	The road does not have another way out,
del un lado le bate la marina,	that the hill, round about, was sliced:
del otro un gran peñol con él confina.[41]	on one side the sea beats against it,
	on the other, a great rock confines it.

(Ercilla, *La Araucana*, 6.38, 1–8)

Francisco de Villagrá and his men got over the stone wall that served as a defense only to be surprised by an abyss where many fell to their deaths. The lines of the poem are effective in conveying not only the drama of the scene but also the particular attributes of the terrain that contributed to deciding the outcome in favor of the Araucanians.

Los bárbaros airados defendían	The barbarians, angry, defended
el paso, pero al cabo no pudieron,	the pass, but in the end they could not,
que por más que las armas esgremían	because for all the weapons wielded
los fuertes españoles los rompieron;	the powerful Spaniards break them;
unos hacia la mano diestra guían,	some lead toward the right,
otros tan buen camino no supieron,	others never knew so excellent a road,
tomando a la siniestra un mal sendero	taking to the left a wrong trail
que a dar iba en un gran despeñadero.	went to a great precipice.

(Ercilla, *La Araucana*, 6.44, 1–8)

The description of landscapes and battles is a constant in the poem.[42] Nature is frequently presented in the context of Araucanian leaders, especially the protagonists Lautaro, Rengo, and Caupolicán. Particularly noteworthy are the events related to Caupolicán's flight and his subsequent capture after the unsuccessful Araucanian assault on the fortress of Cañete in 1558. The scenes are presented in the context of a geography that Caupolicán knew well.[43]

The lines about the battle of Acoma in Villagrá's *Historia*, to which he devotes no fewer than five cantos (27 to 31), recall Ercilla's description of the battle on Andalicán hill.[44] Villagrá uses the expression "peñol soberbio" (proud rock) to refer to the enormous mesa where Acoma is located. The poet combines two related meanings here: a lofty rock, and one that represents arrogance and pride, which for the poet was the attitude of the Acoma people. The mesa is 357 feet high, and in the sixteenth century it was accessed by a type of stairway cut into the rock. Upon encountering the rocky formation of Acoma, Villagrá noted that there were two rocks united by a corridor. In Mercedes Junquera's edition of the poem, she mentions that Villagrá demonstrates that he knew the terrain better than other witnesses, because he describes the division of the rock in two, "united by a narrow corridor replete with fissures and cracks formed by erosion of the terrain."[45]

Y assí, marchando en orden, nos llegamos	Thus, marching in order, we did arrive Before the mighty fort, which consisted
Al poderoso fuerte, el cual constaba	Of two great, lofty rocks upraised,
De dos grandes peñoles lebantados,	The terrible, unconquered sites
Más de trescientos passos devididos	Divided by more than three hundred feet,
Los terribles assientos no domados,	And from one to the other was a neck
Y estaba un passamán del uno al otro,	Of rocks so lofty they equaled
De riscos tan soberbios que ygualaban	The outsized peaks, such as were never
Con las disformes cumbres nunca vistas,	seen,
(Villagrá, *Historia*, 27, 117–24)	

The Spaniards were led by Sargento Mayor Vicente de Zaldívar, who had been named lieutenant governor for this mission. They attacked Acoma Pueblo on January 22, 1599, and for almost three days the violent battle was waged.[46] Villagrá was an active protagonist in the fighting, and his description of the battle is based on his direct experience. He details the Spanish strategy of distracting the Indians, making them believe the soldiers were climbing up the second rock, at which point the Indians left the "first rock" unoccupied, where a group of a dozen Spaniards, including Villagrá, began the ascent to surprise the defenders.

Y estaba un passamán del uno al otro	And there, between the two, was a passage
De rocas tan soberbias que igualaban	Of rocks so lofty that equaled

Con las más altas cumbres que tenían.	The very highest tops of them.
Entendido, pues, esto, con secreto	This, understood, then, secretly
Dexó doce españoles escondidos	He left twelve Spaniards in hiding
Al socaire de un risco muy pegado	Upon a lee of a crag very near
Al primer peñol, y luego al punto	To the first rock, and then at once
Mandó quitar las tiendas, de manera	He ordered the tents struck for the
Que todos claro viesen y notasen	purpose
Que, sin que Castellano allí quedase,	That all might see clearly and note
Al prometido hecho todos juntos	That, no Castilian staying there,
Determinados yban a matarlos.	All, joined for this the promised deed,
	Were coming determined to slaughter
	them.

(Villagrá, *Historia*, 28.307–18)

He notes the drama of the scene when, not having the wooden beam that had been used to cross the second crag, for it had been left on the other side, someone had to leap back to get the beam and place it as a bridge over the first crag. It was Villagrá who did it, and addressing himself to the king, he describes the moment:

Oyendo, pues, aquesto, retíreme	Hearing this, then, I did fall back,
Porque entendí, señor, que a mí dezía,	For, lord, I thought he spoke to me,
Cosa de nueve passos, y qual Curcio,[47]	Some nine paces and, like to Curtius,
Casi desesperado, fui embistiendo	I was running, near desperate,
Aquella primer zanja, y el Sargento,	Towards the first ditch and the Sergeant,
Pensando que pedazos me haría,	Thinking that I would be dashed to pieces,
Asiome del adarga y, si no suelta,	Did grasp me by the shield, and, had
Sin duda fuera aquél el postrer tiento	he not
Que diera a la fortuna yo en mi vida.	Loosed me no doubt that had been
Mas por largarme presto fui alentando	The last test I had made of fortune in
La fuerza de aquel salto de manera	my life.
Que al fin salve la zanja, y el madero,	But, as he loosed me quickly, I gathered
No libre de temor y de rezelo,	Momentum for that leap to such effect
Fuy como mejor pude allí arrastrando	That finally I jumped the ditch and then,
Y, puesto en el passage, los dos puestos	Not free from fear and trembling, I took
Passaron con presteza allí los vuestros.	The log as best I might and dragged,
	And, passage made between the ditches,
	Your men did quickly pass over.

(Villagrá, *Historia*, 30, 193–208)

In other passages of the poem, it is evident that the physical attributes of Acoma Mesa posed a challenge for the Spaniards, who were nevertheless able to take advantage of the terrain. The poem also refers to the use the Indians made of their knowledge of their natural space, such as caves and natural hideouts in the rock. In the poem, Villagrá calls the Indian leader Zutacapán, a fictional name.

Sólo Zutacapán y sus amigos,	Only Zutacapán and they his friends,
Huiendo de cobardes por no verse	Fleeing as cowards lest they see themselves
En manos de Gicombo, se escondieron	Within Gicombo's hands, did hide
En las cuevas y senos que tenía	themselves
La fuerza del peñol, cuia grandeza	Within the caves and hollows which there
Segundo labirinto se mostraba	were
Según eran sus cuevas y escondrijos,	Upon the fortress rock, whose great extent
Sus salidas y entradas y aposentos.	Did show itself a second Labyrinth
	Because of many caves and hiding holes,
	Their entrances and exits and chambers.

(Villagrá, *Historia*, 31, 260–67)

Villagrá, like Ercilla, used the techniques of epic poetry in the realistic description of the drama of battle. In the case of Acoma, the poet devoted many lines to showing the reaction of the Indians, who preferred to be burned to death or die by throwing themselves from the heights of the rock into the void rather than surrender.[48]

Although the description of the landscape and the battles therein is more frequent in Ercilla, both poets offer information that permits the reader to understand and relate the geographical characteristics to the waging of battles. Physical description of the terrain is also used effectively with several purposes: to add more drama, to include the poet as protagonist in those battles in which he participated, to use the occasion to address the king directly—the most important audience for the story—and to incorporate, whenever possible, references to mythology and classical history. The battles of the Spanish American epic are conveyed in a European context but with different geography. Winning the battle had much to do with overcoming geographical impediments, particularly for the Spaniards. With respect to the Indians, the poets underscore that the natives' knowledge of geography gave them an advantage in both Chile and New Mexico. Geography thus played a relatively significant role in the consolidation or lack thereof of Spanish domination in the north and south frontier spaces of the Americas.

In 1598 and 1599, battle victories on both frontiers benefited opposite sides, with the Spaniards being forced to retreat in one case and consolidating their position in the other. On the southern frontier in 1598, Governor Martín García Oñez de Loyola was defeated in Curalaba on the banks of the Río Lumaco and killed, along with fifty soldiers who accompanied him. On the northern frontier, by the beginning of 1599, Spaniards consolidated their position by winning the battle of Acoma. On the southern frontier, the defeat at Curalaba constituted the beginning of a general Indian uprising that lasted several years, during which the Spaniards had to withdraw north of the Río Biobío, and the Spanish cities located south of the river were destroyed. Between 1598 and 1622 the Araucanians continued their successful resistance. Meanwhile, on the northern frontier the Spaniards continued to consolidate their authority at least until 1680, the year of the great rebellion of the Pueblo Indians that obliged the Spaniards to completely abandon New Mexican territory until their return in 1693.

CHAPTER 6

Geographic Landmarks

Que del grande trabajo fatigados
en el largo y veloz curso aflojaron,
y por el gran tesón desalentados
a seis leguas de alcance los dejaron.
Los nuestros, del temor más aguijados,
al entrar de la noche se hallaron
en la estrema ribera de Biobío
adonde pierde el nombre y ser de río.

Exhausted by the great effort
they [the Spaniards] slowed down in the
   long and speedy course,
discouraged by the great tenacity
they left the Araucanians within six
   leagues of reaching them.
Our men, mostly spurred on by fear,
found themselves, as night fell
at the extreme end of the Biobío River,
where it loses the name and form of a
   river.

(Ercilla, *La Araucana*, 7.3, 1–8)

Mas la gran providencia, condolida,
Que tanto es más beloz en socorrernos
Quanto con más firmeza la esperamos,
Al quinto abrió las puertas y fuimos
   todos,
Alegres, arribando el bravo Río
Del Norte, por quien todos padezimos
Cuidados y trabajos tan pesados.

But great Providence, pitying,
Which is always quicker in helping us
As we more firmly trust in it,
The fifth day opened up the door
And we all, happily, did come upon the
   roaring River
Of the North, for which we all had
   undergone
Such care and such enormous toil.

(Villagrá, *Historia*, 14, 100–106)

An Araucanian legend says that "the waters of the rivers have mysterious genies that lie in wait for men."[1] There is no question that in Chile there was a river, the Biobío, whose "genies" impeded the consolidation of the Spanish conquest, at least during the sixteenth century and part of the seventeenth. The Biobío River became a geographic landmark and a natural boundary of the war. The Río del Norte, or Rio Grande, on the Spanish-American northern frontier also became a geographic landmark, although with different characteristics because of the nature of the war in the north, which involved a largely sedentary indigenous population. Just as these two rivers, and others, were important in the conquest, so were other elements of the landscape. In the context of imperial literature, the regional geography woven throughout *La Araucana* and *Historia de la Nueva México* helps define them as epics with a Spanish-American frontier theme.

This final look at both regions and their natural space in part II of this book is devoted to the presence of geographic landmarks that, because of their physical characteristics and location, became part of the historical context of the two poems. The river, the plain, the rocky promontory, and the volcano are the major landmarks that each poet describes. The topographic features that loom large in each poem help identify the nonfictional aspects of the histories they relate. Literary critic Rolena Adorno affirms in her analysis of the polemics of possession that the writings of early Spanish colonial literature (among them the chronicle, the report, and the epic) "do not describe events; they are events, and they transcend self-reference to refer to the world outside themselves."[2] This idea can be applied here to geographic landmarks. Their presence in the poetic discourse of *La Araucana* and the *Historia* indicates the important role of certain physical characteristics of the natural space itself that were as real as the presence of each poet in that space.

These landmarks, as well as frontier geography in general, went on to become active elements ("events") rather than passive elements, not only because they could impede or facilitate the Spanish advance, but also because without them much of the content of the poems would be missing. In fact, landmarks served as inspiration for some of the best lines of the poems.

The objective of this chapter is to analyze the presence of these geographic landmarks in the historical context of the Spanish entrada on both frontiers and to show their importance as active elements in the histories recounted in the poems. These landmarks were essential in the life of the Indians in both Chile and New Mexico for thousands of years before the arrival of the Spaniards. Although the objective here is to study the epic, it cannot be ignored that for the Indians, these landmarks were an active part of their life and culture, whether explicitly present or not in the poetry of Spanish conquest. Undoubtedly, rivers were crucial elements for the survival of human beings before and during the Spanish presence on both frontiers.

After founding Santiago (1541) and La Serena (1544) and going back to Peru for two years, Pedro de Valdivia returned to Chile and began a campaign to consolidate the Spanish presence toward the south. Thus, in 1550 he founded the town of Concepción, in 1551 La Imperial, in 1552 the towns of Valdivia and Villarrica, and, finally, in 1553 Angol. In this last year he founded the fortresses of Arauco, Purén, and Tucapel with the goal of observing Indian movements in the far south and permitting communication between Concepción and the new cities.[3] The foundation of the towns and fortresses symbolized the consolidation (though at times only temporary) of Spanish occupation. Rivers, whose channels always represented a challenge to the Spanish advance, were important landmarks to conquer. The act of crossing them was considered to be another form of possession, as was setting foot on the land.

In his poem, Ercilla left a record of the importance of crossing the rivers in the consolidation of the Spanish occupation. The following lines mention the *entrada* of Valdivia into the region south of the city of Santiago; the region's geography was dominated by important rivers such as the Maule, the Itata, and the Andalién, in whose valley Valdivia founded Concepción:

Después entró Valdivia conquistando	Later Valdivia entered conquering
con esfuerzo y espada rigurosa	by rigorous effort and sword
los promaucaes, por fuerza sujetando	by force submitting the Promaucaes
curios, cauquenes, gente belicosa;[4]	the Curios, the Cauquenes, warlike people;
y el Maule y raudo Itata atravesando,	and crossing the Maule and the impetuous Itata,
llegó al Andalién, do la famosa	arrived at the Andalién, where he founded
ciudad fundó de muros levantada,	the famous city of raised ramparts,
felice en poco tiempo y desdichada,	joyful for a short time and unfortunate,

(Ercilla, *La Araucana*, 1.60, 1–8)

The Biobío and Nibequetén Rivers, which originate in the Andes, are also mentioned. Pedro de Valdivia arrived at the Biobío for the first time from the Nibequetén. Ercilla notes that after crossing the rivers and the Sierra de Andalicán—a mountain chain that, as mentioned in the previous chapter, was the scene of battles—one entered Araucanian territory.

De allí llegó al famoso Biobío	From there he arrived at the famous Biobío,
el cual divide a Penco del Estado,	where Penco is separated from the State,
que del Nibequetén, copioso río,	which from the Nibequetén, a large river,
y de otros viene [Biobío] al mar acompañado.	and from others, comes accompanied to the ocean.
De donde con presteza y Nuevo brío,	From where with speed and new vigor,
en orden Buena y escuadrón formado	in good order and formed squadron
pasó de Andalicán la áspera sierra	he passed through the rough mountain range of Andalicán
pisando la araucana y fértil tierra.	stepping on the Araucanian fertile land.

(Ercilla, *La Araucana*, 1.62, 1–8)

When war was being waged in the south of Chile between 1550 and 1656, the Biobío River represented the natural boundary of the conflict. To cross the river and found settlements south of the river meant solidifying Spanish colonization; to withdraw the settlements and retreat to the river's northern banks implied the failure of domination.[5] This is what happened with the Araucanian rebellion of 1598, which destroyed all the cities south of the Biobío.

In reality, Araucanian territory began farther north, on the banks of the Itata River, but once Valdivia reached the Biobío River, it became the northern limit of the Araucanian advance. Thus, a geographical element—a river—became a historical symbol. The importance of the Biobío was more historical than geographic. As a frontier, its character was more psychological than physical because it did not really constitute an insurmountable barrier. With numerous fords, changes in the current, and shifting sandbanks and gravel, it was easy to cross.[6]

The course of the Biobío River is 211 miles long (approximately 340 kilometers) and in some places as much as 0.62 mile wide (one kilometer). Its waters are augmented by spring runoff and summer and winter rains. From turbulent headwaters at an altitude of 3,772 feet (about 1,150 meters) in Galletué and Icalma Lakes, it finally becomes a river of calm water that empties into the sea. This exit to the South Sea, or Pacific Ocean, and its close proximity to the Strait of Magellan increased the significance of the Biobío, which went beyond being the natural frontier of the war with the Araucanians. The river was a natural entrance into Chilean territory. From the end of the sixteenth century on, the threat of English and Dutch pirates who arrived in the Pacific through the Strait of Magellan made it necessary for the Spanish to reinforce their armed presence on the Chilean coast. Francis Drake, for example, had arrived in the Biobío region in 1578.[7]

Any Spanish campaign aimed at subjugating Araucanian territory had to start by crossing the Biobío, which resulted in more than one battle being waged on its banks. But there were other rivers that also constituted the natural margins of the war. The Biobío and Toltén Rivers were the boundaries of the state of Arauco, where the Araucanians held out until the end, and where the fighting was concentrated. Between the two rivers is another, the Cautín River, which in its last stretch joins with various streams, creating what the Spaniards called the Imperial River. After its confluence with the Cautín, the Imperial drains into the sea. The town of La Imperial was founded in 1551 near the confluence of the Cautín and Imperial Rivers. Valdivia chose the townsite because it was in a zone of dense indigenous habitation and because the river was navigable from the sea. Valdivia compared Cautín to the Guadalquivir River at Seville.[8]

References to rivers in the telling of history are so frequent in *La Araucana* that they become protagonists in the events. More than once Ercilla relies on elegant poetic expressions to refer to the emptying of the river into the sea, almost always in the context of battles. One example is the mention of the Claro River in the description of the military encounters in 1557 between the Spaniards, led by Pedro de Villagrá (cousin of Francisco de Villagrá), and the Araucanians, led by Lautaro.

Éste sin más tardar tomó el camino	He, without further delay, took the road,
en demanda del bárbaro Lautaro	in search of the barbarian Lautaro

y el cargo que tan loco desatino
como es venir allí, le cueste caro.
Diose tal priesa a andar que presto vino
a la corva ribera del río Claro,
que vuelve atrás en círculo gran trecho,
después hasta la mar corre derecho.

and knowing that such crazy blunder
of coming there, will cost him dearly.
He hurried his march and quickly he
 arrived
at the bend of the bank of Claro River,
which returns in a circle for a very great
 distance,
and further on it runs straight into the sea.

(Ercilla, *La Araucana*, 11.47, 1–8)

A similar example is the mention of the Itata River, included in a story about Lautaro. Ercilla's poetic description of the campsite chosen by the Araucanian leader is noteworthy, as are the poet's references to the river and its exit to the sea.

Así el feroz Lautaro caminaba
y al fin de tres jornadas, entretanto
que esperado tiempo se avecina,
se aloja en una vega a la marina,

junto adonde con recio movimiento
baja de un monte Itata caudaloso,
atravesando aquel umbroso asiento
con sesgo curso, grave y espacioso,

Thus the ferocious Lautaro marched,
and at the end of three journeys,
as the awaited time approached,
he camped on a boggy swamp by the sea,

next to where with hefty movement
down from the mountain Itata comes
 copiously,
crossing that shady site
with a slanting course, grave and spacious,

(Ercilla, *La Araucana*, 12.42, 5–8; 43, 1–4)

Siete leguas de Penco justamente
es ésta deleitosa y fértil tierra,
abundante, capaz y suficiente
para poder sufrir gente de guerra.
Tiene cerca a la banda del oriente
la grande cordillera y alta sierra,
de donde el raudo Itata apresurado
baja a dar su tributo al mar salado.

Seven leagues from Penco precisely
is where this delightful and fertile land is,
abundant, capable and sufficient
to maintain people at war.
Nearby, to the East
it has the great mountain ridges and tall
 mountain range,
from where the impetuous Itata
comes down to the sea to pay its tribute.

(Ercilla, *La Araucana*, 12.44, 1–8)

Ercilla's account of the river and the Indian presence there recalls the ancient link that existed between the natives and their rivers and lakes in southern Chile. Rivers were not only active elements in the Spanish conquest; rather, before the conquest, they were important in the organization of Araucanian society. The native people inhabited the areas on the banks of rivers and lakes. Life beside the river was possibly the first element of Indian social organization. Congregated near a river or river basin, families' lives had important connections with the rivers that were for the Indians systems of communication. After the conquest they became divisions or frontiers.[9] Before the arrival of the Spaniards, the Biobío and its basin constituted the region most heavily populated by Indians, together with the coast and the basins of the Cautín and Valdivia Rivers.[10] In the Mapuche language the Biobío was called Butalebu or Butalevo, which means "large river."[11]

On the northern Spanish-American frontier, another large river became the natural boundary of war. Crossing it from the south meant an entrada into Indian territory, although the conquest of this region had different characteristics from that of the southern frontier. The Rio Grande on the northern frontier flows from north to south, not from east to west as does the Biobío, and its course follows a route to what the Spaniards called the interior or "tierra adentro;" entering the territory of sedentary Indians. The Rio Grande was not called thus, either during the colonial period or during most of the period in which the territory belonged to Mexico (1821–46). In these two historical periods it was called Río del Norte or Río Bravo.[12] Villagrá corroborates this in his poem.

Del caudaloso Río que del Norte	Of that wide stream that from the north
Deciende manso y tanto se embrabece	Flows calm, yet swells so much
Que también Río bravo le llamamos.	That we call it the Río Bravo, too.
(Villagrá, *Historia*, 11, 169–71)	

The Río del Norte, today's Rio Grande, flows for some 1,800 miles (around 2,880 kilometers) and is an essential geographic element in the history of the states through which it flows: from Colorado, through central New Mexico and the border between Texas and Mexico, to empty into the Gulf of Mexico.[13] Before the arrival of the Spaniards, groups of Pueblo Indians who spoke Tewa, Tiwa, Keresan, and Piro were located on the banks of the river or its tributaries in elevated zones or terraces. Many pueblos, including those that have survived to this day, are located at the confluence of the Rio Grande and its tributaries.[14]

The Rio Grande was seen for the first time by Spaniards who came from the Gulf of Mexico and called it the Río de las Palmas (River of the Palms), but this name did not extend to the north.[15] The first reference to crossing the river in the chronicles was in the report of Álvar Núñez Cabeza de Vaca, the first Spaniard to cross it.[16] Later, in September 1540, the expedition of Francisco Vázquez de Coronado arrived at the river, coming from the pueblos of Zuni and Acoma, and called it "Nuestra Señora" (Our Lady).

The next expedition to arrive at the Rio Grande was that of Franciscan Agustín Rodríguez and Captain Francisco Sánchez Chamuscado in 1581. They arrived at the river coming from the south and crossed the Conchos River, a tributary of the Rio Grande in what is today the Mexican state of Chihuahua. The Rodríguez-Chamuscado expedition called the Rio Grande the Guadalquivir.[17] In the chronicle of the expedition of Antonio de Espejo in 1582, the name Río del Norte is frequently mentioned, although it is also called Río Turbio (Turbulent River) in its southern part because of its muddy water. Around 1590 the most common name was Río del Norte, with the name Río Bravo applied to the lowest part of the river. The Gaspar Castaño de Sosa expedition in 1591 also explored what he called the Río del Norte.[18]

But it was the group of would-be colonizers led by Juan de Oñate in 1598 that officially made the Río del Norte a fundamental participant in taking possession of the land, a fact Villagrá included in his poem. Before arriving at the Río del Norte, Oñate crossed the Río de las Conchas (today the Conchos River). In describing the Oñate expedition during its passage north through the present-day Mexican state of Chihuahua and arrival at the Conchos River, the poet says that the train of livestock, persons, and wagons stretched three miles long and three miles wide. Villagrá elegantly describes the course of the river and the way in which it empties into the sea, an interesting copy of the Ercillian model.[19]

Hasta llegar [la expedición] con bien a las Riberas	Until, with fortune, it came to the banks Of Río de Conchas, whose name
Del Río de las Conchas, cuio nombre	is taken from the beauty of its shells, it creates
Tomó por la belleza que se crían	
Quales vistosos nácares graciosos,	Like graceful, slightly pearl-mother,
A bueltas de gran suma de pescado,	And, too, its mighty store of fish.
Cuia vertiente vemos que derrama	We saw there that its source bursts forth
Por donde el claro sol su luz esconde	Toward where the glowing sun doth hide his light,
Y a la remota parte de Lebante,	And in some remote place to the Levant
Por torzidos caminos y veredas	It goes by winding roads and trails
Va al poderoso mar restituyendo.	To its waters back unto the sea.

(Villagrá, *Historia*, 10, 48–57)

The poem mentions that the volume of water in the river made it difficult to find a crossing-place.

De donde resulto tentar un vado	Whence they resolved to try a ford
Algo dificultoso y mal seguro,	Somewhat difficult and hardly safe,
Por cuia causa muchos temerosos	For which cause many fearful ones
Asegurar passage no quisieron	Would not attempt a passage
Por no ser de sus aguas caudalosas	Lest by its waters copious they might
Sorbidos y tragados sin remedio.	Be swallowed up and drowned without recourse.

(Villagrá, *Historia*, 10, 64–72)

Here once more Villagrá highlights the figure of Oñate—who demonstrates his horsemanship in crossing the river—comparing him with the Roman military leader Julius Caesar.[20]

Y assí el Gobernador, qual Caio César,
Que sin freno ni rienda gobernaba
La fuerza de caballos bien soberbios,
Assí saltó en un caballo bravo,
De terrible corage, desembuelto,
Notando con aviso y con destreza
Que nunca es eloquente en sus razones
Aquél que las propone si admirados
Con proprias obras y valor de brazos
No dexa a los oyentes, y rendidos
A sólo el apetito blanco y fuerza
Que aspira la corriente de su gusto.

So the Governor, like Caius Caesar,
Who without rein or bridle governed
The spirit of the wildest horse,
Then leaped upon a fearless horse
Of terrible and fearsome mettle,
Noting advisedly, with skill,
That he is never eloquent in reasoning
He who proposes things, unless by his
    own works
And valor of his arms he leaves the ones
Who hear him all surprised, surrendered
    quite
Unto the target, appetite, and course
The current of his will would take.

(Villagrá, *Historia*, 10, 73–83)

The poet uses the moment to give a dramatic tone to the poem, at the same time demonstrating the leadership of Oñate, whose actions Villagrá describes in this way:

Y con estas razones fue bolviendo
Las riendas al caballo poderoso
Y assí se abalanzó al bravo Río,
Y rompiendo las aguas fue bufando
El animal gallardo, desembuelto.

And with these words he then did loose
The reins unto his powerful horse,
And thus did plunge into the rushing
    stream.
The gallant, raging animal,
Snorting, did breast the waves.

(Villagrá, *Historia*, 10, 92–96)

Here a brief note should be made of Villagrá's use of nautical similes, especially in scenes that describe the crossing of rivers such as the Conchos and Río del Norte. Elizabeth Davis has analyzed this topic in depth, concluding that here the poet is making use of the ancient tradition of linking epic poetry and the sea. Furthermore, the personal experience of the poet who crossed the Atlantic five times before the publication of his poem is, according to Davis, another historical reason to understand his interest in images of navigation.[21]

Once across the Conchos River, Oñate sent an advance squad, in which Villagrá took part, to find the Río del Norte. Thus, the Río del Norte became an important geographic symbol in the conquest of New Mexico. The Biobío River in Chile held geopolitical significance similar to that of the Río del Norte. It is also worthy of note that these two rivers are similar in some stretches. They are comparable to one another in their importance to the history of the Spanish conquest. For the Indians on each frontier, they were natural resources for survival, while for the Spaniards they were symbols of imperial positioning, geographic landmarks of penetration. Crossing the rivers implied the continuation of exploration in the quest, not only for the subjugation of the Indians, but also for natural resources (mines in particular), and of the passage to the "other sea"—on the northern frontier, to the Pacific, and on the southern frontier, to the Atlantic. One difference between the two rivers is that while the Biobío constituted a frontier in and of itself, the Río del Norte constituted a route to follow to the interior populated by sedentary Indians.

The long and wide rivers, the enormous lakes, the varied flora and fauna, the expanse of the horizon, the immensity of the space, the towering mountains and volcanoes were all geographical elements that contributed to create, in the minds of sixteenth-century Spaniards, a "savage" (in the sense of untamable) view of the Americas. The vast plains, which to Spanish eyes appeared endless, were seen as veritable oceans of grass. In fact, the nearest comparison for Europeans was the sea, and thus the plains of eastern New Mexico and what are today the states of Texas and Kansas, areas also known for their herds of bison or buffalo, were described as seas.[22]

In the *Relación postrera de Cíbola* ("The Latest Account about Cibola") the land is described as being "as flat as the sea" and there is "such a multitude of cattle that they are beyond counting."[23] Pedro de Castañeda, chronicler of the expedition of Vázquez de Coronado, probably provided the most accurate description with respect to the disorientation to which the Spaniards were exposed in the middle of the plains,

> wandering about the country as if they were crazy, in one direction or another, not knowing how to get back where they started from, although this ravine extended in either direction so that they could find it. Every night they took account of who was missing, fired guns and blew trumpets and beat drums and built great fires. . . . It is worth noting that the country there is so flat that at midday, after one has wandered about in one direction and another in pursuit of game, the only thing to do is to stay near the game quietly until sunset, so as to see where it goes down, and even then they have to be men who are practiced to do it.[24]

Hernán Gallegos, in his account of the Rodríguez-Chamuscado expedition of 1581, stated in reference to the presence of buffalo on the plains that "They are so large that when seen in the midst of a plain they resemble ships at sea or carts on land."[25] These contemporaneous accounts of the expeditions prior to 1598 show that Villagrá did not exaggerate in describing the same plains.

Y gozan de unos llanos tan tendidos	And they enjoy such widespread plains
Que por seyscientas y ochocientas leguas	That for six and eight hundred leagues
Un sossegado mar parece todo,	All seems to be a peaceful sea
Sin género de cerro ni vallado	With no sort of valley or hill

| Donde en manera alguna pueda el hombre | Where a man can in any way Limit his vision or rest it |

Topar la vista acaso o detenerla
  (Villagrá, *Historia*, 17, 95–100)

Clearly the poet relied on the stories told by the group of sixty-some Spaniards who had gone out to hunt buffalo in 1598. The leader of the expedition, Sargento Mayor Vicente de Zaldívar, described the episode. In his account, called the *Relación de la xornada de las bacas*, Zaldívar described the animal in great detail, as well as the frustrated attempt to hunt it using the Spanish technique of the rodeo.[26] José Rabasa, in his book, *Writing Violence in the Northern Frontier*, includes an analysis of Zaldívar's description of the buffalo, which Rabasa titles "Zaldívar's Whimsical Bison." In the words of Rabasa, "Zaldívar recreates by means of the pen what is marvelous and ferocious, fearsome, and laughable—a source of delight even for the melancholic."[27] Zaldívar's description of the bison, to which Rabasa refers, merits being cited here.

> Their shape and form is so marvelous and comical or astonishing that the more you see them, the more you desire to see them, and no one would be so melancholic that if one saw them a hundred times every day one would very willingly laugh each of these hundred times and marvel at the sight of such a fierce animal.[28]

More than one Spanish chronicler included the animal in his descriptions. Álvar Núñez Cabeza de Vaca was the first European to mention the buffalo in an account, which was first published in 1542.

> Cows come here; I have seen them three or four times and eaten them. It seems to me they are about the size of the ones in Spain. . . . They have two small horns, like Moorish cattle, and very long hair, like a fine blanket made from the wool of merino sheep. . . . These animals come from the North all the way to the coast of Florida, where they scatter, crossing the land for more than four hundred leagues. All along their range, through the valleys where they roam, people who live near there descend to live off them, and take inland a great quantity of their hides.[29]

The works of chroniclers of the Indies, such as Gonzalo Fernández de Oviedo y Valdés (1535–47), Francisco López de Gómara (1554), and Juan López de Velasco (1571–74) also include descriptions of hunting buffalo, its utilization by the Indians, and the immediate use that the Spaniards also began to make of this animal, especially as a food source.[30] The presence of the buffalo on the North American prairies fascinated the Spaniards. The view of the buffalo on the plains signified a completely new image that, for the Spaniards who saw them, was at times difficult to describe to people who had never seen them. Villagrá reveals the great impression the buffalo made on the Spaniards.

Con esto, todos juntos se metieron
Los llanos más adentro y encontraron
Tanta suma y grandeza de ganados
Que fue cosa espantosa imaginarlos.
Son del cuerpo que toros Castellanos,
Lanudos por extremo, corcobados,
De regalada carne y negros cuernos,
Lindíssima manteca y rico cebo,
Y como los chibatos, tienen barbas,
Y son a una mano tan ligeros
Que corren mucho más que los venados,
Y andan en atajos tanta suma
Que veynte y treynta mil cabezas juntas
Se hallan ordinarias muchas vezes.

After this all did travel on
Further into the plains and found
Such sum and mighty herds of beasts
That 'twas a frightful thing to imagine
    them.
In size they are like Spanish bulls,
Wooly in the extreme and all
    humpbacked,
Of plenteous flesh and of black horns,
Most splendid lard and rich in fur,
And, like the goats, they have beards,
And they are so swift turning
That they do run much more than deer,
And so many do go in bands
That twenty, thirty thousand head at once
Are often and commonly found.

(Villagrá, *Historia*, 17, 81–94)

Villagrá relates the Spaniards' frustrated attempt to hunt buffalo using the same technique they would use with a herd of cows, that is, driving them into a sort of corral, in the same episode that Zaldívar recounts. Faced with the failure of the operation, they decided to use their firearms.

Todos en buenas yeguas voladoras
Aventando salieron el ganado,
Y assi como la manga descubrieron,
Qual poderoso viento arrebatado
Que remata en un grande remolino,
Assí fue reparando y rebolviendo,
La fuerza del ganado lebantando
Un terremoto espeso, tan cerrado
Que si junto a unas peñas no se halla
La soldadesca toda guarecida
No quedara ninguno que hecho piezas
Entre sus mismos pies no se quedara.
Por cuia causa luego dieron orden
Que el ganado en paradas se matase,
Y todo assí dispuesto, hizieron carne

All mounted on swift and good mares,
They sailed forth to drive the herds
And, as soon as these saw the trap,
Precipitate as a powerful wind
Which ends up in a great whirlwind,
They did stop and whirled to the rear,
The force of the beasts, raising up
An earthquake so heavy and so blinding
That, had the soldiers not found
    themselves
Protected by some nearby rocks,
There would not have been one of them
Not cut to pieces 'neath their hoofs.
Wherefore an order then was given
That these cattle should be killed as they
    stood,
And, all being thus arranged, they made
    meat

(Villagrá, *Historia*, 17, 137–51)

The Indian guides who witnessed the slaughter were frightened, in the words of the poet, to see the weapons of the Spaniards. The buffalo hunt culminated in a show of Spanish force. The firearms represented power, not the skill in hunting, a skill Villagrá attributes to the Apache Indians who killed buffalo "on foot" and whom the poet terms *vaqueros*, "cowboys."

Los quales vieron siempre en estos llanos	We always saw upon these plains
Gran suma de vaqueros que apie matan	Great sums of cowboys, who did kill, on foot,
Aquestas mismas vacas que dezimos	Those same cows we have spoken of,
Y dellas se sustentan y mantienen,	And from them maintained and sustained themselves,
Toda gente robusta y de trabajo,	All robust folk and hard workers,
Desenfadada, suelta y alentada,	Unembarrassed and free and spirited,

     (Villagrá, *Historia*, 17, 158–63)

The plains and the buffalo thus represented elements of local geography that put the Spaniards' survival techniques to the test, although the buffalo also became an important food source.

Crossing the immense prairies was a challenge for the Spaniards; they could easily get lost without visual points of reference. The identification of geographic landmarks was fundamental for Spanish exploration. Those points that could be seen in the distance marked the direction in which to continue the march or to visualize the final destination of a journey. For the Indians, of course, many of these geographic landmarks had been their reference points for thousands of years. The Spaniards gave names in their language to specific places, or renamed those that already had Indian names, as if this automatically implied domination. Thus, they gave names to specific types of geographic features. One of them is known as a *morro*, which in the sixteenth century meant a "hill or a rocky promontory with a flat point."[31] This word had also been used in reference to a hill or sheer cliff, usually next to the banks of a river or the ocean shore. This definition was extended to a construction or building with the characteristics of a coastal fortress. The word "morro" was used for the "end of a pier" and as the name of the fortresses and castles the Spaniards constructed on the coasts of the Americas, as was the case of El Morro in the bay of Havana, Cuba.[32] In any event, it denoted a headland or promontory that could be seen from a distance.

Ercilla mentions in *La Araucana* "el morro de Penco" to identify the hill or group of hills located next to the beach in Talcahuano Bay. In 1550 Pedro de Valdivia founded Concepción adjacent to the Cerro de Penco. The town was destroyed in 1553, and when the expedition of García Hurtado de Mendoza, in which Ercilla participated, arrived there in 1557, they began to rebuild the fortress of Penco, not far from where Concepción was located. Today Penco and Concepción are two different communities, but the geographic aspect of the bay Ercilla described in the sixteenth century continues to look the same. Penco is flanked on the west by what is today called the Tumbes Peninsula and on the northwest by the small island—the poet called it an "isleta"—of Quiriquina, which protected the port from the strong tide. That is where the ship that brought Hurtado de Mendoza, as newly named governor and captain general of Chile, from Peru found safe haven during an impressive storm before arriving at the bay, in July 1557. This event is described in detail by Ercilla, who witnessed it.

The storm's episode looms large because it is the moment in which the poet begins to live his Chilean experience. Perhaps for this reason, the description of the storm is graphic and exaggeratedly long (136 lines in seventeen stanzas). The storm is a perfect event for an epic poem, in which the poet can shine with dramatic details. Part 1 of the poem ends with a description of the storm, a finale that leaves the reader in suspense. In canto 15 (the first canto of part 2) Ercilla continues to describe the storm. The poet ends the tale with the view of the morro of Penco in the horseshoe-shaped bay, a landmark that represented the geographic point the Spaniards so avidly sought.

En esto, la cerrada niebla escura	In this, the heavy fog dispersed
por el furioso viento derramada,	scattered by the furious wind,
descubrimos al este la Herradura,	we discovered to the east the Herradura,
y al sur la isla de Talca levantada.	and to the south the island of Talca
Reconocida ya nuestra ventura	elevated.
y la araucana tierra deseada,	Already recognizing our fortune
viendo el morro de Penco descubierto,	and the desired Araucanian land,
arribamos a popa sobre el puerto;	seeing Penco's promontory uncovered,
	we arrived at the port;

(Ercilla, *La Araucana*, 16.17, 1–8)

The morro of Penco adjacent to Talcahuano Bay was an important reference point on the southern coast of Chile, as was "El Morro" in New Mexico. Villagrá describes El Morro in his poem as "certain lofty cliffs" (*unos peñascos levantados*). This expression understates the real dimension of this landmark, which is two hundred feet (sixty meters) high. However, the poet does not use the term Morro. The Spaniards must have begun to use that name at some point in the seventeenth century, because earlier documents, including Villagrá's, do not. The earliest written documentation of the word "morro" referring to the place about which the poet writes appears in the 1692 campaign journal of Diego de Vargas, in which he refers to the feature by that name at least six times.[33]

The existence of El Morro was first documented in the journal of Diego Pérez de Luxan, chronicler of the expedition of Antonio de Espejo in 1583. They had previously passed by Acoma and through an area covered with lava, where they camped. Four days after their departure from Acoma, they arrived at the place they called "pool of the rock" on March 1, 1583.[34] The name describes the physical characteristics of the place: a prominent sandstone mass with a permanent pool of water at its base, filled by summer rain and winter snow and about twelve feet deep. The outcropping and its pool are located some thirty miles east of Zuni Pueblo and seventy miles west of Acoma Pueblo in New Mexico.

Villagrá reached El Morro in November 1598 on his trip from Acoma, having returned to the area through Santa Bárbara, in what is today north-central Mexico, after having killed two deserters, on the orders of Juan de Oñate. At Acoma he found the Indians in a distrustful frame of mind. Fearing his life was at risk, he departed rapidly, passing over the lava flows that Diego de Luxan had recorded in his chronicle of the 1583 expedition. There, as mentioned, the poet lost his horse in an animal trap and was surprised by a snowstorm. Villagrá, almost dying of hunger and thirst, dramatically describes his arrival at the famous pool of water at the base of the "lofty cliffs."

Hasta que por gran suerte fuy llegando	Until, by great good luck, I reached
Al pie de unos peñascos lebantados,	The foot of certain lofty cliffs,
En cuio assiento y puesto vi que estaba	In which place I did see there was
Un apazible estanque de agua fría,	A pleasant pool of cold water,
Sobre cuyos cristales, casi ciego,	Over whose crystal depths I, almost blind,
Apenas fuy venciendo la gran furia	Scarcely could conquer the great fury
De la insaziable sed que me acababa,	Of that insatiable thirst that all but ended me
Quando temblando, todo estremecido,	When, trembling all over, quivering,
El húmido licor lancé forzado.	I forcibly threw up the damp fluid.

(Villagrá, *Historia*, 19, 249–57)

Three soldiers rounding up horses that had been scattered by a snowstorm found the poet near death at Agua de la Peña, the pool of water at El Morro. He had gone for two or three days without food. A chronicle of Oñate's failed expedition to the South Sea and the salt flats confirms the words of the poet. The governor was exploring the area of the Zuni Salt Lakes some forty miles southeast of Zuni Pueblo with a group of Spaniards when the poet and his rescuers came to meet them.[35]

To reach El Morro, Villagrá had followed the ancient Indian route from Acoma to Zuni Pueblo that passed by the foot of the promontory. That was the natural route to follow, given that El Morro was a landmark that both Indians and Spaniards could see from miles away as a rocky protuberance jutting out of the earth on the vast prairie and long valley. Obviously it was a fundamental point of orientation. Nevertheless, because early reports mention the place as "the pool of the rock" or "water of the rock," it leads one to believe that the site was most valued for its water. It was a place to rest, protected by the enormous rock, after a long journey. Moreover, the ruins of an Indian pueblo on top of El Morro, abandoned long before the arrival of those first Spaniards, is proof that the rock had been an ancient site of human settlement.

Before the arrival of the Spaniards, the place was known as Atsinna, the Zuni word to refer to "a place of writing on stone." In fact, the existence of indigenous petroglyphs on the rock proves this. In addition to the petroglyphs, many other inscriptions of passersby are found on the rock. Among them is the name of Juan de Oñate, who paused at El Morro on April 16, 1605, on his trip back from searching for the South Sea.[36] Oñate's inscription represents the Spaniards' desire to leave a record of their presence in those lands. In the same way as Ercilla had left his lines inscribed on the trunk of a tree in southern Chile, Oñate left his name, proof of the discoverer's need to appropriate in some way what was discovered.

Today El Morro is a point of historical interest that is worth seeing because it constitutes a geographic landmark on which different civilizations have left their mark as they passed by, including inscriptions in English from the nineteenth century. The site is a geographic point in the history of Spanish imperialism; that is, another natural element of the geography of war. Because the landscape is little changed in much of the territory of the southwestern United States and because there are still vast unpopulated areas, it is possible today to see geographic landmarks such as El Morro from a distance.

In the south of Chile, this type of geographic landmark that served as a point of reference for the Indians and Spaniards also existed, and fortunately can be seen and enjoyed today. Among the many landmarks, one in particular is worthy of mention because it is cited in *La Araucana*: the Villarrica volcano. In canto 34 Ercilla describes the journey of Governor García Hurtado de Mendoza's expedition to the south, and eventually its arrival at the "desaguadero" that is today the Canal de Chacao. The poet was not part of this group originally, he joined the governor and his men later, in Valdivia (the Spanish southernmost Spanish settlement in Chile). In the poem, Ercilla mentions Hurtado de Mendoza's journey past the Villarrica settlement and the nearby volcano at the beginning of 1558.[37] The description of the volcano and its surrounding landscape is framed by Ercilla's need to reaffirm the crushing effect of the Spanish military presence in the area.

Pasó [García Hurtado de Mendoza] de Villarrica el fértil llano que tiene al sur el gran volcán vecino, fragua (según afirma) de Vulcano,	He passed from Villarrica a fertile plain that has to the south the great neighboring volcano, a forge (as they affirm) of Vulcan,

que regoldando fuego está contino.
De allí volviendo por la diestra mano,
visitando la tierra al cabo vino
al ancho lago y gran desaguadero,
término de Valdivia y fin postrero,

    (Ercilla, *La Araucana*, 34.46, 1–8)

that continuously belches fire.
From there he turned to the left,
and visiting the land in the end came
to the wide lake and great drain,
where the boundary of where Valdivia is
   the end.

donde también llegué, que sus [Hurtado
  de Mendoza] pisadas
sin descansar un punto voy siguiendo
y de las más ciudades convocadas
iban gentes en número acudiendo
pláticas en conquistas y jornadas;
y así el tumulto bélico creciendo
en sordo són confuso ribombaba
y el vecino contorno amedrentaba;
    (Ercilla, *La Araucana*, 34.47, 1–8)

where I also arrived, that his footsteps
I followed without resting an iota
and from most of the cities summoned
people in number went
talking of conquests and journeys;
thus the warlike tumult growing
in deafening confused noise rumbled
frightened the neighboring surroundings;

Villarrica volcano forms part of a series of volcanic cones in the foothills of the Andes, a chain of hills between the Andes range and the so-called longitudinal valley. Still active, the volcano stands out from the local topography because of its height (9,341 feet).[38] The landscape of the lake of the same name, with the volcano in the background, is of incomparable beauty, even today. Ercilla did not perceive it in that way or note the natural wonder of the place in his poem.[39] The poet also failed to mention that the volcano had a Mapuche name: Rancupillán, "house of Pillán," that is, the house of the deity who lives in volcanoes.[40]

The Spaniards had chosen the area to found a town a few years earlier. Gerónimo de Alderete founded Santa María Magdalena de Villarrica on Valdivia's orders in 1552. The town was on the edge of the lake and at the mouth of the present-day Toltén River, north of the volcano. The town was abandoned two years later. García Hurtado de Mendoza ordered it resettled in 1559, but in 1602 the Araucanians captured it definitively. Apparently the name Villarrica came from the Spanish goal of exploiting nearby gold, which the Indians of the region had told them about, in addition to telling them of the existence of an easily traversed pass through the Andes. The region was fertile and had an agreeable climate.[41]

When the Araucanians attacked Villarrica in 1602, only a handful of Spaniards—thirteen women and eleven men—resided in the town. How could such a small group, at the ends of the Southern Hemisphere, represent the interests of the Spanish crown and the Catholic Church? This is difficult to answer, just as it is difficult to understand the historical phenomenon that has been called a "fever" to found Spanish towns south of the Biobío River. The impulse lasted from Pedro de Valdivia's time up to 1559. From faraway Spain, the goal of establishing a permanent Spanish presence in the south of Chile might have made sense and even been viewed with optimism. In the Americas, however, the reality was different.

While the small Spanish settlement of Villarrica in the south of Chile disappeared in 1602, in the north Oñate attempted to maintain his controversial leadership. His men were in the midst of desertions because of the failure of the conquering enterprise. At the same time, he desperately tried to convince the king that the crown should invest more into the frontier.[42]

Ercilla chose to end his poem optimistically with Hurtado de Mendoza taking possession of the southernmost land that Europeans had set foot on and with Felipe II becoming king of Portugal. The poet left the Americas with a bad taste in his mouth because of his exile, but he did not devote many lines to his plight at the end of his poem and preferred to conclude with a paean to the Spanish empire. In a similar vein, Villagrá chose to end his poem with the Spanish victory at Acoma. Although the poet devoted many lines to the Acomas' valiant defense of their land and liberty, nothing in the final cantos of the poem indicates that Villagrá himself or the Spaniards felt any remorse or doubt about the need for Spanish dominion on the northern frontier.

∼

With regard to the theme of part II—the frontier—*La Araucana* and the *Historia de la Nueva México* help foster an understanding of the Spanish conquest in an American space. The expansion of the Spanish empire in the sixteenth century, generated from Spain by means of capitulaciones, ordinances, and royal cédulas, cannot be understood without its local context and without the voice of its participants. Similarly, the study of the imagery in the poems aids in contributing to a new and richer interpretation of the "first America."[43] The poets' description of geography is congruent with the style of literature of the first two centuries of colonization. This imperial colonial poetry ranges in theme from rituals for taking possession of the land and rules of obedience and vassalage, to examples of the Indians' response, sometimes ambiguous and confused, sometimes defiant. The poems also reflect the characteristics of war as it was waged on the frontier in the sixteenth century, and an understanding of the physical space: from the Spanish impressions in the face of the vast landscape and the appearance of its flora and fauna to the profound knowledge of their natural space demonstrated by the Indians.

Spanish imperial expansion during the reigns of Carlos I and Felipe II is also presented in the two poems. This expansion is expressed through the concept of entrada, the description of expeditions of exploration, the founding of towns, the almost omnipotent royal authority, the Spanish advance to the most remote regions, and the mission of religious conversion. The expansion of empire was fed by a Spanish and Christian pride in carrying their "civilization" to the "ends" of the earth. As was anticipated in the introduction, epic poetry with an American theme contributed to the reinvention of Spain, not the Spain that supported Columbus in his voyages, but the Spain that Carlos I and his son Felipe II built in the sixteenth century: a country whose national profile could not exist or be understood without its American possessions and landscape. The epic genre that the poets chose has been considered inappropriate because it did not suit the literary times. However, the events related in the poems fit the characteristics of the historic times.

Epilogue

Thomas Jefferson's private book collection became the nucleus for the Library of Congress of the United States after the British destroyed the first library. Among the important written works in his collection was a 1776 volume of *La Araucana* by Alonso de Ercilla y Zúñiga.[1] The poem is a significant text, but the fact that the third president of the United States, one of the leaders of the American Revolution, considered it important enough to own is worth highlighting. One wonders if Jefferson were able to read some of the lines in sixteenth-century Spanish. But his ability to read it or not does not diminish the value he saw in the poem as an essential literary piece to have in his library. In 1776, the year Jefferson's copy of *La Araucana* was published and the Declaration of Independence from British colonial rule was signed, New Mexico was still a Spanish colony. The region would not officially become part of the United States until seventy-two years later.

While *La Araucana*, a poem about a remote South American region, was part of Jefferson's library in the eighteenth century and became part of the Library of Congress collections in 1815, the *Historia de la Nueva Mexico*, written about a region that would become part of the United States, was completely unknown in that country and little known even among the Spaniards and their descendants in Mexico and New Mexico. Today, the 1610 edition of the *Historia* by Gaspar Pérez de Villagrá is among the holdings of twenty-one institutions in the United States—probably the highest number of first editions of the book in any country.[2] It is considered part of the literary heritage of two countries: Mexico and the United States (three if we count Spain). Depending on the reader's perspective, the poem can be considered part of Mexican literature and, as such, part of colonial Latin American literature; or it can be claimed as part of the U.S. Hispanic literary patrimony. How did a sixteenth-century criollo, born in Puebla, Mexico, become the first author in the Hispanic literary tradition in the United States? How did a sixteenth-century Spanish soldier become the national poet of Chile?

Today, in the early twenty-first century, both poems have a unique validity that would have been difficult for their authors and their contemporaries of four

hundred years ago to imagine. The year 1997 marked four centuries since the pub-
lication of the first complete edition of Ercilla's *La Araucana*, and 2010 marked
four centuries since the publication of the first edition of Villagrá's *Historia de la
Nueva México*. In these four centuries, each poem has passed through the sieve
of the paradigms of each period and of their respective physical spaces—from
frontier colony and periphery to state and nation.

La Araucana's value as a high-quality example of its genre was true from the
time of its first printing to the present. Numerous testimonies demonstrate that
the poem has received recognition from the moment the first part of the poem
was published in 1569. It has been admired over and over for its artistic merit,
and its style and verses have inspired other epic poems and colonial narratives.
Miguel de Cervantes, the greatest Spanish-language writer of all time, immor-
talized the poem by mentioning it in the pages of his masterwork, *Don Quixote*,
as a work worth keeping.[3] Literary critics have pointed out the quality of its
poetry, and historians have used some passages as source material, particularly
lines that recount events that Ercilla either took part in or saw firsthand. Four
hundred years later, the poem is still considered to be of the same high artistic
quality.

Agustín Cueva stated in 1978 that the poem was "the only authentically
inspired demonstration of conscience in the conquest of America" and that later
examples, which lacked its artistry, had not surpassed it. He called the recre-
ation of battles "Ercilla's greatest aesthetic achievement."[4] Cueva points out that
historical circumstances—particularly the characteristics of the Arauco war—
gave Ercilla an appropriate context to write his epic poem. Ercilla "extols the
native adversary," and his choice of that option allowed him to create an epic of
high quality.[5] The advantage in Ercilla's favor is that he never became a colonizer.
Therefore, he never had to justify native servitude: "he [did] not have time to
acquire the mentality of the colonist, whose type of exploitation and whose con-
frontations with indigenous people produced racist reflexes."[6] Had Ercilla been a
colonizer, perhaps his poem would never have achieved such fame.

There is general agreement among critics that *La Araucana* depicts the heroism
of its Indian protagonists and yet is absolutely identified with Spanish imperial
ideology. For this reason, during the colonial period, the poem was read more as
a Spanish epic than as a Spanish-American epic. By the mid-nineteenth century,
the poem began to be seen as separate from its Spanish identity and instead as a
foundation of Chilean nationality. From that time up to the nineteen-seventies,
generations of intellectuals (Chilean or otherwise) saw in *La Araucana* the
seed establishing the nation of Chile, and they considered Ercilla the country's
"inventor."

Venezuelan writer Andrés Bello in 1862 referred to the poem thus: "Chile is
the only one of the modern peoples whose founding has been immortalized

by an epic poem." Bello was probably the first to state that the poem was the foundational text of Chile. He also saw in the poem "the love of humanity, the worship of justice, a generous admiration of the patriotism and boldness of the defeated."[7] Literary critic Roberto Castillo Sandoval attributes the "canonization" of *La Araucana* not only to Bello but also to earlier sources, such as the colonial author Abate Ignacio de Molina.[8]

But if the true origin of the myth of *La Araucana* as the creator of the Chilean fatherland is pinpointed, it clearly lies in the second half of the nineteenth century. The timing is ironic, for in that period the new Arauco war being waged was against an army no longer Spanish and imperial but national and Chilean, which defeated the Mapuches and proceeded to usurp their lands. This irony, which is nothing more than historical appropriation, is cited by Castillo Sandoval in referring to the final battle in 1883: "Among the victors of the day there appeared the name Caupolicán. This is not, obviously, the celebrated Araucanian hero or some Mapuche leader descended from him but a battalion of the army of the Republic of Chile."[9] In the words of Castillo Sandoval, a phenomenon of transference takes place from the Republic of Chile to the territory of Arauco: "as the name of Caupolicán is definitively Chileanized, Araucanía is appropriated and supplanted by Chile." As Castillo Sandoval notes, Chileans made the Araucanians disappear from the historical map of Chile. Thus, the occupation by the Caupolicán regiment becomes the "reconquest [of] a territory it has a right to possess by virtue of its demonstrated bravery in fighting and its fervent love of the fatherland."[10] Historian Leonardo León Solís has alluded to the same idea in observing that the interpretation of *La Araucana* in the nineteenth century and the first part of the twentieth century is characterized by the "negation of the Mapuche voice" in the poem.

A town called Ercilla was founded in the Araucanian territory in the 1880s in the occupation previously alluded to. The first colonists of Huequén Cerro Nilontraro, as the place was then called, were of Swiss, German, and French origin. In 1885 the decision was made to establish the town formally, and thus Ercilla was born, founded on February 6, 1885, by General Gregorio Urrutia Bahamonde. According to the settlement minister, Aniceto Vergara Albán, the city received the name of the poet "in memory of Captain Alonso de Ercilla y Zúñiga, who, at the time of the conquest, traveled through those fields and exalted it with his celebrated epic poem."[11]

The biography of Urrutia Bahamonde, founding father of Ercilla, suggests one piece of his generation's vision for founding the town: the Chilean army's adoption of the Araucanian "fighting temperament." General Urrutia Bahamonde participated in the Araucanía campaign between 1862 and 1869, fought in the War of the Pacific against Peru and Bolivia, and was General of the Army and Chief of Staff of the Army of the South.[12] Today, the main street of the city of

Ercilla bears the poet's name. The main plaza was finished in 1900 and continues to be the center of the life of the city. It is also witness to protests in defense of Indian rights, mentioned in the introduction to this book.

Editions of *La Araucana* and publications about it from the 1880s and well into the twentieth century, up to the 1930s and 1940s, continued to repeat the Ercillian myth. In Chile, one of the most elevated praises of Ercilla and his poem was that of Antonio de Undurraga, author of the prologue to the 1946 edition of the poem. He attributed to *La Araucana* and its author the ideals that had made the Republic of Chile "an effective democracy."[13] The voluminous publications of Chilean historian José Toribio Medina that deal with *La Araucana* and the life of its author were also published in the first half of the twentieth century. Medina's works doubtless aided the profusion of studies about the poem.[14]

The renowned Chilean poet Pablo Neruda devoted some lines to Ercilla in his *Canto general* (1950). In the poem, Neruda writes about the geography, cultural roots, and political reality of Latin America. The *Canto general* is considered not only one of the literary jewels of the Spanish language, but also an impassioned plea for Latin American unity. It is a journey through the history of the region from its Indian ancestors to the political and social ideals that began to gain ground in the 1950s. In a sort of Latin American ideological hymn, Neruda cites Ercilla in verses that emphasize the latter's nonviolent attitude with respect to the Indians.[15] Neruda also wrote about Ercilla on the occasion of the four hundredth anniversary of the publication of *La Araucana*. Reeditions of Ercilla's poem as well as books and articles about it and its author were published between 1968 and 1971. Praises abound in all of them. The voice of Neruda is included in a short piece entitled "The Messenger," in which Ercilla is referred to as "inventor and liberator." According to Neruda, Ercilla, whom he calls "Dante's messenger," was the person who "in truth" gave the stars to the Southern Cross.[16] In one of the last books published during his lifetime, Neruda again mentioned Ercilla, this time in a much more revolutionary context; denouncing the imperialism of the United States.[17]

By baptizing Ercilla as the "inventor" of Chile, Neruda's words gave the name to a compilation of articles (Neruda et al., *Don Alonso de Ercilla, inventor de Chile*, 1971) by important intellectuals of the day, whose writings reflected the idea of an Ercilla as initiator of the Chilean fatherland. In the publication, literary critic Jorge Román-Lagunas refers to *La Araucana* as the "point of departure of a nation" and adds: "If that nation [Chile] came about not by peaceful conquest or the union of neighboring tribes or voluntary submission or by birth in a bloody struggle, that nation has an epic: *La Araucana*."[18] In the same publication, Victor Raviola Molina analyzes the main points in the poem that reflect an "ethnic reality," such as epic conflict, the use of Indian vocabulary, the customs, and the characters.[19]

Therefore, the 1960s and 1970s witnessed an interpretation of *La Araucana* in which the acknowledgement of Indian elements, together with a Latin Americanist and Chilean nationalist vision, represented a reevaluation of the poem and its author. As Castillo Sandoval explains it, in those decades, the reading of the poem was given a "leftist political seal" that helped the public to perceive "the germ of Chilean national identity"—a vision curiously shared by the political forces of the right.[20] Taking up the nationalist interpretation of the poem, other publications of the same years took it upon themselves to lionize the figure of Ercilla, in some cases giving his poem a more Spanish tinge.[21]

In summary, the myth of Ercilla as inventor of Chile, and of *La Araucana* as the origin of Chilean nationality, persisted for more than a century owing to several generations of intellectuals who mythologized the poet and his poem. Their interpretations went from Hispanophilia to vindication of indigenous races, passing through every sort of nuance until arriving at anti-imperialism. Obviously these generations of writers were steeped in the values of their respective times: the (racist) European Romanticism of the nineteenth century, mixed with the birth of Latin American republics in the search for native elements, but without forgetting Spain, the motherland. In the first half of the twentieth century, this patriotic bent was followed by the strengthening of democratic values in Chile together with the need to pinpoint an origin for this nationalist and republican pride. Finally, the 1950s, 1960s, and early 1970s brought the socialist influence to Latin America, including Chile, and with it an anti-imperialist vision, reinventing a Chile that was proud of its political and economic independence. To put it another way, *La Araucana* in the twentieth century responded to every possible ideal of various historical periods, and the poem was appropriated at the same time by both those on the political right and those on the political left.

The year 1973 put an end to the socialist experiment in Chile with the military coup and dictatorship that interrupted the democratic tradition of the country for sixteen years. By 1989, with the end of the dictatorship, a new generation of intellectuals had begun to reevaluate the poem and its author from an interdisciplinary perspective that was less limited and more pluralistic. More than a century had to pass to overcome the foundational myth of the poem, to arrive at the current time in which writers in various disciplines—literary criticism, history, ethnography, and anthropology—are attempting to provide an interpretation that offers a more complete, or perhaps, less partial view, responding in accordance with a new paradigm.[22]

Thus, today the poem continues to be used and reread, and its discourse is once again analyzed, now in the light of new methodologies that seek to overcome narrow ideology. Each discipline is providing ideas to be rethought and reevaluated. Overall, it is clear that *La Araucana* should be analyzed in the context of the Spanish imperial movement of the sixteenth century and that it should be studied with an understanding of the nuances and ambiguities of its time. But to this interpretation is added an analytical perspective aligned with what literary critics call "cultural studies" and historians call "new history," the latter in the specific context of postcolonialism. Anthropology, ethnography, and linguistics are supporting disciplines that help rediscover the Mapuche voice in the poem, which traverses Ercilla's pro-Indian—albeit ethnocentric—vision.

In the past twenty years, academic criticism in Chile has brought about greater acknowledgement of ethnic minorities, including the Indians—specifically Mapuches—in the country's reconstruction of historical memory. In this new analysis and rereading of the poem, neither Ercilla's mythic Indian nor the "barbarous" Indian seen by the intellectuals of the second half of the nineteenth century is admired. Today the "Mapuche voice" that Ercilla included in the poem is being reinterpreted from various perspectives. Historians and other specialists are studying historical and ethnohistorical data embedded in the poem, such as Mapuche cannibalism, or the interpretation of Lautaro as a disloyal Indian more than a hero.[23]

Also in the past two decades, through a new reading of *La Araucana*, the cultural model that for centuries emphasized Chile's European races is starting to be overcome. Historian Leonardo León Solís states that Chile has always had difficulties "in reencountering its *Indianness*." Referring to the view of the Mapuche people in the past, he adds that "the task that historians face is not easy; it implies, fundamentally, abolishing the idea of a State—a nation that minted other historians—Barros Arana, Góngora, Villalobos—in a gesture of Western arrogance that left most of the poor Chileans of this country without memory or identity."[24]

Numerous scenes depicted in the poem provide information about Mapuche customs, language, and social organization, as well as references to fiestas, parliaments, speeches, and details of battles such as the battle of Tucapel, which no Spaniard survived. The poet's description of these events establishes that he had Mapuche informants. León Solís proposes that Ercilla's principal Mapuche informant was a woman close to the poet, whose life she saved.[25] For this reason the title of the poem was not "La Araucanía" or "Heroic Deeds of the Araucanians," but *La Araucana*, in reference to a woman.[26]

Today, the investigation of Mapuche culture has been reformulated in an attempt to study the ethnicity group by group, each with distinctive characteristics. Subjects such as the parleys between Spaniards and Indians, for example, are studied today from the perspective of international relations, recognizing the parleys as true international treaties. New methodologies and new readings of old documents are providing answers that are compared with episodes in *La Araucana* to confirm or disprove what the poem presents as fact. Although the

Mapuche horseback riders, Chile, circa 1900. *Postcard in the public domain, photographer unknown.*

By the year 1900, Mapuche Indians of Chile had lost the struggle (1860–83) against the military occupation of the Araucanía. Spanish colonization in the sixteenth century, followed by the violent occupation of Indian land by the Chilean army in the nineteenth century, reduced the indigenous communities to small areas of poor-quality land. The Mapuche people were forced to become poor peasants. The Chilean government gave them titles to the lands, but when this photo was taken, only two-thirds of the Mapuches had received property titles. Of ten million hectares of the Mapuche region in southern Chile, the Chilean state gave five hundred thousand hectares back to the Mapuche people. Thus the conflict was never completely resolved.

poem's discourse is from the sixteenth century, an analysis of relations between Spaniards and Mapuches of the seventeenth and eighteenth centuries is useful in fostering an understanding of such a complex history of relations. In addition, *La Araucana*, its author, and its protagonists remain a source of local pride for certain places in Chile. Such is the case with the current celebration of Las Garcíadas in the Chilean city of Cañete.[27]

In reference to Chile's most recent transition to democracy, it is important to point out that for twenty years Chile has been experiencing a new phase, a time of democratic optimism and of some economic success, although still with marked social inequality. This new optimism has translated into a sort of historical pride but with a necessary view to the future. This is how it was seen by Chilean historians who were asked to write about the two hundred years of independence that Chile celebrated in 2010. Their view of the country's history in their articles is linked not only to the present but also to the future.

What is said about Ercilla and his poem when referring to present-day Chile, and what is hoped for in the future? Before examining the topic of the bicentennial, it is important to remember that during the fight for independence in the 1810s and 1820s, Chilean criollos adopted the idea of the Mapuche struggle against the Spaniards as an antecedent to their own struggle. Ercilla and his poem represented part of this discourse. One of the first newspapers supporting independence was called *El Monitor Araucano*. The discourse of pride in Araucanian history shifted around the late nineteenth century, when the Chilean state focused on Araucanía and began its military campaign of extermination of the Indians.

During the bicentennial of independence in 2010, the foundational myth of the poem began to fade in importance. The reflections of present-day Chilean historians refer more to accepting the lack of a national identity and the difficulty of defining one, unless the country's diversity is recognized. As Julio Retamal writes, "We shall be people with an identity when we recognize what we really are, a new society that has American, European, and African roots."[28] Following this line of thought, Emma de Ramón states that, "in a society as racist as the one we have formed, carrying within ourselves the being of the Indians freed from oppression does not encourage us in the slightest . . . the Indian is transformed into another myth that also does not relate to the world we see around us."[29]

Referring specifically to Ercilla and his poem in the national context, De Ramón asserts that the present-day Mapuche people, segregated and condemned to poverty, have no relation to a Caupolicán or a Lautaro. "These epic characters rest on their military glory praised by Alonso de Ercilla; they are not linked to the Indian who crosses the peaks of the *altiplano* or the mud flats of the south."[30] Therefore, having overcome the myth of *La Araucana* as the crucible of Chilean nationality, today's historians study the poem and its period with an optimistic view of the military conflict of the sixteenth century. The analysis of the two centuries following the Spanish conquest demonstrates that the region fostered a culturally rich society that functioned within the framework of inter-ethnic commercial and economic relations.[31] *La Araucana* will continue to form a part of the Chilean memory. At the same time, intellectuals have undertaken the task of giving the poem its rightful place in an appropriate context. Each generation to come will formulate its own response, as Chilean historian Olaya Sanfuentes expresses: "Neither collective memory nor history can remain fixed forever; each generation must remake them and validate them."[32]

What is obvious is the influence of *La Araucana* on the creation of other Spanish-American epic poems, including the *Historia de la Nueva México*. In the context of celebrating the four hundredth anniversary of the publication of the first part of *La Araucana*, in 1967 Julio Caillet-Bois published a book titled *Análisis de La Araucana* in which he included a list of Spanish-American poems

Acoma Pueblo, circa 1880–1885. *Photo by James S. Worth. Center of Southwest Research, University Libraries, University of New Mexico, Pict. Coll., 000–083. Atlantic and Pacific Railway Collection.*

By the date this photo was taken, the Acoma people's traditional, somewhat isolated life was disrupted by the arrival of the railroad in New Mexico. The "Indian Agent," representative of the U.S. government as part of the reservation model established by the mid-1800s, had further interfered with their way of life. This began a process of assimilation that forced schoolchildren to speak English and dress in Western clothes, with many sent to boarding schools. Western farming techniques were imposed without success, since Pueblo people had centuries of farming experience.

inspired by Ercilla's poetry.[33] Villagrá's poem appears on the list. This was possibly the first time that *La Araucana* and the *Historia de la Nueva México* had been linked.

When looking at the modern relevance of Villagrá's poem, it is well to consider not only the history of the poem's various editions but also the publications in which the *Historia* is listed as a work linked to a specific literary heritage. The *Historia* has a different trajectory from that of *La Araucana*, since the *Historia*'s existence is tied to the literary heritages of different countries: Spain, Mexico, and the United States. These overlapping claims make Villagrá's poem a special case.

Villagrá's biographer, Manuel Martín Rodríguez, has done the most complete study to date about the critical reception of the *Historia de la Nueva México*. Contrary to what has been said previously regarding the poem being read only by "a few erudites throughout the centuries,"[34] there is evidence as early as 1619—nine years after its publication—that it was cited at least four times in the seventeenth century.[35] One of these citations deserves special attention because its author—Francisco Murcia de Llana—refers to Villagrá as a writer "who knew how to give [New Mexico] eternal life," opening the door to thinking about the poet as the "father of New Mexico,"[36] recalling Ercilla's role as "creator of the Chilean fatherland."

It is noteworthy that copies of the *Historia* arrived in the Americas in the same century as it was published. Those copies were owned by at least two officials in New Spain—an *oidor* in Guatemala and a New Mexico governor.[37]

It was in the nineteenth century when the *Historia* became the object of a greater number of critical commentaries, as Martín Rodríguez has proved. References to the poem—in French, English, and Spanish—are more negative than positive, especially in the first half of the century. However, the demand for the poem notably increased in the second half of the century. By the 1880s the negative reviews began to mix with some more positive opinions such as the case of the Mexican Francisco Pimentel, who in 1883 included the poem in his *Historia crítica de la literatura y de las ciencias en México*.[38] This is an important reference because the *Historia* here appears in the canon of Mexican literature, and, as a result, becomes part of the Spanish-American literary heritage.

It was also in the 1880s when the poem began to be classified as part of the literary tradition of the United States. In 1887 John Gilmary Shea published his article "The First Epic of Our Country, by the Poet Conquistador of New Mexico, Captain Gaspar de Villagrá," in which he deemed the poem to be the first history of the United States, having been published fourteen years before Captain John Smith's *Generall Historie of Virginia*.[39] One of the main scholars who showed a great interest in the poem was archaeologist Adolph Bandelier, who, with the assistance of his wife, Fanny, and at the request of renowned New Mexico lawyer and politician Thomas B. Catron, transcribed the poem in Spanish, in Mexico City. The transcription was unusual because it included Bandelier's own illustrations.[40] The first published reedition of the poem began to appear in installments on July 30, 1898, in the newspaper *El Progreso*, in Trinidad, Colorado.[41] There is evidence of its publication in sections at least until June 17, 1899. It is quite possible that the poem was not published in its entirety.[42]

After its first edition in 1610, the poem was not published again in a complete edition until 1900, when it was published by Luis González Obregón at the Imprenta del Museo Nacional de México.[43] The first edition of the poem in English was published in 1933 in prose rather than verse.[44] The English edition was particularly useful because it provided valuable documentary information about Villagrá and the historical events included in the poem. The fact that the first edition in English was published in the early twentieth century (1933, reprinted 1967) and not in its original format but in prose, says a great deal about the poem's lack of dissemination to the English-speaking audience. This is not an isolated phenomenon if one considers what New Mexico meant for the United States at the beginning of the twentieth century. New Mexico became part of the

United States after the U.S. invasion of Mexico and the 1848 Treaty of Guadalupe Hidalgo. In 1850 New Mexico was declared a territory of the United States. The role of New Mexico in the historical, literary, and political tradition of the United States was not recognized until many decades after it joined the union as a territory.

It must not be forgotten that the debates about converting New Mexico into the forty-seventh state were full of racism and prejudice. Historian David V. Holtby has written an excellent analysis of the debate that delayed and eventually achieved statehood for New Mexico in 1912. He writes, for example, of the opinions for and against statehood published in *La Voz del Pueblo* and the *Carlsbad Current*. In the latter, New Mexicans were denigrated with racist concepts of the time, such as terming them "a mixture of the descendants of Castilians, Aztecs, Sioux, and Ethiopians."[45] In the opinion of the Carlsbad newspaper, only Anglos should decide about statehood for New Mexico because "there is but one race on the earth qualified by its nature to manage and govern man's destiny—the pure Anglo-Saxon."[46] Albuquerque rancher J. G. Dargen went to Washington, D.C., to argue against statehood. He noted that Hispanics outnumbered Anglos in New Mexico and said in an interview, "The white element in this nation has never yet submitted to the rule of an inferior race."[47] Senator Albert J. Beveridge from Indiana, who led the political opposition to New Mexico's statehood, told an audience in Indianapolis that New Mexico "had a savage and alien population" and argued that Spain's former colonial areas, New Mexico and Arizona, would improve only when "the empire of our principles is established."[48] The jingoism that arose from the 1898 Spanish-American war did not help either; nor the opinion of renowned writers such as Texan historian Walter Prescott Webb, who in 1931 wrote that "without disparagement, it may be said that there is a cruel streak in the Mexican nature" that "may be a heritage from the Spanish of the Inquisition; it may, and doubtless should, be attributed partly to Indian blood."[49]

Therefore, it is not surprising that Villagrá's poem was not mentioned in those years (1850–1912) as part of the literary tradition of the nation. The *Historia* did not speak to the Anglo-Saxon tradition. As literary critic Miguel López notes, "In the United States an epic poem in Spanish about the founding of the state by non-Anglo-Saxons did not conform to the national myth of the Puritan forebears."[50] Racism permeated society, politics, and public opinion.

From a strictly literary point of view, there was little recognition that the poem was worthy literature until well into the twentieth century. The use of the poem as a historical source has been more accepted, although, at times, scholars have made the error of considering the events described by the poet as absolute truth. The poems of both Villagrá and Ercilla lend themselves to historical interpretation because both poets were involved in, or saw firsthand, many of the events they recount.

The *Historia* was included in a literary analysis in English for the first time in 1986 in *Beyond Ethnicity* by Werner Sollors. In this study the author cites Villagrá's poem as part of the literature written by minorities and argues that the epic format is associated with ethnogenesis, that is, the origin of a people.[51] In 1989 the *Historia* was included as part of New Mexican and national literary tradition in Luis Leal's article "The First American Epic." In addition, because the poem as a historical source provides details not found in other documents of the period, especially for the years 1598–99, it has a unique value to both literary critics and historians. In both disciplines, literature and history, the poem is considered an important source for reconstructing the New Mexican past.[52]

By the end of the 1980s, the *Historia* and studies on it became more frequent in both Spanish and English editions.[53] The first bilingual edition in 1992 was a major breakthrough.[54] This edition was essential for making the poem known to an English-speaking audience. It was the first time the poem had been published in English in its original verse format, an advantage to which was added that it could be read parallel to the Spanish. The 1992 edition marked a "before" and "after" in studies of the poem, especially in the United States. Because the text is accessible to a larger and more diverse audience, studies of the poem and its author have multiplied.

The first doctoral dissertation on the poem, completed in 1990, contributed to its dissemination. Its author, Philadelphio Jaramillo, states in his study that Villagrá speaks of American heritage (understood as that of the United States) and that therefore it must be judged according to new parameters.[55] In this new setting, an important development, in the words of Miguel López, is "the cultural identification of the Mexican Americans with their Indian and Spanish heritage, and their efforts to unearth and reclaim their founding texts."[56] The *Historia* became, therefore, one of those texts.

The last decade of the twentieth century and the first decade of the twenty-first century have been the most prolific ones to date for the dissemination and analysis of Villagrá's poem since its first publication in 1610. Over the past twenty years many advances in new documentary information have been made about the poem and its author and in the rereading and new interpretations of the poem. While publications in Spanish in recent years have been devoted to providing further historical data, publications in English have focused on analyzing the poem in the context of the Spanish and Mexican literary heritage of the United States within a history that remains conflictive. Events in the Spanish conquest of New Mexico such as the battle of Acoma represent a history of repression mixed with a legacy of different cultures: "Chicanos, as children of Mexico, Spain, and the United States may see themselves as heirs to this tragic history and literature."[57]

The rereading of Villagrá's poem after 1990 has been shaped by the analytical frameworks of ethnic and cultural identity, historical memory, and appropriation. Not too different from what has occurred with *La Araucana*, the legacy of the *Historia* as a colonial literary text represents the duality of Spanish imperial glory in the conquest, and the Indian past destroyed by the very same conquest. But in the case of the *Historia*, that duality has also passed through a double experience of imperial domination, one by Spain and another by the United States. Thus, Chicano literature includes as part of its origins the writings of those who conquered (from the sixteenth to the nineteenth centuries) and the oral traditions of the suppressed. María Herrera-Sobek and Virginia Sánchez Korrol explain the conflictive origin in the following terms: "Painful questions regarding the Hispanic literary legacy must be acknowledged as this *herencia* is tainted by its inscription in a discourse that can only be characterized as a treatise of domination and of servitude."[58] These new interpretations of Villagrá's poem—and literary texts of Spanish and Mexican heritage in general—seen in the light of a new paradigm, have led to a variety of publications that reflect several academic fields and methodological paths.

The publication of the most complete biography of Gaspar de Villagrá thus far, by Manuel Martín Rodríguez, and a new annotated edition of the poem in Spanish by the same author, have provided an important cache of documents. A third volume by the same author published in the United States completes the trilogy.[59] The works of Martín Rodríguez were published in Spanish, which guarantees wide dissemination to a Spanish-speaking audience. Although historians have cited the poem in the past, the facts Villagrá presents have not always been compared with, proven by, or complemented by other historical documents as Martín Rodríguez does. In addition, that author has studied in greater depth Villagrá's use of prose inserted into the poem and his creative use of metatext. The prose insertions had been previously criticized as showing a lack of inventiveness on the part of the poet, when he was accused of not respecting the canons of the epic. But after all, Miguel de Cervantes, in no less a work than his novel *Don Quixote*, mentioned that the epic could also be written in prose.[60]

The awareness and dissemination of Hispanic culture and its literary heritage in the United States have also relied on an important recovery initiative that is having a direct impact on the teaching of literature and history. "Recovering the U.S. Hispanic Literary Heritage Project" is the title of a broad program that has been translated into action, especially publications. The *Historia de la Nueva México* and its author have been part of this interest in recuperating Hispanic American writing.[61] The "Pasó por Aquí" series from the University of New Mexico Press has also aided in the dissemination of the Hispanic literary heritage, including the 1992 bilingual edition of Villagrá's poem and a subsequent reprint.

The publication of texts about how to teach the early literature of the United States—including Native American literature and French, English, and Spanish colonial texts—aimed at educators and literature students is worthy of mention.[62] Two articles deserve particular attention. In "Resisting Colonialism," Carla Mulford discusses teaching the topic of colonialism in the United States (especially the British and Spanish empires) through colonial texts, including Villagrá's poem. In "Colonial Spanish Writings," E. Thomson Shields and Dana D. Nelson offer examples of colonial texts for teaching, among them the *Historia de la Nueva México*.[63] Another publication that merits citation in this context is *The Latino Reader: An American Literary Tradition from 1542 to the Present*, an anthology of writing by Latino authors. This book includes a transcription of a section of Villagrá's poem.[64]

Compendia of colonial writings of the United States are finally including selections from literary texts and oral history that represent minority cultures, among them, colonial writings about the Spanish presence and Mexican heritage. Such is the case with the anthology *The Literatures of Colonial America*.[65] The texts selected include the Acoma origin myth; the Popol Vuh; and writings of Columbus, Bernal Díaz del Castillo, Gaspar de Villagrá, and John Smith, among others. Other texts refer to Native American cultures, French and English colonization in North America, and the Portuguese and Spanish colonization of South America. The focus of the publication is inclusive, multidisciplinary, multicultural, and continental. Thus, the *Historia de la Nueva México* is studied in a larger geographical and cultural context, very much in accord with the needs and questions of a new generation of readers and writers.

The new readings and interpretation of the two poems have opened a large field of possibilities for the study of specific topics, from linguistics and philology to ethnohistory and anthropology. Topics included in Villagrá's poem, such as customs and theatrical productions (religious dramas and plays such as "Moors and Christians"), native and Spanish-Christian legends (the myth of Aztlan and the apparition of the Virgin Mary and the Apostle Saint James in battles) are taken up by specialists and analyzed with the aid of interdisciplinary methodologies.[66] The poem provides information that contributes to the recognition of the origins of a rich folklore of the region that exists to this day and has contributed to its identity.[67]

The interdisciplinary study by Danna Levin Rojo, cited in chapter 4, is another good example of the use of the *Historia*, in this case as a source to demonstrate the important role of indigenous knowledge and sources in the process of Spanish occupation in the U.S. Southwest, specifically New Mexico. This seminal book presents a new dimension of the relevance of the poem and its author. It is hoped that the poem will continue to attract the attention of scholars who can effectively use it in interdisciplinary analyzes. Numerous studies from a historical and literary point of view, most of them cited in this book, attempt to overcome the assumption that everything Villagrá said is factual. Comparative analysis using other historical documentation and the methodological support of literary criticism are allowing researchers to arrive at much more coherent, complete, and interesting conclusions.[68] It is hoped that this present volume will also serve as an aid to this new history.

It is also exciting to see the production of novels that the *Historia de la Nueva México* and *La Araucana* have inspired, which give a new dimension to the legacy of the two poems. The fictional novel by Chilean writer Herman Schwember titled *Donde otro no ha llegado* takes as its centerpoint an event that led Governor García Hurtado de Mendoza to condemn two of his officials, Ercilla and Juan de Pineda, to death (the sentence was later commuted to exile).[69] A novel by Joseph Bohnaker, *Of Arms I Sing*, contains a fictionalized version of Villagrá's poem and the conquest of New Mexico by Juan de Oñate.[70] When two colonial texts inspire other creative literary works, it is because their literary and historical value still resonates even after four centuries.

To conclude this look at the legacy of the two poems and their respective authors, one final dimension of this heritage merits attention. The *Historia* has been incorporated into the cultural identity and historical memory of the people of New Mexico. Thus, for example, Villagrá's work has been compared to that of Sabine Ulibarrí, an important fiction writer of New Mexico in the twentieth century and an internationally recognized Chicano author.[71] Critic Juan Maura mentions themes that relate to the work of both authors, such as the New Mexico landscape as the "scene of a real focus of history," strong women "as keepers of the survival of a living culture to the present," and the "defiant" figure of the horse as a "symbol of the American epic."[72] Villagrá and Ulibarrí are compared to one another based on their interest in taking up common themes about the land and people of New Mexico, which, according to Maura, "today still maintains similar characteristics" as in colonial times.[73] Both authors infuse the epic element with their own experiences as soldiers on the field of battle. Both are called "poet-soldiers"[74] in light of the reality that both write "testimonial literature, created in a frontier world, a world in which to the present day it is difficult to survive."[75] Considering that Maura's article captures the similarities between Villagrá and Ulibarrí, a New Mexican author who defined himself "as a Chicano writer in exclusively political terms,"[76] one begins to understand how Villagrá's political values and ideals have been associated with those of the Chicano minority of the early twenty-first century.

A second analysis that ties Villagrá to the personal experiences of a Mexican American writer is that of Genaro Padilla and his book *The Daring Flight of My Pen: Cultural Politics and Gaspar Pérez de Villagrá's Historia de la Nueva México, 1610*. Padilla interposes sections of analysis of the poem with memories of his childhood in New Mexico and stories related to his family. Worthy of note is the author's use of poetic analysis as an occasion to include elements of his own identity and memory. Evidently, the recuperation of memory is directly related to the physical space of New Mexico, and therefore, the sense of place is of fundamental importance in claiming a legacy.

This dimension is not present as such in the case of *La Araucana.* In Chile today there is no instance of appropriating the poem to claim an identity. Perhaps the explanation lies in the fact that Ercilla never projected in his life or in his poem an identity that was not purely Spanish. Villagrá, by contrast, was born in the Americas, came from Puebla, and was therefore Mexican. As a criollo, he must have experienced that "sense of place"—although he never said so explicitly. In part, his poem reflects his need to identify with the land of his origin, even though his education, religion, and pride in representing the Spanish empire are clearly identifiable in his poetry. Chapter 4, with the topic of geographic space, made reference to how Villagrá connected his two heritages through the use of indigenous knowledge and the information he acquired through his European education.

Villagrá and the conquistador Juan de Oñate, whom the poet idealized so much in his poetry, were criollos with a divided identity. Villagrá depicts Governor Oñate as an "old Christian" responsible for subjugating the Indians of New Mexico. But at the same time, the poet cites the Aztec roots of the governor's wife, the great-granddaughter of Moctezuma. In a duality of conflicting legacies, Villagrá and his poem represent that divided criollo identity in which the pride of being Spanish American coexists with the criticism of an "ignorant and backward" American race: "Creoles claimed Indians as their biological ancestors; they also derided Indians as innately inferior children to protect or as brutes to exploit."[77] This is the image of the criollo that Villagrá depicts in his ambivalent discourse, "often oscillating between images of respect and outright racism."[78] This discourse should be understood in the context of a conquest lived and recounted by a criollo of the late sixteenth and early seventeenth centuries, and especially in the case of Villagrá, by a criollo who participated in an enterprise of imperial conquest in which he fervently believed. Later in the seventeenth century, and especially in the eighteenth century, Mexican writers began to depict a more clear-cut feeling of Mexican patriotism and pride in the indigenous races. Nevertheless, they were still writing in the imperial language, belonged to an intellectual elite of European extraction, and represented a white, upper social class.[79]

Looking at the composition of the group of people that Oñate, another criollo, led to the conquest of New Mexico, of 338 people whose origin has been recorded, 52 percent were from Spain or Portugal (including the Azores and Canary Islands), while approximately 36 percent were from Mexico, Guatemala, or Cuba.[80] According to scholar David Snow, adding Indians and "others assumed to have been born in the New World,"[81] the expedition had more less an equal number of Europeans and natives of the Americas. What must the atmosphere of this expedition have been like, in which half of the participants were of European origin? How should we think of criollos such as Villagrá and Oñate who were part of a group that was half-European? Does the composition of the expedition tell us something about the mentality of the group, its interests, ambitions, and goals? Although these questions are difficult to answer, the composition of the group is interesting data to consider. This is an aspect to look at in greater depth for future research that adds to the criollo debate in the case of New Mexico.

In his article "Epic, Creoles, and Nation in Spanish America," José Antonio Mazotti analyzes epics written by Spanish American criollos. Although he does not cite Villagrá's *Historia*, his study provides important clues to understanding the poem. Mazotti argues that it is necessary to analyze the epics written by criollo authors of the seventeenth and eighteenth centuries from an interdisciplinary perspective. His aim is innovative and appropriate, presenting three particular elements of this genre in colonial America: the social group of the poet, the epic he wrote, and the concept of ethnic nation.[82] The example of Villagrá and his poem adapts perfectly to this type of analysis, and it is hoped that in the near future other researchers will use this model to explain the *Historia* and Villagrá. There is a need to look in greater depth at the period in which the origins of the phenomenon of Mexican *criollismo* can be placed, and to include Villagrá in that analysis.

As has been mentioned more than once in this book, Villagrá and his *Historia* belong not only to the literary tradition of the Southwest of the United States, but first and foremost, to a greater and more diverse cultural and geographic context. It is of great interest for the author of these lines that recently, this problem has finally been covered in articles such as those of Mazotti or Ralph Bauer, "Toward a Cultural Geography of Colonial American Literatures: Empire, Location, Creolization." Bauer points out that "in its exclusive geographic focus on those colonial territories that would later become the United States, the multiculturalists' metanarrative of early American literary history has been caught in a critical anachronism."[83] The *Historia* today continues to be seen by some critics in the limited and circumscribed context of Spanish-American literature and the Spanish language. Now it and other colonial texts are being reclaimed as part of the literary tradition of the United States, as Bauer makes clear in his article.

> Indeed, by including Álvar Núñez Cabeza de Vaca's *Relación* but not Las Casas' *Historia de las Indias*, Pedro Menéndez de Avilés' letter from La Florida but not Cortés' *Cartas* from México, or Villagrá's epic *Historia de la Nueva México* (about New Mexico) but not Ercilla's epic *La Araucana* (about Chile) based

on the rationales that each of the former dealt with a territory that would later form a part of the United States while each of the latter did not, such a paradigm forecloses on an understanding of these texts within their proper intellectual, historical, literary contexts.[84]

Ten years ago, when the author of these lines began the task of comparing Ercilla and Villagrá and their respective poems, the project was inspired by the idea that the epic poem about New Mexico could better be understood if it were included in a larger historical and literary context. The comparison with the epic of Chile has been deemed the most appropriate, not only because *La Araucana* was the model that Spanish-American epic poems followed, but also because the view from the south of the continent offered a cultural and imperial geography that would give the *Historia de la Nueva México* the continental dimension it deserves.

Appendix

Chronology of Ercilla and Villagrá against the Backdrop of Empire

Year	Ercilla– *La Araucana*	Peru–Chile	Spain	Mexico– Nuevo Mexico	Villagrá– *Historia*
1521				Hernán Cortés takes over Tenochtitlan.	
1522			Las Casas begins campaign to protect Indians.	Mexico City founded on top of Tenochtitlan.	
				Cabeza de Vaca begins his journey in North America.	
1533	Ercilla is born in Madrid.	Conquest of Peru begun by Francisco Pizarro.			
1534?		Birth of Lautaro, Araucanian leader.			
1535		Francisco Pizarro founds Lima.			
1536				Cabeza de Vaca returns to Mexico.	
1538		Peruvian civil war (Pizarro vs. Almagro).			
1539		Pedro de Valdivia signs *capitulaciones* to conquer Chile.		Fray Marcos de Niza and Estevanico to Northern Mexico.	

continued

Year	Ercilla–*La Araucana*	Peru–Chile	Spain	Mexico–Nuevo Mexico	Villagrá–*Historia*
1540		Pedro de Valdivia begins the conquest of Chile.		Vásquez de Coronado's expedition to Northern Mexico.	
1541		Valdivia founds Santiago de la Nueva Extremadura. Francisco Pizarro is assassinated by his own men in Lima.			
1542		Creation of the Viceroyalty of Peru.	New Laws.	Vásquez de Coronado returns to Mexico.	
1543			Felipe named Regent of Spain.		
1544		Valdivia founds La Serena in Chile. Gonzalo Pizarro leads *encomenderos* rebellion in Peru.			
1545		*Encomiendas* restored in Peru.	New Laws repealed.		
1546		Lautaro, captured by Spanish, becomes servant of Valdivia. Valdivia returns to Peru.		Start of silver mining in Zacatecas.	Hernán Pérez and Catalina Ramírez from Castile to New Spain.
1547	Ercilla enters as page in entourage of Prince Felipe.	Gonzalo Pizarro is defeated and executed in Cuzco.			

continued

Year	Ercilla– *La Araucana*	Peru–Chile	Spain	Mexico– Nuevo Mexico	Villagrá– *Historia*
1548		Valdivia returns to Chile as its first governor.			
1550		Valdivia founds Concepción in Chile.	Las Casas–Sepúlveda debate begins (through 1551).		
1551		Valdivia founds La Imperial in Chile.	Felipe becomes king of England for seven years.		
1552		In Chile, Valdivia founds Valdivia. Alderete founds Villarrica. Lautaro flees from Spanish. Caupolicán is Araucano *toqui*; Lautaro named vice-*toqui*. In Peru, new *encomenderos* rebellion.	Las Casas's *Brief Account* published.		
1553	Ercilla travels with Prince Felipe to England.	Los Confines, Angol, and Forts Arauco, Purén, and Tucapel founded in Chile. Valdivia is killed after the battle of Tucapel.			
1554	Ercilla travels to Peru via Panama.	*Encomenderos* defeated in Peru. In Chile, Concepción is abandoned and destroyed.			

continued

Year	Ercilla–*La Araucana*	Peru–Chile	Spain	Mexico–Nuevo Mexico	Villagrá–*Historia*
1554		Lautaro defeats Francisco de Villagrá at the hill of Andalicán.			
1555					Gaspar Pérez is born in Puebla de los Ángeles, Mexico.
1556	Ercilla arrives in Chile with new governor Mendoza.	García Hurtado de Mendoza arrives in Chile as governor.	Felipe becomes official king of Spain as Felipe II.		
1557		Battle of Mataquito; Lautaro defeated by Pedro de Villagrá.	Battle of San Quintín; Spanish defeat French.		
		Lautaro killed in Mataquito.			
	Ercilla participates in the Battle of Lagunillas.	Battle of Lagunillas; Araucanos defeated.			
	Ercilla participates in the battle of Millarapué.	Battle of Millarapué; Araucanos defeated.			
	Ercilla witnesses the execution of Caupolicán.	Toqui Caupolicán captured and executed by impalement.			
1558	Ercilla participates in expedition to Southern Chile.	Governor Mendoza leads expedition to Southern Chile.			
		Osorno is founded in Chile.			

continued

Year	Ercilla– *La Araucana*	Peru–Chile	Spain	Mexico– Nuevo Mexico	Villagrá– *Historia*
1558	Ercilla is imprisoned after a fight.				
	He is released to participate in battle of Quiapo.	Battle of Quiapo; Mendoza defeats Araucanos.			
	Ercilla is forced to leave Chile.				
	He lives two or three years in Lima.	Concepción is refounded.			
1559		Francisco de Villagrá becomes governor of Chile.	Peace Treaty of Cateau-Cambresis between Spain and France. Spanish defeated by Turks (Ottoman Empire).		
1561	Ercilla receives *repartimiento* but turns it down.				
1562	Ercilla returns to Spain.	Francisco de Villagrá dies; Pedro de Villagrá becomes governor.			Hernán Pérez involved in commercial activity in Spain.
1563	Ercilla in diplomatic services in Europe.	Castro is founded in Chiloé Archipelago.			
1565			First Spanish settlement in Philippines.		
1566			Las Casas dies.		Hernán Pérez in Spain, probably for two years.

continued

Year	Ercilla– *La Araucana*	Peru–Chile	Spain	Mexico– Nuevo Mexico	Villagrá– *Historia*
1566					Gaspar Pérez's family probably residing in Mexico City.
1567		Francisco de Toledo becomes viceroy of Peru.			
1568			Rebellion of *moriscos* in Granada (through 1570).		
1569	First part of *La Araucana* is published.				
1570	Ercilla is made a knight of the Order of Santiago. Ercilla marries doña María de Bazán.				Gaspar goes to Spain and begins grammar school.
1571	Ercilla occupies position of book censor in Madrid.		Spanish defeat Turks in battle of Lepanto.		Gaspar begins civil law studies at the University of Salamanca.
1573			New Ordinances for Settlement and Discovery.		
1576	Ercilla in Lisbon for two years.	Chillán is founded in Chile.	Fray Luis de León is released from prison in Valladolid, Spain.		Gaspar finishes law studies, returns to New Spain with his father.
1578	Second part of *La Araucana* is published.				
1580			Felipe II becomes king of Portugal.		

continued

Year	Ercilla– *La Araucana*	Peru–Chile	Spain	Mexico– Nuevo Mexico	Villagrá– *Historia*
1581	Ercilla dedicates himself to financial-commercial activities.			Rodríguez-Chamuscado expedition to New Mexico (through 1582).	
1582	In Portugal, Ercilla participates in the conquest of the Azores.			Beltrán and Espejo's expedition to New Mexico (through 1583).	
1586	Ercilla writes a *Romance* (battle of Spanish vs. French).				
1588			British defeat Spanish Armada.		
1589	Third part of *La Araucana* published.				
1590				Castaño de Sosa's expedition to New Mexico.	
1591				Juan Morlete's expedition to New Mexico.	
1593				Leyva de Bonilla and Gutiérrez de Humana's expedition to New Mexico.	
1594	Ercilla dies in Madrid. His body is taken to Ocaña, Toledo.	Santa Cruz de Coya founded in Chile.			
1595		Battle of Curalaba; Araucanos defeat the Spanish.	Felipe II signs royal cédula for settlement in New Mexico.	Juan de Oñate signs *capitulaciones* with Viceroy Luis de Velasco.	Gaspar resides in Llerena, Sombrerete mines, Mexico.

continued

Year	Ercilla–*La Araucana*	Peru–Chile	Spain	Mexico–Nuevo Mexico	Villagrá–*Historia*
1596		A period of successful Araucanian offensives begins.	Another royal cedula suspends Oñate's expedition.	Oñate's expedition to New Mexico suspended.	Gaspar writes a letter against a local priest in Llerena. Gaspar becomes *procurador general* of Oñate's expedition to New Mexico. He is named member of war council of Oñate's expedition.
1597	First edition of complete *La Araucana* poem, with its three parts.			New viceroy of New Spain: Gonzalo de Zúñiga y Acevedo. Oñate's expedition subject to inspections.	
1598		Valdivia, Los Confines, and Santa Cruz de Coya are destroyed. La Imperial is destroyed.	Felipe II dies on September 13. Felipe III becomes king.	Juan de Oñate's expedition to New Mexico (last inspections in February). First Spanish settlement in New Mexico: San Gabriel. Vicente de Zaldívar's expedition to the plains (hunting buffalo).	Gaspar de Villagrá with Oñate's expedition to New Mexico.
1599		Villarrica is destroyed and rebuilt.		Juan de Zaldívar makes demands to Acoma Indians (December). He is killed.	Villagrá is sent by Oñate to capture and kill deserters.

continued

Year	Ercilla– *La Araucana*	Peru–Chile	Spain	Mexico– Nuevo Mexico	Villagrá– *Historia*
1599				Spanish attack Acoma Pueblo after concluding that the war was "just."	Villagrá acts as legal advisor and participates in the attack.
				Attack on Acoma Pueblo (January 22–24).	Villagrá gives testimony after the battle (February).
					Oñate sends him to Mexico to recruit soldiers and get supplies.
1600		A fort is established in the ruins of Valdivia.			Recruitment in Santa Bárbara; Villagrá takes refuge in church.
1601				Oñate's expedition to northeast plains.	
1602		Arauco and Osorno are destroyed.			
		The fort of Valdivia is abandoned.			
		Second Villarrica is destroyed.			
1605			First part of *Don Quixote* published.	Oñate's expedition to Mar del Sur reaches coast of Gulf of California.	
1610				Pedro de Peralta is named governor of New Mexico.	Publication of *Historia de la Nueva México* in Alcalá de Henares, Spain.

continued

Year	Ercilla– *La Araucana*	Peru–Chile	Spain	Mexico– Nuevo Mexico	Villagrá– *Historia*
1614					Villagrá, Oñate, and other officers convicted.
1615			Second part of *Don Quixote* published.		Villagrá begins appeal in Spanish Court (through 1620).
1620					After sentence, Villagrá dies at sea while returning to Mexico to occupy an administrative post in Guatemala.

Notes

Book epigraph

Edward W. Said, *Culture and Imperialism* (New York: Vintage, 1994), xxiii.

Introduction

1. The term "Araucano" or "Araucanian" is used in this book in addition to "Mapuche." However, Araucano is not used today to refer to the indigenous populations who descend from the native groups colonized by Spaniards. It is now considered a foreign term, given by the enemy. Because the term Araucano is what the Spaniards used in the period analyzed in this book and in which the story of *La Araucana* takes place, it is appropriate to use the word for purposes of this analysis. Historical sources of the time, as well as current scholarship that studies this indigenous group at the time of early Spanish occupation, use the term Araucano. The name Mapuche includes descendants of the people who spoke the Mapuche language and inhabited the regions of central and southern Chile and southwestern Argentina. The Mapuche language group at the time of Spanish contact included three subgroups: the Picunches (people of the north, located between the Choapa and Itata Rivers), Mapuches (also known as Moluches or Nguluches, located in the area known as Araucanía or Arauco, between the Itata and Toltén Rivers), and the Huilliches (people of the south, located south of the Toltén River to the Chiloé archipelago). The geographic space in which *La Araucana* takes place is that of the Arauco region, occupied by the Moluches or Nguluches or Mapuches. In Spanish times the area was called Araucanía. This place name probably originated in the local word *rag ko* (adapted to the Spanish language as *Arauco*), which means "clayey water." Another theory points to the origin in the word *awqa*, in the Quechua language of the Incas, meaning "savage" or "rebel," in reference to the Araucano people who resisted domination; the Inca empire was only able to extend its conquest to the natives located north of Araucanía.

2. Six years later, in 2014, while the words of this introduction were being written, conflict in the comuna of Ercilla continued with some partial victories by the Mapuches, such as the recuperation of their land near the community of Temucuicui. "Comunicado público ante retirada de carabineros de Chile del territorio de Temucuicui," June 26, 2014, *Comunidad Autónoma Temucuicui* (comunidadtemucuicui.blogspot.com, accessed July 5, 2014). The Mapuche struggle to recuperate their land has produced local, national, and international awareness and many reports and articles, as well as the use of the Internet, such as the blog cited above. See, for example: Alicia Bárcena, Juan Catrillanca, et al., *Desigualdades territoriales y exclusión social del pueblo mapuche en Chile: Situación en*

la comuna de Ercilla desde un enfoque de derechos (Santiago, Chile: CEPAL and Alianza Territorial Mapuche), 2012. A vibrant discussion among scholars shows how even today the issue provokes varying positions on the part of historians, not all of whom take the same stand in defense of indigenous rights. See Martín Correa, "La estigmatización del mapuche y la creación del enemigo interno," June 26, 2014, *Comunidad Autónoma Temucuicui* (comunidadtemucuicui.blogspot.com, accessed July 5, 2014).

3. Regarding the execution of Araucanian leaders by the Spaniards, see chapter 2.

4. For details about the Spanish punishment of Acoma people and other consequences of the 1599 battle of Acoma, see chapter 2.

5. Elvia Díaz, "Statue of Spaniard Loses Foot," *Albuquerque Journal*, January 8, 1998.

6. Gilberto Triviños, "Revisitando la literatura chilena: Sigue diciendo: cayeron/ Di más: volverán mañana," *Atenea* 487 (2003): 117.

7. Víctor Toledo Llancaqueo, "La memoria de las tierras antiguas: Tocando a las puertas del derecho," in *El derecho a la memoria*, ed. Felipe Gómez Isa (Zarautz-Guipuzcoa, Spain: Giza Eskubideak Derechos Humanos, 2006), 437.

8. Triviños, "Revisitando la literatura chilena," 116.

9. Gilberto Triviños, "Lecturas de La Araucana: 'No es bien que así dejemos en olvido/ el nombre de este bárbaro obstinado,'" in *Épica y colonia: Ensayos sobre el género épico en Iberoamérica (siglos XVI y XVII)*, ed. Paul Firbas (Lima: Universidad Nacional Mayor de San Marcos Fondo Editorial, 2008), 117.

10. María O'Malley, "Mapping the Work of Stories in Villagrá's Historia de la Nueva México," *Journal of the Southwest* 48, no. 3 (2006): 325.

11. Ibid., 324.

12. Elizabeth B. Davis, *Myth and Identity in the Epic of Imperial Spain* (Columbia: University of Missouri Press, 2000), 10–13.

13. Ibid., 6.

14. Raul Marrero-Fente, *Bodies, Texts, and Ghosts: Writing on Literature and Law in Colonial Latin America* (Lanham, Md.: University Press of America, 2010), 1.

15. Ibid.

16. James Nicolopulos, *The Poetics of Empire in the Indies: Prophecy and Imitation in La Araucana and Os Lusíadas* (University Park: Pennsylvania State University Press, 2000).

17. David Quint, *Epic and Empire: Politics and Generic Form from Virgil to Milton* (Princeton, N.J.: Princeton University Press, 1993).

18. Davis, *Myth and Identity*, 13. Davis draws these conclusions from Frances A. Yates, *Astraea: The Imperial Theme in the Sixteenth Century*, pt. 1; Frances A. Yates, *The Last Descendant of Aeneas*; and Marie Tanner, *The Habsburgs and the Mythic Image of the Emperor*.

19. Said, *Culture and Imperialism*, 9.

20. Ibid., 7.

21. Ibid.

22. José Rabasa, *Inventing America: Spanish Historiography and the Formation of Eurocentrism* (Norman: University of Oklahoma Press, 1993), 123.

23. Ibid.

24. Ibid., 6, 7. Rabasa draws his points from Edward Said and his seminal work *Orientalism*, and also the other important work on the subject by Edmundo O'Gorman: *The Invention of America*.

25. Victor Burgin, *Between* (Oxford, UK: Basil Blackwell, 1986), 55, cited in Linda Hutcheon, *The Politics of Postmodernism* (New York: Routledge, 2002), 3.

26. Rolena Adorno, *The Polemics of Possession in Spanish American Narrative* (New Haven, Conn.: Yale University Press, 2007), 4. See also Adorno, "The Warrior and the War Community: Constructions of the Civil Order in Mexican Conquest History," *Dispositio* 14, nos. 36–38 (1989): 225–46.

27. Adorno, *Polemics of Possession*, 4.

28. Hutcheon, *Politics*, 60, 61, 67, 70, 72, 78, 83, 84.

29. Serge Gruzinski. "Les mondes mêlés de la Monarchie catholique et autres 'connected histories,'" *Annales: Histoire, Sciences Sociales*, 1 (2001): 103–108. Gruzinski cites the chroniclers Bernardo de Balbuena, Juan de Torquemada, Tommaso Campanella, Diego Valadés, el Inca Garcilaso de la Vega, and José de Acosta for Spain, and Antonio de Sousa de Macedo and André Álvarez de Almada for Portugal.

30. Michel de Certeau, "La operación histórica," in *Historia y literatura*, ed. Françoise Perus (Mexico City: Instituto Mora, 2001), 41–42.

31. Ibid., 42.

32. Russel B. Nye, "History and Literature: Branches of the Same Tree," in *Essays on History and Literature*, ed. Robert H. Bremner (Columbus: Ohio State University Press, 1966), 140.

33. Ibid., 153.

34. Gustavo Verdesio, "Colonialism Now and Then. Colonial Latin American Studies in the Light of the Predicament of Latinamericanism," in *Colonialism Past and Present: Reading and Writing about Colonial Latin America Today*, eds. Álvaro Félix Bolaños and Gustavo Verdesio (New York: State University of New York Press, 2002), 1–2. For the concept of "digging in the past" Verdesio cites Walter Mignolo's article "Literacy and Colonization" (1989).

35. Álvaro Félix Bolaños, "On the Issues of Academic Colonization and Responsibility when Reading and Writing about Colonial Latin America Today," in Bolaños and Verdesio, *Colonialism Past and Present*, 37.

36. Walter Mignolo, "Occidentalización, imperialismo, globalización: Herencias coloniales y teorías postcoloniales," *Revista Iberoamericana: Literatura Colonial, Identidades y Conquista en América* 61, nos. 170–71 (January–June 1995): 35.

37. Sergio Villalobos, "Guerra y paz en la Araucanía: Periodificación," in *Araucanía: Temas de historia fronteriza*, eds. Sergio Villalobos and Jorge Pinto Rodríguez (Temuco, Chile: Ediciones de la Universidad de la Frontera, 1985), 7–30.

38. Santa Arias and Mariselle Meléndez, "Space and the Rhetorics of Power in Colonial Spanish America: An Introduction," in *Mapping Colonial Spanish America: Places and Commonplaces of Identity, Culture, and Experience*, eds. Santa Arias and Mariselle Meléndez (Lewisburg, Penn.: Bucknell University Press, 2002), 14.

39. Ibid., 16.

40. Ibid., 15. Although the authors establish some differences between the concepts of space and place, in this volume both will be used almost interchangeably, but in some instances the word "place" will be used to mean a specific location.

41. Álvaro Félix Bolaños, "A Place to Live, a Place to Think, and a Place to Die: Sixteenth Century Frontier Cities, Plazas, and '*Relaciones*' in Spanish America," in Arias and Meléndez, *Mapping Colonial Spanish America*, 275.

42. Julie Greer Johnson, "Ercilla's Construction and Destruction of the City of Concepción: A Crossroads of Imperialist Ideology and the Poetic Imagination," in Arias and Meléndez, *Mapping Colonial Spanish America*, 240.

43. Johnson proposes the idea of landscape "as theater" in Ercilla's poem and specifically in her analysis of the destruction of Concepción (ibid., 241). This concept is applicable to the analysis of the role of landscape found in part II of this book.

44. Alfredo Jiménez, "El Lejano Norte español: Cómo escapar del *American West* y de las *Spanish Borderlands*," *Colonial Latin American Historical Review* 5, no. 4 (Fall 1996): 409.

45. Ibid.

46. Ibid., 412.

47. Bernd Schröter, "La frontera en Hispanoamérica colonial: Un estudio historiográfico comparativo," *Colonial Latin American Historical Review* 10, no. 3 (Summer 2001): 353–54.

48. Jorge Pinto Rodríguez, *La formación del estado y la nación, y el pueblo mapuche: De la inclusión a la exclusión* (Santiago, Chile: Dirección de Bibliotecas, Archivos y Museos, 2003), 29.

49. Ibid.

50. Francisco A. Lomelí, "The Sense of Place in Gaspar Pérez de Villagrá's Historia de la Nueva México," *Camino Real: Estudios de las Hispanidades Norteamericanas* 4, no. 6 (2012): 78.

51. The question has been raised as to whether the first American epic poems of the sixteenth century should actually be considered the beginning of "American literature" (understood as both the Americas). See, for example: Jacques Lafaye, "¿Existen las 'letras coloniales'?" in *Conquista y contraconquista: La escritura en el nuevo mundo. Actas del XVIII Congreso Internacional de Literatura Iberoamericana*, eds. Julio Ortega and José Amor y Vázquez (Mexico City: El Colegio de México and Brown University, 1994), 644.

52. Margarita Peña, *Prodigios novohispanos: Ensayos sobre literatura de la colonia* (Mexico City: Universidad Nacional Autónoma de México, 2005), 15. According to Chilean historian José Toribio Medina, the list of epic poems with American topics published in the sixteenth century influenced by *La Araucana* includes: *Cortés valeroso* (1588) by Gabriel Lasso de la Vega; *Elegías de varones ilustres* (1589) by Juan de Castellanos; and *Peregrino indiano* (1599) by Antonio de Saavedra y Guzmán. Other poems directly influenced by *La Araucana* are *Arauco domado* (1596) by Pedro de Oña; *Cuarta y quinta parte de La Araucana* (1597) by Diego de Santisteban Osorio; and *Purén indómito* (1562?) by Fernando Álvarez de Toledo. See also Salvador Dinamarca, "Los estudios de Medina sobre Ercilla," *Revista Atenea* 107 (Concepción, Chile, 1952): 23–25.

Pedro de Oña based his poem *Arauco domado* on *La Araucana*. However, Oña's description of the conquest of Chile makes the conquistador and governor García Hurtado de Mendoza the great hero of the story, a significant difference from Ercilla's poem. Roberto Castillo Sandoval, "'¿Una misma cosa con la vuestra?': Ercilla, Pedro de Oña y la apropiación post-colonial de la patria Araucana," *Literatura colonial: Identidades y conquista*, special issue of *Revista Iberoamericana* 61, nos. 170–71 (1995): 231–47. Other poems following the model of *La Araucana* and with American themes were published in the seventeenth century. For example, see *Argentina y conquista del Río de la Plata* (1602) by Martín del Barco Centenera; *Guerras de Chile* (1610) by Juan de Mendoza Monteagudo; *Compendio historial, conquista y guerras del reino de Chile* (1630) by Melchor Xufré del Aguila; and *Cautiverio feliz* (1673) by Francisco Núñez de Pineda y Bascuñán.

This list of works influenced by *La Araucana* omits *Historia de la Nueva México*. Pedro de Oña's poem *Arauco domado* shows some similarities with Villagrá's *Historia de la*

Nueva México in that the heroes in both poems are the respective conquistadors. However, one of the most important reasons why the present volume uses Ercilla's poem, and not Oña's, to compare with Villagrá's poem is that Pedro de Oña did not participate in the events that he recounts.

53. The fanciful tales of *Orlando Furioso* were replaced in Spanish and Spanish American epic poetry by accounts of political events and military feats, as well as religious stories focusing on the life of Christ, the Virgin Mary, or the saints. Isaías Lerner, introduction to Alonso de Ercilla, *La Araucana*, ed. Isaías Lerner (Madrid: Ediciones Cátedra, Letras Hispánicas, 1993), 9–10. *La Araucana* and *Historia de la Nueva Mexico* are among the Spanish epics of this Golden Age that used exploration and conquest of the Americas as central topics within the context of Spanish military feats. Both poems also used Ariosto's *Orlando Furioso* as inspiration. Although novels and plays from the Spanish Golden Age have become literary classics, the same did not hold true for epic poetry, despite the fame some poems such as *La Araucana* attained. In an effort to rescue epic poetry from oblivion, Pierce includes a catalog of epic poems published in Spanish between 1550 and 1700 in his study. Both *La Araucana* and *La Historia de la Nueva México* are listed. Pierce, *Epic Poetry*, 330–31, 346.

54. The two poems analyzed here belong to the genre of literary epic poetry of the Spanish Golden Age. In his study of Golden-Age Spanish epic poetry, Frank Pierce defines the literary epic genre as having a historical perspective, in contrast with the *chansons de geste*; the latter, according to Pierce, were meant to be recited and they flourished in primitive societies, their sole purpose being to narrate to their audiences heroic deeds close to their time. Frank Pierce, *The Epic Poetry of the Golden Century* (Madrid: Gredos, 1961), 9–14. In defining epic poetry, Pierce mentions among its characteristics, an interest in "man engaged in activities intimately tied to his religious beliefs and social obligations. To express this, the poet makes a prudent use of literary devices common to the current poetic style, such as rhetorical figures which better harmonize with the narrative and the description, and do not present a threat to the basic requirements . . . the epic requires a central hero whose 'message' we grasp through his yearnings and his feats." Ibid., 322.

55. Alfredo Arteaga, *Chicano Poetics: Heterotexts and Hybridities* (Cambridge: Cambridge University Press, 1997), 134. According to Arteaga, "Oñate may have made it in time to conquer the vast northern territory for the empire, but the epic of his conquest appeared too late to be taken without irony." (130) He adds that the use of the epic genre was "traditionally suited to the task" but its lateness made the genre inappropriate for the time: "The epic's capacity to narrate a people was already supplanted by the emerging genres of history and the novel." (134)

56. Ibid., 141.

57. Paul Firbas, introduction to *Épica y colonia*, ed. Paul Firbas, 10.

58. Ibid., 11.

59. Ibid.

60. Peña, *Prodigios novohispanos*, 15.

1. The Spanish Monarchy

Epigraph 1. Ercilla has the Roman war goddess Bellona speak these lines in reference to the imperial legacy that Felipe II received from his father Carlos V. Ercilla spelled the goddess's name as "Belona." Unless otherwise noted, citations of *La Araucana* in Spanish are from Alonso de Ercilla, *La Araucana*, ed. Isaías Lerner (Madrid: Cátedra, 1993), and translations to English are from Louis Carrera, *A Translation of Alonso de Ercilla's La Araucana* (Pittsburgh: RoseDog Books, 2006), with minor revisions. The first numeral indicates the canto, followed by the stanza and line numbers.

Epigraph 2. Villagrá is alluding to the dispute between Hernán Cortés, the Marqués del Valle, and Antonio de Mendoza, viceroy of New Spain, regarding the right to lead the voyage to what would later be New Mexico. Cortés went to Spain to talk directly to Carlos V regarding his claim. Unless otherwise noted, citations of *Historia de la Nueva México* in Spanish and translations to English are from Gaspar de Villagrá, *Historia de la Nueva México*, eds. and trans. Miguel Encinias, Alfred Rodríguez, and Joseph P. Sánchez (Albuquerque: University of New Mexico Press, 1992). The first numeral indicates the canto, followed by the line numbers.

1. "Maximas para el Palazio por D.D.A.G.," Biblioteca Nacional (hereafter BN), Manuscrito 6150, folios 114–134v.

2. "Maximas," folio 115, Sección Galanteria o donaire. Emphasis in the original.

3. Ibid.

4. John H. Elliot, "Felipe II y la monarquía española: Temas de un reinado," in *Felipe II y el oficio de rey: La fragua de un imperio*, eds. José Román Gutiérrez, Enrique Martínez Ruiz, and Jaime González Rodríguez (Madrid: Sociedad Estatal para la Conmemoración de los Centenarios de Felipe II y Carlos V, Ediciones Puertollano, 2001), 47.

5. Elliot, "Felipe II," 45. The "Philippine Islands" were named in honor of the future Felipe II by the first Spaniards who found them.

6. John H. Elliot, *The Old World and the New, 1492–1650* (Cambridge: Cambridge University Press, 1970), 87. The author provides a good summary of the debate about the role the commerce of the Indies played in the expansion of the Spanish empire in the second half of the sixteenth century. Ibid., 87–96, 121.

7. Elliot, *Old World*, 97.

8. Elliot, "Felipe II," 46.

9. Ibid.

10. Ibid., 45

11. Ibid., 46.

12. Ibid., 44, 47.

13. Henry Kamen, *Imperio: La forja de España como potencia mundial* (Madrid: Punto de Lectura, 2004), 16–17.

14. Manuel Fernández Álvarez, *Felipe II y su tiempo* (Madrid: Espasa Calpe, 1998), 789.

15. Elliot, *Old World*, 97.

16. Fernández Álvarez, *Felipe II*, 788–89. As president of the Royal Audiencia of Lima, Pedro de Lagasca, a priest and administrator, ended the 1546–48 Peruvian rebellion between the Spaniards that was led by Francisco Pizarro's brother, Gonzalo. For his successful role in the matter, Lagasca received the honorific title "peacemaker."

17. Fernández Álvarez, *Felipe II*, 788.

18. Diego de Villalobos y Benavides, *Comentarios de las cosas sucedidas en los Países Baxos de Flandes (1594–1598)*, cited in Fernández Álvarez, *Felipe II*, 788.

19. Fernández Álvarez, *Felipe II*, 793.

20. José Miguel Morales Folguera, *La construcción de la utopía: El proyecto de Felipe II (1556–1598) para Hispanoamérica* (Madrid: Biblioteca Nueva, 2001), 26.

21. Serge Gruzinski, "Les mondes mêlés," 89–90.

22. Ibid., 91–93.

23. Ibid., 96.

24. Ibid., 113–15.

25. Elliot, *Felipe II*, 51.

26. Adorno, *Polemics of Possession*, vii.

27. Elizabeth Davis, "La épica novohispana y la ideología imperial," in *Historia de la literatura mexicana: La cultura letrada en la Nueva España del siglo XVII*, ed. Raquel Chang-Rodríguez (Mexico City: Siglo Veintiuno Editores, 2002), 129.

28. Gruzinski, "Les mondes mêlés," 103–108.

29. Scholar Elizabeth Davis also presents the idea of Villagrá's "transatlantic conscience" in her article "De mares y ríos: Conciencia transatlántica e imaginería acuática en la *Historia de la Nueva México* de Gaspar Pérez de Villagrá (1610)," in Paul Firbas, *Épica y colonia*, 263–86.

30. For specific literary influences of the classical epic poets and those of the Renaissance on Ercilla's *La Araucana*, and the practice of imitation, see Quint, *Epic and Empire*; for the same topic as well as the influence of Luis Camõens' *Os Lusíadas* (1572) on Ercilla, see Nicolopulos, *Poetics of Empire*. For a good post-colonial analysis of the influence of the *Aeneid* on *La Araucana*, see Craig Kallendorf, "Representing the Other: Ercilla's *La Araucana*, Virgil's *Aeneid*, and the New World Encounter," *Comparative Literature Studies* 40, no. 3 (2003): 394–414.

31. Adorno, *Polemics of Possession*, 4.

32. "Prólogo" by Ercilla, *La Araucana*, ed. Isaías Lerner, 69.

33. Ibid. 70.

34. Ibid., 463.

35. In 1561 Felipe II had moved the capital to Madrid, leaving Flanders forever. The battle of San Quintín in 1557 gave Felipe a victory that would reinforce his political and religious authority over France. In 1563 the king had begun the construction of the monastery of El Escorial as homage to the victory in San Quintín. Felipe's power had survived the Spanish disaster against the Turks in 1559 and the disorder in the Netherlands in 1566. The fight against the Ottoman Empire, with the object of defending the commercial routes and the coasts of Italy and Spain from Turkish attacks, kept the king busy until his victory of the battle of Lepanto in 1571. To make a strong front against the Turks, an alliance was forged among Felipe II, Pope Pio VI, and the Venetian senate.

36. "Al Rey Nuestro Señor," in Gaspar de Villagrá, *Historia de la Nueva México*, eds. Victorino Madrid Rubio, Elsía Armesto Rodríguez, and Augusto Quintana Prieto (Astorga, Spain: Biblioteca de Autores Astorganos, 1991), 60.

37. This is a common mistake throughout Villagrá's poem; he often assumes he is talking to Felipe II instead of Felipe III.

38. "Al Rey Nuestro Señor," in Villagrá, *Historia*, eds. Madrid Rubio, Armesto Rodríguez, and Quintana Prieto, 61.

39. "Prólogo," ibid., 62.

40. The first stanza and first four lines of the second stanza of *Orlando Furioso* read:

> Of loves and ladies, knights and arms, I sing,
> of courtesies, and many a daring feat;
> and from those ancient days my story bring,
> when Moors from Africa passed in hostile fleet,
> and ravaged France, with Agramant their king,
> flushed with his youthful rage and furious heat,

> who on king Charles', the Roman emperor's head
> had vowed due vengeance for Troyano dead.
>
> In the same strain of Roland will I tell
> things unattempted yet in prose or rhyme,
> on whom strange madness and rank fury fell,
> a man esteemed so wise in former time.
> (Ludovico Ariosto, *Orlando Furioso*)

Although Ercilla chooses not to write from the same perspective as Ariosto (Ercilla says he will not write about "a lady, nor love, nor the beauty of a gentleman's love song"), he uses the same formula to start the poem. To see more references to the connections between Ercilla's poem and Ariosto's poem, see editor's note in Ercilla, *La Araucana*, ed. Isaías Lerner, 77.

41. Of particular importance is the form Villagrá uses in the dedication of his poem to the king. Villagrá is much more explicit than Ercilla when it comes to the importance of royal authority and that of the Spanish empire and the Catholic Church. Villagrá, *Historia*, eds. Madrid Rubio, Armesto Rodríguez, and Quintana Prieto, 60–61.

42. See editors' notes, Villagrá, *Historia*, eds. and trans. Encinias, Rodríguez, and Sánchez, 3.

43. The first stanza of the *Aeneid* reads:

> Arms, and the man I sing, who, forc'd by fate,
> and haughty Juno's unrelenting hate,
> expell'd and exil'd, left the Trojan shore.
> long labors, both by sea and land, he bore,
> and in the doubtful war, before he won
> the Latian realm, and built the destin'd town;
> his banish'd gods restor'd to rites divine,
> and settled sure succession in his line,
> from whence the race of Alban fathers come,
> and the long glories of majestic Rome.
> (Virgil, *Aeneid*)

For more on the *Aeneid* in Villagrá's *Historia*, see Davis, "De mares y ríos," 263–86. Davis also analyzes the influence of Homer's epic poetry on Villagrá's use of nautical similes.

44. See editors' note in Villagrá, *Historia*, eds. and trans. Encinias, Rodríguez, and Sánchez, 4. "The identification of the epic hero's Christian mission with the Homeric hero Achilles is characteristic of the New World epic. It is highlighted, especially, in the epics narrating the conquest of Mexico."

45. See editor's note in Ercilla, *La Araucana*, ed. Lerner, 749, and editors' note in Villagrá, *Historia*, eds. and trans. Encinias, Rodríguez, and Sánchez, 3.

46. For the influence of Ariosto's *Orlando Furioso* on the Fitón character and his cave in *La Araucana*, see Nicolopulos, *Poetics of Empire*, chap. 2.

47. See editor's note in Ercilla, *La Araucana*, ed. Lerner, 749. It should be noted that although this 1597 edition mentions King Fernando Catholic, the lines of the 1578 edition of the second part say: "but Maximum glorious Carlos Quinto." The reference to "Catholic" in the context of opening the road to a New World makes us think that it refers to Fernando the Catholic of Aragón, husband of Isabel of Castile.

48. Vázquez de Coronado left New Spain by way of Sonora to explore today's U.S. Southwest, reaching as far as southern Kansas (Quivira) in 1540–42; Hernando de Soto left Havana and went to explore the Floridas in 1540–41, reaching as far as the Arkansas

River. For more on the information about distances and mapping acquired from the Coronado expedition, see Maureen Ahern, "'Llevando el norte sobre el ojo izquierdo': Mapping, Measuring, and Naming in Castañeda's *Relación de la jornada de Cíbola* (1563)," in Arias and Meléndez, *Mapping Colonial Spanish America*, 24–50.

49. For more references to the goal of extending the conquest of Chile to the Strait of Magellan and the Atlantic Ocean, see part II of this book.

50. Jerónimo de Vivar, *Crónica de los reinos de Chile* (Madrid: Dastin, 2001), 286–89.

51. See Villagrá, *Historia*, 1.67–71. The lines referring to the Gulf of California as "Sea of Pearls" are cited at the end of chapter 3 of this book.

52. The fact that California was not an island was known in Mexico City by the time of the conquest of New Mexico. However, it is difficult to prove how much of that information was publicly or openly offered to explorers. By 1539 an expedition led by Fernando de Ulloa proved that Baja California was a peninsula and not an island. Apparently the Spanish monarchy was successful in those years at keeping information about its explorations secret, to the point that some "previous discoveries" were unknown to explorers of the lands north of Mexico. As David Weber says, "That Baja California was a peninsula, that New Mexico existed, and other lesser details of geography uncovered during the initial phases of Spanish exploration, became lost from view." David J. Weber, *The Spanish Frontier in North America* (New Haven, Conn.: Yale University Press, 1992), 56. Finally, at the beginning of the eighteenth century some maps, such as the 1701 map by Jesuit Eusebio Francisco Kino, showed the Sea of California (Gulf of California) also known as Villagrá's and Oñate's "Sea of Pearls."

53. George P. Hammond and Agapito Rey, eds., "Instructions to Don Juan de Oñate," in *Don Juan de Oñate, Colonizer of New Mexico, 1595–1628* (Albuquerque: University of New Mexico Press, 1953), 1:67.

54. Alonso de Góngora Marmolejo, *Historia de Chile desde su descubrimiento hasta el año 1575* (Santiago, Chile: Editorial Universitaria, 1969), 44.

55. Ibid., 50–51.

56. For more on the topic of Valdivia's greed, see editor's note in Ercilla, *La Araucana*, ed. Lerner, 134n123.

57. Johnson, "Ercilla's Construction and Destruction," in Arias and Meléndez, *Mapping Colonial Spanish America*, 241.

58. Ibid.

59. Vivar, *Crónica*, 259, 270–72.

60. Fernández Álvarez, *Felipe II*, 119.

61. Ibid., 120.

62. Ibid., 122.

63. Barbara Hadley Stein and Stanley J. Stein, "Financing Empire: the European Diaspora of Silver by War," in *Colonial Legacies: The Problem of Persistence in Latin American History*, ed. Jeremy Adelman (New York: Routledge, 1999), 53.

64. In canto 5 of his poem, Villagrá mentions expeditions to New Mexico prior to the one Oñate led in 1598. One such expedition was led by fray Agustín Rodríguez and Captain Francisco Sánchez Chamuscado in 1581–82, and another was led by Antonio de Espejo in 1582–83. Both expeditions left written accounts. The Rodríguez-Chamuscado's expedition was described by Hernán Gallegos, scribe of the expedition. The details of Espejo's expedition were written in the camp journal by Diego Pérez de Luxan. This account was translated and published in pamphlet form in London in 1587 as *New Mexico: Otherwise, the Voiage of Anthony of Espejo, who in the year 1583 . . . , Translated out*

of the Spanish copie printed first at Madreel, 1586, and afterward at Paris, in the same year (London: Thomas Cadman, 1587. Reprinted in limited ed., Lancaster, Penn., 1928).

65. George P. Hammond and Agapito Rey, eds., "Diego Pérez de Luxan's Account of the Antonio de Espejo Expedition into New Mexico, 1582," in *The Rediscovery of New Mexico, 1580–1594* (Albuquerque: University of New Mexico Press, 1966), 193, 197, 205–206.

66. Maureen Ahern, "La relación como glosa, guía y memoria: Nuevo México 1581–1582," *Revista Iberoamericana* 61, nos. 170–71 (1995): 43. The author focuses on the idea that the accounts of expeditions to New Mexico between 1581 and 1583 were manipulated by the next generation of explorers and colonizers. This idea relates specifically to the topic of the current volume, in that the indigenous resistance and violent reaction by the Spaniards recorded in these accounts are ignored by the next generation, while the reference to silver and gold mines is credited.

67. Hammond and Rey, eds., "Discovery of the Salines of Zuñi," in *Don Juan de Oñate*, 1:406.

68. Ibid., 1:406–407. A league is generally equated to 2.6 miles. Regarding the natives of the area where the salt lake and the mines were found, they were the Jumano and the Cruzados (see notes in Hammond and Rey, "Itinerary of the Expedition, 1596–1598," in *Don Juan de Oñate*, 1:328).

69. Ibid., 1:413.

70. Ibid.

71. Ibid., 1:422.

72. Ibid., 1:423.

73. In his letter of March 31, 1605, the Marqués de Montesclaros wrote: "Just lately letters have come from Don Juan de Oñate, together with samples of ores obtained from the mines that have been discovered. These I had assayed here, and thus far the richest ore produced one-eighth part copper, without any trace of silver." Hammond and Rey, eds., "Marquis of Montesclaros to the King, March 31, 1605," in *Don Juan de Oñate*, 2:1001.

74. Hammond and Rey, eds., "Montesclaros to the King, October 28, 1605," in *Don Juan de Oñate*, 2:1009.

75. Ibid., 2:1010.

76. Ercilla, *La Araucana*, ed. Lerner, 508n81.

77. The Roman war goddess Bellona is a familiar character in the epic poems of Virgil, Lucan, and Ariosto, among others. Ercilla follows this model, but his inspiration comes from *The Labyrinth of Fortune* by Spanish poet Juan de Mena (1411–56). In his poem about the national destiny of Castile, Mena writes about Bellona taking him in her cart to a great plain where the goddess Fortune had her palace.

78. Lerner, ed., introduction to Ercilla, *La Araucana*, 37.

79. José Toribio Medina, *La Araucana de Don Alonso de Ercilla y Zúñiga. Vida de Ercilla* (Santiago, Chile: Imprenta Elzeviriana, 1917), 148–49.

80. Davis, *Myth and Identity*, 37.

81. Ibid., 37–38.

82. Ibid., 38.

83. Paul Firbas, "Una lectura de la violencia en *La Araucana* de Alonso de Ercilla," in *La violencia en el mundo hispánico en el siglo de oro*, eds. Juan Manuel Escudero y Victoriano Roncero (Madrid: Visor Libros, 2010), 91–105.

84. Raúl Marrero-Fente, "Épica, fantasma y lamento: La retórica del duelo en *La Araucana*," *Revista Iberoamericana* 73, no. 218 (2007): 211–26.

85. Lerner, ed., introduction to Ercilla, *La Araucana*, 36.

86. Ibid.

87. Quint, *Epic and Empire*, 159.

88. Ibid.

89. See, for example: Gilberto Triviños, "El mito del tiempo de los héroes en Valdivia, Vivar y Ercilla," *Revista Chilena de Literatura* 49 (1996): 5–23; José Antonio Mazzotti, "Paradojas de la épica criolla: Pedro de Oña, entre la lealtad y el caos," in *Épica y colonia*, 231–61; José Lara Garrido, *Los mejores plectros: Teoría y práctica de la épica culta en el Siglo de Oro* (Málaga, Spain: Universidad de Málaga, 1999); Luis Fernández Restrepo, "Entre el recuerdo y el imposible olvido: La épica y el trauma de la conquista," in *Épica y colonia*, 41–59; Kallendorf, "Representing the Other," 394–414.

90. Jill Lane, "On Colonial Forgetting: The Conquest of New Mexico and its Historia," in *The Ends of Performance*, eds. Peggy Phelan and Jill Lane (New York: New York University Press, 1998), 54.

91. Ibid., 58.

92. Ibid., 59.

93. Davis, "La épica novohispana," 137. Davis also cites Maureen Ahern's study that proves how the accounts of expeditions to New Mexico had a precedent in two types of discourse: one "official and propagandistic" and the other that documents an "intimidatory policy." Villagrá's account could be listed as part of the first type.

94. Peña, *Prodigios novohispanos*, 15.

95. Genaro M. Padilla, *The Daring Flight of My Pen: Cultural Politics and Gaspar Pérez de Villagrá's Historia de la Nueva México, 1610* (Albuquerque: University of New Mexico Press, 2010), 35.

96. Ibid., 29.

97. Ibid., 56.

98. Ibid., 80.

99. Ibid., 89, 98.

100. Manuel Martín Rodríguez, "'Aquí fue Troia nobles cavalleros': Ecos de la tradición clásica y otros intertextos en la Historia de la Nueva México de Gaspar Pérez de Villagrá," *SILVA, Estudios de Humanismo y Tradición Clásica* 4 (2005):139–208.

101. Villagrá writes on this topic in canto 20, titled "Of the excessive trials suffered by the soldiers in new discoveries, and of the poor rewards of their services."

102. M. Martin Rodríguez, "Aquí fue Troia," 186. For more on classical epic poetry's influences in Villagrá's poem, specifically to "justify his own conduct" and the representation of indigenous and Spanish women in the poem, see Antonio M. Martín Rodríguez, "Ariadna en Nuevo México: Mujer y mito en la *Historia de la Nueva México* de Gaspar de Villagrá," *Camino Real: Estudios de las Hispanidades Norteamericanas* 4, no. 6 (2012): 23–41.

103. Manuel M. Martín Rodríguez, "400 Years of Literature and History in the United States: Gaspar de Villagrá's Historia de la Nueva Mexico (1610)," *Camino Real* 4, no. 6 (2012): 15.

104. Lomelí, "Sense of Place," 75–86.

105. Sandra M. Pérez-Linggi, "Gaspar Pérez de Villagrá: *Criollo* or Chicano in the Southwest?" *Hispania* 88, no. 4 (2005): 670.

106. Such is the case in the example that literary critic Jorge Cañizares-Esguerra gives in his article "Racial, Religious, and Civic Creole Identity in Colonial Spanish America," *American Literary History* 17, no. 3 (2005): 420–37. According to him, "creole patriotism

took on different aspects in different periods and geographical regions according to historical contingencies and local political circumstances," but some common aspects of the "creole project" remained consistent (424). One example of this "creole project" cited by Cañizares-Esguerra is Villagrá's *Historia*, specifically its figure of Juan de Oñate. The author cites Oñate as "the crusading knight" who was able to succeed in the conquest of New Mexico, compared to a previous "century of failures in the colonization of New Mexico [blamed] on the effeminate nature of the new Peninsular arrivals." (426) But the strongest example Cañizares-Esguerra uses to demonstrate the creole patriotism of Villagrá's poem is that Oñate is presented as "typical of the creole noble elites, rooted both in old-Christian hidalgo and Aztec blood." (426) The author is referring to Oñate being a "proud great-grandson of Moctezuma." However, Oñate did not have any Indian blood; it was his wife who did, and Villagrá makes reference to the Indian ties of Oñate's wife, not Oñate himself. What Cañizares cites as proof of Oñate's Aztec blood are some lines written by Luis Tribaldo de Toledo, who wrote one of the laudatory poems included at the beginning of Villagrá's *Historia*. In his "Canción Pindarica en Loor del Capitán Gaspar de Villagrá, y Don Juan de Oñate, Descubridor y Conquistador de la Nueva México," Tribaldo de Toledo refers to Cristóbal (de Oñate), father of Juan, as being grandson of Hernan Cortés and great-grandson of Montezuma:

> De aquel gran Cristóbal prenda,
> que en belicosa contienda
> ganó la Galicia Nueva,
> en el mexicano imperio.
> Luz del Artico Hemisferio,
> y de sus grandezas prueba:
> arrimo de aquella idea,
> de nobleza que hermosea,
> la virtud que mayor es,
> donde no alcanza mi pluma,
> nieto de Fernán Cortés,
> biznieto de Moztezuma.
>
> (Tribaldo de Toledo, "Canción Pindarica," in Villagrá, *Historia*,
> ed. Madrid Rubio, Armesto Rodríguez, Quintana Prieto, 72).

Thereafter, the mistake is repeated by Cañizares-Esguerra, who bases his argument of creole patriotism in Villagrá's *Historia* on this error, using the example of "Oñate's split identity" as an important case of the creole project that "continued unabated among creoles throughout the colonial period" (426). The rest of the examples he cites belong to the mid-eighteenth century and beyond. To further complicate things, the editors of the 1991 edition of Villagrá's poem repeat information not completely proved regarding a daughter of Gaspar de Villagrá (María de Vilchez Zaldívar y Castilla) who married Captain Cristóbal Becerra y Moctezuma, great-grandson of the emperor Montezuma ("El autor y el poema de la 'Historia de la Nueva México,'" in Villagrá, *Historia*, ed. Madrid Rubio, Armesto Rodríguez, Quintana Prieto, 17.) On the other hand, Villagrá's biographer Manuel Martin Rodríguez is cautious about this information since his research has not yet been able to prove that Gaspar de Villagrá had a daughter; see Manuel M. Martín Rodríguez, *Gaspar de Villagrá: Legista, soldado y poeta* (León: Universidad de León, 2009), 59.

107. M. Martín Rodríguez, "Aquí fue Troia," 198.

108. It appears that the seven years the poet writes about pertained to the time he spent in school in Spain; first studying grammar (perhaps in Madrid), and then entering civil law studies at the University of Salamanca. Villagrá arrived in Spain with his father in 1569 and went back to New Spain in 1576 (for sources and more details on this part of his life, see chapter 2 and the chronology in the appendix).

109. For example, in canto 1, lines 36–48, Villagrá argues for the importance of putting the story in writing, that the heroes of his account will inspire him to do it, and that his poetry deserves to be read by the king because the poet is a witness to everything he says.

110. For more hypotheses about the way the poets ended their poems, see Quint, *Epic and Empire*, chaps. 3 and 4.

2. The Law

1. Jorge Pinto Rodríguez, "Integración y desintegración de un espacio fronterizo: La Araucanía y las Pampas, 1550–1900," in *Araucanía y Pampas: Un mundo fronterizo en América del Sur*, ed. Jorge Pinto Rodríguez (Temuco, Chile: Ediciones Universidad de la Frontera, 1996), 18.

2. J. M. Ots Capdequi, *El estado español en las Indias* (Mexico City: Fondo de Cultura Económica, 1986), 11.

3. The Laws of Burgos of 1513 were the first to regulate the work of the indigenous peoples, limiting the number of work hours required, requiring they be provided with Christian instruction, and feeding them adequately. Evidently, these norms were not enough to stop the abuses.

4. Ots Capdequi, *El estado español*, 13.

5. Ibid., 16–17. Specifically, the Royal Provision of November 17, 1526. Also, the document included the spiritual goal of the conquest.

6. Las Casas began to change his views about Spanish treatment of Indians after a sermon given in 1511 by the Dominican fray Antonio de Montesinos in Hispaniola. Montesinos challenged his audience, asking what right the Spanish had to keep Indians in servitude and what authority they had to make war against them.

7. Not long after his statement and after being better informed about the origins of African slavery, Las Casas not only regretted his idea but also began to write against African slavery, too. For more on this subject, see Adorno, *Polemics of Possession*, 64–69.

8. Ots Capdequi, *El estado español*, 45.

9. Henry Raup Wagner and Helen Rand Parish, *The Life and Writings of Bartolomé de Las Casas* (Albuquerque: University of New Mexico Press, 1967), 108.

10. Néstor Meza Villalobos, *Régimen jurídico de la conquista y de la guerra de Arauco* (Santiago, Chile: Imprenta Universitaria, 1946), 4.

11. The revolt of the encomenderos in Peru as a result of the New Laws of 1542 began with Gonzalo Pizarro en 1544. The confrontation between the encomenderos' interests and the military forces representing the crown's interests lasted until 1548, when the rebellion was quashed and the leaders decapitated. The priest, Pedro de Lagasca, had been sent from Spain as president of the Real Audiencia of Lima and pacifier of Peru and returned to Spain in 1550 after eliminating the old encomiendas and naming new ones. This was not a solution either. Another rebellion began. A new viceroy, Antonio de Mendoza, quashed the rebellion in 1552, but the conflict continued under the next viceroy, Andrés Hurtado de Mendoza, Marqués de Cañete.

12. Meza Villalobos, *Régimen jurídico*, 8–9.

13. Ibid., 6–7.

14. The topic is more complex than what is briefly presented here. For more details, see Meza Villalobos, *Régimen jurídico*, 3–24. Regarding what Valdivia at some point had accumulated for himself, this source says, "By 1552 he had the entire Lampa Valley. . . . As a result of the conquest of the territories of La Serena by Juan Bohom, he took for himself the Coquimbo Valley. After the conquest of Concepción he assigned himself the Arauco Valley, and he also had an encomienda in the city of Valdivia, in all of which he had estancias. In 1547, it was calculated that his Indian work crews who mined gold produced, after expenses, twelve to fifteen thousand pesos annually; the Indian work crews that mined gold in Quilacoya produced five pounds or more per day." Ibid., 12.

15. Pinto Rodríguez, "Integración y desintegración," 13. The author mentions that this fact was highlighted previously by Pierre Chaunu in his book *Conquista y explotación de los nuevos mundos* (Barcelona: Nueva Clío, 1984), 14.

16. Wagner and Parish, *Life and Writings*, 170–82; Anthony Pagden, introduction to *A Short Account of the Destruction of the Indies* by Bartolomé de Las Casas (New York: Penguin, 1992), xxviii–xxx.

17. Wagner and Parish, *Life and Writings*, 186.

18. Adorno, *Polemics of Possession*, 71–72.

19. In November 1553 another large rebellion of encomenderos began as a result of the latest measures by the Real Audiencia of Lima that eliminated the encomienda's forced Indian labor. The audiencia was following orders from Spain, which had been influenced by Las Casas and Sepúlveda's debate of 1550–51. The rebellion's leader was encomendero Francisco Hernández Girón, whose forces were defeated after some victories, and Girón was decapitated in December 1554. The new viceroy, Andrés Hurtado de Mendoza, Marqués de Cañete, arrived in Lima in June 1556 and had to deal with the last part of the revolt and the trial of the last rebel. For more on this subject, see Juan Manzano Manzano, *La incorporación de las Indias a la corona de Castilla* (Madrid: Ediciones Cultura Hispánica, 1948); Adorno, *Polemics of Possession*, 83.

20. Adorno, *Polemics of Possession*, 83–84

21. William Mejías-López, "La relación ideológica de Alonso de Ercilla con Francisco de Vitoria y Fray Bartolomé de Las Casas," *Revista Iberoamericana* 61, nos. 170–71 (1995): 216. For a biography of Alonso de Ercilla, see José Toribio Medina, *Vida de Ercilla* (Mexico City: Fondo de Cultura Económica, 1948).

22. Mejías-López, "La relación ideológica," 216.

23. Quint finds it significant that the "pro-Indian position" of Ercilla "determines and is determined by his adaptation of the model of the *Pharsalia* and of Lucan's rhetoric of freedom" (*Epic and Empire*, 171). This thesis is also presented in chapter 1 of the current volume. Quint notes Ercilla's contribution, through his poem, to the debate over indigenous rights. For more on Las Casas in the context of Ercilla's poem, see Quint, 168–72.

24. In 1538 Francisco de Vitoria had begun his defense of indigenous rights.

25. Mejías-López, "La relación ideológica," 198.

26. Ibid., 198–99. Fray Gil's ideas went against the authorities' plans and were not well received by the then governor of Chile, García Hurtado de Mendoza, who forced him to return to Lima.

27. The topic is complex, and it is not the purpose here to analyze the doctrines of Las Casas and Vitoria in detail. The arguments listed here focus on the aspects presented in

Ercilla's poem, with the goal of making the subject simpler for the reader, without, of course, losing accuracy.

28. "Prólogo" by Ercilla, *La Araucana*, ed. Lerner, 69.

29. Mejías-López, "La relación ideológica," 205.

30. Among them, Alonso de Ovalle in his *Histórica relación del reino de Chile*, first published in 1646. About this episode as well as the custom of meeting in concilium and the different names used for it, see Carlos Ruiz, "La estructura ancestral de los mapuches: Las identidades territoriales, los longko y los consejos a través del tiempo," *Ñuque Mapufōrlaget*, Working Paper Series 3 (Uppsala, Sweden: University of Uppsala, Centro Mapuche de Estudio y Acción, 2003), 9–10.

31. Davis, *Myth and Identity*, 38.

32. Ibid., 40.

33. Ibid., 39–47. Regarding the topic of encomienda in *La Araucana*, see ibid., 68. Quint also analyzes the topic of disunity among Araucanians, as it appears in *La Araucana*, a common characteristic of epic poetry that attempts to highlight the imperial presence and the "other." See Quint, *Epic and Empire*, 7.

34. Triviños, "El mito del tiempo," 15–22.

35. Ruiz, "La estructura ancestral," 8–29.

36. Horacio Zapater, "Huincas y mapuches (1550–1662)," *Historia* 30 (1997): 445–49; Ruiz, "La estructura ancestral," 8–17. The *lof*, *rewe*, and *aillarehue* organizational groups of the Indians of Araucanía had a strong sense of belonging to their territory. A group of the *aillarehue*, for example, formed the *fütanmapu*, a word that was Hispanicized as *butanmapu*. Their number increased from three to five by the first half of the nineteenth century. These *butanmapu* today give the Mapuches what they call a "territorial identity." Ibid., 8.

37. Pedro de Valdivia, "Cartas al Emperador Carlos V," *Colección de Historiadores de Chile y Documentos Relativos a la Historia Nacional*, 1, no. 54 (Santiago, Chile, 1861), in Zapater, "Huincas y mapuches," 453.

38. Ruiz, "La estructura ancestral," 17.

39. For more details about the impact of firearms and horses on the conquest of Chile, see Zapater, "Huincas y mapuches," 452–53.

40. Góngora Marmolejo, *Historia de Chile*, 59.

41. Davis, *Myth and Identity*, 68. See also Quint, *Epic and Empire*, 168.

42. Restrepo, Luis Fernando, "Entre el recuerdo y el imposible olvido: La épica y el trauma de la conquista." In *Épica y colonia: Ensayos sobre el género épico en Iberoamérica (siglos XVI y XVII)*, ed. Paul Firbas (Lima: Universidad Nacional Mayor de San Marcos Fondo Editorial, 2008), 54.

43. Ibid., 54–56. Restrepo offers a unique analysis of the concept of trauma in the colonial epic using theories from the field of psychoanalysis. In the case of *La Araucana*, he shows how Ercilla's inclusion of those stories makes it possible for the poet to demonstrate his openness to the pain of "the other."

44. On the use of "further/native voices" in epic poetry and also the use of fiction related to Indian stories to denounce violence as in *La Araucana*, see: Quint, *Epic and Empire*, chap. 4; Rolena Adorno, "Literary Production and Suppression: Reading and Writing about Amerindians in Colonial Spanish America," *Dispositio* 11, nos. 28–29 (1985): 1–25; Restrepo, "Entre el recuerdo y el imposible olvido," in *Épica y colonia*, 41–57; Firbas, "Una lectura de la violencia," in *La violencia en el mundo hispánico*, 91–105;

Kallendorf, "Representing the Other," 394–414; Marrero-Fente, "Épica, fanstasma y lamento," 211–26.

45. The amputation of hands as punishment was recorded as early as 1800 BC in the laws, known as Hammurabi Codex, of the Babylonian king Hammurabi.

46. Firbas, "Una lectura de la violencia," in *La violencia en el mundo hispánico*, 101–102.

47. Mejías-López, "La relación ideológica," 207.

48. Fray Gil González de San Nicolás, "Relación de los agravios que los indios de las provincias padecen," *Colección de Historiadores de Chile y Documentos Relativos a la Historia Nacional* 29 (Santiago, Chile: Imprenta del Ferrocarril, 1861–23), 461–466, cited by Mejías-López, "La relación ideológica," 213.

49. This was the same philosophy as the Inquisition held. An unconverted Indian could not be executed; only upon converting and then reverting could he or she be tried and punished as a heretic.

50. Julio Caillet-Bois, *Análisis de La Araucana* (Buenos Aires: Centro Editor de América Latina, 1967), 40.

51. Jaime Concha, "Observaciones acerca de La Araucana," in *Lectura crítica de la literatura americana: Inventarios, invenciones y revisiones*, ed. Saul Sosnowski (Caracas: Biblioteca Ayacucho, 1996), 504–21.

52. The encomenderos' revolt in Ercilla's poem has also been presented by Quint, *Epic and Empire*, 172–73.

53. Ibid., 176.

54. Ibid.

55. Ibid., 178. Quint writes that "The language of chance and luck—another legacy from the *Pharsalia* that runs through the Araucana—denies any ideological explanation for political and military success."

56. Wagner and Parish, *Life and Writings*, 179.

57. Ibid., 173.

58. Caillet-Bois, "Observaciones," 43.

59. "Expediente de licencia para pasar a México a Hernán Pérez de Villagrán, vecino de México, marido de Catalina Ramírez," 1573, Archivo General de Indias (hereafter AGI), Indiferente General, 2054, no. 24. The license of Hernán Pérez (Gaspar's father) to travel to New Spain in 1546 has not been located, but this folder of 1573 contains a mention of 1546 as the year when he and his wife embarked for Mexico on the ship *Santa María de la Mar*. See also M. Martín Rodríguez, *Gaspar de Villagrá*, 30–31. From another license given in 1571 to embark from Spain to Nueva España we know that the parents of Hernán Pérez de Villagrá(n) were Juan Pérez and Elvira Melilla (AGI, Pasajeros, L. 5 E. 3054; AGI, Contratación, 5537, L. 3, F. 446).

60. For the origin of the surname Villagrá or Villagrán see M. Martín Rodríguez, *Gaspar de Villagrá*, 29–30. Regarding Hernán Pérez de Villagrá's occupation as a tanner, looking at the geographical area in Spain where the name Villagrá was from, it seems that this craft was common there and probably Gaspar's father learned it there. The village of Villagrá in the province of Valladolid, Spain, is today called Unión de Campos, also named Villalón de Campos. According to the nineteenth-century *Diccionario geográfico Madoz*, the raising of sheep, cows, and mules, and hunting rabbits and hares were common in the area, with eight leather factories.

61. M. Martín Rodríguez, *Gaspar de Villagrá*, 31–32.

62. Ibid., 33.

63. Ibid., 46–51. The study of Latin grammar was a requirement to begin a course of advanced study. Gaspar must have completed that requirement before starting his law studies. Students could study grammar at the University of Salamanca; however, Gaspar Pérez is not listed among the students registered in grammar studies between 1570 and 1572. Perhaps he took grammar the previous year, 1569, although that is the same year he arrived in Spain. Another possibility is that he studied grammar at another college in Madrid.

64. In November 2001, I found the registration of Gaspar Pérez in the University of Salamanca archives (hereafter AUS). The name "Gaspar Pérez" appears as "natural" (native) of Mexico, New Spain, or natural of the city of Mexico in folders called "Matrícula" on the list of "Legistas" (AUS, Secretaría, Fondo Universitario, "16 de enero 1572," Legistas, Matrícula 290, 1571–72, 78 v.; "8 de diciembre 1572," Legistas, Matrícula 291, 1572–73, 70 r.; "15 de noviembre 1573," Legistas, Matrícula 292, 1573–74, 74 r.; "20 de noviembre 1574," Legistas, Matrícula 293, 1574–75, 72 v.; "2 de diciembre 1575," Legistas, Matrícula 294, 1575–76, 78 r.) See also M. Martín Rodríguez, *Gaspar de Villagrá*, 39–42.

65. In all the registries from 1571 to 1576 that I consulted, students of civil law were from Salamanca or elsewhere in Spain, except for Gaspar Pérez.

66. Luis Rodríguez-San Pedro Bezares and Roberto Martínez del Río, *Estudiantes de Salamanca* (Salamanca, Spain: Ediciones Universidad de Salamanca, 2001), 31. During the second half of the sixteenth century, the field of civil law was the fourth most important in terms of the number of students enrolled, not counting Latin and grammar. The first was canon law, followed by theology, then arts and philosophy, then civil law, and last, medicine. For this topic, see Javier Alejo Montes, *La Universidad de Salamanca bajo Felipe II, 1575–1598* (Valladolid, Spain: Junta de Castilla y León, 1998), 234.

67. Rodríguez-San Pedro Bezares and Martínez del Río, *Estudiantes de Salamanca*, 10–11.

68. Luis Enrique Rodríguez-San Pedro Bezares, *La universidad salmantina del Barroco, período 1598–1625* (Salamanca, Spain: Ediciones Universidad de Salamanca, 1986), 250–51.

69. Manuel Fernández Álvarez, "Etapa renacentista (1475–1598)," in *La Universidad de Salamanca: Trayectoria histórica y proyecciones*, ed. Manuel Fernández Álvarez (Salamanca, Spain: Ediciones Universidad de Salamanca, 1989), 1:89–90.

70. M. Martín Rodríguez, *Gaspar de Villagrá*, 50.

71. Gaspar de Villagrá, *Historia de la Nueva México*, ed. Manuel M. Martín Rodríguez (Madrid: Instituto Franklin, Universidad de Alcalá de Henares, 2010), 469n317.

72. Jill Lane, "On Colonial Forgetting," 57.

73. "Contract of Don Juan de Oñate for the Discovery and Conquest of New Mexico," in Hammond and Rey, *Don Juan de Oñate*, 53–54.

74. "Instructions to Don Juan de Oñate, October 21, 1595," ibid., 65–68. The text says, "Both during the organization and progress of the expedition and after the people have been reduced and placed under obedience to the royal crown, you must observe all that is contained in the royal order issued at Bosque de Segovia on July 13, 1573, containing the royal ordinances for new colonizations and pacifications in new discoveries in the Indies, as well as the contract made with you by virtue of those ordinances for the expedition, and you shall carry a testimonial of the said royal order and capitulation." Ibid., 65.

75. "Memorial for the Viceroy about the Missions in New Mexico," ibid., 79.

76. Ibid.

77. Ibid.

78. Ibid., 522n40; see also Malcolm Ebright, *Land Grants and Lawsuits in Northern New Mexico* (Albuquerque: University of New Mexico Press, 1994), 22. In 1609, the instructions given to Governor Pedro de Peralta regarding his obligations and privileges mention the authorization to "allot Indians in *encomienda*, as many as he think suitable, to persons who have served and who are living in those provinces, without interfering with those granted by Don Juan de Oñate, since these must be preserved." "Governor Peralta's Instructions," in Hammond and Rey, eds. and trans., *Don Juan de Oñate*, 1088.

79. Thanks to historian Rick Hendricks for pointing out this fact and the sources. John L. Kessell, Rick Hendricks, and Meredith Dodge, eds., *Blood on the Boulders: The Journals of Don Diego de Vargas, 1694–1697* (Albuquerque, University of New Mexico Press, 1998), 44, 73, 823, 912, 989.

80. John L. Kessell, *Kiva, Cross, and Crown: The Pecos Indians and New Mexico, 1540–1840* (Washington, D.C.: National Park Service, U.S. Department of the Interior, 1979), 99.

81. Ibid.

82. Pérez-Linggi, "Gaspar Pérez de Villagrá," 668.

83. Ibid., 669.

84. "Contract of Don Juan de Oñate," in Hammond and Rey, *Don Juan de Oñate*, 51. For details about the finances of Juan de Oñate's expedition and the crown's participation, see France V. Scholes, "Royal Treasury Records Relating to the Province of New Mexico, 1596–1683," *New Mexico Historical Review* 50, no. 1 (1975): 5–23. See also George P. Hammond and Agapito Rey, "The Crown's Participation in the Founding of New Mexico," *New Mexico Historical Review* 32, no. 4 (1957): 293–309.

85. Hammond and Rey, "Crown's Participation," 295.

86. Cantos 6, 7, 8, and 9 concern these issues.

87. "Contract of Don Juan de Oñate," in Hammond and Rey, eds. and trans., *Don Juan de Oñate*, 46.

88. This is in reference to the fact that in Spain the Council of the Indies had named Pedro Ponce de León leader of the expedition. According to M. Martín Rodríguez, "Villagrá prepares the reader in this way to react negatively to the petition of the Castilian Pedro Ponce de León." The poet presents here the conflict between *criollos* from New Spain and the *peninsulares* (Villagrá, *Historia*, ed. M. Martín Rodríguez, 468n298).

89. Oñate's expedition was subject to two inspections. The first, by inspector Lope de Ulloa, took place at the campsite in the Mines of Casco (in the valley of San Bartolomé), between December 1596 and February 1597. It was after leaving this campsite, when Oñate was about to cross the Nazas River, that Ulloa handed him the royal cédula and the viceroy's order mandating the suspension of the entrada.

90. This was the visit by inspector Juan de Frías Salazar, between December 1597 and February 1598, that took place while the troops were first by the river San Gerónimo, in Santa Bárbara province, and later moved to the Conchas or Conchos River.

91. The content of this letter does not appear in the documents published by Hammond and Rey, or in Marc Simmons's biography of Oñate. What Villagrá mentions in these verses is similar to what Oñate wrote in a letter to the viceroy after the first inspection and the delay mandated by the king. This letter was written beside the Nazas River on September 13, 1596. If Villagrá's lines are about the content of this letter, the poet did not use it in chronological order, since he places the letter in the poem right after the

second inspection in 1598. If this is the case, it is not new that Villagrá does not use exact chronological order in his poem.

92. Other sections in the poem relate to the same topic of dissembling bad news; for example, regarding the news Captain Zaldívar brought to Mexico City before Vázquez de Coronado's major expedition. It was the viceroy who gave the order not to spread the word that the land was "so poor and miserable" (Villagrá, *Historia*, 3, 325–62).

93. Villagrá, *Historia*, ed. M. Martín Rodríguez, 474n399.

94. Introduction, ibid., 29.

95. Ibid.

96. Tamar Herzog, "La política espacial y las tácticas de conquista: Las 'Ordenanzas de descubrimiento, nueva población y pacificación de las Indias' y su legado (siglos XVI y XVII)," in *Felipe II y el oficio de rey: La fragua de un imperio*, eds. José Román Gutiérrez, Enrique Martínez Ruiz, and Jaime González Rodríguez (Madrid: Sociedad Estatal para la Conmemoración de los Centenarios de Felipe II y Carlos V, 2001), 298. Herzog also cites Francisco de Vitoria and his idea that time would ultimately legitimize the Spanish colonization even if the beginning was bad.

97. Zutacapán was the name that Villagrá gave to the Acoma leader. He also invented the names of the other two: Zutancalpo and Chumpo. See Villagrá, *Historia*, canto 18, "How the Governor went to the fortress of Acoma and the tumult that Zutacapán caused, and the treason that he had prepared."

98. Villagrá, *Historia*, canto 18, 202–304.

99. Ibid., canto 18, 296–98. It has not been possible to confirm from available documents if this episode of attempted murder really happened. However, because the poet uses a large part of a canto to write about it, it seems likely.

100. David Wogan, "Ercilla y la poesía mexicana," *Revista Iberoamericana* 3, no. 6 (1941): 374.

101. Gaspar de Villagrá, *Historia de la Nueva México*, ed. Mercedes Junquera (Madrid: Historia 16, 1989), 39; Villagrá, *Historia*, ed. Encinias, Rodríguez, and Sánchez, 228n1.

102. Villagrá, *Historia*, canto 24, line 29.

103. Ibid., canto 25; below line 17 the poet includes the text titled, "The case which the Governor put, that the holy Fathers might give their opinions upon it." The document, produced by the Franciscans, also appears in "Trials of the Indians of Acoma, 1598," in Hammond and Rey, eds. and trans., *Don Juan de Oñate*, 451–53. Neither version, however, includes the references to the Scriptures and other related writings on which the Franciscan fathers based their judgment.

104. Villagrá, *Historia*, canto 25, "The case which the Governor put, that the holy Fathers might give their opinions upon it." See also: "Trials of the Indians of Acoma, 1598," in Hammond and Rey, *Don Juan de Oñate*, 453. Regarding the question of goods, the Franciscans said, "If the cause of the war is the punishment of delinquents and those guilty, they and their goods remain at his [the king's] will and mercy, according to the just laws of his kingdom and republic, if they are his subjects; and if they should not be, he may reduce them to live according to the law divine and natural by all the methods and means." (Villagrá, *Historia*, canto 25, "The case which the Governor put, that the holy Fathers might give their opinions upon it"); see also "Trials of the Indians of Acoma, 1598," in Hammond and Rey, eds. and trans., *Don Juan de Oñate*, 452.

105. "Trials of the Indians of Acoma, 1598," in Hammond and Rey, *Don Juan de Oñate*, 456; M. Martín Rodríguez, *Gaspar de Villagrá*, 119.

106. "Memorial de Justificación," transcribed and edited by M. Martín Rodríguez, in *Gaspar de Villagrá*, 218, 333.

107. Ibid.

108. Ibid.

109. Ibid., 224, 340.

110. Ibid., 123.

111. Ibid.

112. "Trials of the Indians of Acoma, 1598," in Hammond and Rey, *Don Juan de Oñate*, 471.

113. In the *Historia*, Governor Oñate sends the natives to hang themselves, but he was not actually present in Acoma during the battle or after.

114. Quint, *Epic and Empire*, 102.

115. David Quint, "Voices of Resistance: The Epic Curse and Camoes's Adamastor," *Representations* 27 (1989): 114, cited by M. Martín Rodríguez, "History, Poetry," 91.

116. M. Martín Rodriguez, "History, Poetry," 91.

117. "Trials of the Indians of Acoma, 1598," in Hammond and Rey, *Don Juan de Oñate*, 471–72.

118. Quint, *Epic and Empire*, 104–105.

119. Quint cites similar examples from the *Aeneid*, *Pharsalia*, and also *La Araucana*. Ibid., 103.

120. Ibid.

121. Ibid., 104.

122. Ibid.

123. Ibid., 105.

124. Ibid., 106.

125. M. Martín Rodriguez, "History, Poetry," 93.

126. Introduction to Villagrá, *Historia*, ed. M. Martín Rodríguez, 31.

127. "Memorial de Justificación," in M. Martín Rodríguez, *Gaspar de Villagrá*, 226, 341.

128. Ibid.

129. Ibid., 226, 342.

130. Ibid., 227, 343.

131. Ibid., 233, 341.

132. In the legal proceedings against Acoma, Oñate named Captain Alonso Gómez Montesinos as the defender of the Indians and Villagrá as guarantor (*fiador*). According to Manuel Martín Rodríguez, naming Villagrá with his knowledge of the law gave credibility to the defense process. Curiously, Villagrá did not refer to this position in his Memorial of Services. Ibid., 127.

133. M. Martín Rodríguez, *Gaspar de Villagrá*, 130.

134. Ibid., 130–31.

135. Santa Bárbara was located in the northern province of Nueva Vizcaya, Viceroyalty of New Spain. On the subject of Villagrá as leader of the reinforcement expedition, as well as his activities in Mexico City, preparations for his return, and, finally, the poet's decision not to return to New Mexico, the reader can look to the biography by Manuel Martín Rodríguez, who provides complete information about these events, including documents. Ibid., 139–60.

136. The punishment for the male natives of Acoma above twenty-five years of age was to have one foot cut off and twenty years of personal servitude. Two Indians from the

province of Moqui who were present and fought at Acoma were sentenced to have their right hands cut off and to be set free to convey to their land the news of this punishment. Hammond and Rey, *Don Juan de Oñate*, 477. On the charges and sentence against Oñate as well as those against Villagrá, Zaldívar, and others, see "Conviction of Oñate and his Captains, 1614," in Hammond and Rey, *Don Juan de Oñate*, 1109–38. For the trial of Villagrá, see also M. Martín Rodríguez, *Gaspar de Villagrá*, 249.

137. AGI, "Bienes de difuntos (1620), testamento de Gaspar de Villagrá," Contratación, 573, N. 15, R. 1, doc. 14, 1–21. See also M. Martín Rodríguez, *Gaspar de Villagrá*, 282.

138. M. Martín Rodríguez, *Gaspar de Villagrá*, 61–76, 278–85. According to the biographer, there is no doubt that religious devotion was a strong part of Villagrá's character.

139. Ernesto Mejía Sánchez, "Gaspar de Villagrá en la Nueva España," *Cuadernos del Centro de Estudios Literarios* 1 (1970): 4–16. In 1596, while living in the village of Llerena at the Sombrerete mines in Zacatecas, Villagrá wrote two letters to the Tribunal of the Inquisition denouncing Francisco de Porres Farfán, the priest in Llerena. He accused the priest of errors in interpreting passages on the life of Jesus, of wrongly excommunicating some of the faithful, of speaking ill of the religious Order of St. Francis, and of not preventing the circulation throughout the village of a certain prayer that was falsely held to be miraculous. M. Martín Rodríguez holds that Villagrá's involvement in the episode in Llerena must be interpreted as that of a lawyer applying his legal knowledge to a situation that seemed (according to the letter) out of control. See M. Martín Rodríguez, *Gaspar de Villagrá*, 61–66

140. Margarita Peña, "La poesía épica en la Nueva España," in *Conquista y contraconquista: La escritura del Nuevo Mundo. Actas del XVIII Congreso Internacional de Literatura Iberoamericana*, eds. Julio Ortega and José Amor y Vázquez (Mexico City: Colegio de México and Brown University, 1994), 292–93.

141. M. Martín Rodríguez, *Gaspar de Villagrá*, 65.

142. Davis, *Myth and Identity*, 33–38.

143. O'Malley, "Mapping the Work of Stories," 318. See also Quint, *Epic and Empire*, 117. For the use of mythology to justify Villagrá and Oñate's actions, see A. Martín Rodríguez, "Ariadna en Nuevo México," 23–27.

144. "Cartas de Alonso de Ercilla a Diego Sarmiento Acuña, mayo a diciembre de 1593" (copied by Angel Hernán), in *Códice de la Real Academia de la Historia de D. Alonso de Ercilla.* Biblioteca Nacional de Chile (hereafter BNCH), Sala Medina.

145. Adolfo Aragonés de la Encarnación, *Ercilla-Ocaña: IV Centenario del Nacimiento de Don Alonso de Ercilla Zúñiga, 1533–1933* (Toledo, Spain: Rafael Gómez-Menor, 1933), 55–58.

146. AGI, "Bienes de difuntos (1620), testamento de Gaspar de Villagrá," Contratación, 573, N. 15, R. 1, doc. 14, 1–21. In his will, Villagrá asks his wife, Catalina de Soto, to ask the Congregation of the Society of Jesus in the city of Madrid, where he was a council member, "to be done for my soul the indulgences that are accustomed, as I came with permission from that Congregation."

3. *The Geography of War*

1. It is not surprising that both poets calculate the latitude for their regions accurately. Although it was almost two centuries before the Geodesic Mission to the Equator led by French astronomer Louis Godin (and later by Pierre Bouguer), the findings of which made more accurate measures possible, by the time Ercilla and Villagrá participated

in the conquest and wrote their poems, it was possible to measure latitude based on the method of calculating the earth's size. This method was developed by Roman geographer Claudius Ptolemy (who based his method on Greek mathematician Eratosthenes). Latitude was also measured by astronomical techniques for navigation using the marine quadrant: "The quadrant, a precursor to the modern sextant, allowed a navigator to accurately establish latitude by measuring the angle between Polaris and the horizon; since Polaris is almost directly above the north pole, that angle is effectively the same as one's latitude north of the equator." Other traditional methods included the "reading off a table that listed latitudes by the hours of daylight throughout the year." Larrie D. Ferreiro, *Measure of the Earth: The Enlightenment Expedition That Reshaped Our World* (New York: Basic Books, 2011), 2–3.

2. Note that words such as "geography," "nature," "natural space," and "landscape" are used interchangeably. The reason for this is to simplify the analysis. It is known that geography is the science of the phenomena related to the earth, from a natural and from a human point of view. For purposes of this study, the concept of geography is used in this most traditional meaning (which is the one given by the Greeks), that a geographer is someone who studies (and describes) the earth as a landscape with its natural and territorial elements, and with the human element when applicable.

3. Pedro de Castañeda de Nájera, "Account of the expedition to Cibola which took place in the year 1540, in which all those settlements, their ceremonies and customs," in *The Journey of Coronado, 1540–1542*, ed. and trans. George Parker Winship (Golden, Colo.: Fulcrum, 1990), 116. Herbert E. Bolton, *Coronado on the Turquoise Trail: Knight of Pueblos and Plains* (Albuquerque: University of New Mexico Press, 1949), 138–141 (reprinted 1971). The expedition of Vázquez de Coronado headed north from New Spain to explore the region known as Cíbola (in what is today the U.S. Southwest). The first to mention news of the area was Álvar Núñez Cabeza de Vaca. After fray Marcos de Niza brought exaggerated reports about the wealth of this land and its Indian towns to New Spain in 1538, Viceroy Antonio de Mendoza decided to send Vázquez de Coronado. The Coronado expedition also reached the region the Spaniards called Quivira (on the plains of present-day Kansas) in search of a wealthy area that they never found. For historical context, the causes, and itinerary of the Coronado expedition, see the historical introduction by Winship, *The Journey of Coronado*, 1–92. For a summary and bibliography on the Vázquez de Coronado expedition between 1540 and 1542, see David Weber, *The Spanish Frontier in North America* (New Haven, Conn.: Yale University Press, 1992), 46–49, and Thomas E. Chávez, *Quest for Quivira: Spanish Explorers on the Great Plains, 1540–1821* (Tucson, Ariz.: Southwest Parks and Monuments Association, 1992), 5–8.

4. Álvar Núñez Cabeza de Vaca, *The South American Expeditions, 1540–1545*, ed. and trans. Baker H. Morrow (Albuquerque: University of New Mexico Press, 2011), 25. Cabeza de Vaca arrived at the Iguazú River in January 1542. According to the editor-translator, the reference to *lanzas* in the text is "problematic," and Cabeza de Vaca could mean *lanzamientos*: "the measure of a ship from stem to stern that might yield two hundred feet or more—a reasonable estimate of the impressive mists rising from the falls." Ibid., 215.

5. Richard Flint, *No Settlement, No Conquest* (Albuquerque: University of New Mexico Press, 2008), 13.

6. Keith Thomas, *Man and the Natural World: A History of Modern Sensibility* (New York: Pantheon, 1983), cited in Weber, *Spanish Frontier*, 48, 378.

7. Roderick Nash, *Wilderness and the American Mind* (New Haven, Conn.: Yale University Press, 1975), 22. Even though Nash's analysis seeks to interpret the changing American conception of wilderness (in which "America" is understood to refer to the United States), his study of sixteenth-century European values about wilderness can be applied to the Spanish people and the conquest, especially his concept that wilderness is a "state of mind," that is, it is "what men think it is." Nash explains how the Judeo-Christian tradition greatly influenced the formation of the attitude toward wilderness in the Europeans who came to the New World, in contrast to the Far East cultures in which human beings were understood to be a part of nature. Ibid., 13–21.

8. Nash, *Wilderness and the American Mind*, 7.

9. Gerard Helferich, *Humboldt's Cosmos* (New York: Gotham, 2004), 27, 323.

10. Keith Thomas, *Man and the Natural World: Changing Attitudes in England, 1500–1800* (New York: Oxford University Press, 1983), 15.

11. David Beers Quinn, "New Geographical Horizons: Literature," in *First Images of America: The Impact of the New World on the Old*, ed. Fredi Chiappelli (Berkeley: University of California Press, 1976), 635–36.

12. "Los escenarios naturales en una tierra en donde todo era insólito, parecían interesar no tanto por lo que aparentaban sino, sobre todo, por lo que podían anunciar y ocultar." Horacio Jorge Becco, *Historia real y fantástica del Nuevo Mundo* (Caracas: Biblioteca Ayacucho, 1992), xviii.

13. Sergio Villalobos, Osvaldo Silva, Fernando Silva, and Patricio Estellé, *Historia de Chile* (Santiago, Chile: Editorial Universitaria, 2000), 1:97.

14. The discovery of silver deposits in Zacatecas in 1546 shifted the attention of the Spanish to this area. Mining led to a war against the Chichimeca Indians that would last four decades. Philip Wayne Powell, *Soldiers, Indians, and Silver: North America's First Frontier War* (Berkeley: University of California Press, 1952).

15. "Es la más abundante de pastos y sementeras, y para dares todo género de Ganado y plantas que se puede pintar; mucha y muy linda madera para hacer casas, infinidad otra de leña para el servicio dellas, y las minas riquísimas de oro, y toda la tierra está llena de ello. "Carta de Pedro de Valdivia al Emperador Carlos V. La Serena, 4 de septiembre de 1545," in José Toribio Medina, ed., *Cartas de Pedro de Valdivia que tratan del descubrimiento y conquista de Chile* (Santiago, Chile: Fondo Histórico y Bibliográfico José Toribio Medina, 1953), 42.

16. "el primer escalón para armar sobre él los demás y ir poblando por ellos toda esta tierra a V. M. hasta el Estrecho de Magallanes y Mar del Norte." "Cartas al Emperador Carlos V," in Medina, *Cartas*, 43–44.

17. On the importance of Ptolemy's *Geography* as a collection of the cartographic knowledge of the sixteenth century, see Oswald A. W. Dilke and Margaret S. Dilke, "Ptolemy's Geography and the New World," in *Early Images of the Americas: Transfer and Invention*, eds. Jerry M. Williams and Robert E. Lewis (Tucson: University of Arizona Press, 1993), 263–85.

18. For a literary analysis, definitions, and periodization of *cartas*, *relaciones*, and *historias* or *crónicas* during the discovery and conquest, see Walter Mignolo, "Cartas, crónicas y relaciones del descubrimiento y la conquista," in *Historia de la literatura hispanoamericana: Época colonial*, ed. Luis Iñigo Madrigal (Madrid: Ediciones Cátedra, 1982), 57–116.

19. Ileana Rodríguez, *Primer inventario del invasor* (Managua: Editorial Nueva Nicaragua, 1984), 18.

20. Bernal Díaz wrote his *Historia* in 1555. It was not published until 1632.

21. Rodríguez, *Primer inventario*, 113.

22. Ibid., 114–26.

23. Ibid., 118.

24. Ibid., 139–41. For two different but compatible interpretations of Oviedo's work, see Rodríguez, *Primer inventario*, and José Rabasa, *Inventing America*.

25. Rabasa, *Inventing America*, 138.

26. Juan de Ovando was president of the Council of Indies from 1571 to 1575. Juan López de Velasco was named the first chronicler cosmographer.

27. Morales Folguera, *La construcción de la utopía*. See this source for a complete list of topics of all 135 chapters of the *Ordenanza*.

28. Alonso de Góngora y Marmolejo, *Historia de Chile desde su descubrimiento hasta el año 1575* (Santiago, Chile: Editorial Universitaria, 1969), 13. This *Historia* was taken to Spain after its author's death. The manuscript was published for the first time in 1850.

29. Ibid., 22.

30. For the three historical periods of the *relaciones*, see Mignolo, "Cartas, crónicas y relaciones," 71.

31. For a complete analysis and history of the *Instrucción y memoria* as well as the list of *relaciones* sent from the colonies and deposited in the Archivo General de Indias in Seville, Spain, see Marcos Jiménez de la Espada, *Relaciones geográficas de Indias* (Madrid: Ministerio de Fomento, 1881) and Magdalena Canellas Anoz, "Relaciones geográficas de España y de las Indias," in *Felipe II y el oficio de rey: La fragua de un imperio*, eds. José Román Gutiérrez, Enrique Martínez Ruiz, and Jaime González Rodríguez (Madrid: Sociedad Estatal para la Conmemoración de los Centenarios de Felipe II y Carlos V, 2001), 245–66. On the same subject as well as the new knowledge of American nature in a broader context of medicine and official interest in the natural environment of the New World, see Raquel Álvarez Peláez, *La conquista de la naturaleza americana* (Madrid: Consejo Superior de Investigaciones Científicas, 1993).

32. Rodríguez, *Primer inventario*, 18.

33. "una política destinada a obtener el máximo control y los máximos beneficios de las tierras americanas. . . . La realidad exigía, para un mayor ejercicio del poder, el desarrollo del estudio y del conocimiento, en muchos casos,—como el de las plantas medicinales, las cartas geográficas, la minería etc.—científico del nuevo mundo." Álvarez Peláez, *La conquista*, 137. The same author also mentions the work of physician Francisco Hernández, who in 1577 was sent by Felipe II to research medicinal plants in Nueva España and Peru. Ibid., 105–21.

34. Rabasa, *Inventing America*, 182.

35. Ibid.

36. In addition to the Ordenanza de Descripciones, in the same year of 1573 the Ordenanzas de Descubrimiento, Nueva Población y Pacificación de las Indias, were issued, which were of great importance for the expeditions that took place after this date in the Americas, including that of Oñate to New Mexico. For more about these Ordenanzas, see discussion of the "New Ordinances for Settlement and Discovery of 1573" in chapter 2.

37. Although Ercilla and Villagrá lived, studied, and worked in different periods of the reign of Felipe II, they had access to many of the same written geographic descriptions. Ercilla was in Madrid, closely following the politics of Felipe II during the 1560s and 1570s after his return from Chile. The poet was surely aware of the ordinances related to the Americas, including the preparation of the *relaciones geográficas*. His

wedding in 1570 took place in the palace, and in 1571 he became a member of the Order of Santiago. The second part of *La Araucana* (cantos 16 to 29) was published in 1578. Villagrá, meanwhile, was in Spain between 1572 and 1576 attending the University of Salamanca.

38. For a detailed analysis of specific characteristics of these writings in the context of the imperial literature of the sixteenth century, see Rabasa, *Inventing America*, chap. 2 (Columbus), chap. 3 (Cortés), chap. 4 (Oviedo), chap. 5 (*relaciones* and atlases).

39. See chapter 5 of the current volume for examples from the two poems regarding Spaniards entering lands where no foreigner had ever gone.

40. "La aventura del descubrimiento, la temeridad de la conquista de territorios amplísimos y desconocidos, la sorpresa ante una nueva naturaleza, con flora y fauna nunca soñadas, y la conciencia de que nacían y hacían un Nuevo mundo, propició el desarrollo de un género muy literalizado, pero que en esas particulares circunstancias cobraba nueva vida." Pedro Piñero Ramírez, "La épica hispanoamericana colonial," in *Historia de la literatura hispanoamericana*, ed. Luis Iñigo Madrigal (Madrid: Ediciones Cátedra, 1982), 163.

41. Marcelino Menéndez y Pelayo, *Historia de la poesía hispano-americana* (Madrid: Librería General de Victoriano Suárez, 1913), 2:296. The topic of nature in *La Araucana* is briefly mentioned in Agustín Cueva, "El espejismo heroico de la conquista: Ensayo de interpretación de La Araucana," *Casa de las Américas* 19 (1978): 110, 39.

42. Menéndez y Pelayo cites the descriptions of sunrise and sunset included in canto 2. Menéndez y Pelayo, *Historia de la poesía*, 2:296–97.

43. Giuseppe Bellini, *Nueva historia de la literatura hispanoamericana* (Madrid: Editorial Castalia, 1997), 116.

44. Giuseppe Bellini, "De Ercilla a Gaspar Pérez de Villagrá" (Alicante, Spain: Biblioteca Virtual Miguel de Cervantes, Biblioteca Americana, 2009).

45. Bellini, *Nueva historia*, 116.

46. Fernando Alegría, *La poesía chilena: Orígenes y desarrollo del siglo XVI al XIX* (Berkeley: University of California Press, 1954), 46–47. Alegría mentions the influence of Virgil, Petrarch, and Garcilaso in Ercilla's description of the crystal-clear water in the arroyos running through green plains. The descriptions of the sunrise and of nature on the expedition to southern Chile are examples, according to Alegría, of the realistic characteristic of Ercilla's depiction of geography. In other words, the poet's presence makes the descriptions lifelike.

47. Beatriz Pastor, *Discursos narrativos de la conquista: Mitificación y emergencia* (Hanover, N.H.: Ediciones del Norte, 1988), 398–401.

48. Ibid., 402.

49. Rosa Perelmuter-Pérez, "El paisaje idealizado en La Araucana" *Hispanic Review* 54, no. 2 (1986): 133.

50. Ibid., 132.

51. Jaime Concha, "Observaciones," 515. Concha's purpose in the article is to prove that *La Araucana* belongs to the "primitive epic" and not the "cultured epic" category. To prove his point, he includes the description of the landscape as one of the themes. For purpose of the present study, Concha's analysis is valuable because of his argument that Ercilla did not totally ignore the landscape. Concha calls this characteristic "a minute germ of description" (un menudo germen descriptivista) or "an infinitesimal embryo of portrayal of the geographic outlines" (un embrión ínfimo de pintura del contorno geográfico).

52. The Chacao Channel separates the Chilean continental landmass from the northern coast of Chiloé Island.

53. Rodríguez, *Primer inventario*, 28. For the word "desaguadero" Rodríguez cites as her source "El Desaguadero de la Mar Dulce" by Eduardo Pérez-Valle. The so-called "drainage ditch" was the strait that connected the Atlantic Ocean (North Sea) with the Pacific Ocean (South Sea) through the lake of Granada (Cocibolca or Mar de Agua Dulce), in present-day Nicaragua.

54. Introduction to Villagrá, *Historia*, ed. Mercedes Junquera, 57.

55. Ibid., 56. Junquera says that "The Arabic influence on the Spanish epic continued to give the character of the Crusades to the discovery of America. While Italy had to wait until the fourteenth century for the hero to be humanized, in Spain he never ceased to be. The Spanish hero was always patriotic, as were the Carolingians, gallant, as were the Britons, but realistic as El Cid or the chronicles of Bernal Díaz del Castillo."

56. On the influence of Renaissance poetry in Villagrá's poem, see Erich von Richthofen, "Ercilla y Villagrá, cantor de la conquista del Nuevo México," in *Tradicionalismo épico-novelesco* (Barcelona: Editorial Planeta, 1972), 201–204. On the importance of the role of poets who participated in the events they describe in American poems, as well as the same topic as an influence of the medieval Spanish epic, see Erich von Richthofen, "Tardíos ímpetus épicos españoles: Ercilla, Villagrá, Ayllón," in his *Tradicionalismo épico-novelesco*, 207–13.

57. Bellini, "De Ercilla a Gaspar Pérez de Villagrá."

58. Rodríguez, *Primer inventario*, 18–19. The property of enumerating geographic features as well as mentioning topographic and geographic details in the first stanzas was also common in medieval epics. See E. R. Curtius, *Literatura europea y Edad Media latina* (Mexico City: Fondo de Cultura Económica, 1955), 1:286–87; Peremulter-Pérez, "El paisaje idealizado," 134.

59. In colonial times, a mile was the equivalent of one thousand steps.

60. See editors' note in Villagrá, *Historia*, eds. and trans. Encinias, Rodríguez, and Sánchez, 4.

61. Lomelí, "Sense of Place," 79.

62. Ibid., 78.

63. Ibid., 81.

4. The Indians and Their Natural Space

1. Gregory Cajete, *Native Science: Natural Laws of Interdependence* (Santa Fe, N.M.: Clear Light, 2000), 95.

2. Ibid.

3. Ibid., 91.

4. Ibid., 179–80.

5. Ibid., 210.

6. Ibid., 182–83. In Diné-Navajo tradition, their homeland is bounded by the four sacred mountains, which greatly influence the way of life of the Diné.

7. Ibid., 92.

8. Ibid., 310.

9. Scholar Beatriz Pastor agrees with this connection and draws an interesting analysis from it. Others, such as Isaías Lerner, are not convinced. Pastor, *Discursos narrativos*, 364–67. Editor's note, Ercilla, *La Araucana*, ed. Isaías Lerner, 93.

10. "The representation of specific physical and moral traits of the characterization as a projection of the nature of the American land implies the existence of a natural harmony between man and his environment. . . . The Indian appears characterized . . . in relation to the natural environment from which he comes and in which his true identity is revealed." Pastor, *Discursos narrativos*, 366.

11. Isaías Lerner thinks this explanation is not necessarily geographic but is astrological, and therefore deterministic, according to ideas in the sixteenth century. Editor's note, Ercilla, *La Araucana*, ed. Lerner, 93.

12. Quint, *Epic and Empire*, 161.

13. Sergio Villalobos, *Vida fronteriza en la Araucanía: El mito de la guerra de Arauco* (Santiago, Chile: Editorial Andrés Bello, 1995), 44.

14. Ibid., 45.

15. For more details about the Araucanian people's reasons for military struggle and comparisons with other indigenous groups, see ibid., 44–53.

16. Ercilla, *La Araucana*, "Al lector," ed. Lerner, 463–64.

17. Ibid., 927–28, notes 58 and 59.

18. Pastor, *Discursos narrativos*, 421. For more details on the idea of paradise applied to nature and indigenous people in southern Chile as well as comparisons with other literature that mentions the American land as a paradise (Columbus and Vespucci), see Perelmuter-Pérez, "El paisaje idealizado," 140–43.

19. Although it is not the purpose of this study to analyze in detail the influence on Villagrá of classical epic poetry and its authors, it is important here to stress the difficulty of establishing how much attention Villagrá was paying to nature and the Indian and how much he was employing tools and tropes of the epic genre.

20. Danna A. Levin Rojo, *Return to Aztlan: Indians, Spaniards, and the Invention of Nuevo México* (Norman: University of Oklahoma Press, 2014), 179.

21. Ibid., 173.

22. Ibid., 9.

23. Ibid., 176.

24. Manuel Martín Rodríguez, *Cantas a Marte y das batalla a Apolo: Cinco estudios sobre Gaspar de Villagrá* (New York: Editorial Academia Norteamericana de la Lengua Española, 2014), 93.

25. Lomelí, "Sense of Place," 80–81.

26. See chapter 5 for examples regarding the battle of Acoma and natives' knowledge of their land.

27. These passages are all inspired by Virgil's *Aeneid*. See editors' note in Villagrá, *Historia*, eds. and trans. Encinias, Rodríguez, and Sánchez, 121.

28. From a total of 11,877 lines in the *Historia*, 4,033 are devoted to the theme of the Indian. For this calculation I considered verses that include topics such as indigenous legends (Mexica, for example) and references to indigenous people's origins, brief encounters with indigenous peoples during the Spanish march to the Río del Norte, meeting with the cosmographer Mómpil, Indian love stories (Polca and Milco, Luzcoija and Gicombo), descriptions of indigenous customs and traditions, conversation with indigenous people during the process of Spanish settlement, mentions of indigenous guides, mentions of indigenous leaders and their speeches, discussions between indigenous leaders before the great battle of Acoma, description of Indian fighting in the battle of Acoma, and the suicide of many of them. Some cantos are only about indigenous

topics, such as: 13 (394 lines), 21 (233 lines), 26 (332 lines), 30 (320 lines), 32 (394 lines), and 34 (384 of 389 lines).

29. Serge Gruzinski, *La colonización de lo imaginario: Sociedades indígenas y occidentalización en el México español, siglos XVI–XVIII* (Mexico City: Fondo de Cultura Económica, 2004), 279–80.

30. Carmen Bernard and Serge Gruzinski, *Historia del Nuevo Mundo* (Mexico City: Fondo de Cultura Económica, 1999), 2:9.

5. *Spanish Entrada, Landscape, and Battle*

1. Alexander von Humboldt, *Cosmos: A Sketch of a Physical Description of the Universe*, trans. E. C. Otté (New York: Harper and Brothers, 1858), 2:71.

2. Vol. 2, pt. 1 of *Cosmos* is titled "Incitements to the Study of Nature," and "Description of Nature" is the first of three sections in part 1. Humboldt added as a subtitle of this section: "The Difference of Feeling Excited by the Contemplation of Nature at Different Epochs and among Different Races of Men." In this section he included the description of nature in Ercilla's *Araucana* among many other descriptions of nature from ancient to modern times, including names such as Camões, Columbus, Goethe, and Calderón de la Barca. Ibid., 2:71–72.

3. "The description of the manners of a wild race, who perish in struggling for the liberty of their country, is not devoid of animation, but Ercilla's style is not smooth or easy, while it is overloaded with proper names, and is devoid of all trace of poetic enthusiasm." Ibid., 2:71.

4. Ibid., 2:72, footnote.

5. Ibid., 2:72.

6. Ibid. "The natural descriptions of the garden of the sorcerer, of the tempest raised by Eponamon, and the delineation of the ocean (pt. 1, p. 80, 135, and 173; pt. 2, p. 130 and 161, in the edition of 1733), are wholly devoid of life and animation. Geographical registers of words are accumulated in such a manner that, in canto 27, twenty-seven proper names follow each other in a single stanza of eight lines."

7. "Entrada" and "entrar," Real Academia Española, *Diccionario de la lengua española*, 22nd ed.

8. Ercilla argues that his "history" should be published because of "the harm some Spaniards suffered when their feats remained in perpetual silence, lacking someone to write them down, not because they were minor, but because the land is so remote and distant, and far removed that the Spaniards who have set foot in Peru hear almost nothing about it." "Prólogo" by Ercilla, *La Araucana*, ed. Lerner, 69.

9. Ibid., 69–70. "And if in some way it seems that I appear to be someone inclined towards the Araucanians, dealing with their things and their bravery more extensively than what it appears that barbarians require, if we want to look at their upbringing, customs, ways of making and carrying out war, many have not given them the advantage, and there are a few who, with such great constancy and firmness, have defended their land against such ferocious enemies as are the Spaniards."

10. Patricia Seed, *Ceremonies of Possession in Europe's Conquest of the New World, 1492–1640* (New York: Cambridge University Press, 1995), 70. Seed analyzes the background of this ritual of speech known as "requerimiento" (requirement) and traces it back to the presence of Islam in Spain to prove her point that this ritual was uniquely Spanish. See also Seed, "Taking Possession and Reading Texts: Establishing the Authority of Overseas

Empires," in *Early Images of the Americas: Transfer and Invention*, eds. Jerry M. Williams and Robert E. Lewis (Tucson: University of Arizona Press, 1993), 111–47. For a different interpretation of this topic, specifically related to the New Ordinances for Settlement and Discovery of 1573 and its shared origins with other European nations, see Tamar Herzog, "La política especial," 293–303.

11. Tzvetan Todorov, *The Conquest of America: The Question of the Other* (Norman: University of Oklahoma Press, 1999), 147.

12. Ibid.

13. Ibid., 148.

14. Ercilla mentions the founding of Coquimbo, Penco, Angol, Santiago, La Imperial, and Villarrica. Besides *La Araucana*, four additional sources complete the historiography of the founding of towns and forts during the period that Ercilla covers in his poem (1541–58). These sources are: the letters by Pedro de Valdivia (written between 1545 and 1552), the *Crónica y relación copiosa y verdadera de los reinos de Chile* by Gerónimo de Vivar (finished in 1558), the *Historia de Chile* by Alonso de Góngora Marmolejo (finished in1575), and the *Crónica del Reino de Chile* by Mariño de Lobera (completed by Bartolomé de Escobar after 1584).

15. Andrés Huneeus Pérez, *Historia de las polémicas de Indias en Chile durante el siglo XVI, 1536–1598* (Santiago: Editorial Jurídica de Chile, 1956), 35–43, 60–64.

16. The expedition left the town of Valdivia and after camping beside the Río Bueno crossed the area where Osorno would be founded and came to an area close to the first line of mountains before the Andes (the *precordillera*). From there, they went west to the central valley and arrived at an area with elevations that closed the way to the mouth of Río Maullín. The Indian guide left, and they found themselves trapped in a region with no other option but to go through cliffs, tall trees, and thick foliage. For details of the itinerary of this expedition and chronology of events, see Ángel González de Mendoza Dorvier, *El problema geográfico de "La Araucana" y la expedición de D. García Hurtado de Mendoza* (Madrid: Publicaciones de la Real Sociedad Geográfica, 1947), 3–38.

17. Ximena Toledo and Eduardo Zapater, *Geografía general y regional de Chile* (Santiago, Chile: Editorial Universitaria, 1991), 87–91.

18. Ángel Álvarez Vilela, "La expedición a Ancud en La Araucana, o la recuperación del mérito por parte de Ercilla," *Anales de Literatura Hispanoamericana* 24 (1995): 78.

19. Ibid., 79–82, 86.

20. Ibid., 82.

21. Ibid.

22. José de Acosta, *Historia natural y moral de las Indias* (Madrid: Historia 16, 1987), 260–61. Editor's note in Ercilla, *La Araucana*, ed. Lerner, 929. The fruit has been described as being about the size of a cherry, red in color, and "crowned by four green points."

23. The examples provided about Ercilla as protagonist or witness of the events he recounts demonstrate what Paul Firbas and other scholars have stated: the poet's testimonies link his poem to the *cartas y relaciones del Nuevo Mundo* and not to the Renaissance epic canon. Ercilla describes events in which he took part that reflect the reality of the conquest of a geographically remote region. It was an isolated land in which the poet even wrote some of his poetry on the battlefield (see Firbas, "Una lectura de la violencia," in *La violencia en el Nuevo Mundo*, 96–97.) For this topic and the uniqueness of Ercilla's epic poetry in being a firsthand account from the battlefield, see Michael Murrin, *History and Warfare in Renaissance Epic* (Chicago: University of Chicago Press, 1994), 99–100. Murrin also mentions the influence of Ercilla on other poets such as Villagrá, another example of a "wartime correspondent."

24. In the last part of the expedition, Vázquez de Coronado explored the territory that today is the state of Kansas. He came across some villages by the Arkansas River (near the present town of Lyons in Kansas). The expedition found neither riches nor any great civilization. The events Villagrá mentions in regard to Spanish suffering in these territories as well as the disagreement between the members of the expedition about whether to return to Mexico coincide with the period description of this expedition by chronicler Pedro de Castañeda de Nájera, "Account of the expedition to Cibola," 155–58. To compare the facts with Villagrá's account, see the analysis of the results of Coronado's expedition in Richard Flint, *No Settlement*, 183–94.

25. The Camino Real from Mexico City to present-day New Mexico passed through several Mexican cities and mining settlements, such as Querétaro, Zacatecas, Sombrerete, Durango, and Santa Bárbara. Once past the dunes of the Chihuahuan Desert and the Río del Norte, the trail continued north through the Jornada del Muerto, Piro Pueblos, and Santo Domingo Pueblo. Marc Simmons, *The Last Conquistador: Juan de Oñate and the Settling of the Far Southwest* (Norman: University of Oklahoma Press, 1991), 94–95. For a complete, interdisciplinary study of the Camino Real in colonial times see Gabrielle Palmer, ed., *El Camino Real de Tierra Adentro* (Santa Fe: Bureau of Land Management, New Mexico State Office, 1993).

26. Dan Scurlock, "Through Desierto and Bosque: The Physical Environment of the Camino Real," in Palmer, *El Camino Real*, 1. This article offers excellent information about the flora, fauna, and climate of the Camino Real from Chihuahua to today's capital of New Mexico, Santa Fe. The author 's purpose is to demonstrate the important role that environmental factors played in the *camino*.

27. The document that lists the itinerary of Oñate's expedition was transcribed and published in George P. Hammond and Agapito Rey, *Don Juan de Oñate*, 1:309–28. M. Martín Rodríguez published a useful annotated chart in which the itinerary is transcribed (the footnotes are especially valuable); Martín Rodríguez adds that the document is known as "Ytinerario de las minas del Caxco," and the document includes events up to January 24, 1599 (date of the surrender of Acoma Pueblo). M. Martín Rodríguez, *Gaspar de Villagrá*, 89–107.

28. The place Oñate claimed for the king was south of present-day El Paso, Texas. Its exact location is downstream at La Toma, near modern San Elizario, right next to the Rio Grande and the border with the Mexican state of Chihuahua.

29. In the speech in which he took possession of the land in the name of King Felipe II, Oñate mentioned the place and the fact that he had opened the road to New Mexico (another sign of Spanish occupation of the space was "to open a trail"):

"de suerte que me hallo oy con todo mi campo entero y con más gentes de las que saqué de la Provincia de Santa Bárbola, junto al Río que llaman del Norte y alojado a la Ribera, que es lugar circunvezino y comarcano a las primeras poblaciones de la nueva México y que passa por ellas el dicho Río, y dexo hecho camino abierto de carretas, ancho y llano, para que sin dificultad se pueda yr y venir por él, después de andadas al pie de cien leguas de despoblado, e porque yo quiero tomar la posesión de la tierra, oy, día de la Ascensión del Señor, que se cuentan treinta

"so that I find myself today with all my camp entire and with more people than I took from the province of Santa Bárbara, beside the river that they call of the North and lodged on the bank, which is a place neighboring and adjoining the first towns of New Mexico, and the aforesaid river passes through them, and I have left a road made open for wagons, wide and flat, so that it is possible without difficulty to go and come by it, after having gone on foot through a hundred leagues of uninhabited land; and because I wish to take possession of the land

días del mes de Abril deste presente año de mil y quinientos y noventa y ocho ... en voz y nombre del christianíssimo Rey, nuestro señor, don Felipe, Segundo deste nombre, y de sus subcessores, que sean muchos y con suma felicidad, y para la corona de Castilla y Reyes que su gloriosa estirpe Reynaren en ella."

today, the day of the Ascension of our Lord, which is counted thirty days in the month of April of this present year of one thousand five hundred and ninety-eight ... in the voice and name of the most Christian King, our lord, don Felipe, the Second of this name, and of his successors, may they be many and with the highest felicity, and for the crown of Castile and kings whose glorious stock may reign in it."

(Villagrá, *Historia*, end of canto 14)

For a transcription of the original document of the act of taking possession of Nuevo México on April 30, 1598, see Hammond and Rey, *Don Juan de Oñate*, 1:329–36.

30. This play is considered the first literary piece written in what is today the United States of America, although it has been debated whether the site was actually located south of the Rio Grande. For details see M. Martín Rodríguez, *Gaspar de Villagrá*, 95n107.

31. The words used in this ritual deserve to be cited here, at least in part:

posesión real y actual, civil y criminal, en este dicho Río del Norte, sin excetar cosa alguna y sin ninguna limitación, con las vegas, cañadas y sus pastos y abrevaderos. Y esta dicha possesión tomo y aprehendo en voz y en nombre de las demás Tierras, Pueblos, Ciudades, Villas, Castillos y casas fuertes y llanas que aora están fundadas en los dichos Reynos y Provincias de la nueva México y las a ellas circunvezinas y comarcanas, y adelante por tiempo se fundaren en ellos, con sus montes, ríos y Riberas, aguas, pastos, vegas, cañadas, abrevaderos y todos sus Indios naturales que en ellas se incluyeren y comprehendieren, y con la jurisdicción civil y criminal, alta y baja, horca y cuchillo, mero mixto imperio, desde la hoja del Monte hasta la piedra del Río y arenas dél y desde la piedra y arenas del Río hasta la hoja del Monte.

the Royal tenancy and possession, actual, civil, and criminal, at this aforesaid River of the North, without excepting anything and without any limitation, with the meadows, glens, and their pastures and watering places. And I take this aforesaid possession, and I seize upon it, in the voice and name of the other lands, towns, cities, villas, castles, and strong houses and dwellings, which are now founded in the said kingdoms and provinces of New Mexico, and those neighboring to them, and shall in future time be founded in them, with their mountains, rivers and banks, waters, pastures, meadows, glens, watering places, and all its Indian natives, who in it may be included and comprehended, and with the civil and criminal jurisdiction, high and low, gallows and knife, mere mixed power, from the leaf on the mountain to the rock in the river and sands of it, and from the rocks and sands of the river to the leaf on the mountain.

(Villagrá, *Historia*, 14, "De cómo se tomo y aprehendió la possesion de la nueva tierra.")

32. The name Jornada del Muerto (Dead Man's Journey) was inspired by the story of German trader Bernardo Gruber from Sonora who was accused and condemned to prison in New Mexico by the Holy Office of the Inquisition. On June 22, 1670, Gruber escaped from jail in Santa Fe and headed south. He died in the desert and after his remains were found, the site began to be called "paraje del alemán" (place of the German). New Mexico State Office, Bureau of Land Management, *El Camino Real de Tierra Adentro National Historic Trail* (Santa Fe, N.M.: National Park Service, U.S. Department of the Interior, 2002), 158–59.

33. "Ytinerario de las Minas del Caxco" (o de la expedición de Juan de Oñate, 1797–1599), in M. Martín Rodríguez, *Gaspar de Villagrá*, 97. Also in Hammond and Rey, eds. and trans., *Don Juan de Oñate*, 1:317.

34. Seed, *Ceremonies of Possession*, 95.

35. For a transcription of the original documents that describe these acts of "obedience and vassalage" by the various indigenous peoples of Nuevo México, see Hammond and Rey, *Don Juan de Oñate*, 1:337–62. The editors include the acts of obedience of the following pueblos: Santo Domingo, San Juan, Acolocu, and Cueloze (probably Jumano and Tompiro people, located east of the Manzano mountains), Acoma, Zuñi, and Mohoqui (Hopi).

36. See editors' note in Villagrá, *Historia*, eds. and trans. Encinias, Rodríguez, and Sánchez, 160.

37.

Con cuia puerta luego el Comissario	Through this open door the Commissary
Sembró sus Religiosos, como Christo	Did sow his monks the same as Christ
Sembró el Apostolado, por Provincias,	Once sowed the Apostles, in provinces,
Y assí a san Miguel luego le dieron	And so to San Miguel was given
La Provincia de Pecos y a Zamora	The province of Pecos and to Zamora
La Provincia de Queres y al gran Lugo	The province of Queres, to great Lugo
La Provincia de Emes y a Corchado	The province of Emés, and to Corchado
La Provincia de Zía y al buen Claros	The province of Zía, to good Claros
La Provincia de Tiguas, y con esto	The province of Tiguas, and with this
Dieron a Fray Christóbal la Provincia	They gave to Fray Cristóbal the province
De aquellos nobles Teguas donde el campo	Of those noble Teguas with whom the camp
Quiso hazer asiento. Y allí juntos,	Chose to make halt. And there, together,
Los soldados a una hizieron fiestas	The soldiers, as one man, made holiday
Por bien tan inefable y tan grandioso,	For such ineffable and mighty good.
(Villagrá, Historia, 17, 316–29)	

38. M. Martín Rodríguez, *Gaspar de Villagrá*, 114–18.

39. After his horse was killed in the trap, Villagrá continued on foot, probably leaving his helmet and armor in the middle of what are today the lava fields of the Malpaís National Monument. For documents describing these events, see transcriptions by M. Martín Rodríguez, *Gaspar de Villagrá*, 111–14. Martín Rodríguez includes interesting information about the famous scene described by Villagrá in his poem when he decided to wear his boots backward to confuse the Indians who supposedly were following him. This event does not appear in the documents; therefore it is impossible to prove. However, Martín Rodríguez identifies a source for this story: "he must have read about the trick in the eighth book of the *Aeneid*, when Virgil recounts the episode in which Caco did the same thing in order to steal Hercules' cows." Ibid., 111.

40. The hill of Andalicán is today called Marihueñu. It is a high hill between the canyons of Marihueñu and the Colcura Valley. Andalicán was a name used only during the Spanish conquest. The battle is known today as battle of Marihueñu after the site where it took place. The hill appears today on the maps identified as Cerro or Cuesta de Villagrán (named after the Spaniard Francisco de Villagrá who fought against Lautaro in this battle). To locate the site on the map today, the point of reference is the town of Colcura; the battle took place west of this town (Colcura is near the coast, on the gulf of Arauco, south of the Biobío River).

41. Peñol means "peñón," a term commonly used in the sixteenth century. See editor's note in Ercilla, *La Araucana*, ed. Lerner, 227. "Peñón" means a large, rocky hill or mountain. It also means an elevation that serves as a military defense.

42. The description of the landscape in the battles is essential to the poem as it enhances the realism of the battles; this is typical of epic poetry as explained by Lerner in the introduction to his edition of *La Araucana*. Ercilla, *La Araucana*, 40.

43. See, for example, these lines that describe Caupolicán's hiding:

Y con solos diez hombres retirado,	And with only ten men retired,
gente de confianza y valentía,	people of trust and courage,
ora en el monte inculto, ora en poblado,	now in the uncivilized mountain,
desmintiendo los rastros parecía,	now in town,
y en lugares ocultos alojado	denying the signs it seemed,
jamás gran tiempo en una residía,	and in hidden places housed
usando de su bárbara insolencia	never for a great while in one resided,
por tenerlos en miedo y obediencia.	uses his barbarian insolence
	to make them fearful and obedient.

   (Ercilla, La Araucana, 32.26, 1–8)

44. The last three cantos of the poem (32 to 34) describe scenes after the battle.

45. Villagrá, *Historia*, ed. Junquera, 341.

46. The documents with the itinerary of the expedition offer a general view of the battle, but Villagrá's poem is the only source that gives details.

47. The editors of the poem refer to the fact that Villagrá is citing Curtius, the "Roman youth who sacrificed himself by leaping into the trench of the Forum. See Livy VII." See editors' notes in Villagrá, *Historia*, eds. and trans. Encinias, Rodríguez, and Sánchez, 264.

48. All these events are mentioned in canto 31, with dramatic description.

6. Geographic Landmarks

1. Alicia Morel, *Cuentos araucanos: La gente de la tierra* (Santiago, Chile: Editorial Andrés Bello, 1982), 73.

2. Adorno, *Polemics of Possession*, 4.

3. Villalobos, *Vida fronteriza*, 40.

4. In reference to the Indian groups Promaucaes, Curies, and Cauquenes.

5. Historian Sergio Villalobos has divided the war into three periods: armed conquest (1550–98), Araucanian victory (1598–1622) and de-escalation of fighting (1623–56). See Sergio Villalobos, "Guerra y paz," 9–15.

6. Villalobos, *Vida fronteriza*, 21.

7. Patricia Cerda-Hegerl, *Fronteras del sur: La región del Bio Bio y la Araucanía chilena, 1604–1883* (Temuco, Chile: Ediciones Universidad de la Frontera, Instituto Latinoamericano de la Universidad Libre de Berlín, 1990), 15–18.

8. José Bengoa, *Historia de los antiguos mapuches del sur: Desde antes de la llegada de los españoles hasta las paces de Quilín, siglos XVI y XVII* (Santiago, Chile, 2003), 65–68.

9. Bengoa, *Historia*, 54. According to Bengoa, the lives of the Araucanians were so linked to the rivers that they were called by the same names. For example, the name "Araucanian" came about because they were located around a river called *Ragco*, in what is today the coast of "Arauco," a deformation of Aragco. Ibid., 52–53.

10. Bengoa, *Historia*, 62.

11. Ernesto Wilhelm de Moesbach, *Voz de Arauco: Explicación de los nombres indígenas de Chile* (Temuco: Editorial Millantu, 1991), 32.

12. At the beginning of the United States' occupation in 1846, the term Río del Norte or just Del Norte was still common; some even used the name Río Grande del Norte, but it is uncertain exactly when the name changed to Río Grande. According to historian Robert Torrez, apparently there was no official change in designation, but probably the "newcomers" decided not to use its historical name and "by all indications, the use of Río Grande was common and was notoriously used within a decade, and it has remained so to this date." Robert Torrez, "The River Through Time: Historical Overview of the Río Grande," in *La Vida del Río Grande: Our River—Our Life*, ed. Carlos Vázquez (Albuquerque: National Hispanic Cultural Center, 2004), 5. I have found one source that includes the name Río Grande as early as 1812, although there is the possibility of a problem in the translation; the source is the report presented by don Pedro Bautista Pino to the Courts of Cádiz in the year 1812. According to the English translation, Pino says in his report: "The largest river of New Mexico is the Rio Grande or river of the North." H. Bayley Carroll and J. Villasana Haggard, eds., *Three New Mexico Chronicles* (Albuquerque: Quivira Society, 1942), 23.

13. The Rio Grande "Rises in the East slope of the Continental Divide, near Silverton, Colorado, entering New Mexico northwest of Ute Peak. Flows south through the western half of the state crossing into Texas at Anthony to run into the Gulf of Mexico." T. M. Pearce, ed., *New Mexico Place Names. A Geographical Dictionary* (Albuquerque: University of New Mexico Press, 1965), 134.

14. Today's pueblos are: Taos, Picuris, San Juan, Santa Clara, San Ildefonso, Tesuque, Nambe, Pojoaque, Cochiti, Santo Domingo, San Felipe, Santa Ana, Zia, Jemez, Sandia, Isleta, Laguna, and Acoma. Dan Scurlock, *From the Rio to the Sierra: An Environmental History of the Middle Rio Grande Basin* (Fort Collins, Colo.: Rocky Mountain Research Station, U.S. Department of Agriculture, 1998), 84–85. For more details on pueblos of the Rio Grande region in times of the Spanish presence, see Elinore M. Barrett, "The Geography of Rio Grande Pueblos Revealed by Spanish Explorers, 1540–1598," *Latin American Institute Research Paper Series* 30 (Albuquerque: University of New Mexico, 1997), 1–23.

15. The first Spaniard who saw the river was Alonso Álvarez de Pineda. Pearce, *New Mexico*, 134.

16. Álvar Núñez Cabeza de Vaca, *The Account: Álvar Núñez Cabeza de Vaca's Relación*, eds. and trans. Martin Favata and José Fernández (Houston: Arte Público Press, 1993), 101–103. His journey (1528–36) predated the expeditions of Soto and Vázquez de Coronado in what is today the United States.

17. "Gallegos' Relation of the Chamuscado-Rodríguez Expedition," in Hammond and Rey, eds., *Rediscovery*, 83. This is not the first time that Spaniards named a river after or compared it to the well-known Guadalquivir River in Seville, Spain. In his account, Álvar Núñez Cabeza de Vaca compared the Río Conchos to the Guadalquivir River (Cabeza de Vaca, *Account*, 92) and also compared the Iguazú River in South America to the Guadalquivir. Pedro de Valdivia in his conquest of Chile compared the Cautín River to the Guadalquivir.

18. Torrez, "River," 4.

19. The expedition consisted of four hundred men, fifty-five of whom brought their families; eighty-three wagons; and around seven thousand head of livestock. Editors'

notes in Villagrá, *Historia*, ed. Mercedes Junquera, 167; and in Villagrá, *Historia*, eds. and trans. Encinias, Rodríguez, and Sánchez, 88.

20. Elizabeth Davis explains the meaning of the comparison of Oñate to Julius Caesar; she adduces that the poet might have linked the two because of the Roman leader's famous crossing of the Rubicon (Davis, "De mares y ríos," in *Épica y Colonia*, 270.)

21. Ibid., 263–86.

22. "Buffalo" is properly the name for a similar type of animal from Asia and Africa.

23. "Relación Postrera de Cíbola," in *Narratives of the Coronado Expedition, 1540–1542*, eds. George Hammond and Agapito Rey (Albuquerque: University of New Mexico Press, 1940), 308. This account was translated from a copy of a Spanish text which was part of a larger work written by fray Toribio de Benavente or Motolinía. The document was in the possession of Joaquín García Icazbalceta and is now in the collections of the University of Texas Library in Austin. For more information about the origins of this document, see fray Toribio de Benavente (Motolinía), *Historia de los indios de la Nueva España*, ed. Edmundo O' Gorman (Mexico: Porrúa, 1979), xxxiii–xxxiv. See Chávez, *Quest for Quivira*, 6.

24. Castañeda de Nájera, "Account of the Expedition to Cibola," 134–35.

25. "Gallegos' Relation," in Hammond and Rey, *Rediscovery*, 91.

26. The original of this account is in AGI, Patronato 22, ramo 13, folios 1019v–21r . It was translated to English and published by Hammond and Rey, *Don Juan de Oñate*, 398–405.

27. José Rabasa, *Writing Violence on the Northern Frontier: The Historiography of Sixteenth-Century New Mexico and Florida and the Legacy of Conquest* (Durham, N.C.: Duke University Press, 2000), 135.

28. Cited in Rabasa, *Writing Violence*, 134–35.

29. Cabeza de Vaca, *Account*, 72–73. In 1541 Francisco Vázquez de Coronado and his men were the next Europeans to hunt buffalo after Cabeza de Vaca, in this case on the plains of the present-day states of Kansas and Texas. Pedro de Castañeda, a soldier in the Coronado expedition, described this scene in his "Account of the Expedition to Cibola," cited previously in this book.

30. Gonzalo Fernández de Oviedo y Valdés, *Historia general y natural de las Indias* (Madrid: Ediciones Atlas, 1959); Francisco López de Gómara, *Hispania Victrix. Primera y Segunda parte de la* Historia general de las Indias. *Con todo el descubrimiento, y cosas notables que han acaecido desde que se ganaron hasta el año de 1551; con la conquista de México y de la Nueva España* (Madrid: Rivadeneyra, 1877); Juan López de Velasco, *Geografía y descripción universal de las Indias* (Madrid: Fortanet, 1894).

31. Editor's note in Ercilla, *La Araucana*, ed. Lerner, 471. Regarding the origins of the word "morro," the root could be pre-Celtic: "mor" or "morr" means head, or hill, or hilltop. Also, some Celtic and Mediterranean words suggest an Indo-European root, in which case "mor" means stone or rock. For this topic see Álvaro Galmés de Fuentes, *Los topónimos: Sus blasones y trofeos (la toponimia mítica)* (Madrid: Real Academia de la Historia, 2000), 157.

32. *Larousse Diccionario Enciclopédico* (Mexico City: Larousse, 1985), 427.

33. The journals of Diego de Vargas in the entries for November 8, 9, and 29 and December 1 of 1692 describe the place as a campsite with a water hole. On one of these dates Vargas inscribed his name on the rock. John L. Kessell and Rick Hendricks, eds., *By Force of Arms: The Journals of don Diego de Vargas, New Mexico, 1691–1693* (Albuquerque: University of New Mexico Press, 1992), 543–45, 580–81, 584.

34. "Diego Pérez de Luxan's Account of the Antonio de Espejo Expedition into New Mexico, 1582," in Hammond and Rey, *Rediscovery*, 183.

35. "Expedition to the South Sea and the Salines," in Hammond and Rey, eds. and trans., *Don Juan de Oñate*, 395.

36. Oñate continued the tradition that began with the natives of this area and that would be followed by Spaniards and other travelers through the nineteenth century. Today it is possible to identify the names of the people who "passed by"; next to their names and dates in most cases they included the purpose of their journeys. The site is considered an archive on the rock.

37. See details of this expedition in chapter 5.

38. Alfredo Sánchez and Roberto Morales, *Las regiones de Chile: Espacio físico y humano-económico* (Santiago, Chile: Editorial Universitaria, 1990), 174–76.

39. Accounts contemporary with *La Araucana* that mention García Hurtado de Mendoza's campaign in the area of Villarrica do not mention the beauty of the place either. Such is the case, for example, of the chronicles by Jerónimo de Vivar, *Crónica*, 327.

40. César Fernández, ed., *Cuentan los mapuches* (Buenos Aires: Ediciones Nuevo Siglo, 1999), 257.

41. Carlos Valenzuela Solís de Ovando, *Crónicas de la conquista* (Santiago, Chile Editorial Andíjar, n.d.), 75.

42. Simmons, *Last Conquistador*, 169–71.

43. The concept of the "first America" and its imaginary is presented by Serge Gruzinski in his book *La guerra de las imágenes*.

Epilogue

1. The citation as it appears in the library catalog is: Alonso de Ercilla y Zúñiga, *La Araucana*, parte I–II. Madrid: por D. Antonio de Sancha, año de M.DCC.LXXVI. Se hallará en su casa en la Aduana Vieja [1776].

2. Manuel Martín Rodríguez includes the list of copies of the 1610 edition of the poem, which is found today in various institutions and countries, in his annotated 2010 edition of the poem. Villagrá, *Historia*, ed. M. Martín Rodríguez, 443–45.

3. "Now, here come three together: the 'Araucana' of Don Alonso de Ercilla, the 'Austriada' of Juan Rufo, a magistrate of Cordova, the 'Monserrato' of Christoval de Virves, a poet of Valencia. 'These three books,' said the priest, 'are the best that are written in heroic verse in the Castilian tongue, and may stand in competition with the most renowned works of Italy. Let them be preserved as the best productions of the Spanish Muse.'" Miguel de Cervantes, *Adventures of Don Quixote de la Mancha*, chap. 6.

4. Cueva, "El espejismo heroico," 30, 34. Cueva agrees with Fernando Alegría that the *Arauco domado* by Pedro de Oña (to which *La Araucana* has been compared) "is a failure as an epic." Ibid., 30.

5. Ibid., 30. Cueva says that "it must be remembered that in America the conquistador-colonizer (the two terms are empirically inseparable) found himself caught in a trap, which impeded him from attributing heroic dimensions to the newly subjugated. Either he poetically praised the autochthonous adversary, in order to confer an epic scope to his adventure, but in that case it became incongruent to denigrate him in other ideological manifestations and the justification of servitude broke down, or he justified this, denigrating the Indian, but then all epic possibility disappeared."

6. Jaime Concha, "El otro nuevo mundo" in *Homenaje a Ercilla* (Concepción: Universidad de Concepción, 1969), cited by Cueva, "El espejismo heroico," 32.

7. Cited by Roberto Castillo Sandoval, "¿'Una misma cosa con la vuestra'? Ercilla, Pedro de Oña y la apropiación post-colonial de la patria araucana," *Revista Iberoamericana* 61, nos. 170–71 (1995): 234.

8. Ibid., 232.

9. Ibid., 231.

10. Ibid., 231. The author cites nineteenth-century Argentinian writer and president Domingo Faustino Sarmiento, whose thoughts confirm the common vision of the poem by intellectuals of the second half of the nineteenth century: "The history of Chile is traced on *Araucana*, and Chileans, who must consider themselves defeated with the Spaniards, cover themselves with the glory of the Araucanians . . . these adoptions have been beneficial for forming the fighting character of the Chileans, as seen in the recent war with Peru." Ibid., 232.

11. Acta de Fundación, Ilustre Municipalidad de Ercilla, "Investigación histórica de Ercilla," unpublished manuscript, 7. My thanks to the staff of the Ercilla city hall for a copy of this research report.

12. Ibid., 8.

13. Antonio de Undurraga, Prologue to Alonso de Ercilla, *La Araucana* (Madrid: Espasa Calpe, 2000), 22. The prologue was written for the 1946 Santiago, Chile, edition of the poem. Undurraga points out that Ercilla was the son of a lawyer and that democratic ideals surfaced in his poetry through the balance seen between his view of the Araucanians and Governor García Hurtado de Mendoza.

14. To quote the works by Medina regarding *La Araucana* and Ercilla would require a bibliographic analysis beyond the scope of this work. For this topic see Dinamarca, "Los estudios de Medina," 3–26. On Ercilla's biography, the first and fundamental work that other authors have used as a basis for their own studies is by José Toribio Medina, in the third volume of his collection of five on Ercilla and *La Araucana*: José Toribio Medina, *La Araucana de Don Alonso de Ercilla y Zúñiga. Vida de Ercilla* (Santiago, Chile: Imprenta Elzeviriana, 1917). See also Ricardo Donoso, *Vida de Ercilla* (Mexico City: Fondo de Cultura Económica, 1948). Most of the editions of *La Araucana* include a biography of the poet; the current volume draws most heavily on the editions by Isaías Lerner and Marcos A. Morínigo (Madrid: Clásicos Castalia, 1979); and by Isaías Lerner (Madrid: Ediciones Cátedra, 1993). Together, these two editions offer an excellent analysis of the poem. The works of Frank Pierce are also important to mention: *Epic Poetry* (Madrid: Gredos, 1961) and *Alonso de Ercilla y Zúñiga* (Amsterdam: Rodopi, 1984).

15.

> "Piedras de Arauco y desatadas rosas
> fluviales, territorios de raíces,
> se encuentran con el hombre que ha llegado de España.
> Invaden su armadura con gigantesco liquen.
> Atropellan su espada las sombras del helecho . . .
> Hombre, Ercilla sonoro, oigo el pulso del agua
> de tu primer amanecer, . . .
> Deja, deja tu huella
> de águila rubia, destroza
> tu mejilla contra el maíz salvaje,
> todo será en la tierra devorado.

> Sonoro, sólo tú no beberás la copa
> de sangre, sonoro, solo al rápido
> fulgor de ti nacido
> llegará la secreta boca del tiempo en vano
> para decirte: en vano."
>> (Pablo Neruda, *Canto general*, vol. 1
>> [Buenos Aires: Losada, 1999], 65).

16. "[H]undreds of years before the discovery of America, Dante, from Ravena, predicted and intuited the four stars of the Southern Cross. For me, no one bothered with these stars except for, to be sure, geographers and mapmakers. The first to really see them, having come from Europe, and from a Europe that was more backward, was Dante's messenger, don Alonso Ercilla. To him we owe our constellations. Our other American fatherlands had a discoverer and a conqueror. We also had in Ercilla, an inventor and liberator." Pablo Neruda, "El mensajero," in *Don Alonso de Ercilla, inventor de Chile* (Barcelona: Editorial Pomaire, 1971), 11–12.

17. His work is titled "Incitación al nixonicidio y alabanza de la revolución chilena," cited by Giuseppe Bellini, *Nueva historia*, 112.

18. Jorge Román-Lagunas, "Lo épico y 'La Araucana,'" in *Don Alonso de Ercilla*, 168.

19. Víctor Raviola Molina, "Elementos indígenas en La Araucana de Ercilla," in *Don Alonso de Ercilla*, 81–136.

20. Roberto Castillo Sandoval, "¿'Una misma cosa'?" 234–35.

21. Alfonso Bulnes, *Visión de Ercilla y otros ensayos* (Santiago, Chile: Editorial Andrés Bello, 1970).

22. For this section, I especially thank my Chilean colleagues mentioned in the acknowledgments.

23. Specialists disagree about what aspects of *La Araucana* are possible to study and what aspects cannot be studied because of a lack of details. At the very least, these attempts to reread and reinterpret the poem have contributed to a stimulating debate.

24. Leonardo León Solís, "La Araucana: Una lectura desde la nueva historia," unpublished manuscript, 1. I thank Dr. León Solís for giving me a copy of his paper.

25. León Solís, "La Araucana," 11–12. León Solís arrives at this conclusion using not only the poem but other historical documents.

26. The story that in the opinion of León Solís inspired Ercilla to call his poem "La Araucana," in reference to the woman who provided Ercilla with information and probably saved his life, appears in the list of Chilean legends as presented by Aurelio Díaz Meza in his book *Leyendas y episodios chilenos* (Buenos Aires: Editorial Antártica, 1968), 7–37. The legend is titled "Of how don Alonso de Ercilla y Zúñiga avenged an offense."

27. These festivities are celebrated between January 18 and 30 of each year, and their name comes from the name of Governor García Hurtado de Mendoza, successor of Governor Pedro de Valdivia in the conquest and colonization of Chile. As part of the events, specialists deliver lectures, and teachers from the Liceo de Cañete recite the poem *La Araucana* during a day. Cañete was founded in 1558 by García Hurtado de Mendoza in honor of his father, the Marqués de Cañete, Viceroy of Peru. The Spanish built the Tucapel fort there. As a result of the interest in reconstructing the history of the city, local historian Clímaco Hermosillo Silva published the book *Cañete: Crónicas de cinco siglos* (Concepción, Chile: Cosmigonon, 2002). Ercilla's poem is used as a historical source in parts of the book.

28. Julio Retamal, "Pensando la historiografía del mañana," in *Historiadores chilenos frente al bicentenario*, ed. Luis Carlos Parentini (Santiago, Chile: Comisión Bicentenario, Presidencia de la República, 2008), 405.

29. Emma de Ramón, "Recuerdos y proyecciones en torno al bicentenario," in Parentini, *Historiadores chilenos*, 182.

30. Ibid.

31. Luis Carreño, "Exclusión y prejuicio: La formación del estado nacional," in Parentini, *Historiadores chilenos*, 152.

32. Olaya Sanfuentes, "La trinidad patrimonial: Patrimonio, historia y memoria en la formación de la identidad," in Parentini, *Historiadores chilenos*, 465. The author links the concepts of memory, identity, and history: "Memory is what allows us to place ourselves where we came from; identity leads us to the question about what we are, while history makes us reflect on where to aim our destiny, toward our future, at the same time that it ties us to three times, the past, the present, and the future, in which our individual and collective being unfolds" (463).

33. Caillet-Bois, *Análisis*, 9.

34. M. Martín Rodríguez, *Cantas a Marte*, 209.

35. Ibid., 216–18.

36. Ibid., 217.

37. Ibid., 218.

38. Ibid., 226–30. See also Luis Leal, "The First American Epic: Villagrá's History of New Mexico," in *Pasó por aquí: Critical Essays on the New Mexican Literary Tradition, 1542–1988*, ed. Erlinda Gonzales-Berry (Albuquerque: University of New Mexico Press, 1989), 48.

39. Leal, "First American Epic," 47.

40. The transcription of the *Historia* was made in two copies by Swiss-born archaeologist Adolph Bandelier, who copied the existing original book at the National Museum of Mexico City. At present one of these copies is at Harvard University, in the Hemenway Collection of the Peabody Museum. The other is available at the Fray Angélico Chávez History Library and Photographic Archives of the Museum of New Mexico's Palace of the Governors in Santa Fe, New Mexico. For more information on the transcriptions, see Thomas E. Chávez, "La Historia de la Nueva México: The Cuartocentenario of Juan de Oñate," *El Palacio* 102, no. 2 (1997–98): 38–44.

41. M. Martín Rodríguez, introduction to Villagrá, *Historia*, ed. M. Martín Rodríguez, 32.

42. Ibid. Martín Rodríguez mentions that the editor of the *El Progreso* newspaper in 1898, Isidoro Armijo, used an edition that belonged to the New Mexican writer and lawyer Eusebio Chacón.

43. Gaspar de Villagrá, *Historia de la Nueva México*, ed. Luis González Obregón (Mexico City: Imprenta del Museo Nacional, 1900), 2 vols. The first volume is an edition of Villagrá's poem and the second volume includes documents pertinent to Villagrá. For more information about this edition, see M. Martín Rodríguez, introduction to Villagrá, *Historia*, ed. M. Martín Rodríguez, 32.

44. Gaspar Pérez de Villagrá, *History of New Mexico*, ed. and trans. Gilberto Espinoza, introduction and notes Frederick W. Hodge (Los Angeles: Quivira Society, 1933). Reprinted (Santa Fe, N.M.: Arno Press, 1967). For more information about these editions, see M. Martín Rodríguez, introduction to Villagrá, *Historia*, ed. M. Martín Rodríguez, 32–33.

45. David Holtby, *Forty-Seventh Star: New Mexico's Struggle for Statehood* (Norman: University of Oklahoma Press, 2012), 119.

46. Ibid.

47. Ibid., 120.

48. Ibid., 42.

49. Walter Prescott Webb, *The Great Plains* (New York: Grosset & Dunlap, 1931), 126.

50. Miguel López, "Disputed History and Poetry: Gaspar Pérez de Villagrá's Historia de la Nueva México," *Bilingual Review* 26, no. 1 (2001–2002): 47.

51. Leal, "First American Epic," 48.

52. Ibid.

53. Villagrá, *Historia*, ed. Junquera (the same edition by Junquera was published in Madrid in 2003 by Dastin Press). Other editions are: Villagrá, *Historia*, eds. Victorino Madrid Rubio, Elsía Armesto Rodríguez, and Augusto Quintana Prieto; and Villagrá, *Historia*, ed. M. Martín Rodríguez. For more information about the editions of the poem during the 1980s and after, as well as a critical evaluation, see Martín M. Rodríguez, introduction to Villagrá, *Historia*, ed. M. Martín Rodríguez, 33–34. For more information on Villagrá, the reading of his poem throughout history, and the reception of the poem, see Manuel M. Martín Rodríguez, "La Historia de la Nueva México de Gaspar Pérez de Villagrá: Recepción crítica (con nuevos datos biográficos de su autor)," in *El humanismo español, su proyección en América y Canarias en la época del humanismo*, eds. A. Martín Rodríguez y G. Santana Henríquez (Las Palmas de Gran Canaria: Universidad de las Palmas de Gran Canaria, 2006), 189–253; Manuel M. Martín Rodríguez, "Reading Gaspar de Villagrá (in the Seventeenth Century)," in *Cien años de lealtad: En honor a Luis Leal*, eds. S. Poot Herrera, F. A. Lomelí, and M. Herrera-Sobek (Mexico: UC-Mexicanistas, 2007), 2:1337–46; Manuel M. Martín Rodríguez, "400 Years," 13–19. The most complete análisis of the critical reception of the poem is included in M. Martín Rodriguez, *Cantas a Marte*, 207–77.

54. Villagrá, *Historia*, eds. and trans. Encinias, Rodríguez, and Sánchez. Reprinted 2004.

55. Philadelphio Jaramillo, " Dispositio Textus: Paleographic or Semipaleographic Edition?" *Bilingual Review/ Revista Bilingüe* 17, no. 3 (1992): 276. Cited by López, "Disputed History," 43. Jaramillo adds that the poem must be studied and read in Spanish, especially "by the Hispanists of New Mexican origin who are participants of the Hispanic world and who consider [the poem] the literary and historical source of our cultural roots here in the United States."

56. López, "Disputed History," 45; Leal, "First American Epic," 48.

57. López, "Disputed History," 54.

58. María Herrera-Sobek and Virginia Sánchez Korrol, introduction to *Recovering the U.S. Hispanic Literary Heritage*, eds. María Herrera-Sobek and Virginia Sánchez Korrol (Houston, Arte Público Press, 2000), 3:4.

59. M. Martín Rodríguez, *Gaspar de Villagrá: Legista, soldado y poeta*; Villagrá, *Historia*, ed. M. Martín Rodríguez; M. Martín Rodríguez, *Cantas a Marte*. Mexican writer Moisés Ramos Rodríguez, from Puebla, is also working on a biography of Gaspar de Villagrá.

60. "The freedom, indeed, of this kind of composition is alike favorable to the author, whether he would display his powers in epic (for there may be epic in prose as well as verse) or lyric, in tragedy or comedy—in short, in every department of the delicious arts

of poetry and oratory." Miguel de Cervantes, *Adventures of Don Quixote de la Mancha*, chap. 46.

61. Volumes 1, 2, and 3 of *Recovering the U.S. Hispanic Literary Heritage* were published between 1993 and 2000 by Arte Público Press (Houston, Tx.). See also María Herrera-Sobek, ed., *Reconstructing a Chicano/a Literary Heritage: Hispanic Colonial literature of the Southwest* (Tucson: University of Arizona Press, 1993).

62. Carla Mulford, ed., *Teaching the Literatures of Early America* (New York: Modern Language Association of America, 1999).

63. Carla Mulford, "Resisting Colonialism," in *Teaching the Literatures*, 75–94. E. Thomson Shields and Dana D. Nelson, "Colonial Spanish Writings," in Mulford, *Teaching the Literatures*, 97–111. In "Colonial Spanish Writings" the authors make an important point regarding the value of studying the poem, since it "allows students to see that the writing of history and of literature are not essentially different," and they add, "It is worth asking students to consider how the epic form guides Villagrá's portrayal of events like Oñate's attack on Acoma Pueblo." Ibid., 105.

64. Harold Augenbraum and Margarite Fernández Olmos, *The Latino Reader: An American Literary Tradition from 1542 to the Present* (Boston: Houghton Mifflin, 1997).

65. Susan Castillo and Ivy Schweitzer, eds., *The Literatures of Colonial America: An Anthology* (Malden, Mass.: Blackwell, 2001); and *A Companion to the Literatures of Colonial America* (Malden, Mass.: Blackwell, 2005).

66. In this list we include the article by Enrique Lamadrid, whose analysis centers on legends of miracles and supernatural events mentioned, among other sources, by Villagrá in his poem. Lamadrid's conclusion adds to the topic of the poem as foundational text, in this case linked to miracles that include Hispanics and Native Americans ("Santiago and San Acacio: Slaughter and Deliverance in the Foundational Legends of Colonial and Postcolonial New Mexico," *Journal of American Folklore* 115, nos. 457–58 [2002]: 457–474).

67. For a study of the myth of Aztlán in the *Historia de la Nueva México*, see María Herrera-Sobek, "New Approaches to Old Chroniclers: Contemporary Critical Theories and the Pérez de Villagrá Epic," in *Recovering the U.S. Hispanic Literary Heritage*, eds. María Herrera-Sobek and Virginia Sánchez Korrol (Houston: Arte Público Press, 2000), 3:154–62. Regarding information the poem offers about dramas, one interpretation is that Captain Farfán de Los Godos wrote a version of the *Moros y Cristianos* to be performed as the first theatrical representation along the Rio Grande, near today's San Elizario (close to today's El Paso, Texas) in 1598; see Aurora Lucero White-Lea, ed., *Literary Folklore of the Hispanic Southwest* (San Antonio, Tx.: Naylor, 1953), cited by José B. Fernández, "Hispanic Literature: The Colonial Period," in *Recovering the U.S. Hispanic Literary Heritage*, eds. Ramón Gutiérrez and Genaro Padilla (Houston: Arte Público Press, 1993), 1:253–64. Villagrá, however, mentions in the poem that Farfán de los Godos wrote a piece regarding the success of the Catholic faith, but the poet never says that it was Moros y Cristianos. The poet mentions the representation of Moros y Cristianos in another section of the poem in regard to a moment of celebration when Oñate and his people were settled in San Juan de los Caballeros.

68. One good example is the anthology *Épica y colonia*, edited by Paul Firbas and cited several times in this book. Published in 2008 in Peru, it includes articles by scholars from Latin America and the United States, and the poems by Ercilla and Villagrá are the main subject of some of those studies.

69. Herman Schwember, *Donde otro no ha llegado* (Santiago, Chile: CESOC, 2003).

70. Joseph J. Bohnaker, *Of Arms I Sing* (Santa Fe, N.M.: Sunstone, 1990). In his novel Bohnaker characterizes Villagrá as a kind person in his dealings with indigenous people (he even marries a woman from Acoma) and as critical of the Inquisition. Although the novel is ostensibly about Juan de Oñate through Villagrá's first-person account, it is more about Villagrá than Oñate. In the novel the poet writes his poem while in prison in Seville, where he was detained by the Inquisition because of his crimes during the conquest (specifically the killing of two fugitives who escaped from the colony in New Mexico). In the novel the poet was born in Spain, not in New Spain, and he is writing his poem while telling the story. He appears in the novel as a hero, always looking for the most balanced and just answers and criticizing the negative aspects of the conquest. Although he writes about Oñate with some admiration, in general the poet is more critical of the governor than what he writes in the poem. In the preface, the novelist describes Oñate as indomitable, with visions of glory and adventure, while Villagrá is, in the words of the novelist, a "courageous" captain. The author points out (through the voices of his characters) the differences between creoles and Spanish (considering Villagrá as Spanish and behaving as Spanish).

71. Juan F. Maura, "Gaspar Pérez de Villagrá y Sabine R. Ulibarrí: Pasado y presente de la épica de Nuevo México," *Espéculo: Revista de Estudios Literarios* (Universidad Complutense, Madrid) 8, no. 20 (2002).

72. Maura, "Gaspar Pérez de Villagrá."

73. Ibid.

74. Ibid. Ulibarrí was a volunteer in the U.S. Army during World War II.

75. Ibid.

76. Ibid.

77. Cañizares-Esguerra, "Racial," 426.

78. Ibid., 427.

79. Such are the cases of Sor Juana Inés de la Cruz, Miguel Sánchez, and Carlos Sigüenza y Góngora in the seventeenth century and Francisco Clavijero in the eighteenth century.

80. David Snow, *New Mexico's First Colonists: The 1597–1600 Enlistments for New Mexico under Juan de Oñate, Adelantado and Gobernador* (Albuquerque: Hispanic Genealogical Research Center of New Mexico, 1998), 5.

81. Ibid.

82. José Antonio Mazzotti, "Epic, Creoles, and Nation in Spanish America," in Castillo and Schweitzer, *A Companion to the Literatures of Colonial America*, 480–99.

83. Ralph Bauer, "Toward a Cultural Geography of Colonial American Literatures: Empire, Location, Creolization," in Castillo and Schweitzer, *A Companion to the Literatures of Colonial America*, 38. The author cites William Spengemann, who has pointed out this "proto-nationalist paradigm of early American literary studies" in these terms: "No one wrote in what has been called 'the future United States,' a future that did not exist until it was a past." William Spengemann, *A New World of Words: Redefining Early American Literature* (New Haven, Conn.: Yale University Press, 1994), 49.

84. Bauer, "Toward a Cultural Geography," 39.

Bibliography

Manuscript Collections

SPAIN

Archivo General de Indias (AGI): Indiferente General, 2054; Contratación, 573 (Bienes de Difuntos).
Archivo de la Universidad de Salamanca (AUS): Secretaría, Fondo Universitario (Legistas, Matrículas 290, 291, 292, 293, 294).
Biblioteca Nacional (BN): Manuscritos.

CHILE

Acta de Fundación, Ilustre Municipalidad de Ercilla, "Investigación histórica de Ercilla."
Biblioteca Nacional de Chile (BNCH), Sala Medina: *Códice de la Real Academia de la Historia de D. Alonso de Ercilla.*

Books, Articles, Dissertations, and Manuscripts

Acosta, José de. *Historia natural y moral de las Indias*. Madrid: Historia 16, 1987.
Adorno, Rolena. "Literary Production and Suppression: Reading and Writing about Amerindians in Colonial Spanish America." *Dispositio* 11, nos. 28–29 (1985): 1–25.
———. *The Polemics of Possession in Spanish American Narrative*. New Haven, Conn.: Yale University Press, 2007.
———. "The Warrior and the War Community: Constructions of the Civil Order in Mexican Conquest History." *Dispositio* 14, nos. 36–38 (1989): 225–46.
Ahern, Maureen. "'Llevando el norte sobre el ojo izquierdo': Mapping, Measuring, and Naming in Castañeda's *Relación de la jornada de Cíbola* (1563)." In *Mapping Colonial Spanish America: Places and Commonplaces of Identity, Culture, and Experience*, edited by Santa Arias and Mariselle Meléndez, 24–50. Lewisburg, Penn.: Bucknell University Press, 2002.
———. "La relación como glosa, guía y memoria: Nuevo México 1581–1582." In *Literatura colonial: Identidades y conquista*. Special issue of *Revista Iberoamericana* 61, nos. 170–71 (January–June 1995): 41–55.
Alegría, Fernando. *La poesía chilena: Orígenes y desarrollo del siglo XVI al XIX*. Berkeley: University of California Press, 1954.
Álvarez Peláez, Raquel. *La conquista de la naturaleza americana*. Madrid: Consejo Superior de Investigaciones Científicas, 1993.

Álvarez Vilela, Ángel. "La expedición a Ancud en *La Araucana*, o la recuperación del mérito por parte de Ercilla." *Anales de Literatura Hispanoamericana* 24 (1995).

Aragonés de la Encarnación, Adolfo. *Ercilla-Ocaña: IV centenario del nacimiento de Don Alonso de Ercilla Zúñiga, 1533–1933*. Toledo, Spain: Rafael Gómez-Menor, 1933.

Arias, Santa, and Mariselle Meléndez. "Space and the Rhetorics of Power in Colonial Spanish America: An Introduction." In *Mapping Colonial Spanish America: Places and Commonplaces of Identity, Culture, and Experience*, edited by Santa Arias and Mariselle Meléndez, 13–23. Lewisburg, Penn.: Bucknell University Press, 2002.

Ariosto, Ludovico. *Orlando Furioso. Poema escrito en italiano por Ludovico Ariosto.* Edited and translated by Manuel Aranda y Sanjuan. Vol. 1. Barcelona: Empresa Editorial La Ilustración.

Arteaga, Alfred. *Chicano Poetics: Heterotexts and Hybridities.* Cambridge: Cambridge University Press, 1997.

Augenbraum, Harold, Margarite Fernández Olmos, et al. *The Latino Reader: An American Literary Tradition from 1542 to the Present.* Boston: Houghton Mifflin, 1997.

Bárcena, Alicia, Juan Catrillanca, et al. *Desigualdades territoriales y exclusión social del pueblo mapuche en Chile: Situación en la comuna de Ercilla desde un enfoque de derechos.* Santiago, Chile: CEPAL and Alianza Territorial Mapuche, 2012.

Barrett, Elinore M. "The Geography of Rio Grande Pueblos Revealed by Spanish Explorers, 1540–1598." *Latin American Institute Research Paper Series* 30 (1997): 1–23.

Bauer, Ralph. "Toward a Cultural Geography of Colonial American Literatures: Empire, Location, Creolization." In *A Companion to the Literatures of Colonial America*, edited by Susan Castillo and Ivy Schweitzer, 38–59. Malden, Mass.: Blackwell, 2005.

Becco, Horacio Jorge. *Historia real y fantástica del Nuevo Mundo.* Caracas: Biblioteca Ayacucho, 1992.

Bellini, Giuseppe. "De Ercilla a Gaspar Pérez de Villagrá." Alicante, Spain: *Biblioteca Virtual Miguel de Cervantes, Biblioteca Americana*, 2009.

———. *Nueva historia de la literatura hispanoamericana.* Madrid: Editorial Castalia, 1997.

Benavente, Toribio de, fray (Motolinía). *Historia de los indios de la Nueva España.* Edited by Edmundo O' Gorman. Mexico: Porrúa, 1979.

Bengoa, José. *Historia de los antiguos mapuches del sur desde antes de la llegada de los españoles hasta las paces de Quilin: Siglos XVI y XVII.* Santiago, Chile: Catalonia, 2003.

Bernard, Carmen, and Serge Gruzinski. *Historia del Nuevo Mundo.* Mexico: Fondo de Cultura Económica, 1999.

Bohnaker, Joseph J. *Of Arms I Sing.* Santa Fe, N.M.: Sunstone, 1990.

Bolaños, Álvaro Félix. "On the Issues of Academic Colonization and Responsibility when Reading and Writing about Colonial Latin America Today." In *Colonialism Past and Present: Reading and Writing about Colonial Latin America Today*, edited by Álvaro Félix Bolaños and Gustavo Verdesio, 19–49. New York: State University of New York Press, 2002.

———. "A Place to Live, a Place to Think, and a Place to Die: Sixteenth Century Frontier Cities, Plazas, and '*Relaciones*' in Spanish America." In *Mapping Colonial Spanish America: Places and Commonplaces of Identity, Culture, and Experience*, edited by Santa Arias and Mariselle Meléndez, 275–93. Lewisburg, Penn.: Bucknell University Press, 2002.

Bolaños, Alvaro Félix, and Gustavo Verdesio, eds. *Colonialism Past and Present: Reading and Writing about Colonial Latin America Today.* New York: State University of New York Press, 2002.

Bolton, Herbert E. *Coronado on the Turquoise Trail: Knight of Pueblos and Plains.* Albuquerque: University of New Mexico Press, 1949. Reprinted 1971.

Bremner, Robert H., ed. *Essays on History and Literature.* Columbus: Ohio State University Press, 1966.

Bulnes, Alfonso. *Visión de Ercilla y otros ensayos.* Santiago, Chile: Editorial Andrés Bello, 1970.

Burgin, Victor. *Between.* Oxford, UK: Basil Blackwell, 1986.

Cabeza de Vaca, Álvar Núñez. *The Account.* Edited and translated by Martin Favata and José Fernández. Houston: Arte Público Press, 1993.

———. *The South American Expeditions, 1540–1545.* Edited and translated by Baker H. Morrow. Albuquerque: University of New Mexico Press, 2011.

Caillet-Bois, Julio. *Análisis de La Araucana.* Buenos Aires: Centro Editor de América Latina, 1967.

Cajete, Gregory. *Native Science: Natural Laws of Interdependence.* Santa Fe, N.M.: Clear Light, 2000.

Canellas Anoz, Magdalena. "Relaciones geográficas de España y de las Indias." In *Felipe II y el oficio de rey: La fragua de un imperio,* edited by José Román Gutiérrez, Enrique Martínez Ruiz, and Jaime González Rodríguez, 245–66. Madrid: Sociedad Estatal para la Conmemoración de los Centenarios de Felipe II y Carlos V, 2001.

Cañizares-Esguerra, Jorge. "Racial, Religious, and Civil Creole Identity in Colonial Spanish America." *American Literary History* 17, no. 3 (2005): 420–37.

Carreño, Luis. "Exclusión y prejuicio: La formación del estado nacional." In *Historiadores chilenos frente al bicentenario,* edited by Luis Carlos Parentini, 151–54. Santiago, Chile: Comisión Bicentenario, Presidencia de la República, 2008.

Carrera, Louis. *A Translation of Alonso de Ercilla's "La Araucana."* Pittsburgh, Penn.: RoseDog Books, 2006.

Carroll, H. Bayley, and J. Villasana Haggard, eds. *Three New Mexico Chronicles.* Albuquerque: Quivira Society, 1942.

Castañeda de Nájera, Pedro de. "Account of the expedition to Cibola which took place in the year 1540, in which all those settlements, their ceremonies and customs, are described." In *The Journey of Coronado, 1540–1542,* edited and translated by George Parker Winship. Golden, Colo.: Fulcrum, 1990.

Castillo, Susan, and Ivy Schweitzer, eds. *A Companion to the Literatures of Colonial America.* Malden, Mass.: Blackwell, 2005.

———. *The Literatures of Colonial America: An Anthology.* Malden, Mass.: Blackwell, 2001.

Castillo Sandoval, Roberto. "'¿Una misma cosa con la vuestra'?: Ercilla, Pedro de Oña y la apropiación post-colonial de la patria araucana." *Revista Iberoamericana* 61, nos. 170–71 (1995): 231–47.

Cerda-Hegerl, Patricia. *Fronteras del sur: La región del Bío Bío y la Araucanía chilena.* Temuco, Chile: Ediciones Universidad de la Frontera, Instituto Latinoamericano de la Universidad Libre de Berlín, 1990.

Certeau, Michel de. "La operación histórica." In *Historia y literatura,* edited by Françoise Perus, 31–69. Mexico City: Instituto Mora, 2001.

Chang-Rodríguez, Raquel, ed. *Historia de la literatura mexicana: La cultura letrada en la Nueva España del siglo XVII*. Mexico City: Siglo Veintiuno Editores, 2002.

Chaunu, Pierre. *Conquista y explotación de los nuevos mundos*. Barcelona: Nueva Clío, 1984.

Chávez, Thomas E. "*La Historia de la Nueva México*: The *Cuartocentenario* of Juan de Oñate." *El Palacio* 102, no. 2 (1997–98): 37–44.

———. *Quest for Quivira: Spanish Explorers on the Great Plains, 1540–1821*. Tucson, Ariz.: Southwest Parks and Monuments Association, 1992.

Chiappelli, Fredi, ed. *First Images of America: The Impact of the New World on the Old*. Berkeley: University of California Press, 1976.

"Comunicado público ante retirada de carabinero de Chile del territorio de Temucuicui," *Comunidad Autónoma Temucuicui*, June 26, 2014 (comunidadtemucuicui.blogspot.com, accessed July 5, 2014).

Concha, Jaime. "Observaciones acerca de La Araucana." In *Lectura crítica de la literatura americana: Inventarios, invenciones y revisiones*, edited by Saul Sosnowski, 504–21. Caracas: Biblioteca Ayacucho, 1996.

———. "El otro nuevo mundo." In *Homenaje a Ercilla*, 31–82. Concepción, Chile: Universidad de Concepción, 1969.

Correa, Martín. "La estigmatización del mapuche y la creación del enemigo interno." *Comunidad Autónoma Temucuicui*, June 26, 2014 (comunidadtemucuicui.blogspot.com, accessed July 5, 2014).

Cueva, Agustin. "El espejismo heroico de la conquista: Ensayo de interpretación de La Araucana." *Casa de las Américas* 19, no. 110 (1978): 29–40.

Curtius, Ernst Robert. *Literatura europea y edad media latina*. Vol. 1. Mexico: Fondo de Cultura Económica, 1955.

Davis, Elizabeth. "De mares y ríos: Conciencia transatlántica e imaginería acuática en la *Historia de la Nueva México* de Gaspar Pérez de Villagrá (1610)." In *Épica y colonia: Ensayos sobre el género épico en Iberoamérica (siglos XVI y XVII)*, edited by Paul Firbas, 263–86. Lima: Universidad Nacional Mayor de San Marcos Fondo Editorial, 2008.

———. "La épica novohispana y la ideología imperial." In *Historia de la literatura mexicana: La cultura letrada en la Nueva España del siglo XVII*, edited by Raquel Chang-Rodríguez, 129–52. Mexico City: Siglo Veintiuno Editores, 2002.

———. *Myth and Identity in the Epic of Imperial Spain*. Columbia: University of Missouri Press, 2000.

De Ramón, Emma. See Ramón, Emma de.

Díaz, Elvia. "Statue of Spaniard Loses Foot." *Albuquerque Journal*, January 8, 1998.

Díaz Meza, Aurelio. *Leyendas y episodios chilenos*. Buenos Aires: Editorial Antártica, 1968.

Dilke, Oswald A. W., and Margaret S. Dilke. "Ptolemy's Geography and the New World." In *Early Images of the Americas: Transfer and Invention*, edited by Jerry M. Williams and Robert E. Lewis, 263–85. Tucson: University of Arizona Press, 1993.

Dinamarca, Salvador. "Los estudios de Medina sobre Ercilla." *Revista Atenea* 107 (1952): 23–25.

Donoso, Ricardo. *Vida de Ercilla*. Mexico: Fondo de Cultura Económica, 1948.

Ebright, Malcolm. *Land Grants and Lawsuits in Northern New Mexico*. Albuquerque: University of New Mexico Press, 1994.

Elliot, John H. "Felipe II y la monarquía española: Temas de un reinado." In *Felipe II y el oficio de rey: La fragua de un imperio*, edited by José Román Gutiérrez, Enrique Martínez Ruiz, and Jaime González Rodríguez, 43–59. Madrid: Sociedad Estatal para la Conmemoración de los Centenarios de Felipe II y Carlos V, Ediciones Puertollano, 2001.

———. *The Old World and the New, 1492–1650.* Cambridge: Cambridge University Press, 1970.

Ercilla, Alonso de. *La Araucana.* Translated by Louis Carrera. Pittsburgh: RoseDog Books, 2006.

———. *La Araucana.* Edited by Isaías Lerner. Madrid: Ediciones Cátedra, Letras Hispánicas, 1993.

———. *La Araucana.* Edited by Isaías Lerner and Marcos A. Morínigo. Madrid: Clásicos Castalia, 1979.

Escudero, Juan Manuel, and Victoriano Roncero, eds. *La violencia en el mundo hispánico en el siglo de oro.* Madrid: Visor Libros, 2010.

Fernández, César, ed. *Cuentan los mapuches.* Buenos Aires: Ediciones Nuevo Siglo, 1999.

Fernández, José B. "Hispanic Literature: The Colonial Period." In *Recovering the U.S. Hispanic Literary Heritage*, edited by Ramón Gutiérrez and Genaro Padilla, 1:253–64. Houston: Arte Público Press, 1993.

Fernández Álvarez, Manuel. "Etapa renacentista (1475–1598)." In *La Universidad de Salamanca: Trayectoria histórica y proyecciones*, edited by Manuel Fernández Álvarez, 1:59–101. Salamanca: Ediciones Universidad de Salamanca, 1989.

———. *Felipe II y su tiempo.* Madrid: Espasa Calpe, 1998.

Fernández Carrain, Sergio. *Homenaje a Ercilla, padre de nuestras voces, en el IV Centenario de La Araucana.* Santiago: Boletín de la Academia Chilena de la Historia, 1969.

Fernández de Oviedo y Valdés, Gonzalo. *Historia general y natural de las Indias.* Madrid: Ediciones Atlas, 1959.

Fernández Restrepo, Luis. "Entre el recuerdo y el imposible olvido: La épica y el trauma de la conquista." In *Épica y colonia: Ensayos sobre el género épico en Iberoamérica (siglos XVI y XVII)*, edited by Paul Firbas, 41–59. Lima: Universidad Nacional Mayor de San Marcos Fondo Editorial, 2008.

Ferreiro, Larrie D. *Measure of the Earth: The Enlightenment Expedition That Reshaped Our World.* New York: Basic Books, 2011.

Firbas, Paul, ed. *Épica y colonia: Ensayos sobre el género épico en Iberoamérica (siglos XVI y XVII).* Lima: Universidad Nacional Mayor de San Marcos Fondo Editorial, 2008.

———. "Una lectura de la violencia en *La Araucana* de Alonso de Ercilla." In *La violencia en el mundo hispánico en el siglo de oro*, edited by Juan Manuel Escudero and Victoriano Roncero, 91–105. Madrid: Visor Libros, 2010.

Flint, Richard. *No Settlement, No Conquest: History of the Coronado Entrada.* Albuquerque: University of New Mexico Press, 2008.

Galmés de Fuentes, Álvaro. *Los topónimos: Sus blasones y trofeos (la toponimia mítica).* Madrid: Real Academia de la Historia, 2000.

González de San Nicolás, fray Gil. "Relación de los agravios que los indios de las provincias padecen." In *Colección de historiadores de Chile y documentos relativos a la historia nacional*, vol. 29. Santiago, Chile: Imprenta del Ferrocarril, 1902: 461–66.

Góngora Marmolejo, Alonso de. *Historia de Chile desde su descubrimiento hasta el año 1575.* Santiago, Chile: Editorial Universitaria, 1969.

Gonzales-Berry, Erlinda, ed. *Pasó por aquí: Critical Essays on the New Mexican Literary Tradition, 1542–1988.* Albuquerque: University of New Mexico Press, 1989.

González de Mendoza Dorvier, Angel. *El problema geográfico de "La Araucana" y la expedición de D. García Hurtado de Mendoza.* Madrid: Publicaciones de la Real Sociedad Geográfica, 1947.

Gruzinski, Serge. *La colonización de lo imaginario: Sociedades indígenas y occidentalización en el México español, siglos XVI–XVIII.* Mexico: Fondo de Cultura Económica, 2004.

———. *La guerra de las imágenes: De Cristóbal Colón a "Blade Runner" (1492–2019).* Mexico: Fondo de Cultura Económica, 2003.

———. "Les mondes mêlés de la Monarchie catholique et autres 'connected histories.'" *Annales: Histoire, Sciences Sociales* 1 (2001): 85–117.

Gutiérrez, José Román, Enrique Martínez Ruiz, and Jaime González Rodríguez, eds. *Felipe II y el oficio de rey: La fragua de un imperio.* Madrid: Sociedad Estatal para la Conmemoración de los Centenarios de Felipe II y Carlos V, Ediciones Puertollano, 2001.

Gutiérrez, Ramón, and Genaro Padilla, eds. *Recovering the U.S. Hispanic Literary Heritage.* Vol. 1. Houston: Arte Público Press, 1993.

Hammond, George P., and Agapito Rey. "The Crown's Participation in the Founding of New Mexico." *New Mexico Historical Review* 32, no. 4 (1957): 293–309.

———, eds. and trans. *Don Juan de Oñate, Colonizer of New Mexico, 1595–1628.* 2 vols. Albuquerque: University of New Mexico Press, 1953.

———, eds. *Narratives of the Coronado Expedition, 1540–1542.* Albuquerque: University of New Mexico Press, 1940.

———, eds. *The Rediscovery of New Mexico, 1580–1594.* Albuquerque: University of New Mexico Press, 1966.

Helferich, Gerard. *Humboldt's Cosmos.* New York: Gotham, 2004.

Hermosillo Silva, Clímaco. *Cañete: Crónicas de cinco siglos.* Concepción, Chile: Cosmigonon, 2002.

Herrera-Sobek, María. "New Approaches to Old Chroniclers: Contemporary Critical Theories and the Pérez de Villagrá Epic." In *Recovering the U.S. Hispanic Literary Heritage,* edited by María Herrera-Sobek and Virginia Sánchez Korrol, 3:154–62. Houston: Arte Público Press, 2000.

———, ed. *Reconstructing a Chicano/a Literary Heritage: Hispanic Colonial Literature of the Southwest.* Tucson: University of Arizona Press, 1993.

Herrera-Sobek, María, and Virginia Sánchez Korrol, eds. *Recovering the U.S. Hispanic Literary Heritage.* Vol. 3. Houston: Arte Público Press, 2000.

Herzog, Tamar. "La política espacial y las tácticas de conquista: Las 'Ordenanzas de Descubrimiento, Nueva Población y Pacificación de las Indias' y su legado (siglos XVI–XVII)." In *Felipe II y el oficio de rey: La fragua de un imperio,* edited by José Román Gutiérrez, Enrique Martínez Ruiz, and Jaime González Rodríguez, 293–303. Madrid: Sociedad Estatal para la Conmemoración de los Centenarios de Felipe II y Carlos V, Ediciones Puertollano, 2001.

Holtby, David. *Forty-Seventh Star: New Mexico's Struggle for Statehood.* Norman: University of Oklahoma Press, 2012.

Humboldt, Alexander von. *Cosmos: A Sketch of a Physical Description of the Universe.* Translated by E. C. Otté. Vol. 2. New York: Harper and Brothers, 1858.

Huneeus Pérez, Andrés. *Historia de las polémicas de Indias en Chile durante el siglo XVI, 1536–1598.* Santiago: Editorial Jurídica de Chile, 1956.

Hutcheon, Linda. *The Politics of Postmodernism.* New York: Routledge, 2002.

Jaramillo, Philadelphio. "Historia de la Nueva México del capitán Gaspar de Villagrá: Edición paleográfica, con notas y estudio preliminar." Ph.D. diss., University of Colorado, 1990.

Jiménez, Alfredo, "El Lejano Norte español: Cómo escapar del *American West* y de las *Spanish Borderlands.*" *Colonial Latin American Historical Review* 5, no. 4 (Fall 1996): 381–412.

Jiménez de la Espada, Marcos. *Relaciones geográficas de Indias.* Madrid: Ministerio de Fomento, 1881.

Johnson, Julie Greer. "Ercilla's Construction and Destruction of the City of Concepción: A Crossroads of Imperialist Ideology and the Poetic Imagination." In *Mapping Colonial Spanish America: Places and Commonplaces of Identity, Culture, and Experience,* edited by Santa Arias and Mariselle Meléndez, 237–50. Lewisburg, Penn.: Bucknell University Press, 2002.

Kallendorf, Craig. "Representing the Other: Ercilla's *La Araucana*, Virgil's *Aeneid*, and the New World Encounter." *Comparative Literature Studies* 40, no. 3 (2003): 394–414.

Kamen, Henry. *Imperio: La forja de España como potencia mundial.* Madrid: Punto de Lectura, 2004.

Kessell, John L. *Kiva, Cross, and Crown: The Pecos Indians and New Mexico, 1540–1840.* Washington, D.C.: National Park Service, U.S. Department of the Interior, 1979.

———. "Spaniards, Environment, and the Pepsi Generation." In *New Spain's Far Northern Frontier: Essays on Spain in the American West, 1540–1821,* edited by David Weber, 285–91. Albuquerque: University of New Mexico Press, 1979.

Kessell, John L., and Rick Hendricks, eds. *By Force of Arms: The Journals of Don Diego de Vargas, New Mexico, 1691–1693.* Albuquerque: University of New Mexico Press, 1992.

Kessell, John L., Rick Hendricks, and Meredith Dodge, eds. *Blood on the Boulders: The Journals of Don Diego de Vargas, 1694–1697.* Albuquerque, University of New Mexico Press, 1998.

Lafaye, Jacques. "¿Existen las 'letras coloniales'?" In *Conquista y contraconquista: La escritura del Nuevo Mundo. Actas del XVIII Congreso Internacional de Literatura Iberoamericana,* edited by Julio Ortega and José Amor y Vázquez, 641–50. Mexico: El Colegio de México and Brown University, 1994.

Lamadrid, Enrique. "Santiago and San Acacio: Slaughter and Deliverance in the Foundational Legends of Colonial and Postcolonial New Mexico." *Journal of American Folklore* 115, nos. 457–58 (2002): 457–74.

Lane, Jill. "On Colonial Forgetting: The Conquest of New Mexico and Its *Historia.*" In *The Ends of Performance,* edited by Peggy Phelan and Jill Lane, 52–69. New York: New York University Press, 1998.

Lara Garrido, José. *Los mejores plectros: Teoría y práctica de la épica culta en el siglo de oro.* Málaga, Spain: Universidad de Málaga, 1999.

Las Casas, Bartolomé de. *A Short Account of the Destruction of the Indies.* New York: Penguin, 1992.

Leal, Luis. "The First American Epic: Villagrá's History of New Mexico." In *Pasó por aquí. Critical Essays on the New Mexican Literary Tradition, 1542–1988,* edited by Erlinda Gonzales-Berry, 47–62. Albuquerque: University of New Mexico Press, 1989.

León Solís, Leonardo. "La Araucana: Una lectura desde la nueva historia." Unpublished manuscript in possession of the author.

Levin Rojo, Danna A. *Return to Aztlan. Indians, Spaniards, and the Invention of Nuevo México.* Norman: University of Oklahoma Press, 2014.

Lomelí, Francisco A. "The Sense of Place in Gaspar de Vilagrá's Historia de la Nueva Mexico." *Camino Real: Estudios de las Hispanidades Norteamericanas* 4, no. 6 (2012): 75–86.

López, Miguel. "Disputed History and Poetry: Gaspar Pérez de Villagrá's Historia de la Nueva México." *Bilingual Review* 26, no. 1 (2001–2002): 43–55.

López de Gómara, Francisco. *Primera y segunda parte de la* Historia general de las Indias. *Con todo el descubrimiento, y cosas notables que han acaecido desde que se ganaron hasta el año de 1551; con la conquista de México y de la Nueva España.* Madrid: Rivadeneyra, 1877.

López de Velasco, Juan. *Geografía y descripción universal de las Indias.* Madrid: Fortanet, 1894.

Madrigal, Luis Iñigo, ed. *Historia de la literatura hispanoamericana.* Madrid: Ediciones Cátedra, 1982.

Manzano, Juan. *La incorporación de las Indias a la corona de Castilla.* Madrid: Ediciones Cultura Hispánica, 1948.

Marrero-Fente, Raúl. *Bodies, Texts, and Ghosts: Writing on Literature and Law in Colonial Latin America.* Lanham, Md.: University Press of America, 2010.

———. "Épica, fantasma y lamento: La retórica del duelo en La Araucana." *Revista Iberoamericana* 73, no. 218 (2007): 211–26.

Martín Rodríguez, Antonio M. "Ariadna en Nuevo México: Mujer y mito en la *Historia de la Nueva México* de Gaspar de Villagrá." *Camino Real: Estudios de las Hispanidades Norteamericanas* 4, no. 6 (2012): 23–41.

Martín Rodríguez, Manuel M. "'Aquí fue Troia nobles cavalleros': Ecos de la tradición clásica y otros intertextos en la *Historia de la Nueva México* de Gaspar Pérez de Villagrá." *SILVA: Estudios de Humanismo y Tradición Clásica* 4 (2005): 139–208.

———. *Cantas a Marte y das batalla a Apolo: Cinco estudios sobre Gaspar de Villagrá.* New York: Editorial Academia Norteamericana de la Lengua Española, 2014.

———. "La formación intelectual de Gaspar de Villagrá." In *El humanismo español entre el viejo mundo y el nuevo,* edited by J. M. Nieto Ibáñez and R. Manchón Gómez, 385–93. Jaén and León, Spain: Universidad de León–Universidad de Jaén, 2008.

———. "400 Years of Literature and History in the United States: Gaspar de Villagrá's *Historia de la Nueva Mexico* (1610)." *Camino Real: Estudios de las Hispanidades Norteamericanas* 4, no. 6 (2012): 13–19.

———. *Gaspar de Villagrá: Legista, soldado y poeta.* León, Spain: Universidad de León, 2009.

———. "La Historia de la Nueva México de Gaspar Pérez de Villagrá: Recepción crítica (con nuevos datos biográficos de su autor)." In *El humanismo español, su proyección en América y Canarias en la época del humanismo,* edited by A. Martín Rodríguez and G. Santana Henríquez, 189–253. Las Palmas de Gran Canaria, Spain: Universidad de las Palmas de Gran Canaria, 2006.

———. "History, Poetry, and Politics in Gaspar de Villagrá's Historia de la Nueva México." *Camino Real: Estudios de las Hispanidades Norteamericanas* 4, no. 6 (2012): 87–100.

———. "Reading Gaspar de Villagrá (in the Seventeenth Century)." In *Cien años de lealtad: En honor a Luis Leal*, edited by Sara Poot Herrera, F. A. Lomelí, and María Herrera-Sobek, 2:1337–46. Mexico: UC-Mexicanistas, 2007.

Maura, Juan Francisco. "Gaspar Pérez de Villagrá y Sabine R. Ulibarrí: Pasado y presente de la épica de Nuevo México." *Espéculo: Revista de Estudios Literarios* (Universidad Complutense, Madrid) 8, no. 20 (March–June 2002).

Mazzotti, José Antonio. "Epic, Creoles, and Nation in Spanish America." In *A Companion to the Literatures of Colonial America*, edited by Susan Castillo and Ivy Schweitzer, 480–99. Malden, Mass.: Blackwell, 2005.

———. "Paradojas de la épica criolla: Pedro de Oña, entre la lealtad y el caos." In *Épica y colonia: Ensayos sobre el género épico en Iberoamérica (siglos XVI y XVII)*, edited by Paul Firbas, 231–61. Lima: Universidad Nacional Mayor de San Marcos Fondo Editorial, 2008.

Medina, José Toribio. *La Araucana de Don Alonso de Ercilla y Zúñiga. Vida de Ercilla.* Santiago, Chile: Imprenta Elzeviriana, 1917.

Medina, José Toribio, ed. *Cartas de Pedro de Valdivia que tratan del descubrimiento y conquista de Chile.* Santiago, Chile: Fondo Histórico y Bibliográfico José Toribio Medina, 1953.

———. *Vida de Ercilla.* Mexico: Fondo de Cultura Económica, 1948.

Mejía Sánchez, Ernesto. "Gaspar de Villagrá en la Nueva España." *Cuadernos del Centro de Estudios Literarios* 1 (1970): 4–16.

Mejías-López, William. "La relación ideológica de Alonso de Ercilla con Francisco de Vitoria y Fray Bartolomé de Las Casas." *Revista Iberoamericana: Literatura Colonial, Identidades y Conquista en América* 61, nos. 170–71 (January–June 1995): 197–217.

Menéndez y Pelayo, Marcelino. *Historia de la poesía hispano-americana.* 2 vols. Madrid: Librería General de Victoriano Suárez, 1911 [vol. 1], 1913 [vol. 2].

Meza Villalobos, Néstor. *Régimen jurídico de la conquista y de la guerra de Arauco.* Santiago, Chile: Imprenta Universitaria, 1946.

Mignolo, Walter. "Cartas, crónicas y relaciones del descubrimiento y la conquista." In *Historia de la literatura hispanoamericana: Época colonial*, edited by Luis Iñigo Madrigal, 57–116. Madrid: Ediciones Cátedra, 1982.

———. "Occidentalización, imperialismo, globalización: Herencias coloniales y teorías postcoloniales." *Revista Iberoamericana: Literatura Colonial, Identidades y Conquista en América* 61, nos. 170–71 (January–June 1995): 27–40.

Montes, Javier Alejo. *La Universidad de Salamanca bajo Felipe II, 1575–1598.* Valladolid, Spain: Junta de Castilla y León, 1998.

Morales Folguera, José Miguel. *La construcción de la utopía: El proyecto de Felipe II (1556–1598) para Hispanoamérica.* Madrid: Biblioteca Nueva, 2001.

Morel, Alicia. *Cuentos araucanos: La gente de la tierra.* Santiago, Chile: Editorial Andrés Bello, 1982.

Mulford, Carla. "Resisting Colonialism." In *Teaching the Literatures of Early America*, edited by Carla Mulford, 75–94. New York: Modern Language Association of America, 1999.

———, ed. *Teaching the Literatures of Early America.* New York: Modern Language Association of America, 1999.

Murrin, Michael. *History and Warfare in Renaissance Epic.* Chicago: University of Chicago Press, 1994.

Nash, Roderick. *Wilderness and the American Mind.* New Haven, Conn.: Yale University Press, 1975.

Neruda, Pablo. *Canto general.* Vol. 1. Buenos Aires: Editorial Losada, 1999.

———. "El mensajero." In *Don Alonso de Ercilla, inventor de Chile*, by Pablo Neruda, et al., 11–12. Barcelona: Editorial Pomaire, 1971.

———, et al. *Don Alonso de Ercilla, inventor de Chile.* Barcelona: Editorial Pomaire, 1971.

New Mexico State Office, Bureau of Land Management. *El Camino Real de Tierra Adentro National Historic Trail.* Santa Fe, N.M.: National Park Service, U.S. Department of the Interior, 2002.

Nicolopulos, James. *The Poetics of Empire in the Indies: Prophecy and Imitation in La Araucana and Os Lusíadas.* University Park: Pennsylvania State University Press, 2000.

Nye, Russel B. "History and Literature: Branches of the Same Tree." In *Essays on History and Literature*, edited by Robert H. Bremner, 123–59. Columbus: Ohio State University Press, 1966.

O'Malley, María. "Mapping the Work of Stories in Villagrá's 'Historia de la Nueva México.'" *Journal of the Southwest* 48, no. 3 (2006): 307–30.

Ots Capdequi, J. M. *El Estado español en las Indias.* Mexico: Fondo de Cultura Económica, 1986.

Padilla, Genaro M. *The Daring Flight of My Pen: Cultural Politics and Gaspar Pérez de Villagrá's Historia de la Nueva México, 1610.* Albuquerque: University of New Mexico Press, 2010.

Pagden, Anthony. Introduction to *A Short Account of the Destruction of the Indies*, by Bartolomé de Las Casas, edited by Anthony Pagden, xxviii–xxx. New York: Penguin, 1992.

Palmer, Gabrielle, ed. *El Camino Real de Tierra Adentro.* Santa Fe: Bureau of Land Management, New Mexico State Office, 1993.

Parentini, Luis Carlos, ed. *Historiadores chilenos frente al bicentenario.* Santiago, Chile: Comisión Bicentenario, Presidencia de la República, 2008.

Pastor, Beatriz. *Discursos narrativos de la conquista: Mitificación y emergencia.* Hanover, N.H.: Ediciones del Norte, 1988.

Pearce, T. M., ed. *New Mexico Place Names: A Geographical Dictionary.* Albuquerque: University of New Mexico Press, 1965.

Peña, Margarita. "La poesía épica en la Nueva España." In *Conquista y contraconquista: La escritura del Nuevo Mundo*, edited by Julio Ortega and José Amor y Vázquez, 289–301. Mexico: Colegio de México and Brown University, 1994.

———. *Prodigios novohispanos: Ensayos sobre literatura de la colonia.* Mexico City: Universidad Nacional Autónoma de México, 2005.

Perelmuter-Pérez, Rosa. "El paisaje idealizado en La Araucana." *Hispanic Review* 54, no. 2 (1986): 129–46.

Pérez-Linggi, Sandra M. "Gaspar Pérez de Villagrá: *Criollo* or Chicano in the Southwest?" *Hispania* 88, no. 4 (2005): 666–76.

Perus, Françoise, ed. *Historia y literatura.* Mexico: Instituto Mora, 2001.

Phelan, Peggy, and Jill Lane, eds. *The End of Performance.* New York: New York University Press, 1998.

Pierce, Frank. *Alonso de Ercilla y Zúñiga.* Amsterdam: Rodopi, 1984.

———. *The Epic Poetry of the Golden Century.* Madrid: Gredos, 1961.

Piñero Ramírez, Pedro. "La épica hispanoamericana colonial." In *Historia de la literatura hispanoamericana*, edited by Luis Iñigo Madrigal, 161–88. Madrid: Ediciones Cátedra, 1982.

Pinto Rodríguez, Jorge, ed. *Araucanía y Pampas: Un mundo fronterizo en América del Sur*. Temuco, Chile: Ediciones Universidad de la Frontera, 1996.

———. *La formación del estado y la nación, y el pueblo mapuche: De la inclusión a la exclusión*. Santiago, Chile: Dirección de Bibliotecas, Archivos y Museos, 2003.

———. "Integración y desintegración de un espacio fronterizo: La Araucanía y las Pampas, 1550–1900." In *Araucanía y Pampas: Un mundo fronterizo en América del Sur*, edited by Jorge Pinto Rodríguez, 11–46. Temuco, Chile: Ediciones Universidad de la Frontera, 1996.

Powell, Philip Wayne. *Soldiers, Indians, and Silver: North America's First Frontier War*. Berkeley: University of California Press, 1952.

Quinn, David Beers. "New Geographical Horizons: Literature." In *First Images of America: The Impact of the New World on the Old*, edited by Fredi Chiappelli, 2:635–58. Berkeley: University of California Press, 1976.

Quint, David. *Epic and Empire: Politics and Generic Form from Virgil to Milton*. Princeton, N.J.: Princeton University Press, 1993.

Rabasa, José. *Inventing America: Spanish Historiography and the Formation of Eurocentrism*. Norman: University of Oklahoma Press, 1993.

———. *Writing Violence on the Northern Frontier: The Historiography of Sixteenth-Century New Mexico and Florida and the Legacy of Conquest*. Durham, N.C.: Duke University Press, 2000.

Ramón, Emma de. "Recuerdos y proyecciones en torno al bicentenario." In *Historiadores chilenos frente al bicentenario*, edited by Luis Carlos Parentini, 179–83. Santiago, Chile: Comisión Bicentenario, Presidencia de la República, 2008.

Raviola Molina, Víctor. "Elementos indígenas en La Araucana de Ercilla." In *Don Alonso de Ercilla, inventor de Chile*, by Pablo Neruda, et al., 81–136. Barcelona: Editorial Pomaire, 1971.

Restrepo, Luis Fernando. "Entre el recuerdo y el imposible olvido: La épica y el trauma de la conquista." In *Épica y colonia: Ensayos sobre el género épico en Iberoamérica (siglos XVI y XVII)*, edited by Paul Firbas, 41–59. Lima: Universidad Nacional Mayor de San Marcos Fondo Editorial, 2008.

Retamal, Julio A. "Pensando la historiografía del mañana." In *Historiadores chilenos frente al bicentenario*, edited by Luis Carlos Parentini, 403–405. Santiago, Chile: Comisión Bicentenario, Presidencia de la República, 2008.

Richthofen, Erich von. *Tradicionalismo épico-novelesco*. Barcelona: Editorial Planeta, 1972.

Rodríguez, Ileana. *Primer inventario del invasor*. Managua: Editorial Nueva Nicaragua, 1984.

Rodríguez-San Pedro Bezares, Luis Enrique. *La universidad salmantina del Barroco, período 1598–1625*. Salamanca, Spain: Ediciones Universidad de Salamanca, 1986.

Rodríguez-San Pedro Bezares, Luis Enrique, and Roberto Martínez del Río. *Estudiantes de Salamanca*. Salamanca, Spain: Ediciones Universidad de Salamanca, 2001.

Román-Lagunas, Jorge. "Lo épico y 'La Araucana.'" In *Don Alonso de Ercilla, inventor de Chile*, by Pablo Neruda, et al., 168. Barcelona: Editorial Pomaire, 1971.

Ruiz, Carlos. "La estructura ancestral de los mapuches: Las identidades territoriales, los longko y los consejos a través del tiempo." *Ñuque Mapuförlaget*. Working Paper Series 3. Uppsala, Sweden: University of Uppsala, Centro Mapuche de Estudio y Acción, 2003.

Said, Edward W. *Culture and Imperialism*. New York: Vintage, 1994.

———. *Orientalismo*. Barcelona: De Bolsillo, 2002.

Sánchez, Alfredo, and Roberto Morales. *Las regiones de Chile: Espacio físico y humano-económico*. Santiago, Chile: Editorial Universitaria, 1990.

Sánchez, Joseph. "From Santa Bárbara to San Juan de los Caballeros: Villagrá's 'Historia' and the 'Itinerario' of Juan de Oñate's Expedition of 1598." *Camino Real: Estudios de las Hispanidades Norteamericanas* 4, no. 6 (2012): 43–73.

Sanfuentes, Olaya. "La trinidad patrimonial: Patrimonio, historia y memoria en la formación de la identidad." In *Historiadores chilenos frente al bicentenario*, edited by Luis Carlos Parentini, 461–65. Santiago, Chile: Comisión Bicentenario, Presidencia de la República, 2008.

Scholes, France V. "Royal Treasury Records Relating to the Province of New Mexico, 1596–1683." *New Mexico Historical Review* 50, no. 1 (1975): 5–23.

Schröter, Bernd. "La frontera en Hispanoamérica colonial: Un estudio historiográfico comparativo." *Colonial Latin American Historical Review* 10, no. 3 (Summer 2001): 351–85.

Schwember, Herman. *Donde otro no ha llegado*. Santiago, Chile: CESOC, 2003.

Scurlock, Dan. *From the Rio to the Sierra: An Environmental History of the Middle Rio Grande Basin*. Fort Collins, Colo.: Rocky Mountain Research Station, U.S. Department of Agriculture, 1998.

———. "Through Desierto and Bosque: The Physical Environment of the Camino Real." In *El Camino Real de Tierra Adentro*, edited by Gabrielle Palmer, 1–11. Santa Fe: Bureau of Land Management, New Mexico State Office, 1993.

Seed, Patricia. *Ceremonies of Possession in Europe's Conquest of the New World, 1492–1640*. New York: Cambridge University Press, 1995.

———. "Taking Possession and Reading Texts: Establishing the Authority of Overseas Empires." In *Early Images of the Americas: Transfer and Invention*, edited by Jerry M. Williams and Robert E. Lewis, 111–47. Tucson: University of Arizona Press, 1993.

Shields, E. Thomson, and Dana D. Nelson. "Colonial Spanish Writings." In *Teaching the Literatures of Early America*, edited by Carla Mulford, 97–111. New York: Modern Language Association of America, 1999.

Simmons, Marc. *The Last Conquistador: Juan de Oñate and the Settling of the Far Southwest*. Norman: University of Oklahoma Press, 1991.

Snow, David. *New Mexico's First Colonists. The 1597–1600 Enlistments for New Mexico under Juan de Oñate, Adelantado and Gobernador*. Albuquerque: Hispanic Genealogical Research Center of New Mexico, 1998.

Sosnowski, Saul, ed. *Lectura crítica de la literatura americana: Inventarios, invenciones y revisiones*. Caracas: Biblioteca Ayacucho, 1996.

Spengemann, William. *A New World of Words: Redefining Early American Literature*. New Haven, Conn.: Yale University Press, 1994.

Stein, Barbara H., and Stanley J. Stein. "Financing Empire: The European Diaspora of Silver by War." In *Colonial Legacies: The Problem of Persistence in Latin American History*, edited by Jeremy Adelman, 51–68. New York: Routledge, 1999.

Thomas, Keith. *Man and the Natural World: A History of Modern Sensibility.* New York: Pantheon, 1983.

Todorov, Tzvetan. *The Conquest of America: The Question of the Other.* Norman: University of Oklahoma Press, 1999.

Toledo, Ximena, and Eduardo A. Zapater. *Geografía general y regional de Chile.* Santiago, Chile: Editorial Universitaria, 1991.

Toledo Llancaqueo, Victor. "La memoria de las tierras antiguas: Tocando a las puertas del derecho, políticas de la memoria mapuche en la transición chilena." In *El derecho a la memoria,* edited by Felipe Gómez Isa, 421–40. Zarautz-Guipuzcoa, Spain: Giza Eskubideak Derechos Humanos, 2006.

Torrez, Robert. "The River through Time: Historical Overview of the Río Grande." In *La Vida del Río Grande: Our River—Our Life,* edited by Carlos Vázquez. Albuquerque: National Hispanic Cultural Center, 2004.

Triviños, Gilberto. "Lecturas de La Araucana: 'No es bien que así dejemos en olvido/ el nombre de este bárbaro obstinado.'" In *Épica y colonia: Ensayos sobre el género épico en Iberoamérica (siglos XVI y XVII),* edited by Paul Firbas, 113–31. Lima: Universidad Nacional Mayor de San Marcos Fondo Editorial, 2008.

———. "El mito del tiempo de los héroes en Valdivia, Vivar y Ercilla." *Revista Chilena de Literatura* 49 (1996): 5–23.

———. "Revisitando la literatura chilena: Sigue diciendo: cayeron/ Di más: volverán mañana." *Atenea* 487 (2003): 113–33.

Undurraga, Antonio de, ed. Introduction to *La Araucana de Alonso de Ercilla.* Madrid: Espasa Calpe, 2000.

Valenzuela Solís de Ovando, Carlos. *Crónicas de la conquista.* Santiago, Chile: Editorial Andújar, n.d.

Vázquez, Carlos, ed. *La Vida del Río Grande: Our River—Our Life.* Albuquerque: National Hispanic Cultural Center, 2004.

Verdesio, Gustavo. "Colonialism Now and Then: Colonial Latin American Studies in the Light of the Predicament of Latinamericanism. In *Colonialism Past and Present: Reading and Writing about Colonial Latin America Today,* edited by Álvaro Félix Bolaños and Gustavo Verdesio, 1–17. New York: State University of New York Press, 2002.

Villagrá, Gaspar Pérez de. *Historia de la Nueva México.* Edited by Luis González Obregón. 2 vols. Mexico City: Imprenta del Museo Nacional, 1900.

———. *Historia de la Nueva México.* Edited by Victorino Madrid Rubio, Elsía Armesto Rodríguez, and Augusto Quintana Prieto. Astorga, Spain: Biblioteca de Autores Astorganos, 1991.

———. *Historia de la Nueva México.* Edited by Manuel M. Martín Rodríguez. Madrid: Instituto Franklin, Universidad de Alcalá de Henares, 2010.

———. *Historia de la Nueva México, 1610.* Edited and translated by Miguel Encinias, Alfred Rodríguez, and Joseph P. Sánchez. Albuquerque: University of New Mexico Press, 1992.

———. *Historia de Nuevo México.* Edited by Mercedes Junquera. Madrid: Historia 16, 1989.

———. *History of New Mexico.* Edited and translated by Gilberto Espinoza. Introduction and notes by Frederick W. Hodge. Los Angeles: Quivira Society, 1933. Reprinted Santa Fe, N.M.: Arno Press, 1967.

Villalobos, Sergio. "Guerra y paz en la Araucanía: Periodificación." In *Araucanía: Temas de historia fronteriza*, edited by Sergio Villalobos and Jorge Pinto Rodríguez, 7–30. Temuco, Chile: Ediciones de la Universidad de la Frontera, 1985.

———. *Vida fronteriza en la Araucanía: El mito de la guerra de Arauco*. Santiago, Chile: Editorial Andrés Bello, 1995.

Villalobos, Sergio, and Jorge Pinto Rodríguez, eds. *Araucanía: Temas de historia fronteriza*. Temuco, Chile: Ediciones de la Universidad de la Frontera, 1985.

Villalobos, Sergio, Osvaldo Silva, Fernando Silva, and Patricio Estellé. *Historia de Chile*. Santiago, Chile: Editorial Universitaria, 2000.

Vivar, Jerónimo de. *Crónica de los reinos de Chile*. Madrid: Dastin, 2001.

Wagner, Henry Raup, and Helen Rand Parish. *The Life and Writings of Bartolomé de Las Casas*. Albuquerque: University of New Mexico Press, 1967.

Webb, Walter Prescott. *The Great Plains*. New York: Grosset & Dunlap, 1931.

Weber, David J., ed. *New Spain's Far Northern Frontier: Essays on Spain in the American West, 1540–1821*. Albuquerque: University of New Mexico Press, 1979.

———. *The Spanish Frontier in North America*. New Haven, Conn.: Yale University Press, 1992.

Wilhelm de Moesbach, Ernesto. *Voz de Arauco: Explicacion de los nombres indígenas de Chile*. Temuco, Chile: Editorial Millantu, 1991.

Williams, Jerry M., and Robert E. Lewis, eds. *Early Images of the Americas: Transfer and Invention*. Tucson: University of Arizona Press, 1993.

Winship, George Parker, ed. and trans. *The Journey of Coronado 1540–42*. Golden, Colo.: Fulcrum, 1990.

Wogan, David. "Ercilla y la poesía mexicana." *Revista Iberoamericana* 3, no. 6 (1941): 1–79.

Zapater, Horacio. "Huincas y mapuches (1550–1662)." *Historia* 30 (1997): 441–504.

Index

Page numbers in italic type refer to maps, figures, or illustrations.